THE 'CONQUEST' OF ACADIA, 1710: IMPERIAL, COLONIAL, AND ABORIGINAL CONSTRUCTIONS

The conquest of Port Royal by British forces in 1710 is an intensely revealing episode in the history of northeastern North America. Bringing together multilayered perspectives, including the conquest's effects on aboriginal inhabitants, Acadians, and New Englanders, and using a variety of methodologies to contextualize the incident in local, regional, and imperial terms, six prominent scholars form new conclusions regarding the events of 1710. The authors show that the processes by which European states sought to legitimate their claims, and the terms on which mutual toleration would be granted or withheld by different peoples living side by side, are especially visible in the Nova Scotia that emerged following the conquest. Important on both a local and global scale, *The 'Conquest' of Acadia* will be a significant contribution to Acadian history, native studies, native rights histories, and the sociopolitical history of the eighteenth century.

JOHN G. REID is a professor of history at Saint Mary's University.

MAURICE BASQUE holds the Chaire d'études acadiennes at the Université de Moncton.

ELIZABETH MANCKE is an associate professor of history at the University of Akron.

BARRY MOODY is a professor of history at Acadia University.

GEOFFREY PLANK is an associate professor of history at the University of Cincinnati.

WILLIAM WICKEN is an associate professor of history at York University.

THE 'CONQUEST' OF ACADIA, 1710

Imperial, Colonial, and Aboriginal Constructions

John G. Reid
Maurice Basque
Elizabeth Mancke
Barry Moody
Geoffrey Plank
William Wicken

UNIVERSITY OF TORONTO PRESS
Toronto Buffalo London

© University of Toronto Press Incorporated 2004
Toronto Buffalo London

Printed in Canada

ISBN 0-8020-3755-0 (cloth)
ISBN 0-8020-8538-5 (paper)

Printed on acid-free paper

National Library of Canada Cataloguing in Publication

The 'conquest' of Acadia, 1710 : imperial, colonial, and aboriginal
constructions / John G. Reid ... [et al.].

Includes bibliographical references and index.
ISBN 0-8020-3755-0 (bound)   ISBN 0-8020-8538-5 (pbk.)

1. Acadia – History.   2. Port Royal Habitation (N.S.).   3. Nova Scotia –
History – To 1784.   4. Canada – History – 1663–1713 (New France).   5. Micmac
Indians – Nova Scotia – History – 18th century.   6. Great Britain – Colonies –
America – Administration.   I. Reid, John G. (John Graham), 1948–

FC2043.c66 2004   971.6'01   C2003-901165-8
F1038.c664 2004

University of Toronto Press acknowledges the financial assistance to its
publishing program of the Canada Council for the Arts and the
Ontario Arts Council.

This book has been published with the help of a grant from the Canadian
Federation for the Humanities and Social Sciences, through the Aid to Scholarly
Publications Programme, using funds provided by the Social Sciences and
Humanities Research Council of Canada.

University of Toronto Press acknowledges the financial support for its
publishing activities of the Government of Canada through the
Book Publishing Industry Development Program (BPIDP).

Contents

Acknowledgments

This book has been in active preparation since 1996, when the six team members agreed to collaborate on a new treatment of a subject that all of us had been researching (though from a variety of perspectives) and that all of us believed had been inadequately studied before. Over the years we have benefited from the assistance of many people, and it is a pleasure to acknowledge these debts.

The research assistants who have contributed at various stages of the volume's emergence include Chris Alders, Nicole Barrieau, Dan Conlin, Raymond Cyr, Carol Goodine, Heidi MacDonald, Bill Miles, and Steven Schwinghamer. Also, a number of scholars have read portions of the manuscript and commented on them to our great benefit: we thank especially Catherine Desbarats, Naomi Griffiths, J.K. Hiller, Richard R. Johnson, David Jones, Tina Loo, and Alan Taylor. We are grateful, too, to the anonymous readers for the University of Toronto Press and the Humanities and Social Sciences Federation of Canada.

Research for the project was funded in part by grants from the Social Sciences and Humanities Research Council of Canada and from the Canadian Embassy in Washington, DC. Through a grant from the International Council for Canadian Studies, we were able to meet as a team for an intensive two-day workshop and planning session. Publication was assisted by a subvention awarded through the Aid to Scholarly Publications Programme of the Canadian Federation for the Humanities and Social Sciences. Also, internal research grants were made available through our own institutions. We gratefully acknowledge all of this invaluable support.

We offer sincere thanks also to our editors at the University of Toronto Press. Gerry Hallowell provided the initial encouragement, and it was continued by Len Husband. Frances Mundy saw the book through its later stages, and James Leahy provided expert copy editing.

For a team of six authors, supportive family members and friends are too numerous to mention by name. But this in no way alters the warmth and sincerity with which we thank one and all.

Introduction

John G. Reid, Maurice Basque, Elizabeth Mancke,
Barry Moody, Geoffrey Plank, and William Wicken

On 5 October 1710 (O.S.), a force composed of New England militia
and British marines accepted the French surrender of the fort at Port
Royal, military headquarters of the colony of Acadia.[1] At the most extensive – though highly controvertible – estimation, the colony's boundaries could be taken by French or British observers to correspond to the
later dimensions of Canada's Maritime provinces, with the possible
additions of the Gaspé Peninsula and a piece of the state of Maine
extending southwestward to the Penobscot River. Within that territory,
the clear majority of the population was aboriginal: perhaps some 3500
Mi'kmaq and 500 Wulstukwiuk (Maliseet), and 600 Passamaquoddy and
Penobscot if the southwestern extension is included.[2] The Acadian colonial population may have approached 2000. Port Royal was the largest
single settlement, but other substantial clusters of villages were located
on the Minas Basin and on the Isthmus of Chignecto. Unlike the native
population, the Acadians were rapidly increasing at a rate that doubled
their overall numbers approximately every twenty years.[3] Following the
conquest of 1710, and the attribution of Nova Scotia to Great Britain by
the Treaty of Utrecht three years later, British soldiers and colonists –
located chiefly at Annapolis Royal (as Port Royal was renamed) and
intermittently at the fishing settlement of Canso – numbered some 400,
except when reinforced in time of war.[4]

Boundaries remained a matter of dispute. The Treaty of Utrecht provided for the cession from France to Great Britain of the territory
known as 'la nouvelle Ecosse autrement dite Acadie,' but its definition
was a masterpiece of ambiguity: 'en son entier, conformement à ses

anciennes limites, comme aussi ... la Ville de Port-Royal, maintenant appellée Annapolis Royale, et généralement ... tout ce qui dépend desdites Terres et Isles de ce Païs-là.'⁵ As diplomatic disputes evolved over the ensuing four decades, British and French positions would diverge radically over the extent of the territories surrendered at Utrecht. Nevertheless, statements made in 1710 left no doubt that the fall of Port Royal was regarded by contemporary colonial and imperial officials as a remarkable development. The Massachusetts governor, council, and assembly were triumphant in their message of congratulations to Queen Anne, 'Possessor of that important Fort and Country, not only by conquest, but of indubitable right, annex'd to your Majesty's Imperial Crown.' The other side of the coin was represented by the mood of shock and desperation manifested in the response of the French minister of marine, Jérome Phélypeaux, comte de Pontchartrain. 'Je pense continuellement,' wrote Pontchartrain in December 1710, 'aux moyens de pouvoir reprendre ce poste important avant que les anglois y soient solidement establys.'⁶ Neither imperial rival, of course, grappled seriously with the reality that the territory largely remained under native control regardless of its delineation.

This book, therefore, is a study of an important but ambiguous conquest. The events of 1710 lacked the apparent decisiveness of the conquest of Canada half a century later. Leaving the existing Acadian population, at least temporarily, with the option of staying in the nominally British Nova Scotia, the events also lacked the human tragedy and the destructive ironies of the *grand dérangement* that would begin in 1755. Yet the conquest of Acadia had its own profound implications for the history of northeastern North America in the first half of the eighteenth century, and as a geopolitical event it has never received due attention from historians. It was a key element in the framing of the North American issues in French–British treaty negotiations of 1711–13, notably in compelling French negotiators to find an uneasy balance between safeguarding the economic interests of the lucrative North Atlantic fisheries and the strategic interests of retaining a sufficient territorial bridgehead to assure access to the Gulf of St Lawrence, and thus to Canada. The conquest of Acadia also precipitated the creation – tenuous as it was at first – of a new colonial society in British Nova Scotia, and posed new and difficult questions of identity for Acadians. For the native population, its significance was not initially clear, but in the longer term native involvement in the continuing competition between ill-defined European territorial claims had both diplomatic and military consequences.

In all of these respects, the conquest's immediate results engendered changes that became evident only incrementally, gathering force over time. To adopt *Annales* terminology, the conquest requires examination on at least three historical levels. In the shortest term, it can be studied as an event. It also revealed and influenced the course of social, cultural, economic, and political transitions that existed in what Fernand Braudel defined as *le temps conjoncturel*. Finally, it demands evaluation in the context of the *longue durée*: does the conquest merely have a conjunctural significance, or does it speak to the historian of deeper currents and more extended chronologies?[7]

If the significance of the conquest of Acadia exists on different levels of analysis, it was also an intricate process in a different sense. It is easy enough to create a narrative of the conquest from official imperial and colonial documentation, and the opening chapter of this study does so as a benchmark. But the truth is that there is no single valid narrative, and to pretend to construct one would do violence to complexities that were characteristic not only of Mi'kma'ki-Wulstukwik/Acadia/Nova Scotia, but also (with local variations) of early modern North America as a whole. The events that are central to this book were experienced differently by native inhabitants, Acadians, and British and French officials, and by British colonists in New England and then in Nova Scotia. Accordingly, even the most traditional principles of historical methodology will tell us that the historian's narrative will vary according to the questions that are asked; thus the diversity of approaches taken by the authors, chapter by chapter. If it succeeds in its task, however, this book is no mere collection of essays. Rather, it represents a coordinated effort to portray a multilayered reality – unfettered either by traditional assumptions that geopolitical events have exclusively geopolitical significance, or by the kind of teleological blinkers that have too often caused the conquest of Acadia to be seen only as a precursor of other geopolitical events later in the eighteenth century. The geographical core of the book's analysis lies in the territory where Mi'kma'ki, Acadia, and Nova Scotia overlapped: in modern terms, peninsular Nova Scotia. Events and processes taking place in neighbouring territories are prominently examined where the analysis demands it: the French colony of Île Royale, and especially Louisbourg; Wulstukwik and the portion of Mi'kma'ki falling within modern New Brunswick; and northern New England. Also considered is the persistent influence of Massachusetts. In a wider sense, however, the context includes the entire North Atlantic world.

This study argues that a fully contextualized history of the conquest of Acadia has much to reveal both about the world of the North Atlantic in the early eighteenth century and about the constant negotiation and renegotiation of relationships among imperial, colonial, and native interests in North America itself. The processes by which European states sought to legitimate their claims, and the terms on which mutual toleration would be granted or withheld by different peoples living side by side, are especially visible in the Nova Scotia that emerged following the conquest. Yet these issues were neither unique nor local in their significance. In existing historiography, they have too often been obscured by the inability or the reluctance of authors to explore the interconnections of imperial, colonial, and aboriginal history. The inability of earlier generations of historians to do so stemmed from the lack, until the last thirty years or so, of the social and ethnohistorical approaches that have been developed within that time. Much of the literature on geopolitical developments simply predates these crucial historiographical changes. More recently, historians who have been preoccupied with exploring the insights of social history have tended to assume that geopolitical events and imperial influences are largely irrelevant to an understanding of societal characteristics. A more realistic perspective, this book contends, can be based on the recognition of a constant three-way dialogue – sometimes formal and sometimes not, sometimes punctuated by violence but more often not – involving the representatives of the imperial states and of local societies both colonial and aboriginal.

This analysis is, of course, built in part on the work of those authors within the existing historiography who have already explored the existence of negotiated relationships in early modern North America. In varying contexts, the works of Edward Countryman, Jack P. Greene, and Richard White come to mind.[8] More generally, the recent studies in the history of the British empire that have come to be grouped under the heading of 'the new imperial history,' analogous work on the empire of France, and studies of the Atlantic world more generally, are also directly relevant insofar as they deal with the relationship of the imperial state with colonial and aboriginal peoples. Examples are the works of authors such as C.A. Bayly, J.F. Bosher, H.V. Bowen, Nicholas Canny, and P.J. Marshall – as well as the first two volumes of the *Oxford History of the British Empire*, edited respectively by Canny and Marshall.[9] Also germane are the previous studies of the individual authors of this study, ranging over a variety of intellectual terrains that are here juxtaposed and correlated.[10]

The earlier historiography of the conquest of Acadia itself presents a mottled picture. In the study of Canadian history, references to 'The Conquest' have usually referred to the events of 1759–60 in the St Lawrence valley, to an extent that implicitly categorizes that event as the only eighteenth-century conquest worthy of the name. Over the ensuing centuries, the conquest of Canada came to assume a profound ideological significance in successive struggles to define the dynamics of nationality among the Québécois, just as Acadian intellectuals of the nineteenth and twentieth centuries debated the lessons that might or might not be learned from the expulsion of 1755–62.[11] Against such ideological juggernauts and the academic literatures that corresponded to them, the conquest of 1710 stood little chance. It could all too easily be dismissed as just one of the episodes leading up to the Treaty of Utrecht, which in turn could be seen as a failed attempt to reconcile the essentially irreconcilable French and British interests that would finally clash in the climactic events of the 1750s and 1760s. Not for this conquest the grandeur of disputes as to whether it was, as was debated passionately of the conquest of Canada, a catastrophe or a mere incident for those conquered. Not for this part of Acadian history the acrimony of rival contentions that it was, as was argued of the *grand dérangement*, an act of wanton cruelty or a regrettable but unavoidable military measure. Instead, at least until the late 1960s, interpretations of the conquest of Acadia fell into three principal categories. What all of them had in common was a view of the conquest as incidental to the unfolding of larger chains of events.

First, the conquest of Acadia could be interpreted as a strategic stepping-stone to the conquest of Canada. This view had the merit of being founded on a body of evidence generated by contemporaries who saw the attack on Port Royal – and previous attempts since 1690 – in just this way. For example, Samuel Vetch's celebrated tract of 1708, 'Canada Survey'd,' identified the seizure of Quebec and Montreal as crucial to the chances of British displacement of the French from North America.[12] The failure of the naval expedition to the St Lawrence led by Sir Hovenden Walker in 1711 ended any possibility that the conquests of Acadia and Canada would occur in successive years, but that did not prevent historians from linking the two and assigning priority to the second, in significance if not in time. In the early twentieth century, Herbert Levi Osgood wrote of the capture of Port Royal that 'this petty operation figures in history as the conquest of Acadia,' but saw in it and in the Walker expedition primarily 'an anticipation of what was to occur with decisive results a half-century later.'[13] The point was later taken up in greater detail by Guy Frégault, who wrote extensively on Acadian matters even though his main interests lay always in Canada. With the fall of Port Royal, Frégault observed in 1956, 'une colonie française vient de tomber dans l'empire anglais pour n'en plus sortir.' The logical culmination, delayed as it was following Walker's failure, was the elimination of France as an imperial power in North America.[14] Thus, the conquest of Acadia was significant as 'une préfiguration' of events still to come.[15]

A second historiographical approach to the 1710 conquest centred on its significance for Acadian society, and was profoundly influenced by Acadian clerical nationalism. It portrayed the Acadians as responding to the conquest in ways that demonstrated their existing qualities of virtue and piety, and presaged the exercise of the same characteristics at the time of the expulsion. For this approach, the crucial body of primary source evidence lay in the French and British official correspondences that followed the Treaty of Utrecht and dealt with the question of whether or not the Acadians would leave Nova Scotia to resettle on Île Royale or Île Saint-Jean. The same material was used by different authors in this tradition to make different arguments – either that British authorities unjustifiably prevented Acadians from leaving, or that most Acadians decided for themselves that they would not abandon their ancestral lands. Either way, the key inference was that by 1710 the Acadians had developed into a people characterized by piety, simple rural values, and a desire for peace. For Antoine Bernard, 'les trois pivots de toute société durable: religion, famille et propriété, existèrent en Acadie dès la première heure et servirent de base à son développement ethnique,'[16] and it was the same qualities that in the wake of the conquest 'continuaient de soutenir le petit édifice français d'Acadie.'[17] The emphasis on pastoral virtues, with the conquest as an early testing ground for their resilience, became until the 1960s a virtually unassailable orthodoxy in the historiography of the Acadian people, and influenced in turn the work of non-Acadian writers such as L.H. Gipson and Andrew Hill Clark.[18]

A third historiographical approach drew upon official colonial correspondence and other documentation originating in Massachusetts to portray the conquest of 1710 as a consolidation of New England's rightful, or at least inescapable, sphere of influence. New England resentment of the raiding warfare of French and native forces, and of the French privateers operating from Port Royal in the years immediately prior to the conquest, was easily established. 'Port Royal,' complained

Governor Joseph Dudley and others in 1709, 'is become another Dunkirk.'[19] Thus, Thomas Hutchinson's eighteenth-century history of Massachusetts set the conquest in the context of the 'barbarities' of frontier warfare, and English-speaking Nova Scotia historians of the nineteenth century took up the theme, in the words of Beamish Murdoch, that the conquest was 'the only mode of relieving the frontier English settlers from the sudden surprizes of the Indians,' and thus from the 'cowardly mode of warfare pursued by their neighbors.'[20] The view of the conquest of Acadia as an event significant primarily for its New England origins and its success in extending British rule northeastward was then carried into two treatments of greater sophistication that were published in the twentieth century. In the interpretations of J.B. Brebner and Gustave Lanctôt, the theme of New England resistance to French and native aggression was replaced by a more detached analysis of the strengths and limitations of New England influence after 1710. Brebner, writing in 1927, portrayed the conquest as inaugurating yet another phase of Acadia/Nova Scotia as 'New England's Outpost,' but he also pointed out the political and military weakness of the new British regime.[21] Lanctôt, in 1941, agreed. 'En définitive,' he argued, 'malgré son nouveau drapeau et sa nouvelle garnison, l'Acadie ne changea guère.' Yet Lanctôt did maintain that the Acadians experienced material benefits from the conquest: peace and prosperity, with secure access to New England markets as well as the new prospect of trade with Louisbourg.[22]

For New England, on the other hand, Lanctôt argued that the conquest had proved to be 'une assez mince victoire économiquement et politiquement,' considering that France still held Canada and Cape Breton Island.[23] This point hinted at the view that the 1710 conquest could be seen as a stepping-stone towards 1759–60, just as Brebner's insistence that the Acadians after the conquest 'continued their bucolic existence' reflected the approach that stressed the persistence of simple moral values.[24] The three historiographical traditions that portrayed the conquest as an incident in larger continuing processes were not mutually exclusive. Yet, individually or in combination, they allowed for little debate as to whether there were also forces of change that were created or prompted by the events of 1710.

From the 1970s onwards, fresh approaches towards Acadian history, and towards the more general history of northeastern North America in the colonial era, began to be explored. New findings emerged to cast doubt on the earlier assumptions regarding the 1710 conquest,

although no major study focused on the circumstances and results of
the conquest considered for their own sake. In 1973, George A. Rawlyk
took issue with Brebner's contention that the eighteenth century saw
the steadily increasing assertion of expansionist energies by New
England. For Rawlyk, New England's interest in Acadia/Nova Scotia was
intermittent, and was driven by specific concerns involving military security and the safeguarding of the fisheries. Thus, while there might be
scope for elements of continuity in New England involvement, spanning
the era of the conquest, there was no guarantee of it.[25] Donald F. Chard,
in a series of articles, went a step further. The military contingencies of
the years surrounding the conquest had profound economic and strategic significance, Chard argued, bringing about new dynamics of conflict
and prompting New Englanders to pursue their economic interests in
the region in novel ways. The threat from French privateers, first at Port
Royal and later from Louisbourg, was deemed by Chard to be genuine
enough to lend some credence to the often-drawn contemporary comparison with Dunkirk.[26] The aftermath of the conquest saw French–New
England conflicts in the Canso area that formed the context for
attempts by New England to set limits on the French fishery, represent-
ing for Chard 'a calculated effort by New Englanders to formulate imperial policy for their own ends.'[27]

Other historians explored imperial issues more directly. Ian K. Steele
saw the events of 1710 as an 'easy conquest' that made no essential break
with the 'recurring patterns' of native–French–British rivalries that characterized the first half of the eighteenth century. For James D. Alsop,
the years leading up to the conquest provided revealing evidence of the
influence on British imperial approaches of private individuals – or
'projectors' – such as Samuel Vetch.[28] The 1987 treatment by Robert
Sauvageau, of the significance of Acadia/Nova Scotia in the 'guerre de
cent ans des Français d'Amérique' that the author assigned to the years
from 1670 to 1769, was historiographically provocative in portraying the
Acadians as warriors in the French cause rather than as an essentially
nonmilitary people. For Sauvageau, the failure of the French to hold or
recapture Port Royal was a turning point that demonstrated the failings
of the officers who governed both Acadia and Canada, and that left the
Acadians to fight an increasingly unequal battle.[29] Thomas G. Barnes,
on the other hand, emphasized in 1990 the legal rather than the military implications of the conquest, putting the ultimate blame on Whitehall for the 'juridical failure' of the British regime in Annapolis, the very
benignity of which he believed had allowed Acadian leaders to draw

ambiguous conclusions regarding the rigour and the stability – or the lack thereof – of British rule.[30]

Social and economic questions, meanwhile, were examined by Jean Daigle and William Godfrey. Daigle's 1975 doctoral thesis established that Acadian merchants were far from passive participants in their pre-conquest trading relationship with counterparts from New England. Although the size and strength of the Massachusetts economy gave the New Englanders an advantage in sheer economic muscle, the Acadian *entrepreneurs-commerçants* pursued their own goals with skill and success in Daigle's view. The era of the conquest, however, saw this achievement undermined. First, the growing number of French privateers disrupted trade and even competed with the Acadian merchants as suppliers of goods to the colony. Then, following the conquest, the *entrepreneurs-commerçants* were no longer needed as intermediaries between Acadia and New England, and a significant number took employment with Massachusetts merchants as sea captains or pilots.[31] A further result of the conquest was indicated in Godfrey's biographical study of the British major-general born in Annapolis Royal in 1714 and baptized 'Jean Baptiste Bradstreat.' Bradstreet was the son of a British officer and his Acadian wife, and his family background was one example of the changed circumstances brought about by the presence of the British garrison and the beginnings of intermarriage.[32]

Socioeconomic and demographic issues relating to the Acadians were raised also in works by Gisa Hynes, Leslie Choquette, Bernard Pothier, and Corinne LaPlante. Writing in 1973 on demographic characteristics of Acadians at Annapolis Royal, Hynes focused on two consequences of the conquest: the end of immigration from France, and the exclusion from Nova Scotia of the religious orders. The lack of immigrants led, Hynes argued, to an increase in marriages between cousins, while the unavailability of formal education by members of religious orders produced a decline in literacy.[33] For Choquette, however, the most salient elements of Acadian population history remained essentially undisturbed by the conquest: geographical mobility, and a political outlook that was 'essentially modern' in the individualism that was based on a commercial economy.[34] Additional evidence of the economic context of geographical mobility in the era of the conquest was provided by Pothier in an analysis of the sixty-seven Acadian families who chose to resettle on Île Royale following the Treaty of Utrecht, showing that most were headed not by farmers but by navigators and artisans.[35] Conversely, LaPlante argued that the decision of most Acadians not to remove was a voluntary and realistic one based on reluctance to abandon a productive base of agricultural land.[36]

The ongoing work of Naomi Griffiths, while recognizing the economic and demographic continuities that spanned the conquest era, has also explored the subtleties of the political choices that were thrust before Acadians at this time. Writing in 1973, Griffiths interpreted the conquest as inaugurating a period during which the Acadians, denied any certainty as to whether the British regime would prove to have been permanently established by the Treaty of Utrecht or whether it might subsequently be erased by military or diplomatic means, had to find a way through the dangerous thickets of allegiance to Great Britain or to France. The result by 1717, she argued, was the articulation of a strategy of neutrality, influenced by the earlier history of Acadian pragmatism but explicitly formulated as a response to the changed circumstances after 1710.[37] Returning to this question in 1992, Griffiths dealt explicitly with the significance of the conquest era as '[the Acadians'] circumstances were altered from those of a people on the periphery of French power to those of a border people of the English empire.'[38] While none of these changes represented, for Griffiths, an immediate barrier to increasing Acadian economic complexity and prosperity, this author's studies of the wider aspects of Acadian societal development and identity raised significant questions regarding continuity and discontinuity at the time of the conquest.

So too did studies in a native context. Writing in 1979, L.F.S. Upton declared that following the Treaty of Utrecht, 'the new situation gave the native people a new importance in European eyes'; the French looked upon native populations as sources of auxiliary forces, while the British sought a form of pacification that would secure their rule in Nova Scotia.[39] Olive P. Dickason explored in 1976 the nature of the alliance between the Mi'kmaq and the French at Louisbourg, recognizing that the French depended upon native cooperation for both economic and military reasons, and that the Mi'kmaq position of strength ensured that influence was the most that French officials – or religious missionaries – could hope to exert.[40] Writing again on the subject in 1992, Dickason reaffirmed that the Mi'kmaq rejected any notion that either the events of 1710 or the Treaty of Utrecht placed them under any obligation to the Nova Scotia regime, and resisted British encroachments both by sea and by land.[41] Mi'kmaq repudiation of British assertions and a strategy of armed resistance when necessary – though ultimately against overwhelming odds – were also central to the treatment of this era by Daniel N. Paul in 1993.[42]

Taken as a whole, the existing literature on the conquest of Acadia is inconclusive. Without significant exception, the older studies portrayed the conquest as an incident of limited significance within a larger series of events. Treatments from the 1970s onwards have been more varied, and important and provocative questions have been raised as to whether or not the conquest made a difference in a range of economic, political, and cultural contexts. The difficulty has been, however, that if the conquest has not invariably been seen in the recent literature as incidental to other events, it has usually been treated as incidental to the historiographical questions broached by historians who have examined it en route to their explorations of other themes. The purpose of this book is to invert the pattern. A variety of historiographical approaches will be brought to bear, but always using the conquest of Acadia as a refractive prism – and with the ultimate goal of assessing the conquest as an event and as an episode both in conjunctural time and in the *longue durée*.

The book's treatment of the conquest will be structured in four principal parts. A preliminary chapter, 'The "Conquest" of Acadia: Narratives,' will stand alone as a benchmark narrative of the conquest and its surrounding events. While based largely on well-known British and French sources, it will also introduce the different narratives that arise from considering the events as construed by Mi'kmaq and Acadians. These themes will be developed more fully as the book progresses. The second section, 'Precursors,' will consist of two chapters tracing back into the seventeenth century the origins of the conquest and of imperial and colonial responses to it. The first of the chapters, 'Elites, States, and the Imperial Contest for Acadia,' will set the conquest in a long-term context of early modern developments in the North Atlantic world. The second, entitled 'Family and Political Culture in Pre-Conquest Acadia,' will examine the rootedness of Acadian responses to English/British incursions from 1690 onwards in a political culture profoundly shaped by family connections.

The third section, 'Agencies,' will focus on further influences that were essential to the moulding of the conquest's results. The first of three chapters, 'New England and the Conquest,' will not only explore New England's participation in the conquest itself but will show how the actions of New Englanders created Mi'kmaq and Acadian grievances that long influenced the relationships of these peoples with the post-conquest British regime. 'Mi'kmaq Decisions: Antoine Tecouenemac, the Conquest, and the Treaty of Utrecht,' the chapter that deals most centrally with native agency in the era of the conquest, will demonstrate that the limitations of written evidence must not distract historians from understanding the Mi'kmaq experience as situated in Mi'kmaq villages. The Mi'kmaq were far from being mere adjuncts of imperial and colonial processes, and their history cannot properly be represented by privileging the traditional notion of its being fatally intertwined with external influences. The third chapter of the section, 'Imperialism, Diplomacies, and the Conquest of Acadia,' will examine diplomatic responses to the 1710 conquest, emphasizing that both formal and informal diplomacies were at work.

In the fourth section, 'Transitions,' three chapters will examine longer-term processes of which the conquest formed a crucial part. 'Making a British Nova Scotia,' will analyse the British effort to consolidate the conquest by establishing an effective regime at Annapolis Royal, and the reasons why this was a tenuous enterprise at best. The chapter 'The Third Acadia: Political Adaptation and Societal Change' will build on the earlier exploration of Acadian political culture to demonstrate how Acadian responses to the conquest were political as well as diplomatic, but existed in a climate of social and economic change. The final substantive chapter, 'Imperial Transitions,' will portray the imperial dimensions of the conquest as offering some opportunities to British officials to forge tools for dealing with the stresses of an increasingly multiethnic empire, but at the same time laying bare the problems arising from disjunction between metropolitan policy and colonial conditions that would prove costly to the empire later in the eighteenth century. Imperial history in this sense will imply, of course, the interpretation of empire as constructed to include the agency of non-British peoples as well as colonists and imperial authorities. That this is an important theme of the book as a whole will be confirmed in the Conclusion, where the importance of juxtaposing different narratives of an event such as the conquest will be reaffirmed as a contribution to our understanding of the complexities of early modern northeastern North America.

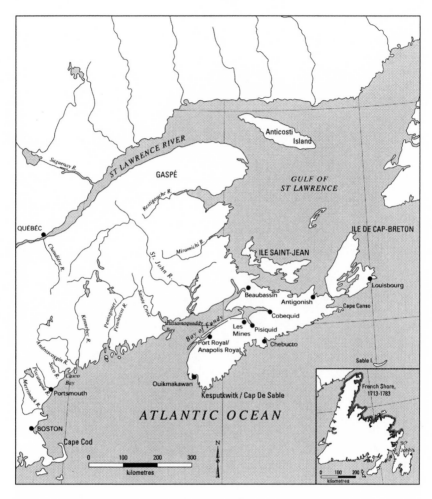

Map 1: Acadia/Nova Scotia and Surrounding Areas of Northeastern North America

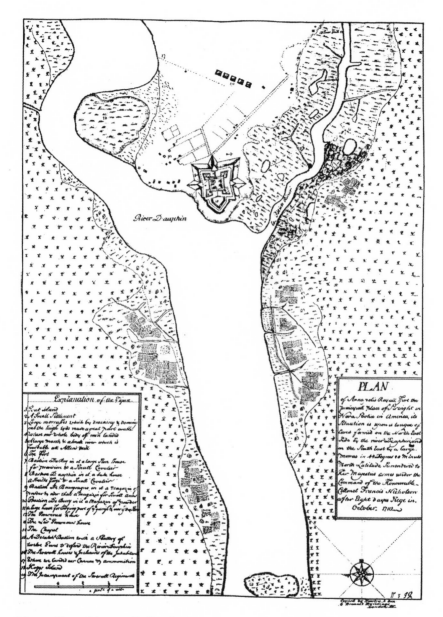

Map 2: Plan of Annapolis Royal, 1710

PART ONE: THE EVENT

1

The 'Conquest' of Acadia: Narratives

John G. Reid

Anne to *New England Nicholson* Commands
To save it from base Neighbours savage hands
Who comes regardless of his Life & Coyn
New English Troops to *British* Fleet doth joyn
And to Block up that Port *Matthews* fore runs
Till dread nought ships are come with Bombs and Guns
Brave *Francis* Quell'd the *Francks* & sent them going
With ease he stopt the strutting Coxcombs Crowing
Thus *Supercass* his Goverment & Name
And Castle Lost and hastens home with shame
Port Ryall is become Annopolis
And Nova Scotia doth revive in this
For a North Britian now doth rule the roast
And Vetch and Hobbey to defend her Coast
For in the year seventeen hundred and ten
By Nicholson Anne got Her own again
Victorious Anne she and Her Great Allies
Triumph in European Victories
But this *American* is all Her own
Under the Conduct of Her Nicholson
Dear Christ confirm what Thou hast wrought thy Dove
From hence forth cover with thy Wings and Love[1]

Many different narratives of the conquest of Acadia could be constructed. Many were told at the time, no doubt, although few have

survived. Judge Samuel Sewall's tribute to 'Brave *Francis*' Nicholson and the 'North Britian' Samuel Vetch was written in Boston in October 1710. The poem was statelier in its original Latin than in the translation, which foreshadowed the writing style of another North Briton of doubtful celebrity, William McGonagall. Yet Sewall's portentous view of the conquest touched on most of the elements that made the event, at least in the eyes of the victors of Annapolis Royal, a prodigious triumph. Well it might, as Sewall had written the poem for immediate dispatch to Nicholson at Annapolis Royal.[2] The freeing of New England from the threat of Port Royal, with its privateers and native allies; the victory of Protestantism over the Catholic foe; the united military might of New England and Great Britain; the benefits of the union of England and Scotland, including the reassertion of the British right to an ancient Scottish claim; and, of course, the heroism of the expedition itself: all were themes that Sewall managed to work into the few 'Distichs' that he modestly offered to Nicholson, 'such as they are.'[3]

The poem, with the construction it places on the story of the Conquest, provides a point of departure for a benchmark narrative – not a definitive one – based on the accounts of British and French protagonists. As this chapter will show, the battle for Port Royal was not prolonged. After a siege lasting a week, the French governor agreed to terms of capitulation on behalf of the outnumbered garrison. Three more days saw the fort in British hands, and within a further two weeks the defeated troops had been dispatched to France. The remaining issues were more complex. Tentative Mi'kmaq–British negotiations were followed by skirmishing, with the British coming off worse. Initial British efforts to govern the Acadian population were also inconclusive. An equilibrium of sorts prevailed by 1712, but it was fragile. Much depended by that time on diplomatic exchanges, conducted formally in the Netherlands and in France and informally in the new 'Nova Scotia.' The formal negotiations in Europe could proceed in blissful ignorance of the variety of constructions that could be put on the conquest and its surrounding events. The informal but equally crucial negotiations among British officials and the non-British peoples were more directly affected by the existence of parallel narratives.

Samuel Sewall, as a diarist, had recorded Nicholson's arrival in Boston in mid-July 1710, with a small naval fleet and some 400 British marines.[4] How much of a threat the expedition posed to the French control of Port Royal was open to doubt at that time. Nicholson's instructions looked forward to the capture not only of Port Royal itself, where Vetch was then designated to command, but also of 'other places in Nova Scotia.'[5] Whether Nova Scotia, as a British colony, existed outside of the cartographic fantasies of imperial officials was a point yet to be determined. Whether Port Royal, or anywhere else, could be captured also remained to be seen. The last attempt in 1707 had ended in disgrace and recrimination. Despite the successful landing of some 1100 New England troops near the French fort in the late spring of that year, ten days passed without any serious attempt to move siege artillery over the marshland terrain. An ignominious retreat was followed some weeks later by an equally ineffective attempt under new commanding officers. The lieutenant-governor of New Hampshire was not alone in thinking of the episode, from the English perspective, as a 'Horible Shamefull miscariage.'[6] Another fiasco ensued in 1709. Pressed by Governor Joseph Dudley of Massachusetts and by Vetch, through his influential tract of 1708 entitled 'Canada Survey'd,' the British Board of Trade had successfully advocated the dispatch of a British and New England expedition to seize control of Quebec. The New England forces were gathered in Boston during the summer, and preparations started for a related assault on Montreal from New York. Only on 11 October did news reach New England that the promised British naval and military force had been diverted to Spain, and hasty attempts to organize a late autumn assault on Port Royal soon proved unworkable.[7] Nicholson, who had been in charge of the land forces supposedly to advance on Montreal, promptly departed for London to argue on behalf of the Massachusetts colony that Port Royal should be the target of a new assault in the following year.[8]

Nicholson succeeded in this task and in securing the commitment of the marines, whose presence in itself made the expedition more formidable than that of 1707. The force of 1710 also outdid its predecessor of 1709, solely by the fact of its physical arrival in Boston. Yet serious questions remained. Prior to leaving Plymouth, Nicholson had observed that the marine contingent, supposedly 500 strong, numbered only 397 on the muster rolls, and that almost half of those were untried and possibly unhealthy recruits who would be unreliable in battle.[9] The defences of Port Royal itself had been supplemented by the successful efforts of the Governor of Acadia, Daniel d'Auger de Subercase, to recruit the services of privateers from the French West Indies. In May 1710, Vetch complained from Boston that even in Massachusetts Bay itself the privateers had taken nine vessels in five days.[10] More generally, the recent history of combined military and naval assaults on defended positions – whether in

North America, the Caribbean, or in western Europe – was one in which failure was the norm. A success such as that temporarily attained by Sir William Phips at Port Royal in 1690 was the exception that proved the rule.[11] All things considered, it seemed likely to the French minister of Marine in May 1710 that the British would be sufficiently discouraged by their past setbacks, and the British treasury sufficiently swamped with competing demands for funds, that Subercase could safely be advised that 'il paroist que vous n'avez beaucoup a craindre d'Eux.'[12]

Subercase was not so sure. Well informed in early 1710, from prisoners taken by the privateers, on the movements of New England militia forces and on the comings and goings of warships in Boston harbour, the governor found some hope in the evident lack of enthusiasm in New England for a spring attack on Port Royal. Should a British fleet appear, however, the situation would be dangerous again. In that case, Subercase remarked, 'je Crains que le passé ne leur soit une lesson pour lavenir et quils ne profitent des fautes quils ont faites.'[13] Subercase worried too about shortage of munitions in the Port Royal fort, the absence of needed reinforcements, and about his inability to adequately provide supplies for native allies whose sympathy for the French cause had been in doubt more than once in the immediately preceding years.[14] The weaknesses of the garrison, moreover, were reported in detail to Governor Dudley in August 1710 by Simon Slocomb, a fishing captain who had been taken by a privateer and had spent part of June and most of July at Port Royal before his release. Although Slocomb had not been allowed to observe the fortifications directly, he had kept his eyes open while exercising along the shore and had conversed with fellow prisoners and Acadian inhabitants. The garrison consisted of only some 200 ill-equipped French troops, Slocomb reported, and 40 Canadiens: 'he saw but very few Souldiers, and those very ragged without Stockens and onely Indian shoes.'[15]

To be sure, the British expeditionary force had logistical troubles of its own. As Nicholson complained to London in mid-September, the New England colonies had lacked instructions to prepare for the fleet's arrival. Rumours had been spreading since May about the approach of 'six Men of War, with a Thousand Marines,' but similar reports had circulated in 1709 and the province was still struggling to pay the bills for the substantial costs of raising and supporting troops for the expedition that had failed to materialize. Nicholson reported that in 1710 the lack of preparation and 'the vast expence and disapointment of last Year' made it a slow business to assemble ships, munitions, and other supplies.[16] Further confusion may have been caused when British authorities abruptly decided in mid-July – the ministry in flux, as Tories steadily displaced Whigs – to order Vetch and Nicholson to collaborate with an additional fleet in an autumn attack on Canada, only to cancel the plan seven weeks later.[17] Finally, on 18 September, the unwieldy fleet set sail from Nantasket. The flagship *Dragon*, three other frigates, and a bomb ship made up the naval contingent, joined by the Massachusetts *Province Galley* under its experienced commander – and veteran of the Phips expedition – Cyprian Southack. The frigate *Chester*, commanded by Thomas Matthews and regularly stationed in New England, had gone on ahead. Some thirty-six other vessels made up the expedition, including supply ships and hospital ships, but not counting the open sloops that carried artillery tools and lumber. Troop transports carried some 1500 provincial and allied native troops, as well as the marines and a company of grenadiers – New Englanders trained for several months in siege warfare by the Huguenot regular Captain Paul Mascarene. Of the provincial forces, Massachusetts contributed some 900, while smaller contingents came from Connecticut, Rhode Island, and New Hampshire.[18]

For three days the fleet coasted northeastwards, until it encountered a minor setback while at anchor off the islands known as the Wolves, just outside Passamaquoddy Bay and east of Campobello. Fog, tidal currents, and bad weather cost several vessels their anchors and cables, but did not forestall the remaining short voyage to reach the entrance to the Port Royal basin three days later.[19] In the meantime, the fleet had met with a brigantine dispatched from *Chester* to carry to Boston four deserters from the Port Royal garrison. For the British, this was significant news. Matthews had blockaded the gut some days before, as Subercase had admitted to France on 13 September (the 24th, N.S.). At the time, the governor had been confident in the solidarity of the garrison, but he reported a week later that defeatism in the ranks had led to desertions. Subercase's own morale had also suffered by this time, as his letter to the minister of Marine revealed:

> Mais enfin, Monseigneur, je vous supplie de croire que je ne sçaurois pas faire l'impossible. Je suis comme dans une prison ou je ne puis rien faire entrer, n'y d'ou je ne sçaurois rien faire sortir, et la recolte a esté très mauvaise au Port Royal; outre cela, je n'ay pas un sol et nôtre credit est Epuisé.[20]

After meeting with the other vessels, the brigantine turned back

towards Port Royal, escorting a single transport. The main fleet followed
on the 24th, finally riding at anchor off Goat Island, at the mouth of the
Port Royal River and some ten kilometres short of the fort. Matthews
was already there with another eight French deserters, and two more
French soldiers arrived during the evening. The British themselves lost
'three Irish and one Dutchman' to desertion, but they could better
afford it.[21] Not that all the indications were favourable for the invaders.
When the brigantine and the transport entered the gut, they were
met by 'several Vollyes of small shot' fired by 'a parcel of Indians.'[22]
Although cannon fire from the ships ended the exchange without damage on either side, the incident raised the possibility of Mi'kmaq opposition. Resistance from the isolated and now-depleted garrison was one
thing. The antagonism of the native inhabitants was something else altogether. The Mi'kmaq had long been willing to accommodate a French
presence in their territory. This was seen in their acceptance of missionary priests, their tolerance of Acadian settlement, and their willingness
to trade. None of it, however, implied a surrender of autonomy or military capacity. The expansion of Acadian settlements in population and
extent was a nonstate phenomenon that posed no affront to the contin-
uation of overall native control. Thus, any Mi'kmaq opposition had necessarily to be taken seriously by British forces. Nevertheless, from the
time of the initial incident at the gut, native interventions in the siege of
Port Royal – while enough to belie Samuel Vetch's assertion of 1707 that
the Mi'kmaq 'never had any Warr with the English' – were neither determined nor decisive.[23] The contest for Port Royal in the autumn of 1710,
to an extent unusual in the campaigns of the era, would have the character of a largely French–British dispute.

A more serious setback for the British force came on the afternoon of
24 September, when the first entry into the Port Royal River itself was
attempted by the transport ship *Caesar*. Grounding his vessel close to
shore, Captain Jeremiah Tay – who had been plying the northeastern
coasts since the early 1690s – was calm or complacent enough to refuse
offers of help. When the wind swept the *Caesar* on to the rocks in the
evening, Tay drowned along with crew members and twenty-three soldiers from the company he was carrying. The company commander and
some twenty-five others struggled ashore.[24] With the other companies
intact, however, a council of war met on board Nicholson's flagship the
Dragon and selected the next day, 25 September, for reconnaissance on
shore and a possible landing in force. One group of officers, supported
by 200 marines, went ashore on the south side of the river – the side

where the fort and the main settlement were located. Vetch, Mascarene, and the grenadiers explored the north side. The main landing took place in the afternoon. The force was divided, with Vetch joined by two of the four New England regiments on the north side, and Nicholson heading the remainder in a more direct approach to the fort. There were hints of discord. While later accounts defined the strategic purpose of the north side landing as leading towards an eventual upriver crossing to permit assaults on the fort from both east and southwest, one officer informed the Board of Trade that Vetch's real purpose was to enjoy his own command rather than having to defer to Nicholson. Vetch never went near the fort, Colonel Robert Reading recalled, until the siege was over.[25]

Be that as it may, both sides of the river were within range of the cannons of the fort's defenders. Fire was intermittent and caused no injury at first, while the response of the British bomb ketch apparently was equally ineffective. The next four days were more deadly, as casualties began to accumulate from exchanges of cannon fire and bombs, and from small arms skirmishes where the woods met the marsh. An attempt by Vetch to set up mortars across the river from the fort was thwarted by the muddy ground, but a combined force of marines and grenadiers on the south side succeeded in entrenching a position within '400 paces' of the fort. By 29 September, four days after the landing, all the British cannon had been landed, and no single concentrated attack had been launched by the defenders.[26] It was in this context that the first direct communication took place between Subercase and Nicholson, when a French party emerged abruptly from the fort in the early afternoon under a flag of truce. What began as a request by Subercase for refuge in the British camp for the families of the French officers, and their maid-servants, soon became a dispute over military etiquette. The French envoys, Nicholson complained, had not been announced by drumbeat so that they could be blindfolded and securely escorted into the British camp. Exchanges of letters continued through the afternoon and evening, Nicholson agreeing to shelter 'the Ladies that are with Child, and those that have young Children,' but ended with a French officer under arrest as a spy and Subercase threatening to cut off all further negotiation.[27]

Subercase also detained a British officer in reciprocation: 'You have one of my Officers and I've one of yours, so that now we are equal.'[28] William Elliot spent what must have been an interesting evening in the fort. He was introduced to the women and children, shared toasts with

Subercase, and responded to the governor's heavy-handed military badi-
nage with some of his own. 'Inform me where the Generals Quarters
are,' Subercase asked, 'and if you'l Ingeniously tell me, neither Morter
or Cannon Ball shall come that way. To which the said William Elliot
Reply'd sometimes in a Bottom, sometimes in a Hill, sometimes in a
House, sometimes under a Hedge, and sometimes betwixt two Bear
Skins.' With apparent resolution, Subercase also informed Elliot that
'he would not give up, his Government without Resistance, and to tell
Col. Vetch that he came of an indifferent Errand for he would still be
Governour.'[29] Yet this was no more than bravado, and Subercase knew
it. The next day passed in intermittent skirmishing, while British cannon were hauled to upland positions threatening the fort and one of
the New England regiments on the north side of the river advanced to a
position opposite Hog Island. By the morning of 1 October, a Sunday,
Subercase offered capitulation in an undated note to Nicholson. Hostilities continued, with British mortars now within 100 metres of the fort,
while Nicholson sent in a formal demand for surrender. The response
denied the British claim to Nova Scotia but assented to negotiations for
'an honourble [sic] and Advantageous Capitulation.' By the end of the
day, a truce had been agreed.[30]

   The subsequent discussions were quick and, by all indications, easy
enough. When the articles of capitulation were signed on 2 October, they
dealt mainly with the honourable departure of the garrison and the privateers. The only one that was replete with future complexities was the
provision for the status of the Acadians: 'that the Inhabitants within Cannon shot of the Fort of Port Royall [defined as extending three miles
around], shall Remain upon their Estates, with their Corn, Cattle and
Furneture, During two Years, in Case they are not Desirous to go before,
The[y] taking the Oaths of Allegance and Fidility to Her Sacred Majesty
of Great Brittain.'[31] To sort out what all of that meant, not to mention
what it implied for Acadians outside of Port Royal, would be the work of
decades rather than years or months. For the time being, however, civil-
ities and ceremonials prevailed, at least for those of the officer class on
both sides. Boats were sent upriver by Nicholson to retrieve those of the
'French Ladies' who had travelled out of the immediate area of the fort.
'They Breakfasted with the General,' read the expedition journal, 'and
were conducted into the Fort; Sir Charles Hobby led in Madam Bonaventure,
and the rest were led in by other Officers.' The next morning a number
of Acadians – men, women, and children – also emerged from refuge in
the woods, although they were not treated to breakfast.[32]

The main ceremony took place on 5 October. With the victorious troops drawn up outside the fort, Nicholson, Vetch, and Hobby – one of the regimental commanders and now to be Vetch's second-in-command – advanced to meet Subercase halfway across the bridge spanning the defensive ditch. The defeated governor, chivalrous to the last, made a gracious speech:

> Sir, I'm very sorry for the misfortune of the King my Master in Losing such a Brave Fort, and the Territories adjoyning; but count myself happy in falling into the hands of so Noble and Generous a General, and now deliver up the Keys of the Fort, and all the Magazines into your hands, hoping to give you a Visit next Spring.[33]

With that, the ragged garrison marched out with drums beating and flags flying. The British, Vetch holding the keys to the fort, marched in to begin a series of celebrations that included drinking royal toasts and firing guns in salute, and extended too to the ceremonial hoisting of the Union flag of Great Britain and the symbolic renaming of Port Royal in honour of Queen Anne. 'The General,' the expedition journal recorded simply, 'gave the Place the name of Annapolis Royal.'[34]

More mundane tasks remained for both armies. During the two days following the transfer of the fort, 200 of the marines were assigned to the continuing garrison, along with 250 New England volunteers. Stores were moved into the fort, while artillery was reembarked on the ships and preparations began for the return of the fleet and the remaining troops to Boston. On one day, 'some Indian's in the woods' fired on the crew of a boat, but the incident was isolated. By 14 October, the transports were loaded and ready. Delays intervened while Nicholson prepared for departure on board the *Dragon*, and to allow for wood and water to be taken on. Some of the vessels left on the 18th. The main fleet followed the next day, reaching Boston a week later.[35] The French, meanwhile, had to contend with the tedium of awaiting their agreed passage to La Rochelle or Rochefort. Finally, on 13 October, they were embarked on a frigate and two brigantines: 149 soldiers, with 109 officials, officers, and families. The six-day wait before the vessels sailed was eased by Nicholson's provision of wine, beer, rum, 'all sorts of Liquor,' and 'several sorts of Spice for the Women and Children.' Subercase for one, although initially disappointed by the quality of the food and water on board, departed well satisfied with the 'particular favours and Civility' that had made the entire episode a model of what a capitulation should be.[36]

Nevertheless, for all concerned – the native and Acadian populations, and the garrison – the ensuing winter would bring hard questions. One was the issue of what exactly the British had captured through the surrender of Port Royal. Even the imperial documents surrounding the expedition were vague on the matter. References to 'Nova Scotia' in either Nicholson's commission or his instructions were sparse, and they were incidental to the delineation of the main purpose of 'the reduction of Port Royal and any of the Country and Places adjacent belonging to the enemy.' Vetch's duties as commander were defined only in reference to Port Royal itself.[37] Yet neither Vetch nor the other leaders of the expedition were long content to remain so modest. A proclamation on 12 October, by Nicholson and the seven other members of the council of war, formally announced the conquest to all the inhabitants of 'L'Accadie and Nova Scotia.' Both this, and a further proclamation directed to British colonists elsewhere in North America, referred to 'the dominions of L'Accadie and Nova Scotia,' although the latter document also admitted that 'the season of the year will not allow the totall reduction of this large country of Nova Scotia.' Two days later, the members of the council of war again joined together to inform Queen Anne that 'in great measure the large country of Nova Scotia is again reduced to your large Empyre in America' and to solicit titles for themselves through a revival of the order of knights-baronets of Scotland that had formed part of the effort to establish the colony of New Scotland during the reign of James VI.[38] Undismayed by the silence that greeted this request, Vetch was ready by late January of 1711 to inform the British secretary of state, Lord Dartmouth, of an unorthodox personal initiative: 'I think fitt to acquaint your Lordship of my haveing taken the title of Governour for her Britannick Majesty of all the territorys of Accadie and Nova Scotia, though they are not yett wholly reduced, this ... I doe not out of the least vanity, but to assert Her Majesty's soveraignety to the same.'[39]

While the seventeenth-century claims and counter-claims that led to the odd juxtaposition of the terms 'L'Accadie' and 'Nova Scotia' were of arcane origin, the issues at stake were no mere abstractions.[40] The conflicting imperial claims of France and Great Britain, and the boundary implications of each, would fuel for several months in 1712 and early 1713 the negotiations leading to the Treaty of Utrecht. Even thereafter, the terms of that treaty left ample scope for the disputes that contributed frequently to French–British tensions in North America. They also did nothing to recognize the even more crucial reality of native control.

Meanwhile, the more limited question of what the conquest of Port Royal implied for the wider territories claimed as 'Nova Scotia' had immediate importance for both Acadian and Mi'kmaq inhabitants. Vetch attempted to put the best face on matters in reporting to Dartmouth in early 1711 that 'the inhabitants within the Banlieu which Containts a league round the ffort have all taken the oath of aledgeance to her Majesty.' The Acadians outside the area covered by the terms of capitulation, he continued, were 'absolutly at her Majestys discretion nor have I given them any tearms of protection though they have frequently applyed for it and offered to take the oath of aledgeance.'[41] Acadian perspectives were not necessarily the same. As early as November 1710 a group of leading Port Royal inhabitants had written to the governor of New France, Philippe de Rigaud de Vaudreuil, to complain of 'la maniere dure avec laquelle Mr. Weische [Vetch] nous traitte.'[42] It was true that some of the Port Royal Acadians had taken an oath of allegiance, as some had done in 1690 under Phips's short-lived regime, but divisions persisted.

By the following spring even Vetch had to admit that the takers of the oath were 'but few' and that they were 'threatned and made uneasy by all the Others who Call them Trayters.'[43] The behaviour of those further up the Annapolis River, and in the Minas and Beaubassin settlement clusters, gave little evidence that they understood their position to be as tenuous as Vetch had described it: 'they are become prisoners at discretion and ... both their persons and Effects are absolutely at the Disposal of the Conquerors.'[44] A visit by Paul Mascarene to the Minas communities in mid-November went off amicably enough, but had more of the air of a diplomatic mission than of a triumphal tour. The inhabitants responded well to Mascarene's invitation that they should not 'take an umbrage' at his arrival with a small party of soldiers, and they selected deputies who were agreeable to the payment of at least part of a sum of 6000 livres and 20 pistoles a month demanded by Mascarene for what he described delicately as 'Contributions ... designed for a present to our Governour.' Mascarene could remember nothing that was actually paid, however, beyond a small initial consignment of furs.[45] The boot was soon on the other foot, when the Annapolis commissary, Peter Capon, was seized by 'three or four Fellows' while on a trip upriver. Capon was released only on payment of a ransom of 20 pistoles obligingly advanced to him by the inhabitant Pierre LeBlanc, at whose house he had been dining when the incident occurred. Efforts to uncover the 'Banditti' responsible failed to bear fruit.[46]

The attitude of nearby Mi'kmaq to the Annapolis Royal regime was also complex. While native leaders informed Vetch on a number of occasions during the first winter that they were considering expulsion of the garrison from its dilapidated fort, late February brought an apparent change. After successfully demanding a hostage from Sir Charles Hobby – in command during Vetch's temporary absence in Boston – a group of Mi'kmaq from LaHave offered negotiations on the basis that 'they were resolv'd hence forward to offer no Violence to any of the English, unless they first began with them.' An amicable meeting was followed by a further visit some days later by a Mi'kmaq father and son from Cape Sable, who received gifts from Hobby and promised that 'the Indians would send their Chiefs here to sign Articles of Peace.'[47] However, for whatever reason, negotiations went no further. By June, Vetch was complaining that he was powerless to curtail the activities of 'Sckulking partys' of Mi'kmaq who were intimidating Port Royal Acadians who had been prevailed upon to cut wood for repair of the fort.[48] Mi'kmaq and Acadian inhabitants responded to the early British presence at Annapolis with, depending on time and place, either good humour or hostility. Both approaches undoubtedly owed something to the expectation that the conquest, such as it had been, might soon prove short-lived. As rumours of a French counter-attack heightened the tensions of the spring of 1711, Vetch pleaded for reinforcements for his sickly and quarrelsome troops: 'wee have not one person to befrind us save what are within the Garison and those Including the sick near two hundred men short of what allways should be.'[49]

In reality, the prospect of a French thrust against Annapolis Royal was receding rapidly during the winter and spring of 1711, although native intervention continued to be a more active possibility. The initial reaction of the French minister of Marine, the Comte de Pontchartrain, was to waste no time in regaining control of Acadia. While it is not certain from which quarter Pontchartrain was first informed about the fall of Port Royal, the governor of French Newfoundland was forwarding 'la facheuse nouvelle' as early as 6 November 1710 (26 October, O.S.).[50] The minister was fully informed by late December, and well into January was pressing the Intendant of the Marine at Rochefort – and former Intendant of New France, François de Beauharnois de la Chaussaye – for urgent action on the mounting of an expedition. 'Vous connoissez,' Pontchartrain reminded the Intendant, 'combien il est Important de reprendre ce poste, avant que les Ennemis y soient solidement Etablis, la conservation de toute l'amerique septentrionale et le commerce des pesches le demandent egalement.'[51] Within a few weeks, however, it had become clear that the demands of ship owners and suppliers for their participation would be too much for the already over-strained royal treasury. By mid-March, Pontchartrain had effectively given up on the immediate retaking of Port Royal. The most likely means of accomplishing the goal, he informed Beauharnois, involved forming a merchant company for the thorough reestablishment of Acadia and its trading economy. This would require efforts to gain the interest of merchants from a series of ports – La Rochelle first and foremost, but also St-Malo, Bayonne, and Nantes – and nobody pretended that it would be anything but slow work.[52]

There were other possibilities, but they too had their drawbacks. The missionary Antoine Gaulin, a priest of the seminary of Quebec who served as vicar-general of Acadia as well as continuing after the surrender of Port Royal to live among the Mi'kmaq, was anxious for intervention from French Newfoundland. The complications were twofold. One was the weakness of the French headquarters in Newfoundland, Plaisance. Governor Costebelle, during the summer of 1711, commented sympathetically to France on Gaulin's request for officers and troops, but concluded that 'we are too far distant from one another for that. I have much ado to furnish an Indifferent Guard to the Different posts that I Employ. The few troops that are here are Extraordinaryly fatigued.'[53] Secondly, Plaisance had gained in strategic and diplomatic importance. For it now to fall, as Pontchartrain had reflected in January, would turn defeat at Port Royal into a wider disaster and jeopardize the French fisheries in the North Atlantic.[54] French Newfoundland's defences, therefore, could not be depleted. Then there was the possibility of an attack from Canada. Governor Vaudreuil had lost no time in requesting reinforcements for the purpose, and in July 1711 he was instructed to consider whether a winter assault could be successful – though without any guarantee of further troops or supplies from France.[55] In the shorter term, however, a large British combined force was gathering in Boston and preparing to ascend the St Lawrence River on its way to Quebec. At Rochefort, Beauharnois had orders that the necessary strengthening of Canada must be accomplished even if 'vous devez faire l'impossible pour surmonter les difficultés quil pourroit y avoir,' but the purpose was firmly to defend Canada rather than to regain Port Royal.[56]

An assertion of native authority, on the other hand, would be capable of more immediately threatening the tenuous British hold on Annapolis. French strategists were well aware that this was so, and took steps to encourage it. In early 1711, Vaudreuil commissioned Bernard-Anselme d'Abbadie de Saint-Castin as French commander in Acadia. His Penobscot mother, Pidianske, was the daughter of the leading Penobscot chief of the early 1690s, Madockawando. His father, the first Saint-Castin to live at Pentagoet, had arrived as a French officer in 1670 and had been adopted by the Penobscot. Bernard-Anselme had fought at the head of Abenaki forces during the unsuccessful New England attack at Port Royal in 1707; in October 1710 he had visited Nicholson at Annapolis and had then departed for Quebec with news of the capitulation.[57] Vaudreuil's commission to Saint-Castin represented, in effect, a plea for Abenaki assistance. Similarly, supplies left France in the spring of 1711 that were intended to enable Gaulin to prompt Mi'kmaq raids on the Annapolis Royal garrison.[58] French authorities were in no position to exert pressure on either the Mi'kmaq or the Abenaki, and repeatedly expressed anxiety that British diplomatic overtures to those peoples might be effective in much the same way as the French had reached an understanding with the Houdenasaunee a decade before.[59] Nevertheless, the balance between hostility and negotiation in both Abenaki and Mi'kmaq relationships with the British was always a delicate one. The late spring of 1711 saw Mi'kmaq parties impeding British efforts to strengthen the defences of the Annapolis fort.[60]

Also, a force of some 40 Abenaki landed from Pentagoet in early June, and promptly ambushed a British detachment on its way up the Annapolis River with the garrison's engineer in an attempt to speed the flow of timber for repairs to the fort. Proceeding, according to Vetch's account, 'with too much Confidence (having never before hardly mett with any resistance),' the British force of sixty-four allowed itself to be separated into smaller groups and was effectively annihilated. The eighteen killed included the engineer, while eleven were wounded and almost all the others taken captive. One soldier escaped to regain the comparative security of Annapolis Royal two days later.[61] The strict military cost of the defeat at 'Bloody Creek' was serious enough, for a beleaguered garrison that had been reduced during the winter by disease and desertion. More important still was what it signified. The missionary Gaulin reported that 'Cette action a si fort relevé le courage des habitants françois et des sauvages' that the Mi'kmaq had abandoned for the time being all thought of responding to British offers of negotiation, while many Acadians had moved upriver from the environs of the fort and expected the garrison soon to be expelled. Mascarene's later recollection was that after the defeat of the detachment the Acadians remaining at Annapolis had 'turned haughty and imperious – and threatn'd no less than to take us – by assault – and put every one of us "to the Edge of the Sword."'[62] Generalizations could be misleading when it came to the attitudes of peoples whose divisions were not always convenient for the likes of Gaulin and Mascarene to recognize. Nevertheless, the affair at Bloody Creek had shown graphically, despite Mascarene's occasional eastward forays on the Bay of Fundy, the weakness of the British hold on anything outside of the fort. It also lent conviction to the declarations frequently made over the years by Mi'kmaq speakers to the effect that, as cited by a later British lieutenant-governor, 'although the English conquered Annapolis, they never did Menis [Minas] and these other parts of the Province.'[63]

As 1711 went on, worse was to follow for the British in northeastern North America. The expedition destined for Quebec under the command of Admiral Sir Hovenden Walker set sail from Boston at the end of July. Its complement of some 7500 troops and marines, most of whom had been transported from Great Britain itself, determined that the fleet would consist of some seventy sail, including nine warships and two bomb ketches.[64] In every respect, this enterprise made its predecessors – whether the Phips attempt on Quebec, or any of the expeditions against Port Royal – look small by comparison. It also had a direct effect on the British presence at Annapolis Royal. Vetch left for Boston in mid-July, reporting when he arrived that 'the French Indians in L'Acadie summon'd the fort at Annapolis a few dayes after they had defeated the party he sent to cutt timber to repair it; that they afterwards block'd it up for four dayes and then retir'd.'[65] Vetch sailed with the expedition, in command of the New England troops, while at Annapolis Sir Charles Hobby earned the wrath of the senior commanders by accepting two companies of New Englanders for the garrison while refusing orders to release the equivalent number of marines for service against Quebec.[66] The 100 or so marines did eventually set out for Quebec, but as matters turned out no reinforcement would have made any difference to the outcome. On the evening of 23 August, when the Walker fleet was some distance west of Anticosti Island and closer to the north shore of the St Lawrence than its navigators believed, a severe storm caused the wreck of seven transport vessels and a storeship. Estimates of the number of those drowned reached 1000, and in the wake of the disaster Walker abandoned the attempt on Quebec.[67]

While the failure of the expedition underlined the inability of British

forces in this war to move decisively outside of the limited bounds of
their own colonies of settlement to offer any serious challenge to
French or – more importantly – to native ascendancy over much larger
territories, from the particular perspective of Annapolis Royal it resulted
in some stabilization of the British position. As the fleet straggled back
to Boston, Vetch stopped at Annapolis to change the garrison. The survivors of the original New England troops, and the 40 or so remaining
marines, were replaced by fresh New Englanders headed by a new lieutenant-governor, the Anglo-Irish officer Thomas Caulfeild.[68] The commander of the land forces on the expedition, General John Hill, had
also allocated to Vetch a number of New England native troops. When
the promised company returned directly to Boston in the confusion of
the retreat, and was disbanded, Vetch set to work on his brother-in-law
John Livingston to raise a force of Mohawks. Livingston's close ties with
the Houdenasaunee had earned him the nickname 'the Mohauk,' and
early in 1712 he arrived at Annapolis Royal with a company of fifty-
eight.[69] The garrison continued to have its difficulties, notably in terms
of logistics and in obtaining funds for wages and other expenses. Vetch
regularly pleaded with British imperial authorities for support, but had
little success in shaking the influential opinion represented by the view
of the former Plantations Secretary, William Blathwayt, that the
expenses of this outpost in 'a desolate Countrey' might best be met by
the Massachusetts colony whose fisheries it protected.[70] For the time
being, though, the garrison carried on. By May 1712, the new engineer
at Annapolis, George Vane, felt able to report that 'we have passed this
winter very peaceably.'[71]

It was true that a new, though fragile, equilibrium had been established. Immediately prior to the 1710 conquest of Port Royal, reports
had been reaching France from critics of Subercase that in Acadia 'les
choses sont a un point que si les anglois se presentoient bien loin que
les habitants se missent en Estat de les chasser il seroit tres a craindre
qu'ils se joignissent a eux.'[72] Although Acadian complaints about 'the
tyranny of Mr. Subercase' had quickly surfaced after the defeated governor's departure, fears that Acadians would make common cause with
the British were not entirely fulfilled. Some Acadians had taken oaths of
allegiance, and Vetch reported that more did so in the early autumn of
1712.[73] This rapprochement apparently continued in the succeeding
months, partly because Caulfeild had a realistic idea of the need for a
negotiated relationship with the Acadian inhabitants. Caulfeild,
reported the engineer Vane, 'has intierly gained the affections of the

people, by his affable and just Gouverment.' This contrasted, Vane went on, with the abrasive behaviour of Vetch, who had 'raised Excessive contributions, and committed abondance of Extortions, using the people more like slaves than any thing Else.'[74] Vetch also reported in November 1711 on renewed negotiation with Mi'kmaq representatives who had offered that 'if wee would allow them the same Liberty [of trade] as they had from the ffrench Garison and sell them all sorts of Goods for their furrs particularly pouder and small shott without which they Could not subsist they would never go no more to Canada.'[75] Native toleration of the British presence at Annapolis Royal would depend ultimately on British behaviour. Yet for the moment, with French–British hostilities subsiding after what turned out to be the final campaigning season of the current war between the imperial claimants, the elements existed for dialogues to begin among all those who had been affected by the French surrender at Port Royal.

The shift of events to a diplomatic trajectory was mirrored in western Europe by the opening of the peace congress at Utrecht in January 1712.[76] There and in bilateral French–British negotiations, the issues raised by the fall of Port Royal would be debated along with other North American matters for more than a year. What, if any, relationship these discussions bore to anything recognizable as reality in northeastern North America itself was not always clear, although there were occasional flashes of insight. The British envoy Matthew Prior noted in early 1713, in a comment directed at negotiations over Hudson Bay but capable of wider application, that treaty provisions at Utrecht were 'no otherwise advantageous or prejudicial to Great Britain than as we are better or worse with the Native Indians.'[77] As far as Annapolis Royal was concerned, historical (or ahistorical) understandings of the significance of the events of 1710–12 were central to all of the interactions that might now determine the future relationships of indigenous and settled populations with pretenders to imperial power.

From the perspective of a Samuel Sewall – and of other New Englanders who were inclined to celebrate the fall of Port Royal even though they might approve less heartily of imperialists of the stripe of Nicholson and Vetch – the events surrounding the conquest were very nearly self-sufficient in a historical sense. The ancient Scottish claim to the territories colloquially known to New Englanders as 'Nova Scotia' imbued the conquest with an attractive symmetry, but it was essentially very recent history that was both surmounted (the failures of 1707 and 1709) and glorified (the Union of 1707) in the triumph of 1710. The victory

over the forces of Catholicism, meanwhile, had an overwhelmingly pre-
sentist significance within a struggle that was punctuated by celebrations
of anniversaries of past events but retained its current and ongoing
urgency for British Protestants on either side of the Atlantic. The cultural context was supplemented too by the imaginative visions of empire
that were becoming evident in 1710 through the celebrations of the visit
to London of 'four Indian kings,' whose Houdenasaunee connections
helped to solidify support for the Walker expedition as a sequel to the
seizure of Port Royal.[78] The mythology of empire that surrounded the
1710 conquest, as the achievement of the new British nation, was a
recent and emerging construction no matter how much earlier historical developments were mined for the legitimacy they might lend.

From a British diplomatic viewpoint, meanwhile, the details of the
precedents for a British presence in 'Nova Scotia' had a greater significance, but it was an essentially practical one: to be able to claim convinc-
ingly the restoration of a reinvented status quo, in order to protect and
advance strategic and commercial interests. French negotiators too
argued over the merits of precedent, and resisted concessions that
would disrupt both past claim and present interest. During preliminary
discussions in Paris in July 1711, Matthew Prior listened to the French
secretary for foreign affairs – Jean-Baptiste Colbert, Marquis de Torcy –
quote Louis XIV's personal reaction to the British demands in North
America: 'you ask in America all that which [with] our sweat and our
blood we have been endeavouring for a hundred years to build.' Torcy
had been especially vehement in defence of French Newfoundland.
'Voici encore une autre impossibilité ... la terre neuve,' the chancellor had protested while enumerating the effronteries of the British position. Prior's
response was a discreet silence, secure in the reflection that 'some tem-
perament might be found in the negotiations upon this head from our
being already possessed of Port Royal, and consequently of Acadie ...
and knowing likewise that it is not of so great consequence to us,
provided we remain [in the final treaty] possessed of their part of
Newfoundland.'[79]

Acadian and native perceptions of the significance of the surrender
of Port Royal rested on other historical understandings altogether. Control of the Port Royal fort had changed hands on several occasions during the seventeenth century. Acadians, statistically, lived long lives, and
collective memory was informed by the experience of elders who could
clearly recall earlier British intrusions.[80] Invasion inevitably brought
threats and disruptions. It also brought opportunities, as had been well

understood in the 1650s by those Acadians who had taken advantage of a loose English regime to burst the bounds of the seigneurial system, or by Acadian merchants who lost little time after the Phips incursion of 1690 in claiming trading rights with New England because they were 'Included and under the present Subjection of those parts to the Crowne of England.'[81] Conquests of Port Royal, however, had never been permanent, and the short-lived Phips episode was a prime example. Thus, while a pragmatic search for necessary accommodations had been generally effective in facilitating a collective Acadian survival in the face of changing regimes, it was not a pragmatism that necessarily bred unity or harmony. The opportunities that invasion brought were often individual rather than collective, and the fact that there was room for debate as to how long each regime would last meant that bitter disputes could arise – as in 1711 – between those who looked for a further change and those who preferred to gamble on continuity. From an Acadian perspective, therefore, the conquest of 1710 was not an unfamiliar development. But it was a momentous one nevertheless, as past experience indicated that it would bring both individual opportunity and collective stress. Any comprehensive Acadian narrative of the conquest would have to begin, not in 1707, but in 1654 at the latest.

A Mi'kmaq narrative would begin even earlier.[82] The capture of Port Royal was not altogether welcome to either Mi'kmaq or adjoining peoples, as emerged clearly from the intermittent Mi'kmaq–British hostilities during the ensuing year and from the Abenaki intervention of June 1711. Yet changing control of the fort was also a familiar phenomenon for native inhabitants, and in a way distinct from the Acadian experience. Whereas each new Port Royal regime signified for the Acadians the arrival of a potentially intrusive force, for the Mi'kmaq the occupants of the fort – whoever they might be at a given time – had continuously represented both an opportunity for trade and an alien presence that, although it might be resented at times, was amenable to military intimidation if necessary. That the diplomatic initiative should be taken by the Mi'kmaq in February 1711, and that trade should be prominent in the discussions, was fully in accord with past practice. The close Mi'kmaq relationship with the French in the original Port Royal habitation from 1605 onwards had begun soon after the colony had moved from St Croix Island. 'L'hiver venu,' recorded the contemporary account of Marc Lescarbot, 'les Sauvages du païs s'assembloient de bien loin au Port Royal pour troquer de ce qu'ils avoient avec les François.'[83] When the Scots arrived in 1629, they were approached within days by 'two Salvages in a Canow,' described by a Scottish observer as speakers of a Basque-influenced trade language who were 'subtill in their truckings.' Further trading sessions and gift exchanges followed.[84] Although direct evidence of Mi'kmaq or other native contacts with the English regime of 1654–70 is sparse, trade took place on an ongoing basis even if the principal English claimant to 'Nova Scotia' found it convenient at times to complain of 'the hazard and trouble to drive on this poore Trade with the Natives.'[85] As long as the British or the French presence was confined within trading forts, at Port Royal or in other locations such as at the mouth of the Wulstukw (St John) River, it constituted a longstanding element of the native experience that could be tolerated with wariness or benevolence as the occasion demanded. There was no reason to suppose that the British regime of 1710 should be an exception, unless in certain definable contingencies: if the British tried to assert themselves militarily outside of Annapolis Royal itself, or if diplomatic failure were to highlight the advantages of a restored French regime. In such circumstances, the native rebuke could be sharp and effective.

As a historical event, therefore, the British conquest of Port Royal in 1710 could be described through a number of different narratives, which will be further explored in subsequent chapters of this study. Seen from the narrowest of chronological perspectives and through New England eyes, the conquest was a dramatic affair and a welcome discontinuity. That it might be expendable in British diplomatic exchanges was not, for the time being, a serious concern. In longer historical context, the conquest could be seen as the latest in a series of upheavals that had presented, over a period of almost 60 years, both opportunities and serious dilemmas to Acadian inhabitants. In the longest view, the conquest represented a change of the guard at Annapolis Royal that might cause barely a ripple in the established predominance of the Mi'kmaq and their neighbours. All of these narratives were possible when the conquest took place. Whether it as an event would bring about changes in the telling would depend on the immediate and longer-term interaction of the peoples and interests involved.

PART TWO: PRECURSORS

2

Elites, States, and the Imperial Contest for Acadia

Elizabeth Mancke and John G. Reid

The British seizure of Port Royal in 1710, and the formal cession of an ill-defined territory by the French in the Treaty of Utrecht three years later, did not represent the first time that Europeans had exchanged entitlements in the region. French, English, and Scottish claims to Acadia or Nova Scotia (the nomenclature changing with the possessor) had figured explicitly in the negotiation of several treaties prior to 1713: the Treaty of Saint-Germain-en-Laye (1632), the Treaty of Breda (1667), and the Treaty of Ryswick (1697). The French charters to Acadia and Canada overlapped with English charters to New England and with the Scottish charter to New Scotland. Over few places in the seventeenth-century Americas did Europeans contest their claims so repeatedly and inconclusively as those to Acadia, a region of which the many conflicting definitions of boundaries would encompass at most a territory stretching from the Penobscot River on the southwest (now in Maine) to Cape Breton on the northeast and to the Gaspé on the northwest.[1] Following the 1710 conquest and 1713 cession, however, the French and British never again exchanged the heart of Acadia (the peninsula of present-day Nova Scotia). The finality of this cession was influenced by a variety of factors, but in an imperial sense it represented an important phase in the gradual extension of state formation in Britain and France into overseas dependencies.

Paradoxically, Acadia was an important diplomatic and imperial issue despite the dismal assessments of the colony by officials of both France and Great Britain. Governor Louis-Alexandre Des Friches de Meneval had described the colony dismissively in 1688: 'ce pays est si peu fait qu'on peut dire qu'il ne l'est point du tout qu'il manque presque généralement de touttes choses et qu'excepté la pesche de la morue il y a peu de moyens connus jusques icy qui puissent servir à le rendre bon.'[2] Twenty-three years later, and two years before the signing of the Treaty of Utrecht, the retired but still-influential British imperial official William Blathwayt took a similar view. Nova Scotia was, Blathwayt remarked, 'at present a desolate Countrey ... Chiefly usefull for Protecting the [Massachusetts] Fishery.'[3] Yet, in 1713 – as in 1631, during the negotiations leading to the Treaty of Saint-Germain – the disposition of Acadia/Nova Scotia threatened to be an issue contentious enough to break the chances of Anglo–French peace.[4] The origins of this paradox of Acadia's marginality as a colonial venture and its prominence in treaty negotiations lay in the tension between overseas expansion and state formation that had been emerging in the course of the sixteenth and seventeenth centuries.

In the early seventeenth century, the governments of France, England, and Scotland had neither the financial nor the institutional resources to undertake empire-building directly. Instead all three delegated colonization and governance to companies or proprietors.[5] Over time, the French and English metropolitan governments increased their supervision of the extra-European territories they claimed as dependencies, through such means as regulation of trade and the building of fortifications. They established bodies to oversee such regulations as existed in colonial, trade, and maritime matters: in England, a series of committees and councils for trade and plantations preceded the establishment of the Board of Trade in 1696, while in France colonies were administered under the aegis of the Ministry of Marine, advised from 1700 by the Conseil (later the Bureau) de Commerce.[6] As late as the turn of the eighteenth century, the establishment of royal institutions of government within the colonies themselves – as in Virginia (1625), Canada (1663), or Massachusetts (1685) – was a phenomenon associated only with the failure of company or proprietary governments to operate in an adequate or acceptable manner.[7] In Acadia/Nova Scotia following the Treaty of Utrecht, however, neither Great Britain nor France gave any sign of delegating governance of the parts of old Acadia they each controlled. Britain established a royal government in Nova Scotia. The French retained Cape Breton and constructed Louisbourg as a naval base, commercial entrepôt, and administrative centre for the fishery.

The existence of broad similarities in the mechanisms that England, Scotland, and France first used to sponsor transoceanic expansion and the similar timing in the growth of state involvement overseas did not preclude the emergence of dissimilar outcomes for the French and British. Differences in seventeenth-century state formation led, in the eighteenth century, to a contrast between the respective fiscal bureaucracies. Although recent studies have shown the British fiscal apparatus to have been more efficient and stable than that of the French, Parliament's control of taxation and spending meant that a Privy Council committee such as the Board of Trade lacked independence in mobilizing funds to support the advice it dispensed. Not until the 1740s did Parliament begin voting substantial sums for intracolonial developments. The French government, on the other hand, was not dependent on a legislative assembly for monies, and so had greater discretion (if not always the wisdom) to decide to invest heavily in a place like Louisbourg. Thus the configuration of governmental institutions affected in each case the role of the state in colonial affairs,[8] and the conquest of Port Royal provides a revealing illustration of the pivotal transition from delegated governance of colonies to direct metropolitan governance by both France and Great Britain.

Beyond fiscal imperatives, the more general relationship between European states and their early modern colonies is not well understood in either chronologies or particulars. Major events, such as Louis XIV's takeover of New France from the Compagnie des Cent-Associés in 1663, or the British government's passage of the Sugar Act in 1764, are widely accepted as threshold moments of state intervention into colonial affairs rather than as stages in long and evolving relationships.[9] What the case of Acadia/Nova Scotia shows, however, is that the 1713 transition was not a sudden shift in metropolitan policies. Rather, it was the culmination of century-long processes in both France and Britain. The protracted struggle by competing private interests and European states, as well as by natives, to define, control, and stabilize the region, makes an analysis of the roles of the French and British metropolitan governments and their interactions with colonial interests a window onto the broader question of the mechanisms European states used in their attempts to bring North American territory under their control.

The concept of 'the state' is problematic in itself. Scholars of early modern state formation generally concur on a number of characteristics that came to define the modern state. They included a sovereign central authority, a defined territory, the dominant (though not monopoly) control of coercive force, and an array of relatively uniform institutions that reached to the limits of the territory. Not that these characteristics were attained tidily or according to any single pattern of development. Each of them represented a complex process, and the combinations among them varied with each individual state. The two English revolutions of the seventeenth century reflected, among other things, the tensions and contradictions of state formation, as in France did the transition from the era of the Frondes to the personal rule of Louis XIV. Insofar as consolidation and bureaucratization were effected in early modern European states, the trend in scholarship on state formation has been to attribute it to the exigencies of war, in particular the raising of money and men, resulting in what has come to be called the fiscal-military state.[10]

The emergence of these attributes of statehood came in the same era during which many western European states – notably Spain, Portugal, the Netherlands, France, and England – were engaged in sponsoring overseas expansion with countervailing tendencies. Overseas expansion made territorial boundaries outside the core of European states imprecise and contested, at the same time that boundaries within Europe were in the process of being defined with ever-greater precision and defended with ever-greater vigour. Overseas ventures could thus greatly complicate this already difficult and expensive element of state formation.[11] Agents of expansion developed or adapted institutions, such as joint-stock companies and colonial governments, that carried the potential of challenging state institutions. European monarchs delegated the control and exercise of coercive force to subjects operating beyond their realms, while simultaneously reining in local armies within their realms.[12]

Yet most studies of state formation in the early modern era give little heed to, if they do not ignore altogether, the place of overseas expansion and empire-building in the definition of states.[13] Despite the seeming contrariness of state formation and overseas expansion, the centripetal forces within states may have shared much in common with the centrifugal forces that pulled Europeans to Africa, Asia, and the Americas. Recent studies that qualify the fiscal–military interpretation of early modern state formation offer a reminder that the characteristic functions of states encompassed far more than making war, extending also to such roles as dispute resolution and regulation of the socially 'deviant' (such as the wandering poor or unwed mothers). In these matters, 'local notables' often approached monarchs seeking legitimation for policy innovations in the provinces. Thus central authorities did not necessarily initiate or execute the practices that led to state coalescence;

nor did the innovations place financial demands on early modern states that would require quantifiable increases in central revenues. But they did forge bonds of shared governance between provincial elites and state authorities. Early modern state formation was not inherently an outcome of coercion and conquest of territorial margins, but was often achieved through a symbiotic process of cultural and political 'elite co-option' that legitimated provincial elites at the same time that they acknowledged central authority.[14] The utility of elite co-option in the process of state coalescence lay in the very ambiguity of who co-opted whom, whether elites on the periphery or elites at the centre.

Overseas expansion provided new, unknown, and unstable arenas for elite co-option as cash-strapped monarchs negotiated with merchants, nobles, and, in England, a rising gentry over what privileges and obligations would inhere in any venture.[15] The colonies established by the French and English in the seventeenth century were begun by elites who petitioned monarchs for charters for overseas commerce and colonization; monarchs granted them based on how a colony or commercial venture could serve strategic state interests, such as French and English competition with the Spanish. Elite negotiation for overseas expansion was often on the same continuum as negotiation over intrastate power. Pierre Du Gua de Monts, who received the first charter for Acadia from Henri IV in 1603, was a prominent Huguenot who had fought with Henri during the Wars of Religion. De Monts's associate, Jean de Biencourt de Poutrincourt, had fought against Henri IV until 1593 but then had benefited from the monarch's reconciliation with Catholic opponents. In England, many of the early colonial enthusiasts were gentlemen soldiers, such as Sir Walter Raleigh and his half-brother Sir Humphrey Gilbert, who had fought for Elizabeth I against the Spanish and in Ireland, and had urged her to support Protestants in the Low Countries.[16] Joint-stock companies – for example, the East India Company and the Hudson's Bay Company – became major financiers of the English/British state and their shareholders were often prominent members of government whose investments abroad often intersected with policy at home.[17]

The establishment of colonies by France, England, and Scotland illustrates this shifting and evolving process of elite positioning and negotiation vis-à-vis themselves, their respective states, and interests overseas. In the particular case of seventeenth-century Acadia/Nova Scotia, the small settler population and persistent international competition magnified and exaggerated the role of elites, engendered competition

among them, made them dependent on legitimation from Europe
rather than locally, and encouraged the intervention of the French and
English states. The origins of the process lay, however, in the preceding
century.

European interventions in Acadia were commercial long before they
were colonial. The direct origins of Acadia as a colony lay in the legacy
of commercial expansion during the previous century and the place of
merchant elites in the Atlantic economy. During the sixteenth century,
dynastic uncertainties, religious conflicts, and the cost of exploration
and colonization combined to keep England, Scotland, and France
minor players in overseas expansion compared with their Iberian rivals.
Henry VII of England had sanctioned John Cabot's voyages to Newfoundland in 1497 and 1498, but did not fund them.[18] Scotland's Stuart
monarchs had no direct involvement in the Americas. Francis I of
France financed Verrazzano's reconnaissance of the east coast of North
America in 1524, Jacques Cartier's voyages to Canada during the 1530s,
and finally the unsuccessful Cartier–Roberval attempt at colonization in
the St Lawrence Valley from 1541 to 1543. Royal and aristocratic under-
writing of French colonial ventures resumed briefly in the early 1560s,
with short-lived misadventures in Brazil and Florida, but did not survive
the escalation of civil war in France during that decade.[19]

The absence of royal financing, however, did not deter the rapid
expansion of private French and English overseas activity. Merchants
operating from France's Atlantic ports pursued the dyewoods trade in
Brazil and the Caribbean, as well as trade with South American natives.
English merchants sought a northern sea route to Asia, funding arctic
exploration along the Scandinavian and Russian coasts and then in
North American waters. French and English corsairs preyed on Spanish
shipping in the Caribbean. Both countries had large numbers of fishing
vessels that annually trolled the banks and the inshore fishing grounds
off Newfoundland. Over the sixteenth century, and especially with the
upsurge of European demand for beaver pelts during the 1580s, the fur
trade developed out of the fishery as increasing numbers of native
inhabitants in the northeast travelled to the Gulf of St Lawrence and the
Atlantic coast to trade furs to fishers in return for metal and cloth
items.[20]

By the later decades of the sixteenth century, merchants, nobles, and,
in the English case, gentry had acquired enough wealth to negotiate
more costly and permanent ventures, with French and English monarchs
anxious to compete overseas but financially unable to sponsor such

ventures directly.[21] English colonial attempts in Newfoundland and at Roanoke were unsuccessful during the 1580s, as was the attempt of Troilus de La Roche de Mesgouez to settle a French colony on Sable Island in 1598. That the attempts were made, however, was a testament to the ongoing commercial traffic into which the projected colonies were intended to tap. Two further processes were also reaching crucial phases as the seventeenth century opened. Increasing state awareness of the revenue possibilities that flowed from overseas trade was being reflected in royal efforts to harness merchant capitalism by chartering companies with varying degrees of size and elaboration. English examples included the Muscovy Company (1555), the Spanish Company (1577), the Levant Company (1593), and the East India Company (1600), while French initiatives included the grant of 1600 to the Huguenot merchant Pierre de Chauvin de Tonnetuit – nominally under the authority of La Roche de Mesgouez – of a ten-year monopoly of the North American fur trade. Northeastern North America was only one among many possible fields of overseas commercial expansion, with widely divergent resource bases and geographical configurations, but the value of the region's fisheries and fur trade was now beyond dispute.

The second process had to do with the consolidation of state institutions in England, Scotland, and France through the removal of internal and external threats to existing monarchies. In 1598 France's King Henri IV effectively ended the wars of religion by issuing the Edict of Nantes, extending religious toleration to Huguenots, and signing the Treaty of Vervins to end war with Spain. Five years later, James VI of Scotland succeeded his cousin, Elizabeth I, on the throne of England. James's ambitions to bring about a full union of England and Scotland went unrealized, but peace with Spain was a goal achieved in the Treaty of London in 1604. Freed from immediate military pressures, each monarchy was now in a position to begin the long-postponed task of redefining the role of the state vis-à-vis the overseas commercial expansion that had proceeded regardless of internal and international political uncertainties.

Colonial grants in northeastern North America followed quickly on these developments. The French patent issued to de Monts in 1603 called for colonization of an area extending from the 40th to the 46th degree of latitude, with a ten-year monopoly of the fur trade both on the Atlantic coast and on the St Lawrence. The English charter of 1606, for Virginia, defined two overlapping territories that were to be colonized under the authority of separate groups of investors in London and Plymouth. The Plymouth group would have responsibility for 'north Virginia,' extending from the 38th to the 45th degree of latitude. The Acadia and Virginia charters marked the beginning of lasting French and English colonization in North America, and of competing claims to territory. They also led to settlement, tenuous and small in scale as it initially was. An unsuccessful French attempt at St Croix Island in 1604 led on to the building of a *habitation* at Port Royal, on the other side of the Bay of Fundy, in the following year. English efforts in 1607 centred on Jamestown, in south Virginia, and a short-lived north Virginia settlement at Sagadahoc, on the Kennebec River in present-day Maine.[22] With vicissitudes, the settlements at Jamestown and Port Royal persisted, although over time they produced markedly dissimilar colonies. Jamestown became the first settlement in the colony of Virginia that by the eighteenth century was territorially the largest in British North America and economically and demographically parallel with Massachusetts's dominance in New England. Port Royal became the sometimes capital of Acadia, sometimes Nova Scotia, a marginal and contested colony.

Thus, colonies did not initiate French and English involvement in the Americas. Rather they elaborated and extended existing interests, as well as created new ones. On the one end of the spectrum were colonies, such as Virginia, where settlers 'planted' themselves and relatively quickly began producing agricultural products for sale back in Europe. These ventures, requiring local governments, internal ownership of land, and residential labour forces, became, definitionally, colonies of their European societies.[23] At the other end of the spectrum were commercial outposts, most particularly Newfoundland, which – while economically more valuable to England than Virginia – was an extension of early modern Europe rather than a colony. European-based merchants lobbied to continue the sixteenth-century practice of treating the island as a hinterland of their provincial maritime economies, with seasonal labour forces based in Europe, little, if any, year-round settlement, and limited development of the civilian institutions of government. Fish from Newfoundland was imported into England duty-free, as though it were domestically produced, in contrast to 'colonial' products, such as tobacco, that were taxed as imports.[24] For the state, maintenance of territorial control was the element of state formation that continued to have central importance in efforts to be competitive in North America. Nevertheless, although it was too soon in the early seventeenth century to identify mercantilist thinking as a systematic influence on state behaviour, the respective state authorities did now have certain emerging fiscal incentives to take an interest in North America. Encouragement and protection of overseas merchant interests promised (even if not always delivering) both political and fiscal benefits. Exactly how the state's support would be directed, of course, could vary widely according to the geography and resources of specific territories, including the encouragement of settlement in Virginia and its eventual discouragement in Newfoundland.

Acadia was a hybrid, not entirely an economic hinterland of Rouen or La Rochelle or St Malo, but not entirely necessary as a colony to make it useful for European needs. European, but especially French, interests in the region clashed over whether Acadia could be effectively utilized and controlled from Europe, or whether it should develop as a colony.[25] The Atlantic linked Acadia to Europe as much as it distanced it, and made its non-native presence as much early modern European as colonial North American. The ambiguous condition of Acadia began with its first chartering in 1603. De Monts and his associates – 'marchands tant de cette ville de Rouen, Saint-Malo, la Rochelle et Saint-Jean-de-Lux' – intended to establish a year-round trading post for the fur trade. The duc de Sully, chief minister of Henri IV and preoccupied with reestablishing French monetary stability and economic growth after the wars of religion, resisted the diversion of energies on expansion and adamantly opposed spending royal funds on overseas ventures. In offering the charter and the associated fur-trade monopoly, the crown required de Monts to transport 100 colonists per year to Acadia. Balking at 100, he negotiated the number down to 60 per year, still an unachievable goal.[26]

The obligation to undertake colonization in Acadia was a negotiated compromise between merchant interests and Henri IV's desire to secure French claims to American territory through year-round occupation without crown expense.[27] Within months, each side had discovered that its co-option by the other had become untenable. The crown's harnessing of commerce and colonization to one yoke proved less than adequate in practice. Merchants who invested with de Monts soon found that the costs of colonization were disproportionately high in relation to any trade benefits that flowed from lesser reliance on seasonal voyages. Even more damaging in the short term, merchants who found themselves suddenly excluded from the fur trade complained vociferously and used their political muscle to make the royal government back down. In 1607 the crown abruptly revoked the trading monopoly and de Monts abandoned the Port Royal settlement. It was a clear indication that, for the state, the immediate need to appease provincial interests was greater than the desire to have colonies in North America. The Atlantic ports, with their large Huguenot merchant communities, were potentially centrifugal forces for a king seeking to consolidate his power in a recently unified, but not stabilized, France.[28]

For the time being, these problems were far from unique. In a wider French context, the tension between the crown's desire for colonization and the merchants' desire for commerce would plague not just Acadia, but Canada and Louisiana, as well. The French crown tried in each situation to oblige private companies to recruit colonists, but merchants proved dismal labour recruiters and deftly capable of exploiting the private advantages of corporations while ignoring, if not undermining, the corporate interests. Only in the French West Indies did promoters succeed in attracting large numbers of colonists.[29] In general, the historical record shows that merchant concerns, whether French or English, did not make good colonizing agents. Early English settlement attempts in Newfoundland also manoeuvred in vain between the Scylla of inadequate profits and the Charybdis of the hostility of competing merchants.[30] London's established overseas merchants, having learned that colonization held no ready profits, invested instead in the Asian, African, European, and Mediterranean trades in which they provided the commercial link between foreign production and English consumers.[31]

In England, however, alternative models of colonization were created that could be applied to certain specific areas of mainland North America and were not overly dependent on metropolitan-based elites. The emergence of tobacco as a cash crop on the Chesapeake effectively removed in that region the conflict of interest between trade and colonization, which were now necessary counterparts in cultivation and export. Around the rim of Massachusetts Bay, and increasingly inland, sheer weight of numbers – produced in part by religious motivations and in part by the more general dislocation of rural English society by economic change, land consolidation, and population growth – enabled settlers rapidly to alter the physical environment to favour agriculture, and overcome native resistance. It was in these circumstances that much of the initial cost of English colonization in these areas was funded by the gentry, small merchants, and thousands of middling folk through company investment or resettlement in the Americas, the latter being particularly true of the Puritans.[32] France, by comparison, had no similar dislocation of the working poor that made labouring in the colonies more attractive than poverty at home. As well, French migration patterns – while not insubstantial within France and elsewhere in continental Europe – did not extend to a preexisting tradition of offshore agricultural colonization similar to England's colonization of Ireland or the Iberian colonization of the Canaries, Azores, Madeiras, and Cape Verde islands.[33] Thus the challenge of enticing French subjects to become agricultural settlers in North America stymied French colonial efforts and their recruitment was a persistently recurring item on the state agenda.

The weakness of French colonial settlement enabled elites and people with French institutional affiliations to wield power and influence conspicuously in colonies, especially by comparison with the English colonies. By the second decade of the seventeenth century, four interrelated, but often antagonistic, groups of French elites had emerged in various configurations and alliances. All had strong institutional, familial, or business ties to France and would dominate regions of New France and the French Antilles for the next century and a half. The group with the oldest and most fragmented ties to the Americas were the merchants, many of them Huguenot, who had pioneered commerce to the Americas.[34] Catholic clergy, from the bishop of New France to the religious orders, formed another group. Royally commissioned office holders and military personnel, both officers and troops, comprised the third and fourth groups. These groups were not exclusive of one another and many individuals could be counted in more than one: military officers were often colonial office holders; priests negotiated alliances with Natives; merchants had family members in religious orders; colonial officials engaged in trade. The French state tried to use all four to consolidate its interest in American territory, often with the result of creating or furthering competition among them, and thereby necessitating state involvement in a colony to try to reconcile differences.

In Acadia, as in other colonial contexts that paralleled its hybrid status between early modern Europe and colonial North America, colonial promoters emerged to attempt a reconciliation of commercial and settlement interests. Their role as members of a bridging elite demanded certain identifiable capabilities and attributes. One was the ability to relate colonization to wider matters of state. With Acadia a disputed territory between potential colonizing powers, a promoter's capacity to defend it against the raids of foreign rivals (without the benefit of state funding) was inevitably high on the list of recommendations on this score. In a political culture in which personal relationships were crucial, an avenue of direct access to the apparatus of the state was also essential – ideally, through kinsfolk or feudal superiors who were close to the royal court. The ability to mobilize capital was a third requirement, and one that called for ties to merchant communities in the metropolis or the Atlantic ports. The more direct the ties the better, although social stratification determined that the same individual was not necessarily well equipped to forge links both on the Atlantic wharves and in the bosom of the state. Finally, the ability to negotiate successfully with aboriginal inhabitants was indispensable in a region where any ambition to consolidate a European claim had to be tailored according to the overwhelming reality of native control, and the recognition that the small, coastal non-native settlements existed purely on native sufferance. As did Governor Thomas Gorges soon after his arrival in the nearby colony of Maine in 1640, a successful colonial promoter had to be able to record without irony that 'the Great Sagamour hath been with me to welcome me to his country.'[35]

From 1603 to the 1710 conquest, French interests competed among themselves for control of Acadia. A number of factors contributed to the volatility. The paucity of non-elite French colonists exaggerated the role of elites, while the marginal economic value of Acadian colonization – as opposed to the value of seasonal fishing and fur-trading voyages – made the return on either economic or political investments risky, and thus aggravated a sense of threat. Elite tendencies to treat the colony's real property and public offices as personal, heritable property – often in conflict with another person's claims – contributed to fierce competition among the French claimants for Acadia. After the revocation of the trading monopoly in 1607, de Monts and his associate Samuel de Champlain shifted their attention to the St Lawrence, and in 1608 the latter established a trading post and settlement at Quebec. Biencourt de Poutrincourt, another associate of de Monts who had been granted a seigneurie in 1608 that included Port Royal, resumed French settlement on the Bay of Fundy in 1610. His claim was the first of three competing lineages of claims that spawned intra-French armed conflict over the seventeenth century. His son, Biencourt de Saint-Just, succeeded him upon his death in 1615, and moved the settlements around to the south shore to prosecute the fishery. Biencourt died in 1623 or 1624, and the running of the affairs of the small French group that remained in Acadia devolved upon his associate Charles de Saint-Étienne de La Tour.

English and Scottish claims complicated La Tour's position. In 1620, a new English charter had revived and extended the English claim to what was now known as 'New England,' defining it as lying between the 40th and 48th lines of latitude. The Scottish charter of 1621 had then granted to Sir William Alexander, as the colony of New Scotland, an area including all of the later Maritime provinces of Canada, and the Gaspé. The evidence suggests that the English and Scottish patents were intended, despite their overlap, to be complementary; but both competed with the French claim to Acadia.[36] The conflict assumed a new importance with the outbreak of war in 1627 between France and the kingdoms of Charles I. Not only was Quebec captured in 1629 and held for three years by the sons of Gervase Kirke, an English merchant operating out of both London and Dieppe, but also Alexander's son established for a similar period of time a small Scottish settlement at Port Royal. Among the achievements of the Kirkes was the capture at sea of Claude de Saint-Étienne de La Tour, the father of Charles. Taken to England, the senior La Tour negotiated with Alexander for two baronetcies in Nova Scotia for himself and his son. The younger La Tour, however, rejected Alexander's offer, having received French support from the newly established Compagnie de la Nouvelle-France, or Compagnie des Cent-Associés. To strengthen French claims to Acadia, the crown made Charles de La Tour lieutenant-general in 1631, and in the following year the Scots evacuated Port Royal in compliance with the terms of the Treaty of Saint-Germain-en-Laye. Ironically, Nova Scotia would be revived in 1656 as an English colony, after the English capture of key Acadian settlements and with the assistance of a formal justification generated by Charles de La Tour on the basis of the Scottish baronetcy he had rejected in 1629.

The other two French claims for Acadia originated with the French repossession in 1632. Isaac de Razilly, an adviser to Cardinal Richelieu – to whom he was related, and whose family of du Plessis was also the feudal superior of the Razilly family – commanded the fleet sent to retake Acadia in the name of the Cent-Associés. With Razilly were his two lieutenants, Charles de Menou d'Aulnay and Nicolas Denys, each of whom after Razilly's death in 1635 would claim parts of Acadia. D'Aulnay's claim conflicted directly with that of Charles de La Tour. In the competition among the three, the French government, after ill-judged attempts to arbitrate the dispute, eventually condemned La Tour as the aggressor; both La Tour and d'Aulnay curried favour with New England interests; d'Aulnay stormed La Tour's fort on the St John River in 1645; upon d'Aulnay's death in 1650, his La Rochelle creditor Emmanuel Le Borgne emerged as a new claimant, sending out his own armed fleet to claim his due; La Tour and Madame d'Aulnay attempted to thwart Le

Borgne by consolidating their competing claims through marriage. So, in brief, the story went.[37] In 1654, the competition for Acadia was again internationalized when an errant English fleet seized Port Royal and other outposts. In English eyes, Acadia returned to being Nova Scotia. The Cromwellian regime appointed Sir Thomas Temple governor, after he had participated in buying out the claim of La Tour through his Scottish baronetcy, while the French government, to assert its claim, made Le Borgne governor and lieutenant-general of Acadia. Le Borgne continued his economic, and now political, claims to Acadia by sending out fleets to attack the English settlements.[38]

Amidst all of these entangling claims, the core of the future Acadian population settled in and around Port Royal during the 1630s and 1640s, most arriving under the sponsorship of d'Aulnay. Although the fur trade and the fishery remained important to the settler communities, cultivation of diked and drained Bay of Fundy marshlands was crucial to subsistence and ultimately produced surpluses for export. By mid-century the Acadian population, while still numbering only some 300, was embarking on a long period of rapid population growth and was beginning a process of geographical expansion that within three decades would see new settlements made on other areas of Fundy marshland – notably at Beaubassin and on the Minas Basin – as well as further up the Port Royal valley. According to Nicolas Denys, this expansion first became evident during the years of loose English occupation under the rule of Temple. Its causes undoubtedly had to do with demographic growth, and familiarity with the landscape and with the agricultural opportunities that awaited on the upriver marshes, but the English intervention may well have contributed by loosening the constraints of seigneurial landholding structures. Seigneurial relationships had been enforced under the rule of d'Aulnay, but from now on had little effective influence on Acadian communities.[39] By the time the English claim to Nova Scotia was again relinquished under the 1667 Treaty of Breda, and a French imperial presence formally reestablished in 1670, there were some 500 Acadian settlers, of whom some 70 percent lived in the Port Royal region and the remainder were scattered around the coasts of the region.[40]

Beyond the defence of French territorial claims in international negotiations, and occasional interventions to encourage one promoter or censure another, the state played no direct role in the early settlement of Acadia. The conflicts between competing French interests might seem in themselves to signify little more than the contemptible squabbles of those who fancied themselves big fish in the smallest of ponds. Yet their implications were not so petty. From a metropolitan perspective, elite disputes that embroiled colonial interests created dangers that went beyond the limited significance of the small settlements that had been established. They disrupted longstanding patterns of access to fisheries and the fur trade and threatened merchants' commercial interests. The involvement of foreign merchants, such as the New Englanders with whom La Tour traded on a regular basis from 1641 onwards, internationalized elite rivalries.[41]

The underlying difficulty lay in the failure of elite co-option as a means of safeguarding imperial concerns. It was difficult for any of the French colonial promoters of the pre-1670 period to combine all of the attributes that contributed to success. D'Aulnay, through the Razilly family, had the right contacts at court, especially prior to the death of Richelieu in 1642, and had access to capital through Le Borgne. Limited evidence suggests, however, that d'Aulnay had a troubled relationship with native neighbours, and that although his military strength extended to effective assaults during the late 1640s on both La Tour and Denys, the financial price was great enough to impel Le Borgne to legal action to try to recover some of his ill-judged investments in d'Aulnay's cause.[42] La Tour had his own sources of merchant support, derived from the Cent-Associés, and had ties of both friendship and kinship in native communities; in one document, no doubt with some exaggeration, he described himself as 'Grand Sagamos des Souriquois, Etcherines, Pantegois et Quiniban.'[43] However, La Tour was dangerously short of metropolitan political connections, and any military power he wielded was dependent at key points on the expensive and uncertain services of New England mercenaries. Elite co-option presupposed the existence of a credible elite, and the weaknesses of the available colonial promoters were only too clear.

The hybrid nature of Acadia also contributed to the deficiencies of promoters. A long coastline provided many widely separated opportunities for resource exploitation. Much of the European presence was seasonal, and even insofar as year-round installations had been established where nodal points had emerged in the fishery and the fur trade, these were tiny islands of French settlement separated by the ocean and the much larger geographical area of native-controlled territory. Efforts at agriculturally based colonization, primarily at Port Royal, represented as yet only minor exceptions to this pattern. In this region of continuing interactions between metropolitan-based merchants – through their agents and employees – and the native population, the position of the colonial promoters was inevitably precarious. While a convincing case could be made that settlement had advantages for the state, if it helped to consolidate French control over coastal waters and over the commercial approach routes to the Mi'kmaq, Etchemin, and Abenaki, no single colonial promoter had the resources to attain those goals in such a large and diverse geographical context.[44]

After the French repossession of Acadia in 1670, the area became a jurisdiction of New France. As was also true by now of Plaisance, in Newfoundland, Acadia would have a royally appointed governor who reported to France through the governor general resident in Quebec.[45] In theory, the French intended the new arrangements to eliminate the problems of elite competition that had emerged so strongly prior to the English intervention of 1654. With clear lines of communication to Quebec and to Versailles, and with matters of internal finance and bureaucratic organization taken care of by a subdelegate of the Intendant of New France, the roles of the governor would be more straightforward than in earlier years: to take responsibility for defence, to correspond with neighbouring English colonies, and to maintain a harmonious relationship with First Nations. Secure in these expectations, imperial officials – including Jean Talon, the Intendant – confidently expected Acadia to take its place in a hemispheric trading system that would contribute substantially to realizing the mercantilist goals that had been increasingly defined in the mid-seventeenth century. By this time, the presence of non-Iberian commercial and colonial spheres of influence in North America had become so persistent that Spain had abandoned its pretence to a monopolistic role, and had its hands full even in defending its direct interests in the Caribbean.[46] The real economic competition now involved England, France, and the Netherlands. Although the Netherlands had been effectively expelled from any colonial interest in North America through the conquest of New York in 1664, England and France retained competing territorial interests. Mercantilist thinking adapted to meet new circumstances. The goals now included not only the defence of merchant interests, but also the building of imperial linkages that were more aggressive than defensive in their efforts to restrict the commercial expansion of competing empires while also raising revenues to support military and political projects in Europe.

The French state, in the era of Jean-Baptiste Colbert as chief minister, was especially influenced in a mercantilist direction by its involvement in the management of overseas territories such as the colony of Canada in the St Lawrence Valley and the need for revenue to sustain European wars. In early 1671, Versailles confided to Talon the hope that Acadia's growing cattle herds and other agricultural commodities would soon put the colony 'non seulement en estat de se soustenir par elle mesme, mais aussy de fournir aux isles françoises de l'Amerique quelque partie de ce qui leur est necessaire, pour la subsistance de ceux qui les habitent, et pour leurs autres besoins.'[47] Talon's encouraging reply looked forward to exports of salt beef to the French West Indies, but did include the caution that existing Acadian trade links with New England would first have to be broken.[48]

Here Talon touched upon a central issue. New England merchants had forged strong trading links with Acadia, and breaking them had political as well as economic implications. The Acadian economy had not stood still since 1654. Not only had population continued to expand at a modest but perceptible rate, but also New England merchants had tightened their grip on the colony's external trade.[49] Given the unattractiveness of such a small market for French-based merchants – not to mention the disastrous example set by the losses of Le Borgne and others – the notion that effective alternatives could be found outside of New England was unrealistic. Starting with Hector d'Andigné de Grandfontaine, who arrived to reclaim Acadia for France in 1670, successive governors were instructed to break the ties with Boston.[50] But they did not have the tools to do so.

Nor was that all that they lacked. The cash-strapped French state was in no position to provide military assistance on any but the smallest scale, and the initial absence of even the most rudimentary bureaucratic structure compromised the new regime's ability to discharge effectively the internal duties of dispute resolution or fiscal management. Complicating matters further was the rapid turnover of governors: between 1670 and 1710, eleven governors or deputies governed Acadia, averaging less than four-year tenures.[51] While these new governors could not privatize their positions as effectively as had La Tour, d'Aulnay, Denys, and Le Borgne, they nonetheless found themselves captive to the endemic problems of Acadia. One after another, they succumbed to the necessity of endorsing – and even privately participating in – the New England trade, and became embroiled in disputes with and among the Acadian colonists. This in turn underlined a serious limitation to the feasibility of mercantilist projects, in that colonial territorial claims did not necessarily coincide with economic spheres of influence. Just as commercial enterprises had long preceded colonization, so in this part of northeastern North America the state (be it English, French, or Scottish) had conspicuously failed to make its claims coterminous with patterns of commercial activity.[52] Not only that, but over immense areas territorial control had not even been wrested from the nonstate, aboriginal populations. Elsewhere, as in Virginia and in Canada, the royalization of government originally undertaken when private enterprise proved incapable of safeguarding territory had enjoyed some local success in resolving this difficulty. But empires remained ramshackle affairs, no stronger than their weakest links.

Only with the 1687 appointment of Louis-Alexandre Des Friches de Meneval, a professional soldier, did the French government begin actively to create a governmental structure in Acadia that showed some reasonable if modest aspiration to expanding territorial control and lessening elite infighting. Equipped with a naval vessel and a small infusion of troops, Meneval had instructions to eliminate New England traders and fishers from Acadian waters. By 1689, however, England and France were at war, and Meneval was captured in the 1690 New England attack on Port Royal led by Sir William Phips. The governor's short period in office illustrated yet further pressures that threatened the stability of the quasi-royal regime in Acadia. Some of these factors were external. Competition with New England for the fisheries off the Acadian coast had become acute during the 1680s, after the establishment of the French Compagnie de la Pêche Sédentaire at Chedabouctou. Smouldering hostilities, expressed as reciprocal ship seizures and occasional armed raids by New Englanders, formed a volatile source of conflict.

From 1688 onwards, New Englanders also fought – with little success – against Abenaki forces seeking to expel the English colonists from their territory. Often mistakenly at first, and with more accuracy from 1690 on, New Englanders suspected the French of assisting their native antagonists.[53] Where New England observers were correct from the beginning was in taking seriously the Abenaki threat to all of the English colonies in the region. In the spring of 1700, Governor Bellomont of Massachusetts informed the Board of Trade that if the Abenaki and the Houdenasaunee should ever join simultaneously with the French, 'they would in a short time drive us quite out of this Continent.'[54] Such an endangerment of the entire English status quo in North America, and its connection with the military role of the Acadian regime in support of the Abenaki, raised the possibility of unprecedented imperially based conflict in the northeast.[55]

The governorship of Meneval also brought to the forefront certain internal challenges to the effectiveness of the French royal regime. Small as the Acadian population remained – approaching 1000 by 1690[56] – the emergence of a community-generated elite was already clear. The existence of a creole elite, in contradistinction to the official elite, implied that yet another negotiated relationship would be required. The potential difficulties involved were illustrated in 1688, when the subdelegate Mathieu de Goutin married into the Tibaudeau family of Port Royal. After Meneval had condemned the marriage – referring disdainfully to the bride as 'la fille d'un paysan' and waging an ongoing battle against her father's trade in liquor to native recipients – the governor's position became increasingly untenable vis-à-vis the united opposition of a key official and a leading Acadian family.[57] More generally, the existence of an emergent Acadian elite implied the possibility of a new form of elite co-option: by New Englanders with economic or political ambitions in the region. The Boston merchant John Nelson, a nephew of Sir Thomas Temple, had built up by the mid-1680s enough of a trading network to justify maintaining a permanent storehouse at Port Royal.[58] In 1690, after seizing military control of Port Royal at the head of a New England expedition, Sir William Phips (who had himself taken a turbulent route to elite status) took oaths of allegiance from a number of leading inhabitants and appointed some to be members of an Acadian council to rule in the name of Massachusetts. Although the council never functioned effectively, individual Acadians saw opportunities and acted on them. As late as 1696, the Acadian merchant Pierre Lanoue petitioned Massachusetts authorities for trading privileges 'according to the promise made by Sir William Phips to the Inhabitants of Port Royal.'[59]

Thus, elite co-option proved not only to be an uncertain tool of governance in Acadia, but also one that could cut in different directions. The official hiatus from war between 1697 and 1701 did little to stabilize the region before the outbreak of the War of the Spanish Succession that would see the 1710 conquest of Acadia, this time by British regulars and commissioned officers, and the cession in 1713. For over a century elite rivalries had contributed to the destabilization of Acadia. Perhaps, not surprisingly, they did not all disappear with the British takeover. Legalistic claims pursued by seigneurial heirs plagued attempts by governors to establish policies for land distribution. The agricultural settlers remained wary of governmental control. And New Englanders continued to assert a defining role in the region. But the British response was also shaped by a different history of colonial development and elite interaction.

The relationship of the British government with elites in most of its colonies diverged sharply from the experience of the French. English colonization had succeeded with little royal prodding and the success of agricultural colonies had a discernible tendency to distance colonists from English-based elites. In the New England colonies, Puritans had arrived with the intent of establishing a new, albeit religious, elite autonomous from the hierarchy of the Church of England and the king's ministers.[60] Less intentionally, though ultimately just as successfully, other English colonies, whether in the Chesapeake, the West Indies, the mid-Atlantic, or the Lower South, developed creole elites who self-consciously leveraged their interests against those of the metropole. The demographic and economic success of the English colonies, the relatively rapid development of creole elites, and the financial and political autonomy of their governments led to greater independence from, and at times defiance of, the metropolitan government.[61]

There were some exceptions to this pattern. The small English presence in Rupert's Land was directly controlled by commercial interests based in England, while in Newfoundland a small though well-established residential population coexisted during the fishing season with much larger numbers of seasonal dwellers connected with West Country merchant enterprises. The failure of Maine as an autonomous colony, after nearly six decades, is significant because its problems paralleled so many of those experienced in Acadia. Its major sponsor, Sir Ferdinando Gorges, remained in England and sent out agents rather than settling himself. Colonial communities were small and experienced repeated difficulties in reaching agreement with the Abenaki, and they never developed a creole elite. At the same time, Massachusetts challenged Gorges's control, bought out his grandson in 1678, and ultimately absorbed the Maine settlements. The tension between Massachusetts and Gorges resembled the elite rivalries that destabilized Acadia, and this was one of the few instances when the English government was drawn into mediating opposing elite claims in the Americas. Massachusetts's purchase of 1678 did not wholly quiet contested claims or metropolitan concerns about the ambitions and power of the Bay Colony, and in 1679 New Hampshire was established as a royal colony.[62]

Unlike the French government, which employed various stratagems to buttress faltering colonial ventures, the English government found itself trying to curb the increasing independence of its colonies. But the peculiar strengths and weaknesses of state institutions in France and England gave their respective officials significantly different tools for managing overseas dependencies. Because Parliament voted virtually no funds for the management of colonies, and the Crown had few independent revenues, colonists often disregarded or subverted the piecemeal attempts to bring them under greater metropolitan control. New Englanders were notorious for flouting the Navigation Acts, first passed in the 1650s. The Privy Council used its powers to revoke colonial charters and to stay the royal hand in granting new charters for proprietary and company charters. The last colonial charter was to William Penn in 1681. But the royalization of colonies, beginning with Virginia in 1625, did little to check colonial autonomy. Many royally appointed governors, rather than being paid out of parliamentary appropriations or the crown's civil list, were dependent on colonial assemblies for their salaries, thus obliging them to build alliances with colonial elites.

The Privy Council's curbs on royal grants and Parliament's regulation of colonial trade were simultaneously enhancements of the bureaucracy of the English state, restraints on royal power, and checks on the growing power of colonies. Their immediate impact on the internal development of colonies was minimized by the existence of increasingly cohesive colonial societies that presented relatively united fronts against too much pressure from the metropolitan government. Nowhere in seventeenth-century British America, except Maine, were there the sustained conflicts among colonial elites that characterized Acadia, and to a lesser extent other French colonies. Bacon's Rebellion in Virginia in 1676 and Leisler's Rebellion in New York in 1689 drew on class and ethnic divisions, respectively, rather than elite rivalry, a more common source of division in the jurisdictions of New France and the French Antilles.

Part of the explanation for the differences in French and English experiences has to do with how elites were legitimated. In English colonies elites found legitimation for their authority from colonists and hence had less need for metropolitan affirmation than did their French counterparts. Few English colonists arrived with close institutional affiliations with the Court, Parliament, the Church of England, the aristocracy, or elite merchants similar to the connections that French colonial elites had to France. Rather, larger settler populations, and the need to finance colonies through intracolonial taxation, contributed to the establishment of assemblies and fostered the emergence of new elites without personal ties to the metropole.

From the first chartering of Acadia and Virginia to the Treaty of Utrecht, the states of both Britain and France had increased their role in overseas colonies vis-à-vis the private role of subjects. Initially both states had limited their financial involvement. Through charters they had delegated to private interests the responsibility for funding overseas settlement, recruiting settlers, and governing colonies. The demographic strength of English colonies and the demographic weakness of French colonies meant that the English state intervened to curb the power of colonies while the French state intervened to buttress colonies and to negotiate among competing elites. In Acadia, government through co-opted colonial promoters was replaced, following the English-influenced interlude from 1654 to 1670, by a form of royal government that failed in practice to resolve the longstanding instabilities caused by elite competition. Indeed, a rival form of elite co-option from New England introduced new complications. After 1713, both Britain and France chose directly to govern the parts of old Acadia they retained, although the antecedent causes – in terms of both imperial demography and the respective roles of seventeenth-century state formation – were almost opposite.

On the French side, the building of Louisbourg was an extension of early modern France as much as it was an addition to colonial New France. It provided a North American administrative centre for the fishery after the French cession of Plaisance. As an entrepôt, it provided a transfer point between French ports and Canada and between Canada and the French Antilles. As a naval base, it extended the metropolitan naval interest to the west side of the Atlantic. To some extent, Louisbourg represented an abandonment of Acadia as a colonial endeavour and the development of Île Royale as an extension of metropolitan commercial, military, and political interests. On the British side, Nova Scotia was the first colony acquired after the chartering of Pennsylvania in 1681, and its royal government illustrated the eclipse of delegated governance within the British empire in the Americas. The officials of the new regime would turn out for the most part to be sojourners in the colony, their permanent connections to Great Britain or New England matched by few integrative ties with the numerically and territorially dominant non-British peoples. There was still plenty of room for doubt as to whether they could overcome the longstanding problems of seventeenth-century Acadian governance and make out of Nova Scotia a recognizable part of an eighteenth-century empire.

For the historian, however, the troubled imperial and colonial history of Acadia can support important conclusions regarding the inherent tensions existing within a seventeenth-century empire. State formation and empire-building did not necessarily coexist easily. Existing models of North American colonization do not satisfactorily encompass the varieties of imperial expansion that existed even in North America. Colonization and empire-building were not the same process, and at times they could come in conflict. The availability of commercially viable resources and the presence or otherwise of substantial non-native populations were other important variables. In the case of Acadia, demographic weakness made governance by elite co-option an attractive strategy to the French state, while at the same time the hybrid nature of Acadia precluded the emergence of an elite that was equal to the task. Instead, elite rivalries destabilized the colony and dangerously disrupted both existing and putative metropolitan mercantile networks. Half-hearted attempts at royal intervention in 1670 and 1687 failed to bring about significant change. Direct royal regimes in both Île Royale and Nova Scotia after 1713 underline, though in opposite ways, the intersecting roles of imperial demography and state formation in the emergence of a North Atlantic world.

3

Family and Political Culture in Pre-Conquest Acadia

Maurice Basque

When the small French garrison of Port Royal laid down its arms in October 1710, the Acadian population was not witnessing a first. In fact, Port Royal and its vicinity had been attacked several times by English forces since the early seventeenth century. Samuel Argall's raid in 1613 was the first in a series of temporary English conquests of Acadia, later followed by Robert Sedgwick's 1654 expedition and Sir William Phips's capture of Port Royal in May 1690. Even the newer Acadian settlements of Beaubassin on the isthmus of Chignecto and Grand Pré in the Minas Basin region had experienced their share of destructive English raids between 1690 and 1710. Writing about this troubled period of Acadian history, Jean Daigle points out: 'The Acadians realized that they were powerless to control their future, which was unfolding elsewhere. Frequent raids confirmed and reinforced the attitude of accommodation which they developed and applied with regard to both the French and the English.'[1] Accommodation meant that Acadians would rely heavily on adaptability and political pragmatism,[2] which accordingly implied different scenarios. After the British conquest of Port Royal in 1710, officially confirmed by the Treaty of Utrecht in 1713, the vast majority of Acadians became 'neutral French' while a small group of them rejected neutrality and went further than accommodation. Rather, they sided clearly with the French or the British. Members of this group did not belong only to the elite stratum of Acadian society, but could also be found among ordinary farmers, labourers, and fishermen, who would potentially stand to gain economically by selling their goods or their services to one camp or the other. The root of this behaviour can be traced back to the 1690s.

Historians, though, have rarely examined the diversity of Acadian responses to these conflicts for the period prior to 1710 and for the five decades Acadia was under British rule before the dramatic years of the *grand dérangement*. They have generally portrayed Acadian political behaviour of the time as a whole, lacking any form of complexity. This interpretation is intimately linked to the traditionally accepted view that Acadian colonial society was a homogeneous world made up of more or less apolitical, prosperous peasants, a classless community of sorts.[3]

Generations of historians have been influenced by John Bartlet Brebner's reading of Acadians' reaction to military and political events, specifically that Acadian colonial society was not politically minded.[4] According to Brebner, such a simple and rustic peasant society could not conceive of political strategies and certainly was not able to negotiate in political terms with representatives of New England or with French imperial authorities. Brebner's legacy can be found in the works of George A. Rawlyk, who very seldom considered the internal dynamics of Acadian politics.[5] Such is also the case with Michel Roy's revisionist essay on Acadian history in which he describes the pragmatic attitude of accommodation put forth by the Acadians as a mere survival strategy. Roy's thesis rested on a relatively simple argument: after the conquest of 1710, Acadians were living in a conquered land and could not be neutral, or even accommodating, because they were a vanquished society.[6]

In recent years, some historians have criticized this interpretation of Acadian political behaviour. Naomi Griffiths proposes a very different view, arguing that after 1710, accommodation became the cornerstone of Acadian political culture, causing Acadian leaders to consciously adopt neutrality as a deliberate political strategy.[7] Other historians, such as John G. Reid, Josette Brun, Thomas Garden Barnes, and Maurice Basque, have agreed with the interpretation of Acadian neutrality as an intended political gesture having its roots in the two decades preceding the conquest of 1710, but also argue that some groups in Acadian society were not all that neutral.[8] Informing one camp that enemy troops were approaching, supplying food, shelter, and ships to the French or British troops, and even actively taking part in battles cannot be considered neutral behaviour. To understand Acadian responses to the 1710 conquest of Port Royal more fully, it is necessary to examine the intricate nature of this emerging political culture based on neutrality, and on close but sometimes conflicting family networks, by paying particular attention to the role played by different groups in Acadian society at a time when the colony was affected by violently conflicting interests between the French and the English. Another fundamental element to be borne in mind when assessing the Acadians' responses to English attacks is of a more geographical nature. Since Port Royal, Beaubassin, and the Minas Basin settlements did not experience these raids in the same way, their reactions were different. While some settlers eagerly fought back these English attacks, others, such as Beaubassin's prominent settler Germain Bourgeois, chose instead to negotiate. Many families, possibly exasperated by the frequency of these destructive raids, simply chose to leave and remove themselves to new Acadian communities that were relatively safe.

During the last decade of the seventeenth century, the inhabitants of Acadia were frequently reminded of the state of war between France and England in faraway Europe. The War of the League of Augsburg (1689–97) had a brutal impact on the Acadian colony. In 1690, Acadia had a population of roughly 900 inhabitants of European descent, scattered in three major settlements – Port Royal, the oldest one and the capital, had close to 600 settlers compared with Beaubassin and Minas Basin, with approximately 150 and 50 respectively. The remainder lived in very small clusters such as in the Cape Sable region, which counted only a few families.[9] The Acadian colony was still very much a marginal one. In the words of John G. Reid, the Euramerican settlements in this region of the northeastern American colonial world 'had only a tenuous existence ... Whatever the achievements of European colonization elsewhere in America they had come here to a low ebb by 1690.'[10] A world dominated mainly by agriculture, Acadia relied heavily on New England trade for a variety of products including metal tools, sugar, molasses, and rum. Historian Jean Daigle's PhD thesis title neatly summed up the particular relationship between French Acadia and English America in a few words: *Nos amis les ennemis*, 'Our friends the enemy.'[11]

Acadia's existence had been marked by violent external and internal conflicts since its establishment by the French in 1604. As previously mentioned, Virginia-based Samuel Argall's devastating raids in 1613 on the Jesuit mission of Saint-Sauveur in present-day Maine and on the habitation of Port Royal inaugurated a long history of Acadian vulnerability to attacks from the English colonies. Such would be the case in the 1690s. In August 1689, New Englanders were shocked to learn that the English fort of Pemaquid on the Kennebec River had fallen to a Wabanaki attack. News of two other defeats in early 1690 at Schenectady, New York, and at Salmon Falls, New Hampshire, raised the spectre of a powerful French and native alliance looming dangerously over the English colonies.[12]

In the wake of these attacks, Massachusetts authorities decided to
strike back at the French by neutralizing their Acadian borderlands.
Boston sent a military expedition commanded by Sir William Phips to
capture Port Royal and to raid other French settlements on the coast of
Acadia in April 1690. In early May, the 700-strong English force easily
obtained the surrender of the French fort with its 100 soldiers. Even if
Port Royal had a population of about 600 at the time, only some 40 inhabitants were reported to be present at the fort acting as a local militia.[13] The French governor, Louis-Alexandre Des Friches de Meneval,
hastily accepted a capitulation, which secured the property of Acadian
settlers. But he was soon to learn that Phips was not a man of his word.
While Meneval and other officials were taken prisoner, the English
troops looted the small Acadian town. Arriving in Port Royal twelve days
after the departure of the Massachusetts expedition, the Canadian-born
military officer Joseph Robinau de Villebon (who would become commander-in-chief of Acadia in 1691) summarized the destructive impact
of Phips's troops at Port Royal: '[They had] spent twelve days in pillage,
removing the cannon and what little fortification had been made, cutting in two all the palisades which the settlers had built for the King,
destroying the church and committing the worst sacrilege.'[14] Numerous
Acadian houses and barns were burned down, livestock was killed, and
many personal effects were taken back to Massachusetts for public
sale.[15]

The local French inhabitants thus got a bitter taste of what it meant to
be part of the French imperial realm, with little effective French military
protection from their powerful New England neighbours. In the fall of
1689, some Acadian settlers of Port Royal, alongside soldiers of the garrison, had worked on the demolition of the old fort with a view to building a new and larger one which would encompass the church, the
presbytery, a mill, the garrison quarters, and the governor's house. This
was the grand plan of the King's general engineer in New France, Vincent Saccardy, who had arrived in Port Royal in early October. The demolition of the Port Royal fort started without the consent of governor
Meneval and was interrupted because of winter. In November, Saccardy's feud with Meneval led to his return to France, leaving the fort
unfinished and in a weakened state. When the Acadian inhabitants of
Port Royal sighted Phips's ships in their harbour in early May 1690, they
knew they were without any solid defensive military infrastructure.[16]

Acadian reactions to the events of May 1690 varied. Some fled to
safety in the surrounding woods while others witnessed the pillage of

their dwellings and the killing of their livestock. Just before leaving Acadia, Phips ordered the men of Port Royal and of the Minas Basin area to assemble in the ravaged Port Royal church, surrounded by his armed troops:

> Et ayant pris tous les noms des habitans, ils les firent entrer dans l'esglise, et ayant fermé les portes, ils dirent quil falloit quils prétassent serment de fidelité au Prince d'orange, et a marie d'angleterre, Comme Roy et reyne d'Angleterre, Sinon et a faute de ce quils seroient tous faits prisonniers de guerre Et qu'on bruleroit les maisons.[17]

Being held at gunpoint, the French inhabitants pledged allegiance to the English crown. The English flag was raised over Port Royal and Phips appeared to be satisfied with the outcome of this public demonstration of loyalty. But as George A. Rawlyk noted, the pledge of allegiance ordered by Sir William Phips was 'in the naive hope that a few meaningless words would transform the Acadians into ardent supporters of "their most Excellent Majesties William and Mary." '[18] Rawlyk was right. As soon as Phips left, the French settlers reaffirmed their allegiance to Louis XIV in a public ceremony conducted by the *lieutenant civil et criminel* of Acadia, Mathieu de Goutin.[19]

But a closer look at Phips's raid on Port Royal illustrates that all the French inhabitants of the Acadian capital did not react as one. A good case in point is Charles Melanson, an inhabitant of Port Royal of Huguenot origin, whose deceased father, Pierre Melanson dit Laverdure, had lived in England and whose mother, Priscilla, was living in Boston and had remarried there in 1680 to an English captain, William Wright.[20] On the morning of 9 May, two days before the capitulation of Port Royal, Sir William Phips sent for Melanson, who came aboard his ship and probably informed him of the poor state of the French fort and garrison.[21] The behaviour of Charles Melanson exemplifies the complex ties that linked some inhabitants of Port Royal to New England. Melanson's eldest daughter, Marie Melanson dit Laverdure, was married to David Basset, a Huguenot trader who was master of the English vessel *Porcupine* in the raid against the Acadian capital.[22] These close family ties to Boston (and to a prominent member of Phips's expedition) made Charles Melanson, who was himself half French and half English, an involuntary if not a natural ally of the English. Melanson's knowledge of the English language, both spoken and written, was also a valuable commodity for the English raiders.[23] His dwelling must have been spared during the looting of Port Royal, and we can easily imagine the resentment of other Acadian families whose houses were reduced to ashes. But this resentment would not prevent the ongoing trade with New England merchants, who would regularly visit Acadian settlements with their essential goods during the two final decades of the French regime in Acadia. Ordinary Acadian farmers, lacking Charles Melanson's privileged family ties with Boston, had two choices: either leave or rebuild their dwellings and continue dealing with the people who were responsible for their demise. This first generation of Acadian settlers was learning quite fast that life in the New World could be very similar to that of the Old in that border regions like Acadia were from time to time submitted to brutal attacks by the very neighbours they were forced to trade with.

Even though Charles Melanson was one of the rare Acadians to be singled out in the narratives of the raid of 1690, he was not the only settler with links to New England.[24] Many members of his immediate and extended family network were relatively well known in Boston commercial and political circles. At the time of the 1690 raid, he was the father-in-law of two prominent men in Acadian society, Jacques de Saint-Étienne de La Tour and Abraham Boudrot, and brother-in-law of Pierre Arseneau, an Acadian pilot and trader who dealt with Boston merchants.[25] The *sieur* de La Tour was the eldest son of the well-known former French governor of Acadia, Charles de Saint-Étienne de La Tour and Charles's third wife Jeanne Motin de Reux. The de La Tours were certainly the oldest Acadian elite family, with very close ties to other elite families and a long history of contacts with Massachusetts. The *sieur* de La Tour's brothers-in-law included his sister Marie's husband, Alexandre Le Borgne de Bélisle, seigneur of Port Royal, and two men of the d'Entremont family, seigneurs of Pobomcoup (Pubnico): Abraham Mius de Pleinmarais, husband of Marguerite, and Jacques Mius d'Entremont de Pobomcoup, husband of Anne. Le Borgne de Bélisle and the d'Entremonts were no strangers to Massachusetts traders, having done business with them intermittently over an extended period.[26] As for Abraham Boudrot, he was an important Acadian trader who also had close ties with Boston. His father, Michel Boudrot, one of the eldest settlers of Port Royal, had been *lieutenant général civil et criminel* at Port Royal in the 1680s and was the patriarch of a large and prosperous clan.[27] Charles Melanson's eldest brother Pierre had also married into an elite family, his wife being Marguerite Mius d'Entremont. Pierre Melanson was one of the founders of Grand Pré in the early 1680s and the leading settler of that new community, where he was appointed the first militia captain of Minas Basin by Villebon in the 1690s.[28]

Considering all these profitable connections, it is surprising that Charles Melanson did not become a member of the council of leading Acadian notables that Sir William Phips put in place in Port Royal before leaving Acadia.[29] Since no English soldiers were to be stationed in Port Royal, Phips decided that this council would provide a system of indirect rule whereby Massachusetts could claim political control over the region. Members of this council were reportedly elected by the inhabitants of Port Royal, but it is more likely that they were chosen by Phips himself.[30] Phips even had a ten-article constitution written for the council in which the members were ordered, among other things, to arrest and seize French vessels, 'enemies of the English Crown ... in His Majesty's name.'[31] There is a good possibility that, given the circumstances, these men had no other choice. The leading inhabitants went a step further than simply pledging the oath of allegiance to William and Mary. Even though it was probably only a symbolic gesture, membership on this council meant more than accommodation with the Massachusetts authorities. Given the fact that all the members were high-ranking men in Port Royal, it must have appeared to the majority of the French inhabitants that 'their' elite had crossed over to the enemy's side and had accepted becoming subjects and officials of the English crown.

However, good ties with the English were not to be disregarded. Recent Acadian history reminded the eldest members of the Port Royal community that in the decades prior to 1690, many Frenchmen living in Acadia had had a very pragmatic attitude concerning their loyalty to the French crown. The best example was certainly Charles de Saint-Étienne de La Tour, who like his father Claude de Saint-Étienne de La Tour, did not seem to lose sleep when shifting allegiances between Paris and London.[32] One should also keep in mind that the 'interregnum' years between Major Robert Sedgwick's capture of Port Royal in 1654 and the return of Acadia to France in 1670 left the French population in the colony under nominal English rule.[33] In the Port Royal of 1690, some men and women like Michel Boudrot and his wife Michelle Aucoin, Jacques dit Jacob Bourgeois and his wife Jeanne Trahan, daughter of the late *syndic* and blacksmith Guillaume Trahan, would probably propose a more nuanced approach on reaching an acceptable compromise or accommodation with the New Englanders since they had already experienced English attacks.[34]

A few days after Phips and his men left Port Royal, François Perrot, a former governor of Acadia, sailed into the Port Royal harbour. The same French inhabitants who had sworn allegiance to William and Mary told Perrot that they had been forced to do so:

> quils en avoient une telle douleur, Et demanderent tous, qu'on en fit un acte pour servir a la posterité, Lequel fut jnceré au greffe Port royal, Et qu'on envoyast un copie a la Cour, Et une a Monsieur le Comte de fronte-nac, Et quils Suplioient Sa majesté de ne pas les abandonner Et quils estoient prests d'exposer leurs vies pour leurs chère patrie Et ne les pas obliger a renoncer a leur religion et embrasser l'anglicane.[35]

Despite these public displays of loyalty to the French crown, as soon as Phips left, the new French commanding officer in Acadia, Joseph Robinau de Villebon, chose not to settle in Port Royal, but transferred the administrative centre of the colony to a fort at Jemseg on the St John River, judging that this location offered better security against English attacks than Port Royal. Furthermore, the St John River offered the possibility of being closer to the Wabanaki, the native allies of the French with whom they could bring war to the New England borders.[36] Upon his arrival in Port Royal, Villebon met with his first sergeant, Charles Chevalier dit La Tourasse, whom Phips had named president of his Nova Scotia Council. As a strategy to avoid further attacks from New England, Villebon thought it best that Chevalier stay on as president of the council, writing in July 1692 that 'without such compromises one could not exist in this country.'[37] Chevalier's title was not only symbolic, since there is documented proof that, until 1693, when he resigned from his position, the inhabitants of Port Royal and even of Beaubassin considered him to be a leader, as well as an intermediary between Massachusetts authorities and the French command.[38]

For ordinary French settlers in Acadia, the rivalry between France and England in the New World was played in their own backyards, forcing them to take a very careful reading of the political barometer of their region. Even Chevalier's wife, Catherine Bugaret, the widow of a Port Royal justice official, Claude Petitpas de LaFleur, volunteered to play a role as an intermediary between French-Acadian and English interests when she accompanied Abraham Boudrot to Boston in 1693 (she died on the way) to participate in prisoner exchange negotiations. Wrote Villebon in his journal in January 1693: 'Knowing the confidence the English had in her, I was persuaded she would manage everything for the best.'[39] The aforementioned Abraham Boudrot's behaviour was also ambivalent. When doing business in Boston, he acted as a friendly ally of the English, even being protected by Sir William Phips himself when Boston customs officials accused him of illegal trade in Massachusetts. At the same time, Boudrot had privileged contacts with Villebon, paying him what appear to have been regular visits at his fort on the St John River and informing him of what was happening in Boston, even providing him with information on the condition of English forts.[40]

These examples illustrate how the French population of Acadia was caught between the British hammer and the French anvil. Since Phips's raid on Port Royal, they had forcibly become William and Mary's subjects, had publicly repudiated their oath of allegiance by stating that they would give their lives for France, only to learn that the new French colonial administration under Villebon thought it good strategy to maintain nominal New England rule in Port Royal. Villebon's decision almost encouraged Acadians to wave both French and English flags at the same time. This policy was certainly a very pragmatic one, given the military and political context, but it incited Acadian leaders, traders, and even ordinary farmers to play a dangerous game of living on the edge. On arriving in Port Royal in 1691, Villebon must not have been surprised to see the English flag still flying over the town.[41] These strategies of shifting allegiances from one side to another were certainly not a consequence of the New World environment. Since the sixteenth century, numerous European regions were torn by civil and religious wars that forced more than one village to try to adopt the practice of neutrality when confronted with invading armies. Local elites were also known to temporarily play the accommodation card only to withdraw it when the legitimate authorities recaptured the village.[42] Their local patronage networks of tenants, farmers, and labourers usually followed their patrons' chameleon behaviour, since their very livelihood depended on it. A client had to follow his patron.[43] One should also keep in mind that many inhabitants of Acadia at the time of Phips's capture of Port Royal were originally from central western France, a region that had had its share of political and religious conflicts in the second half of the sixteenth century and the first half of the seventeenth century. Individual and collective memories of shifting allegiances in old Europe were certainly not erased when they crossed the Atlantic Ocean. A Port Royal farmer in 1690 was more likely preoccupied with getting access to New England products than declaring allegiance to the distant Sun King in faraway Versailles.

In this light, Acadian behaviour in troubled times was typical of what French villagers in France would have also done. Acadian traders such as Abraham Boudrot and Charles de Saint-Étienne de La Tour, the late French governor's son and namesake, exemplified local elites who dealt with opposing sides. Both these traders benefited from Phips's protection and could be found doing business again in Boston harbour, no doubt playing on the fact that they were now English subjects in light of their recent pledge of allegiance and arguing that their trade was now legal.[44] For their part, New England merchants were conspicuous in Acadian waters, selling goods to the settlers of Port Royal, Beaubassin, and Minas Basin.[45]

For Massachusetts merchants, the Port Royal capture of 1690 sparked renewed interest in Acadian markets. A group of Bostonians, including John Nelson and John Alden, who were already very active in Nova Scotia, sought a monopoly on trade in Acadia. In exchange for this monopoly, Nelson and his associates promised the General Court that they would pay for the construction of an English fort at Port Royal and for its garrison. The project was accepted and Colonel Edward Tyng, a military officer of experience who had served in Maine, was made commander of Port Royal and governor of Nova Scotia in 1691.[46]

These commercial ventures meant more political debate and more pressure for Acadian settlers. As they would soon find out, the oath of allegiance that they had pledged to William and Mary in 1690 did not appear to have been sufficient for Massachusetts authorities, especially at a time when French privateers were patrolling the Bay of Fundy. In fact, the General Court had sent John Alden to Port Royal in November 1690 and March 1691 to assess the French inhabitants' loyalty to the English crown.[47] Tyng himself came to Port Royal the same year and met with the leading notables. In 1692, Phips sent a warship to Port Royal commanded by Captain Richard Short. Short had the difficult mission of convincing the Acadian settlers to actively participate in the fight against the French; a vague promise of neutrality was all that he received.[48] In August 1695, another mission was more convincing; the English frigate *Sorling* under the command of captain Emes Fleetwood sailed in the Port Royal harbour and its presence convinced fifty-eight inhabitants to sign a new oath stating that 'Wee do Swear and Sincerely Promise That wee will be Faithful and bear True Allegiance to his Majesty King William King of England Scotland France and Ireland So help us God.'[49] The signatories included Louis Petit, parish priest of Port Royal; Emmanuel LeBorgne, member of the local seigneurial family; Charles Melanson; and a majority of ordinary farmers like brothers Charles and Prudent Robichaud.

The Acadians responded to these repeated demands in a prudent manner. The majority of them appeared to have preferred a form of neutrality in which they could continue to trade with the English while avoiding conflicts with their native neighbours and maintaining communication with the French administration of the colony. They were also becoming more aware that dealing with the English was not always reserved to the small elite group of Acadian society and that since 1690, many of the ordinary Acadian farmers had had contacts with New Englanders, sometimes very brutal ones, as when some Port Royal dwellings were burned down to the ground. A few leading Acadians, though, were far from neutral, such as Charles Melanson, who asked for and received a militia captain commission from Massachusetts lieutenant-governor William Stoughton in 1696. His correspondence with Stoughton clearly indicates that he kept the Massachusetts official informed of the presence of French ships. Even Louis Petit, parish priest at Port Royal, did not hesitate to act as an informer for New Englanders.[50] While Melanson was playing the English card, his brother Pierre at Grand Pré played the French one, informing Villebon, in his capacity as captain of the local militia, of the presence of English ships in Acadian waters.[51] The Melansons perhaps thought that having players in both camps would protect their family interests. This strategy was also consistent with Abraham Boudrot's ambivalent comportment, as he befriended Phips and Villebon simultaneously. There were other small Acadian groups, mostly made up of young adults, who likewise did not practise neutrality. Rather, they served as crew on French privateering ships like the ones commanded by the feared Pierre Maisonnat dit Baptiste and François Guyon. Baptiste even lived in Port Royal at the time, having wed around 1693 Madeleine Bourg, Abraham Boudrot's niece.[52] Acadia was a small world; small enough that the English authorities knew that those French privateers did not lack privileged contacts with the Acadians. As John G. Reid has noted, Acadian reactions to these events 'had strong elements of pragmatism, but it was a pragmatism that was neither comfortable nor united.'[53]

Yet in 1696, that brand of pragmatism and uneasy compromise was replaced by outright violence. Acadian leaders and the rest of the inhabitants learned the hard way that walking the fine line of accommodation did not always protect them from destructive blows. Such was the case when a military expedition commanded by Benjamin Church laid the Beaubassin settlement to waste as a retaliatory measure to French and native raids on Massachusetts's northeastern borders. A prominent settler of Beaubassin, Germain Bourgeois, had much experience trading with Boston merchants. Being the local militia captain at Beaubassin, Bourgeois tried to convince Church, paper in hand, that the Acadians of his village had sworn allegiance to King William at the time of Phips's expedition at Port Royal, thus granting them the protection of the English crown. The document had little effect, and the fact that Bourgeois was the brother-in-law of Charles Melanson did not appear to count for much either. Church noted in his journal that he was not persuaded by Bourgeois but at least spared his dwellings: such was not the case for some of the other houses of Beaubassin, which were burned to the ground. Before leaving Beaubassin, Church proceeded to what was now a familiar scene on Acadian soil: he exacted a new oath of allegiance from the villagers.[54]

Church's raid on Beaubassin provided an example of another aspect of the Acadian responses to attack. In the absence of an established administrative infrastructure, it was left to an Acadian-born settler, Germain Bourgeois, to try to negotiate with Church. Beaubassin had no fort, no French garrison, and no governor. Instead, Bourgeois appears to have benefited from the lessons of the Port Royal raid of 1690 by putting forth not neutrality, but rather membership in the British realm, as a means of protection. Given his frequent voyages to Port Royal and to Governor Villebon's forts on the St John River, Bourgeois certainly knew the importance that both French and British officers attached to these oaths of allegiance. Yet Acadians in the 1690s also came to realize that pledges of allegiance might mean very little.[55]

The War of the League of Augsburg (1689–97) had a destructive impact on Acadia, and news of the signing of the peace treaty at Ryswick in 1697, which gave Acadia back to France, must have been welcomed by Acadian settlers, many of whom had lost their dwellings, livestock, and even some family members during this war. One lesson that must have been learned from the damaging English raids was that the French inhabitants of Acadia did not respond in any uniform manner and that the *grande famille acadienne* of the last decade of the seventeenth century had its black sheep as well as its favoured sons.[56]

For a few years, the French inhabitants of Acadia could breathe more easily. When Joseph Robinau de Villebon died in 1700, his successor, Jacques-François de Mombeton de Brouillan, decided to reside in Port Royal, where he ordered the reconstruction of the fort beginning in the summer of 1701.[57] The building of a new fort was good news for those settlers who believed that a stronger French military presence in Port

Royal could protect them from further English raids. On the other hand were those who believed that fortifications simply meant more problems. Brouillan had ordered the Grand Pré settlers to erect a fort in their little village, but the inhabitants refused.[58] Perhaps some of them had in mind the 1690 capture of Port Royal, where the presence of a fort had proved to be ineffective.

The settlers of Minas Basin had, until now, been spared by English raiders. Many contemporaries describe them as strong-headed, prosperous farmers who traded extensively with other Acadian settlements and with New England vessels. Villebon was well aware of this situation, having sent many vessels to Minas Basin for supplies.[59] Brouillan confirmed in 1701 that they were a well-off group having considerable livestock. However, he was offended by their nonchalance in regards to his administration, stating that they were so unaccustomed to formal government that they lived like true republicans, having no respect for royal authority or justice.[60]

The relatively peaceful settlement of Grand Pré was to be thrown into turmoil because of events at sea and on the New England borders. The actions of French privateers like Baptiste and Guyon, as well as French and native military raids on English frontier settlements, again made Acadia the target of New England's fury. In 1704, Benjamin Church returned to Acadia, commanding a new expedition. When he arrived at Minas Basin, his expedition was met by an armed force consisting of many Acadian men who were hiding in the woods to exchange fire. Before leaving the region, Church and his troops burned and pillaged Minas Basin, even destroying the *aboiteaux*. Acadian reaction to the Church raid in Grand Pré was quite different from the response to the Beaubassin raid of 1696 or to the Port Royal raid of 1690. Here, there was no evidence that any Acadians were spared by raiders because of privileged links with New England. True to their reputation as strong-headed settlers, and in the absence of a French garrison, Grand Pré men fought back, even though their village would subsequently be burned down. About thirty civilian prisoners were taken by the English, a much higher number than was recorded for the earlier raids on Port Royal and Beaubassin.[61]

The year 1704 saw yet another English attack on Port Royal. Margaret Coleman's well-documented and vivid narrative of this raid shows that things had changed somewhat in the Acadian capital. Acadians' reaction to the attack was more aggressive than in 1690. Seemingly, many of them obeyed Governor Brouillan's order to fight like militia, even though he showed little respect for them. There is also an account of how some Acadian farmers deliberately destroyed their dikes so that the incoming enemy troops would have to pass through flooded fields;[62] the English forces retreated, doing little damage.

Massachusetts authorities were disturbed by this failure to destroy Port Royal, which they saw as a nest of privateers. In 1707, two further attacks were launched by the New England colonies against the Acadian capital. Acadia had a new governor, Daniel Auger de Subercase, who would not witness the same Acadian response to attack as did Brouillan in 1704. In early June 1707, the first English expedition, commanded by Colonel John March, reached Port Royal, and in the first days of fighting the New England men had forced the French soldiers and the Acadian militia to retreat. After these brief encounters, Acadian militiamen abandoned the field. Was it because the English forces were gaining the upper hand? What is clear is that Subercase did not trust the Acadians and moved back to the fort. Eventually, the English left, but the damage was enormous; houses were burned, livestock killed, and property stolen. In August of the same year, another English raid was repulsed, Subercase this time having the active support of many Acadian militiamen.[63]

The raid against Port Royal of 1704 and the two in 1707 demonstrated that the community seemed better prepared than before to defend itself against the English. These attacks differed from the previous ones on Port Royal and Beaubassin because of the presence of native troops fighting on the French side. Yet the French inhabitants too were certainly more prominent on the battlefield than during previous attacks. The Acadian Pierre Granger even managed to impress Brouillan with his martial prowess and was named militia captain during the August raid of 1707. Ironically, Granger's father Laurent was English, and Pierre himself was the brother-in-law of the anglophile Charles Melanson.[64] Many prominent Acadian families by now had privileged links with the French officers at the fort. When the French troops inside and outside the fort of Port Royal were exchanging fire with the invading English, there were Acadians who had a personal stake in the fate of the defending French. Madeleine Melanson, daughter of Grand Pré militia captain Pierre Melanson, had married ship's captain Louis Simon Le Poupet de Saint-Aubin de La Boularderie in 1702, while her sister Anne had wed Port Royal's master cannoneer, Thomas Jacau de Fiedmont, in 1705. In 1707, at the tender age of 13, Anne Mius d'Entremont de Pobomcoup married Antoine de La Boulais de Saillans, a French ensign; her sister Marie had married François Dupont Duvivier, a vessel commander, in 1705, while in 1709, her other sister Jeanne was wedded to Duvivier's brother, Louis Dupont Duchambon. Because they belonged to a noble family, the Mius d'Entremont women were particularly acceptable as potential marriage partners for French officers. The Saint-Étienne de La Tour family was not to be left out either: in 1705, Marguerite de Saint-Étienne de La Tour married a French sergeant, Jean-François Villatte. Her niece, Jeanne de Saint-Étienne de La Tour, had already married the French military surgeon Jacques David dit Pontif in 1703.[65] The Acadian-born Charles de Saint-Étienne de La Tour served as a French officer during the March raid of 1707.[66] Even French privateers joined elite Acadian families. Pierre Maisonnat dit Baptiste married Germain Bourgeois's sister Marguerite in 1707, while Louis-Pierre Morpain wed an Acadian noble lady, Marie-Josèphe d'Amours de Chauffours, in 1709.[67]

If the Acadian elite families now had a personal stake in the presence of French officers in the colony, the same cannot be said of all Acadians. Even though the parish registers of Port Royal indicate a few marriages between soldiers and local Acadian women, and even though French military officers often served as godfathers to many children of the area, relations between the military and the rest of the population were not always cordial. Militia duty and active combat were no *parties de plaisir* for Acadian farmers. Having to rebuild a house following an English raid was a trying task at best. Even local French soldiers were reported in 1705 to be getting out of hand, killing some of the settlers' livestock and plundering their goods.[68] It must have come as no surprise to their neighbours that some Acadian families decided to move elsewhere, to the newer settlements of Grand Pré, Beaubassin, and Cobeguid.[69] Furthermore, the presence of French troops and privateers in Port Royal meant that Acadia would almost always be in a state of conflict with New England. In the decade prior to the conquest of 1710, the Acadian economy suffered much from this state of war. French supply ships were rarely seen and most imported goods were brought in by the privateers. Trade with New England was reduced to the point that French local administrator Mathieu de Goutin wrote in 1707, 'le pays est denue de tout: il n'y a aucun commerce.'[70]

Truly, on the eve of Francis Nicholson's capture of Port Royal in 1710, Acadians had had no uniform experience in their dealings with British and French colonial authorities. In absolute numbers, Port Royal had suffered the most from the raids since 1690, whereas prosperous Grand Pré had only experienced one such raid. Oaths of allegiance had been pledged to both William and Mary and Louis XIV, some within a few weeks of each other. Neutrality had made its appearance in Acadian political culture, but the Acadians sailing on French privateers' ships and those informing Boston about those same ships were certainly not neutral. The conquest of 1710 would only accentuate these different elements of the Acadian political world. Acadian elders who had witnessed violent conflicts while living in France must not always have considered Acadia to be a paradise, Nicolas Denys's 'Pays de Cocagne.' The world they had left behind could still teach them a lesson or two when the time came for them to deal with invading forces in their new land of abundance.

PART THREE: AGENCIES

4

New England and the Conquest

Geoffrey Plank

The lands of the Mi'kmaq and the Acadians were never isolated. From the early seventeenth century onward, several transportation and communication links tied the peoples of the region to the outside world. Following routes they had taken for centuries, the Mi'kmaq travelled by sea to Labrador, west and south along the New England coast, and eastward out into the Atlantic, perhaps as far as Newfoundland. They also took an overland trail up the St John valley to the St Lawrence River and on to Quebec.[1] Acadians travelled the land route to visit Canada, and at least until 1710 they maintained direct links by sea to France.[2] After 1714 a new route opened through Louisbourg that allowed the Acadians and the Mi'kmaq to trade and communicate, directly or indirectly, with partners in the ports of the French empire. In the opposite direction, French, Canadian, Iroquoian, and Algonkian traders, travellers and correspondents exploited most of these various channels of communication to reach the Mi'kmaq and the Acadians. There were many well-travelled routes in and out of Acadia and Nova Scotia in the first half of the eighteenth century, but only one between the province and the British empire. With the exception of a few fishermen who visited the Atlantic coast in the summertime, the vast majority of British subjects who came to Acadia or Nova Scotia between 1690 and 1749 came through New England. Messages, passengers, and trade goods arriving in the province from Great Britain were transshipped in Boston.

These circumstances guaranteed New England's influence over imperial policy in Acadia and Nova Scotia. Though the New Englanders did not always take the initiative in promoting military action, until 1758 every expeditionary force raised to attack the French in Acadia or on neighbouring Cape Breton Island mustered in New England. The officers involved in attacking the French colonies spent weeks or months in Boston prior to sailing northeast, and they raised troops among the New Englanders. New England did not contribute soldiers to the garrison in Annapolis Royal after the War of the Spanish Succession ended in 1713, and only a few New Englanders ever sat on Nova Scotia's provincial council. Nonetheless, New England strongly influenced the new provincial administration, in part because many of the colony's office holders spent their winters in Massachusetts.[3]

The principal leaders of the expedition that conquered Acadia in 1710 were not New Englanders. Francis Nicholson, the commander-in-chief, was English, and his deputy Samuel Vetch was a Scot. Both of them had much closer ties to New York than to Boston, and they never had any intention of establishing Nova Scotia as a cultural, economic, or political outpost of New England. Nonetheless, in order to get to Acadia they had to pass through Boston. The necessity of making that passage, and dealing with the New Englanders on a continuous basis thereafter, affected nearly everything they subsequently did.

Compared with Nova Scotia in the period from 1710 to 1744, the New England colonies were large, and expanding rapidly; a total population of more than 100,000 grew to approximately 300,000 by the early 1740s.[4] Only a minority of New Englanders concerned themselves with the affairs of Acadia or Nova Scotia, and that minority grew smaller, proportionately, as the colonies expanded to the north and west. Every year a small group of New England merchants visited coastal communities along the Bay of Fundy and engaged in trade with the Acadians, but by far the largest group of New England colonists with interests in Nova Scotia were the fishermen and merchants who sailed the waters off the Atlantic coast. As a group these men had very little contact with the residents of the mainland, and so long as they enjoyed unimpeded access to the Atlantic waters, they had no interest in cultivating close relations with either the Mi'kmaq or the Acadians.

The New Englanders plying the waters off the Atlantic coast were ordinarily indifferent towards the peoples of Nova Scotia. Nonetheless it was the fishermen and ocean-going merchants, more than any other colonists, who influenced the New England governments' policies in the region. Those who depended on the sea for a living often had strong economic interests in maintaining access to the coastal waters off Nova Scotia, and they were passionate advocates for political intervention

when they thought that their interests were threatened or that they had
been wronged. Especially after the mid-1720s, when a small base for the
fishery was established on the island of Canso offshore, they seldom
thought about the mainland except in the context of war.[5]

Even before the conquest of 1710, some New Englanders knew Acadia
well. At least since the middle decades of the seventeenth century a few
New England merchants had traded with the Acadians and the Mi'kmaq
along the coasts of the Bay of Fundy, and a contingent of Acadian merchants had carried goods (primarily furs and agricultural products) to
Boston.[6] The New Englanders involved in this trade, along with others
who travelled the Atlantic, wanted to keep the sea lanes open, and most
of them believed that the best way to do so was to establish British naval
supremacy on the Bay of Fundy and the Atlantic coast. In wartime,
piracy and privateering made trade more expensive and dangerous. For
this reason, if for no other, merchants were among the strongest supporters of the 1710 expedition against Port Royal.[7]

The other group of New Englanders with persistent interests in
Acadia were the fishermen. Continuously at least since the 1620s, New
Englanders had been catching fish off Acadia's Atlantic coast, often
landing on the peninsula's shore to dry their catch. Though scuffles occurred before the start of the Anglo–French wars in 1689, the Mi'kmaq
and the Acadians generally tolerated the fishermen's presence, since it
barely interfered with anything they wanted to do. But the outbreak of
the wars made the fishermen insecure. Like the merchants' ships, New
England's fishing vessels were vulnerable to privateers. The fishermen
were also attacked by regular French naval forces, and on occasion by
Mi'kmaq warriors in coastal waters and on land.[8] The attacks terrified
the fishermen, and fishing activity declined sharply during the wars. As a
result of these circumstances, many New England fishermen, like the
merchants, supported the British operation that seized Acadia from the
French in 1710. The removal of the French garrison from the Acadian
capital promised to weaken France's naval presence in the region and
thereby provide the fishery greater security. The conquest also satisfied
a desire for retribution that many fishermen had been cultivating for
years.[9]

Retribution mattered to the New Englanders. When they entered
combat, most New England colonials intended to exact justice, often
against an entire enemy nation. This was not simply the outlook of New
England's angry soldiers, all of whom were volunteers. Vengeance was a
matter of official policy, endorsed by the governments of New England,

sanctioned by the colonists' religious pastors, and rewarded by the military command. In their various campaigns against the Acadians and the Mi'kmaq around the turn of the century, New Englanders flooded fields, burned houses and crops, killed livestock and dogs, and offered bounties for the scalps of men, women, and children. The bounties were offered only for the scalps of Algonkians, and the New Englanders' violence can be explained in part as the product of generations of intermittent, ferocious warfare with native peoples. Surprise attacks, captive-taking, torture, and ritual execution – all of these practices, common among native peoples, appeared demonic to the New England colonists' eyes.[10] Divine justice mandated a violent response, and the New Englanders were crueller to native peoples than they were to anyone else.[11]

Nonetheless, the policy of inflicting violence on noncombatants extended to the New Englanders' campaigns against the Acadians as well as those against the Mi'kmaq. In part this can be explained through a process of assigning guilt by association. At least since the 1670s, many New Englanders suspected that the French and the Acadians were encouraging native forces to attack New England.[12] But there were deeper cultural roots to the New Englanders' desire for communal, retributive justice. Through most of the seventeenth century, in annual artillery sermons and on other occasions, New England's religious ministers had advanced a set of teachings on warfare that suggested that the New Englanders should aspire to serve God in all of their wars. This meant that they had to fight for righteous causes – they could not enter battle in pursuit of glory or riches, but only to do good.[13] It also meant that they had to purify themselves before battle, because God would punish sinners with ruin. And it was not just the soldiers who had to purify themselves. Any sin in the community, even at home, might trigger defeat. These teachings encouraged the New Englanders to interpret their military fortunes as a measure of their standing before God. Triumph was an indication of God's favour. Disappointment and suffering proved that the people had sinned. The solipsistic New Englanders employed this analysis most often to assess their own moral standing, but they applied it also to enemy nations. If the enemy nation suffered, the suffering was evidence of God's wrath against them.

One of the most dramatic examples of the New Englanders' approach to warfare can be found in an episode from the early years of the War of the Spanish Succession, the 1704 Massachusetts raid on Acadia. The attack was planned in retaliation for an event that the New Englanders called the 'Deerfield massacre,' a bloody attack on an outlying settlement in Massachusetts carried out by Algonkian warriors with French support. Responding to public pressure, Massachusetts governor Joseph Dudley commissioned Major Benjamin Church for a campaign against the Acadians.[14] Wary of a prolonged engagement in Acadia, Dudley warned Church not to attack the French military, but told him instead to march his troops through the populated sections of the province and 'use all possible methods for burning and destroying ... the enemies' housing, and breaking of dams of their corn grounds.'[15] Despite stiff Acadian resistance in the Minas Basin region, Church did as he was told. According to the official account, when he was finished only five houses remained standing in the countryside of Acadia. The dikes protecting the Acadians' wheat fields were broken, and most of the farmland destroyed. Though the French suffered no losses in terms of specifically military assets, the expedition was heralded as a success.[16]

The 1704 assault proved that New Englanders could be enthusiastic fighters, and within a few years of the attack Samuel Vetch, Francis Nicholson, and other British imperial promoters decided to exploit the New England colonists' zeal in order to expand the empire. But there would be trouble in that strategy. The British empire-builders and the New Englanders did not share a common understanding of the nature and purpose of combat.

Vetch came to Boston in 1705. As a Scot and a politically active Whig, he had devoted much of his career to the project of establishing colonies for Scotland on the continent of North America. Vetch participated in Scotland's most ambitious imperial project in the seventeenth century, the effort in the 1690s to plant a Scottish colony at Darien, on the isthmus of Panama. After that project failed he moved to New York and became a merchant. During the short years of peace between 1698 and 1702 he traded with French colonists in Newfoundland, Acadia, and Quebec. But Vetch never came to love his trading partners; as he travelled through New France he drew mental maps of the landscape, which he would shortly use to plan an expedition to conquer the French settlements. He hoped eventually to establish colonies of Scots on the conquered lands.[17]

In 1705, within weeks of Vetch's arrival in Boston, Massachusetts governor Joseph Dudley asked him to participate in a diplomatic mission to Quebec to secure the release of war captives, including some of the townspeople of Deerfield. Accompanied by Dudley's son, Vetch went to Quebec and successfully negotiated the release of some prisoners.[18]

A year later, perhaps to reward Vetch for this accomplishment, Dudley gave him permission to visit Acadia. The resulting scandal provided the immediate inspiration for Dudley's decision to assist Vetch in his plan to conquer New France.

During his travels in Acadia Vetch stopped at Canso Island and traded with the Mi'kmaq (perhaps through French or Acadian intermediaries) for furs. The transaction violated Massachusetts law. Vetch carried his cargo to Plymouth, where the townspeople apprehended him and re-ferred him to the authorities in Boston for trading with the enemy. The subsequent criminal trial (Vetch was found guilty on reduced charges) received a great deal of local attention because Vetch's activities had the potential of implicating the governor in treason.[19]

Dudley was a Tory and a conformist in the rites of the Church of England, and he had influential, vocal enemies in Massachusetts, partic-ularly within the local clergy.[20] But he also had powerful supporters in England. Vetch sailed for London to talk to Dudley's friends after the trial, in an effort to secure exoneration. Cotton Mather, the New England minister most hostile to the governor at that time, opposed Vetch's errand with petitions and pamphlets which he arranged to have published in London. Mather accused Dudley of using Vetch's services to aid the Mi'kmaq and the French in Acadia. He did not suggest merely that the governor took a share of Vetch's profits. More dramatically, he argued that Dudley had wanted to assist the enemy war effort in order to ensure that the conflict in North America would continue indefinitely and enable the governor to increase his revenues. 'It is my Belief, and it seems very plain to me, that the Governour intends to forward the French and Indian Enemy to Destroy all they can and keep the Country alarm'd, thereby to put them to ... vast Charges ... [T]here was never such Taxes on the Poor People as now.'[21]

It was while this scandal was breaking that Vetch and Dudley began to lobby the ministry for assistance in the project of conquering both Aca-dia and Canada.[22] They had divergent motivations for pursuing this project. Vetch wanted to serve Scotland by planting Scottish colonies on the conquered lands. Dudley wanted to silence his critics by proving his loyalty to the cause of New England and his enmity to the Acadians, the Mi'kmaq, and the French. Dudley benefited from his association with the project almost immediately. Several of his most outspoken oppo-nents, including the prominent merchant Sir Charles Hobby, who was in London in 1706 petitioning for the governor's ouster, dropped their opposition to his remaining in office as soon as Dudley's support for the

Canada expedition was announced.[23] Cotton Mather also softened his oppositional rhetoric after the governor proposed attacking Acadia, though years would pass before he was fully reconciled with him.

In 1707 Mather gave conditional support to the idea of creating a 'Scotch Colony' in Acadia or Canada. But he did not like Dudley's association with the project, and he warned that 'if any assistance from New England should be expected in this matter, it is of absolute necessity that the country have a Governour whom the People may somewhat rely on.'[24] Dudley did not resign from the project as Mather wished; on the contrary, the governor worked strenuously on behalf of the expedition. In the spring of 1707 the governor raised an army of over one thousand men. Escorted by a British warship, the forces sailed to Port Royal, where the expedition foundered as a result of dissension among the officers and men. The episode was embarrassing; it did not serve Dudley's political purposes, but it reinforced his determination to see the conquest of New France through to its completion.[25]

By 1709, after Vetch's further lobbying efforts had failed to secure adequate military aid from Britain, the supporters of the project had recruited the assistance of another man with values at odds with those of most New Englanders: Francis Nicholson, an old Tory colleague of Dudley's and a military officer with extensive experience in colonial administration. Nicholson worked with Vetch in London and helped gain the ministry's backing for a large-scale, well-funded, and well-supplied invasion of New France. Nicholson had his own reasons for supporting the conquest. He was a devout Anglican, and, among other things, he saw the project as a way to bring Protestant Christianity to the native peoples of the north.[26]

Early in the spring of 1709, with Nicholson's assistance, Vetch convinced the ministry to give him instructions for a summer campaign against Canada.[27] The government granted Vetch a military commission, assigned him eleven officers of the regular British army, and sent him, with Nicholson as an assistant, to New York to raise 1,500 troops from New York, New Jersey, Connecticut, and Pennsylvania.[28] According to their orders, Vetch and Nicholson were to proceed to Boston only after they had completed this round of recruitment in New York. Once in Boston, they were to raise another 1,200 men from Rhode Island and Massachusetts. Late in the summer, after the troops had been raised and naval support had arrived from Great Britain, they were to launch attacks on Quebec and Montreal.

The men started their recruitment efforts in Massachusetts because an errant wind took them into Boston instead of New York. More than 1,200 New Englanders enlisted for the expedition.[29] Along with the New Englanders, hundreds of other colonists volunteered for service in New York. (Strong Quaker elements in the assemblies of New Jersey and Pennsylvania prevented those colonies from contributing troops.)[30] In addition to the colonials, Vetch and Nicholson recruited support from a wide variety of native groups, including Iroquois from the vicinity of New York, and Algonkians from New Jersey, Connecticut, Rhode Island, and the southern coast of Massachusetts.[31] Nonetheless, the 1709 expedition was cancelled. Vetch, Nicholson, and the colonial governors had succeeded in recruiting a sufficient number of fighting men, but they did not have the naval support they needed to sail up the St Lawrence River against hostile fire. The ships that the ministry had promised for the project earlier in the year were detained in Europe, and therefore the conquest of New France had to be postponed.[32]

In 1710, owing in large part to the efforts of Nicholson, who spent the winter lobbying the ministry in London, a scaled-down expedition was authorized. Nicholson was given the command this time. Along with Vetch as a subordinate officer, he was instructed to seize Acadia, and the ministry provided enough naval support to make the project work. In the meantime, however, the New Englanders' enthusiasm for the expeditions had begun to fade. While local clergymen had volunteered to accompany troops in 1709, none would join the New England forces in the attack on Acadia one year later.[33]

Though more than a thousand provincial soldiers from New England participated in the action, the attack on Port Royal in 1710 was dramatically unlike most New England operations against Acadia. The expedition was targeted narrowly and efficiently on the French fort, and the siege caused relatively little collateral damage. By the standards of 1704 there was very little violence against civilians, and though the provincials seized some ships as plunder, the Acadians' farms remained secure. Their homes and personal property were protected by order of the commanding officers.[34] At least part of the explanation for the distinctiveness of the 1710 operation lies in the fact that the commanders were not New Englanders.

Some of the officers' actions following the fall of Port Royal seemed calculated to please the New England colonials, however. Within days of the capitulation, Vetch and Nicholson sent Major John Livingston on a diplomatic mission to Quebec with instructions to negotiate the release of a number of New Englanders taken captive during the previous eight years of war, including some of the residents of Deerfield.[35] To provide Livingston with bargaining power, the commanders issued a proclamation declaring that all of the Acadians beyond the immediate vicinity of the fort were 'prisoners at discretion' and could serve as hostages to secure the French-held captives' release. Vetch also presided at a council of war that sent a memorial to the Queen reminding her of a promise that had been allegedly given to the men who enlisted for the expedition that they would receive Acadian land. The document also vaguely hinted that Massachusetts might assert charter rights over the conquered province.[36]

Nonetheless, most of the actions Vetch and Nicholson took after the French surrender in October 1710 angered the New England soldiers who participated in the campaign. Most of the offending actions stemmed directly from new instructions the commanders had received in the summer of 1710 from the ministry in London, which effectively redefined the purpose of the expedition. The Port Royal campaign had been authorized originally by a Whig-dominated ministry which might have looked approvingly on the project of moving the Acadians and replacing them with Scots, New Englanders, or other English-speaking settlers.[37] But in the summer of 1710 before the attack on Acadia, the ministry in London, increasingly influenced by Tories, amended its instructions to Vetch and Nicholson and directed them to 'give all encouragement to such of the French inhabitants [Acadians] as shall come over to us, or to make a timely submission, by offering them the continuance of all such lands, estates and privileges, as they do at present possess under the French Government.'[38] In pursuance of these instructions, when he negotiated the surrender of Port Royal Nicholson promised the French commander that the Acadians in the vicinity of the fort would be allowed to remain in their homes.[39] This arrangement accorded with Tory policy, but it infuriated most of the New Englanders. When they enlisted for the attack in 1710, most of them had expected to punish the Acadians and gain plunder.[40]

Some of the New Englanders also wanted to take the Acadians' land. Strictly speaking, the capitulation agreement had not prevented them from doing so, and Sir Charles Hobby, the highest-ranking officer from New England, acquired land in spite of the terms of capitulation by buying lots in the renamed town of Annapolis Royal from resident Acadians.[41] But few of the soldiers were willing or able to pay for land in Nova Scotia, and the decision to respect the Acadians' title inhibited them from staying in the province.[42] This was hardly a problem for most of

them, however. It is unlikely that many of the colonials wanted to stay in
Nova Scotia.

When they enlisted, most of the New England soldiers had wanted to
serve the military for a short term and return to their homes. They had
not expected an extended tour of duty. Nonetheless, almost immediately after the French surrendered in 1710, Vetch announced that more
than two hundred New Englanders, along with an equal number of British marines, would stay and hold the fort until reinforcements arrived.
The colonials protested immediately.[43]

Garrison duty was dull, it paid poorly, and it kept the men away from
their families. The New Englanders were serving under officers who
seemed foreign to them. For example, the commander-in-chief of the
garrison, Vetch, was self-consciously Scottish, one of his chief advisers
(his principal liaison with the Acadians) was a French Protestant named
Paul Mascarene, and the permanent chaplain of the garrison, John Harrison, was a minister of the Church of England. For the most part the
colonials could avoid the chaplain, but they could not ignore their commanding officers. They threatened to desert en masse if they were not
placed under a New Englander's command.[44] Sir Charles Hobby was
appointed as one of the garrison commanders in order to placate the
colonials, but this hardly settled the problem. For the next twelve
months, in other words for as long as the New Englanders remained in
Annapolis Royal, there were constant disputes over the chain of command, as colonial soldiers quarrelled with regular troops, and British
officers tried to assert the prerogatives of rank.[45]

Almost every element of life in the garrison made it seem alien to the
New Englanders. They were surrounded by a French-speaking, Catholic
village, and when they moved beyond the immediate protection of the
fort, they exposed themselves to the possibility of attack by warriors
from the Mi'kmaq or other native groups. Within the fort, most of the
officers of the garrison came from across the ocean, and after the summer of 1711, when the garrison was augmented by a contingent of British and Irish regulars, most of the soldiers seemed to the New
Englanders foreign as well. The British and the Irish worshiped God
according to rites that most of the New Englanders rejected and often
behaved without the pious decorum normal in New England. Some of
the Irish were secretly Catholic, and several of them escaped to live (at
least temporarily) among the Mi'kmaq, the French, or the Acadians.[46]

But by the time the British and Irish reinforcements arrived in 1711,
the cultural divides within the garrison had been overshadowed by

other difficulties. Approximately 450 soldiers had been assigned to Annapolis Royal in 1710.[47] The fort was crowded, dirty, and under-supplied.[48] In the spring of 1711 disease struck, and by mid-summer dozens of men lay dying. The numbers contained in Vetch's reports and other contemporary records do not exactly add up, but in June, Vetch reported that 116 soldiers had died in the previous two months.[49] According to another estimate 340 had died by July. Certainly a large part of the garrison had succumbed before the end of the year.[50] In the summer of 1711 Vetch went to New England to ask for new troops to replace the dead and the survivors he still had in the garrison.[51] Not surprisingly, none of the colonial governments seriously considered his request. Thoroughly disgusted with New England, Vetch returned to Annapolis Royal in October 1711 only to discover that the remaining New Englanders had deserted, more than 150 boarding a supply ship on its return trip to Boston.[52] Vetch responded angrily and, among other things, dismissed Sir Charles Hobby from the provincial administration, by which he further alienated himself and his government from New England.

The events of 1710 and 1711 contributed greatly to the New Englanders' disillusionment with imperial expansion, and the death rate suffered by the garrison almost certainly convinced many New England colonists that Nova Scotia was no place to live.[53] But there were longer-term causes of the New Englanders' failure to give sustained military or political support to the new colonial government of Nova Scotia. While most politically active New England colonists had supported attacking the Acadians, few of the New Englanders had ever felt strongly about conquering and resettling the province. The merchants trading with Acadians had wanted a secure environment to facilitate their business, but as long as their ships were protected from piracy and privateering they were willing to trade in French-ruled islands and regions of the mainland, as their behaviour after the war would demonstrate, when they traded extensively with the French at Louisbourg.[54] New England's fishermen, like the merchants, wanted security, but as long as they could work in peace most of them exhibited little concern about which empire nominally ruled the land.[55]

Congregationalist clergymen had supported combat as a tool of retribution, but they generally believed that justice could be served without the conquest of territory. Though their teachings occasionally conflicted with their temperaments, orthodox New Englanders professed that self-aggrandizement was inconsistent with righteousness. The same rule applied to individuals and nations. Preaching to their artillery companies, New England ministers emphasized that the biblical Israel had not expanded beyond its God-given bounds. Neither, the ministers said, should New England.[56] Implicit in their analysis was the assumption that the French colonies were foreign lands. The New Englanders had never compared Acadia or Canada to the promised land, but rather to Babylon, a dangerous place the righteous should avoid.[57]

Given the New Englanders' weak and wavering support for the project of establishing a viable colony in the Bay of Fundy region, Vetch probably would have preferred to carry out his administrative duties without asking for assistance from New England. But his situation made that almost impossible. He had difficulty bargaining for supplies from the Mi'kmaq or the Acadians and virtually no reciprocal contact with anyone in Great Britain from the fall of 1710 through 1713. A few New Yorkers helped him, but it was the New Englanders, Boston merchants in particular, who lent Vetch the money and supplies he needed to carry him through the early years. They did this not because they loved Nova Scotia, but rather for profit, and they were eventually paid for their services. Nonetheless, without their help, Vetch's garrison could not have survived.[58]

Vetch knew that he would have to depend on the New Englanders, but his Scottish pride and belligerent personality made it difficult for him to correspond with them diplomatically. According to one unsympathetic observer, in the winter of 1711 Vetch denounced all New Englanders as liars and haters of the monarchy, and he accused them all of operating under the influence of witchcraft beliefs.[59] Vetch maligned New England at his peril. He had very few influential friends in the imperial administration, and his position as governor was insecure. In 1712 his one-time ally, Francis Nicholson, began a political campaign to supplant him. Nicholson had allies among the Anglicans in Boston, and with their help, and the assistance of well-connected friends in London, Nicholson succeeded in 1713 in taking Vetch's place as governor of Nova Scotia.[60]

Nicholson did not last long in the post, however, and when he left office in 1714 Vetch and Hobby competed for the governorship.[61] Had Hobby secured the post for himself, Nova Scotia's long-term relationship with New England might have been significantly different, but after Vetch returned to office officials in the New England colonies kept their distance from him. And at least until the founding of Halifax in 1749 they would not have close ties with any of Vetch's successors.[62] Nonetheless, throughout that period the most successful administrators in Annapolis Royal were those who could gain the ear of men in Boston.

Though few New Englanders contemplated settling Nova Scotia or cared deeply about the provincial administration, important constituencies in Massachusetts and the other New England colonies remained interested in events there. Merchants and fishermen both wanted security at sea, and when they felt that their security was threatened they would call on their own colonial government to protect them. If they felt that they had been injured, the New Englanders seldom hesitated to seek retribution, and when they thought that they were exacting justice, provincial boundaries often seemed to matter less to them than the need to punish wrongdoers. Responding to complaints from fishermen in 1718, for example, the Massachusetts authorities intervened unilaterally with force in Nova Scotia. The New Englander most responsible for securing the intervention was Cyprian Southack, an English-born merchant who, in addition to owning several fishing vessels, served as commander of the Massachusetts Galley *Anne.*[63] In 1713, operating on instructions from the Massachusetts government, Southack sailed to the Atlantic coast of Nova Scotia to survey the region and determine whether it was safe for the New England fishing fleet.[64] He took the *Anne* in convoy with a few of his own fishing ships, two of which were seized by French privateers. Though Southack was upset by the loss, he saw enough to convince himself that once peace was fully restored, Nova Scotia would be a good base for the fishery. He sent his conclusions to the Board of Trade and probably also to Samuel Vetch.[65]

In 1715 Southack returned to Nova Scotia in his own sloop, the *Hannah.* He brought with him two other fishing vessels, a schooner and another sloop. Coming ashore at Cape Roseway, near the southern tip of the peninsula, he and his crew built two houses to serve as shore residences and to facilitate the drying of fish. The crews of the fishing vessels then took turns, leaving one crew behind while the other two plied the waters offshore. Later in the summer other fishing vessels came to join them in their camp, including one from Piscataqua, in present-day Maine, and another from Marblehead, Massachusetts. After a few weeks (Southack's account is unclear as to the chronology) the fishermen were approached by two visitors: a French-speaking Mi'kmaq man named Jo. Muse, and an Acadian man (probably François Tourangeau, a 73-year-old resident of Cape Sable, or one of his sons) whom Southack identified as French.[66] The visitors told the New Englanders to leave, and warned them that 'one hundred Indians' were on their way to destroy the camp. Southack fled and Mi'kmaq warriors burned his out-post down.[67]

Tourangeau and Muse did Southack a favour by telling him that the Mi'kmaq warriors were coming. Other fishermen in the area that sum-mer who had not been forewarned were taken captive.[68] But Southack was hardly grateful for the warning he received. He interpreted Tou-rangeau's behaviour as evidence of a conspiracy, and he concluded that the Acadian man was acting on behalf of the French, who, aiming to reduce New England's fishing activities, had directed the Mi'kmaq to destroy his camp. Southack resolved to drive the French fishermen away from Nova Scotia, and eventually he decided to challenge them at Canso, one of a small group of islands off the northeastern tip of the province, at the mouth of the straight that separates mainland Nova Scotia from Cape Breton Island.

Canso had been used intermittently as a base for fishing operations since early in the seventeenth century. French-speakers and Basques had dried fish on the island for more than one hundred years, and at least since the 1680s English-speakers had often joined them there.[69] Fishermen and privateers from the rival empires had occasionally fought among themselves over Canso, but the island had not been the object of protracted fighting, nor engaged the attention of the regular armed forces of New England, the French colonies, Great Britain, or France, before 1718.[70] Perhaps as early as the winter of 1716 Southack learned that French fishermen were visiting Canso to dry their fish.[71] By 1718 he had relayed this information to Richard Philipps, the newly appointed governor of Nova Scotia, who was still in London, and the governor of Massachusetts. Philipps notified the British ministry, who in turn sent a protest to France. In the meantime the New Englanders took action. In September, at the urging of Southack and some other angry fishermen, the government of Massachusetts sent the frigate *Squirrel* to Canso.[72] The commander of the *Squirrel* ordered the French to leave, and after they refused he seized two fishing vessels, which he escorted to Boston.[73]

As it was drafted in 1713, the Treaty of Utrecht provided that the islands of the Maritime region belonged to France, and that mainland Nova Scotia belonged to Great Britain. Arguably, a literal reading of the text suggested that the French held sovereignty over Canso, since it was an island. But according to the way Southack read the treaty, the rocks hugging the shore of Nova Scotia were not islands. They were part of the mainland and therefore belonged to Great Britain. Southack claimed that Canso was a rock. A prestigious body of plenipotentiaries met at the royal palace at Versailles in 1720 to resolve the dispute, but they never came to an agreement, and the controversy was settled on the ground.[74]

At least until 1718, Southack and other aggrieved masters of the New England fishery had habitually appealed to their own provincial governments to help them, but after the 1718 raid the authorities in New England delayed further action pending a resolution of the negotiations at Versailles.[75] This shift in policy left the fishermen without protection, and in 1719 Southack reported losing ten fishing vessels to French pirates or privateers.[76] Various fishermen from France and New England spent the fishing season of 1719 fighting, wrecking each others' drying stages, and making Canso inhospitable.[77] In the meantime, Richard Philipps left England to assume his post at Annapolis Royal, and en route he spent the winter of 1719 in Boston, where he heard the insistent complaints of the fishermen.[78] He responded strongly. He travelled to Nova Scotia with a fresh contingent of troops, and within months of his arrival he went to Canso personally and oversaw the construction of fortifications.[79]

The construction of the fort established one place in Nova Scotia – Canso Island – where the interests of Nova Scotia's provincial government and those of the New Englanders converged. For the next two decades, under the protection of the island's garrison, dozens of New England fishing vessels visited Canso every summer. They were joined every season by merchants, and a small number of permanent civilian innkeepers and others soon began providing services to the fishermen, merchants, and military men. Apart from the soldiers Philipps assigned to Canso, most of the other residents and visitors came from New England. The island had become 'New England's outpost,' even if the rest of Nova Scotia had not.[80]

The placement of a year-round British garrison at Canso persuaded the French to stay away, but Mi'kmaq warriors continued to resist the fortification and settlement of Canso for the next four years.[81] Many of the fishermen helped defend the island, and when they engaged Mi'kmaq men in combat, the fighting could be brutal. On one occasion two vessels manned by New England fishermen waged a two-hour naval battle with Mi'kmaq warriors in captured sailing ships. The New Englanders tossed bombs and set fire to the Mi'kmaq's vessels. The warriors tried to swim to land, but the fishermen fired on them in the water. They reported killing twenty-two men, though only five bodies washed ashore. As a warning to

the survivors the New Englanders decapitated the corpses and set the severed heads on pikes near Canso's fort.[82]

This display of heads accorded with New England's established practices in wars with the Mi'kmaq and other Algonkian peoples. At least
since the 1630s New Englanders had employed terror and exemplary
violence in the conduct of their 'Indian wars.' Mutilating the bodies of
the dead served as a moral statement, answering perceived 'savagery' in
kind and thereby exacting justice. The tactic also reflected a compre-
hensible military logic. Given their unfamiliarity with the landscape and
their small numbers, the New Englanders could not hope to pursue the
tactics of conventional warfare and policing in Nova Scotia. If they
wanted to demonstrate their power over the Mi'kmaq people, they had
few alternatives but to exploit momentary advantages and inflict exemplary punishment on unfortunate individuals. For the strategy to work,
every killing had to serve as a warning in order to intimidate people the
New Englanders could not physically subdue.

In their dealings with the Mi'kmaq in the early 1720s, the New
Englanders had a message to convey, a warning to deliver, but they had
few ways to express themselves to the Mi'kmaq except through violence.
Few if any of the native people on the Atlantic coast could speak
English, and though some of the New Englanders were familiar with the
French language, it remained difficult for them to speak with the
Mi'kmaq except in the context of formal meetings with the assistance of
translators. Such formal meetings rarely occurred, because the absence
of communication made them difficult to convene. These problems
were compounded, at least until the garrisoning of Canso, by the transitory nature of the New England fishing camps and by the migrations of
the Mi'kmaq. Longstanding antagonisms and cultural alienation also
inhibited conversation. At the time of the outbreak of sustained hostilities, no habits of productive interaction had been established and no
close relationships had been formed between the fishermen and the
local native people. When they met, they communicated almost exclusively through gestures. And if the intended message was belligerent,
the gesture would be violent.

The five severed heads encircling the fort at Canso served as an
emblem of the fishing community's relationship with the Mi'kmaq in
1720. Later, less brutal gestures would serve similar purposes. Though
they did not seek close relations with the native people, the New
England fishermen were seldom so crudely violent. After 1725 the most
important message conveyed between the Mi'kmaq and the New

Englanders was that both groups wanted to maintain the distance between them. The Mi'kmaq shunned Canso and refused to visit the settlement there. The New Englanders, for their part, withdrew from most of Nova Scotia's mainland Atlantic coast.

In 1725 the provincial government of Nova Scotia entered into an agreement with the Mi'kmaq that they believed constituted a comprehensive settlement.[83] The authorities reduced the compact into writing and conducted events with Mi'kmaq leaders at Annapolis Royal in 1726 ceremonially ratifying the terms of the treaty. But the New England fishermen and their military allies along the Atlantic coast did not negotiate with the Mi'kmaq primarily through words. They were more likely to convey messages through their physical behaviour. By their actions after 1725 the New Englanders seemed to concede that the Mi'kmaq controlled most of the mainland coast, but no such concession appeared in the written treaty, and as a result, future generations of colonists could claim ignorance of the arrangement. In the late 1740s many New Englanders promoted and applauded the founding of Halifax, apparently unaware that the placement of the settlement violated patterns of behaviour that had formed the basis of the colonists' coexistence with the Mi'kmaq for twenty-five years.

The events surrounding the settlement of Canso in the 1720s demonstrate that hundreds of New England colonists retained strong, direct interests in Nova Scotia after the conquest in 1710, particularly merchants and fishermen. In pursuit of their interests they could act decisively, but the New Englanders' concerns were concentrated on the Atlantic coast. A few New England merchants continued to trade with the garrison and inhabitants of Annapolis Royal, but the volume of trade at Nova Scotia's capital was small. The markets at Louisbourg were much larger and attracted a greater share of the New Englanders' attention.[84] Overall, New England's commercial activities hindered rather than advanced the establishment of British authority on the mainland of Nova Scotia.

By refusing to settle in the Bay of Fundy region or elsewhere on the mainland, by neglecting the needs of the British garrison and the colonial administration after the conquest, by trading with the French at Louisbourg in violation of provincial legislation, and in general by pursuing their own ends without regard to the interests of the government of Nova Scotia, the people and governments of New England helped assure that the provincial government would have difficulty governing the Bay of Fundy region effectively. After 1722, when the fiscally conservative Robert Walpole rose to power in Great Britain, the administrators of Nova Scotia would have little financial or logistical support from anywhere outside their own province. These circumstances would change only in 1744, with the onset of renewed imperial war.

Furthermore, the actions of the New England colonials in their wars in Acadia before 1710, coupled with the New Englanders' behaviour during skirmishes with the French and the Mi'kmaq from 1718 through 1725, helped establish a pattern of interaction among all the residents of the region that made Nova Scotia difficult to govern. The Acadians and the Mi'kmaq remembered their grievances against the New Englanders, remained on guard against large-scale violence, and dealt with all English-speakers warily. The primary challenge of the administrators of Nova Scotia, especially after 1722 (when the prospect of large-scale assistance from London disappeared) was to gain the inhabitants' trust. They made great strides in that direction, but much of their progress was lost in 1744, when, along with a set of other disruptive events, the New England volunteers returned.

The men who first summoned New England's fighting forces back to Nova Scotia at the start of the War of the Austrian Succession were fishermen, who pleaded for intervention following a French attack on the fort and fishery at Canso. Massachusetts governor William Shirley recognized a political opportunity in their request for support, and launched a series of military adventures on an unprecedented scale.

The New England soldiers who came to Nova Scotia in 1744 to reinforce the garrison at Annapolis Royal, and those who enlisted later for campaigns against the French at Louisbourg and elsewhere in the Maritime region, generally resembled their fathers, grandfathers, and uncles who had come to Acadia at the time of the 1710 conquest. They remained home-centred men, and though warfare had disrupted their lives, the plans they made for themselves kept them squarely within the borders of New England. Judging from their journals and their actions in moments of combat, most of the soldiers were violently hostile to Catholics and native peoples, and though they were eager to participate in quick punitive measures they were wary of committing themselves to extended tours of service across the local seas.

The fighting men resembled their immediate predecessors, but the religious and political leadership of the New England colonies had changed. New England's pastors, under parallel influences from Anglicanism and evangelicalism, had adopted more of an imperial outlook, and often looked favourably on the establishment of permanent outposts in newly conquered colonial territories. Similarly, the New Englanders' political leaders, Shirley most prominently, saw New England as a set of provinces within a larger, expanding empire. Through the 1740s and the 1750s Shirley and his supporters struggled to break down the New Englanders' common tendency toward isolationism and xenophobia. To a great extent under Shirley's influence, by 1755 the New England colonies were contributing troops to expeditions in Nova Scotia that represented, in almost all of their features, joint efforts of New Englanders and other representatives of the British empire. The relocation of the Acadians at the end of that year's campaigns represented a new departure in New England's approach to the peoples of Acadia. Far from holding the Acadians at arm's length, the policy was to engulf them in a hostile embrace. The relocation program was always controversial in New England. Many New Englanders – most of them, in all likelihood – preferred to stay isolated, protected from exposure to Acadians or native peoples, at home.

5

Mi'kmaq Decisions: Antoine Tecouenemac, the Conquest, and the Treaty of Utrecht

William Wicken

The conquest of 1710, at the time, was not a significant event for the Mi'kmaq. It only became so afterwards, as the British attempted to extend their economic and political control over the region. This is because the Mi'kmaq, unlike the Acadians, were not farmers. They did not keep livestock, they did not enclose their land, and they did not live along the major river systems which flowed into the Bay of Fundy; for these reasons they were less vulnerable to British attack than were the Acadians, whose fields and livestock had been ravaged by New England raiders in earlier conflicts.[1] The Mi'kmaq were a nomadic people, living in coastal areas during spring and summer and moving inland during the winter. However, as the British presence along the eastern coast of Nova Scotia expanded after 1713, many Mi'kmaq communities were forced to deal with the changed political situation precipitated by the Treaty of Utrecht, eventually resulting in the signing of a treaty with British authorities in 1726.

This change can be illustrated through the life of Antoine Tecouenemac, who at the time of the siege was sixteen years of age. His story reveals something about those Mi'kmaq who chose not to be present at the siege but whose lives would become infected by the narrative it set in motion. Indeed, it is precisely because the narrative's tempo quickened after 1710 that we know more about Antoine than about his father, Paul Tecouenemac. This is the paradox in which Antoine would live his life – that his existence as a historical figure resulted from the intensification of French–English rivalry but that colonization would gradually restrict his ability to act upon his world independently of the forces arrayed against him.

Antoine Tecouenemac was the son of Paul and Marie Agathe Tecouenemac. In 1708, Antoine had four siblings – two brothers and two sisters – a household size not unlike others of his generation. Antoine was fourteen. His brother Guillaume was seventeen, Philippe eight, Marie twelve, and Cecile only one year old. Remarkably, Antoine's mother was fifty years of age in 1708, suggesting perhaps that Cecile was a relative's child, not her own.[2]

The reason so much is known about Antoine's family is because of the nominal census made of seven Mi'kmaq villages in 1708. The author of the census was the abbé Antoine Gaulin, a young and enterprising French Catholic missionary who had laboured among the Mi'kmaq from about 1704. Gaulin was no impartial census-taker, but an individual whose salary was paid by the French crown in recognition of his services, though such monies were never enough to subsidize all of his work.[3] The Mi'kmaq were his charges and the service he performed was instruction in the Catholic faith, which in turn rendered the Mi'kmaq better candidates for defending New France from the New England hordes. Though Gaulin was not likely to perceive his work in such a fashion, he believed that it was better for the Mi'kmaq to live in a world where French Catholics held sway than one where they did not. For these reasons, Gaulin's 1708 census illustrates French colonial perceptions of the Mi'kmaq, providing a means to evaluate the importance that French officials placed upon their aboriginal allies for defending Port Royal.

In 1706 and 1707, Gaulin had journeyed to each of the seven Mi'kmaq villages in what is now mainland Nova Scotia and Cape Breton. At each place, the good father had recorded the names and ages of every village member. Each individual was listed relative to village and family membership. However, the way Gaulin divided the population at the end of the census was significant. Females were divided according to their marital status: women, girls, and widows. Men, however, were divided differently. Though married men were listed separately, the rest of the male population was divided according to age: those fifteen years of age and older, and those who were younger than fifteen. It was this information regarding the male population that commanded both Gaulin's attention and that of his superiors at Port Royal and Versailles. This is suggested in the last column of the table at the end of the census in which

Gaulin tallied the total number of warriors, that is, men and boys fifteen years and older. No doubt, the figures regarding the size of the population formed an important part of Gaulin's census-taking. More critical for French military and political officials was the total number of Mi'kmaq warriors who might be recruited to defend Port Royal from British attack.

Gaulin's census recorded 842 Mi'kmaq, a total that could not have incorporated all Mi'kmaq living in the Atlantic region in 1708. There are two problems with the census. First, Gaulin's total only encompassed those communities located on mainland Nova Scotia and Cape Breton Island and therefore did not include other villages, namely those situated along the eastern coast of present-day New Brunswick and the Gaspé coast. For instance, we know from a census made later, in 1735, that these other villages might comprise as much as 35 per cent of the total Mi'kmaq population living in the Atlantic region.[4] More difficult to gauge is the number of people who lived within Gaulin's catchment area but were not enumerated. The size of this group is unknown. However, it only stands to reason that the timing of Gaulin's visit to communities – during summer – and the large areas he canvassed, must have resulted in inadvertent omissions from his census.

Regardless of the problems with the census, Gaulin's efforts were much appreciated by French officialdom, as the Mi'kmaq were integral to securing the region from the English. Versailles was unwilling to expend much to shore up Port Royal's defences. To be sure, the fort at Port Royal had been rebuilt in 1704, more soldiers assigned to guard its walls, and the Acadians organized into militia companies.[5] Still, there were only slightly more than 200 French regular soldiers and 180 Acadian militiamen who comprised the potential fighting force arrayed against the 1900 British and New Englanders sailing towards the head of the Annapolis Basin in September 1710. Therefore, the 240 Mi'kmaq warriors (out of the overall population of 842) whom Gaulin recorded in his census in 1708 provided French officials with some sense of the number of Mi'kmaq who might, they hoped, be rallied to withstand a British assault.

Indeed, Gaulin's census of 1708 can be understood as part of a broader policy initiated by French military and religious officials to employ the Mi'kmaq as a military force against New England. This strategy dated at least from the late seventeenth century, when proposals were made that the Mi'kmaq be relocated to an area where they might serve French military interests more satisfactorily. Such a proposal had first been made in 1698 by Gaulin's predecessor, Louis-Pierre Thury. In a letter to the minister of the Marine in Versailles, Thury proposed that the entire Mi'kmaq mainland population be resettled along the Piziquit (Avon) River.[6] According to Thury, by placing the mission between eastern and western regions of the mainland, French Acadia would be made more secure from enemy attacks as the Mi'kmaq could then be easily deployed. The plan would also assist in bringing the faith to the Mi'kmaq, as their settlement at one location would render their Christianization much easier in teaching them not only the precepts of the Catholic faith but also the rudiments of agriculture. Thury, of course, realized that any effort would be foolhardy without providing the Mi'kmaq with the skills they would need to live year-round at the mission. For this task, he requested the financial support of the crown in the form of provisions to feed the Mi'kmaq initially, as well as the materials needed to build a self-sustaining economy. This material support included 400 tools to clear the land, 50 fishing lines, 200 codfish hooks, 200 to 300 hatchets, and two large shallops.[7] Thury's proposal was approved by the minister of the Marine, who in April 1699 expressed the King's approval for establishing a permanent mission, though providing only 2,000 of the 6,000 livres requested.[8]

Despite royal approval, the plan went nowhere, probably because of Thury's death in 1699 and the resumption of conflict between France and England two years later. Thury's successor, Gaulin, later resuscitated the idea as did Jacques-François de Mombeton de Brouillan, governor of Acadia from 1701 to 1705.[9] Two years later, their plans led to the building of a mission, but at Chebuctou and not at Piziquit as Thury had originally envisioned.[10] The mission's location was derided by some Mi'kmaq, who complained to Gaulin that Chebuctou was too distant from their hunting areas and 'too exposed to the English who come there every day.' As a result, the mission was relocated to the Rivière Sainte-Marie in the centre of the Bay of Islands, an area renowned for its abundance of moose, beaver, and other wild game.[11]

Though the size of Gaulin's mission is not known, it likely consisted of the local Mi'kmaq as well as families from outlying areas. People from other regions did not relocate there, as indicated by Gaulin's complaint in 1708 that 'he was continually occupied in going to all the places where the Mi'kmaq live to instruct and hold them in obedience.'[12] It is probable therefore that the mission Gaulin established along the Rivière Sainte-Marie existed in name only, populated by families who normally lived there.

Gaulin's lack of success was also symptomatic of French difficulties in recruiting the Mi'kmaq to assist in defending Port Royal. The Mi'kmaq refused to cooperate, resisting suggestions that they abandon their community interests in order to protect the King's need to protect his sovereign power over Acadia from English usurpation. Indeed, it is likely that some Mi'kmaq tended not to see their own interest to be irrevocably submerged with French imperial interests, but more pragmatically grounded on their allies' ability – or inability – to provide them with guns, powder, shot, and other manufactured goods.[13] And so, we may surmise that individual communities chose either to not answer Governor Subercase's plea for assistance in defending Port Royal, or to abandon their French allies when the victory of the New Englanders had become clear. Indeed, this may have been the Tecouenemac family's response to the siege, reflecting a closer identification with their familial and societal interests than with France's imperial ambitions. If Antoine Tecouenemac was not at Port Royal on 2 October 1710 when Subercase formally surrendered to Colonel Francis Nicholson, then where was he?

Some historians would have us believe that Antoine Tecouenemac lived in Acadia up until 1713, and afterwards in Nova Scotia. Stephen Patterson, for instance, writes of the 'Nova Scotia Indians.'[14] Such linguistic turns of phrase subsume Antoine into a European world order, as though his identity would henceforth be closely associated with the world that French and later British settlers and their governments would create. Such toponymical inventions belie the realities of the eighteenth-century world that Antoine inhabited. After all, the Acadian population in 1710 was settled mostly in small communities along rivers flowing into the Bay of Fundy, while a small number of families lived scattered along the eastern coast of the mainland. And in the period after 1710, the British presence in the region was minuscule, confined until 1749 to Annapolis Royal and a small garrison at Canso. The rest of the mainland was inhabited by the Mi'kmaq, and rarely, if at all, did either the British or the Acadians venture onto their lands. These areas, which comprise the bulk of the landmass of what we know today as mainland Nova Scotia, cannot be so easily called 'Acadia' or 'Nova Scotia,' as those terms were legal fictions used by France and Great Britain to justify the exclusion of other European nations from the region. This land was not Acadia, or Nova Scotia, but Mi'kma'ki, the land of the Mi'kmaq, and it was in this fashion that Antoine Tecouenemac and his family conceptualized their world.

But while Antoine Tecouenemac lived in Mi'kma'ki, he was also closely identified with a specific geographical landscape. According to the 1708 census, Antoine lived at a place called 'Cap de Sable,'[15] though Antoine himself more likely thought of this place as Kesputkwitk. In later censuses compiled first by the abbé Gaulin and then by other missionaries, the term 'Cap de Sable' would be used to locate a community of Mi'kmaq living on the southwestern mainland. In 1708, their population was given as 97, in 1721, 94, and in 1735, 167.[16] This pattern of persistent residency by distinct communities of Mi'kmaq families was repeated in the censuses made of other Mi'kmaq communities living on mainland Mi'kma'ki and Unamaki (Cape Breton) in the 1700s, showing that areas where the Mi'kmaq lived remained constant from the 1600s to 1735. The censuses show that succeeding generations of families continued to reside in areas inhabited by their parents and grandparents. In this sense, Antoine's identity was merged with a specific landscape, not several, much in the same way that other Mi'kmaq of his generation were associated with other geographical areas of Mi'kma'ki.

The Tecouenemac family lived in coastal areas during spring, summer, and fall. This conclusion is suggested in scattered reports made by New England fishermen and colonial officials regarding their encounters with Mi'kmaq people. In March 1706, for instance, John Curtiss from Marblehead stated that he was aboard a vessel which put into Pubnico, 'where came on board us several French and Indians to whom we sold sundry Goods, particularly Shott.'[17] On 4 November 1715, Peter Capon, under orders from the Massachusetts General Court to recover fishing vessels hijacked by some local Mi'kmaq, met some families at the Pubnico River, though he had also been there on 31 August and only encountered Acadians.[18] Six years later, Captain Paul Mascarene, an officer from the British fort at Annapolis Royal, reported that the Mi'kmaq 'happened to be in some number about' Pubnico during the early part of September and as a result had likely taken provisions from a vessel shipwrecked there.[19]

While this evidence gives a strong indication of the presence of Mi'kmaq along the southwestern coastal mainland during the summer months, it does not tell us the size of Antoine Tecouenemac's community or its location. We might ask, for instance, if the 97 people enumerated as residents of 'Cap de Sable' in 1708 lived continuously together between March and November or if they divided into smaller family groupings. After all, the work of various researchers has concluded that the Mi'kmaq in the early eighteenth century were a semi-nomadic people who were for the most part dependent upon fish and animal populations for their subsistence.[20] Were there sufficient resources along the coastline to sustain a population of this size over the spring, summer, and fall?

On this question, there are no definitive answers, though most researchers have suggested that families tended to live in at least two different sites between March and November. During the early spring, families lived along river systems, near to favoured fishing sites. At some time during the late spring they moved towards coastal areas, living as members of a larger community. For this reason, it is fair to assume that abbé Gaulin's 1708 census, which records 97 Mi'kmaq living at 'Cap de Sable,' reflects this summer congregation of families. However, sometime during the late summer or early fall, families began moving inland, often settling near favoured fish runs that had been temporarily vacated during the late spring.

Antoine Tecouenemac's family appears to have engaged in this kind of movement. They lived at least from March to May at a village called 'Ouikmakanan.' The identity of the Tecouenemac family's spring village is suggested in the deposition of a Joseph Vigé, who recounted meeting Antoine Tecouenemac in early April 1736, at an Indian village where Vigé happened 'to be ... fishing for Eels.'[21] A memorial written by French officials earlier in the century recounted that between the Chebogue and Pubnico Rivers was a place where 'can be fished a prodigious quantity of eels in the months of April and May.'[22] Half a century later this spot was said to be the location of a Mi'kmaq village called 'Ouikmakanan' or 'place of eels.'[23] However, none of these documents precisely determines the village's location. There is little reason to doubt that the French writers had visited the village, but they had no incentive to explain further as it held no importance for either the French or the British.

Evidence from later documents suggests that the village where Antoine Tecouenemac and his family lived was situated on or near Robert's Island, which lies southwest of the Argyle River. The first document dates from 1771 and is a commission given by the governor of Nova Scotia, Lord William Campbell, to Francis Alexis to 'Fish, Hunt and Improve lands ... in the Creek – called Ell [sic] Creek.'[24] This allotment of land stemmed from a petition to the government by Alexis and his people, suggesting the importance of the area to the Mi'kmaq. Though the location of this site is not specified, a report issued by the government surveyor Charles Morris in 1820 provides more details. In this area, wrote Morris, 'are places of resort for the Indians particularly at Eel Bay near the Tusket River, where they take Eels in great quantities.'[25] Finally, there is the information recorded by a local historian, Jackson Ricker, who in a 1941 book recounted the oral history of the region as related by his father. In one of these stories Ricker wrote that during the 1870s, every spring nine or ten canoes of Mi'kmaq camped on Robert's Island, located adjacent to the Argyle River northeast of Pubnico. 'One of the attractions of Roberts Island,' he writes, 'was the eel fishing at Goose Bay.'[26] From all of the preceding information, Robert's Island seems to have been the most likely location of Ouikmakanan.

The village itself appears to have been situated on agriculturally useful land – a 1701 memorial indicated that the soil was 'of a black colour' and very admirable. Suggestive of the land's fertility was the presence of four arpents of chicabens,[27] a vine which grows throughout the southern and middle regions of Nova Scotia. In 1692, Antoine Laumet dit de Lamothe Cadillac had noted that chicaben 'was a root that one found in the earth like truffles and which is very good to eat.'[28] In English this plant is known as the groundnut and in Latin, *Apios tuberosa*. Attached to the roots of the groundnut are anywhere from five to fifty tubers which resemble sweet potatoes in appearance. Two to five centimetres in length, these tubers can be boiled and eaten. According to a twentieth-century commentator, they are rich in vitamins and can be gathered at any time of the year.[29] The vine appears to have been plentiful throughout the region as it also grew in abundance at Cap Fourchu situated three and a half leagues to the northeast.

As the name of the village suggests, Ouimakanan was a 'place of eels,' a place in close proximity to river systems frequented by eels migrating to and from the sea. Eels are a catadromous fish, meaning that they spawn in the ocean. There is only one place, however, where they are known to spawn: the Sargasso Sea, located east of Florida and south of Bermuda. The eggs deposited in the sea by female adults gradually drift northeastward towards the coast of North America, and arrive in eastern Canadian waters a year after hatching, sometime between April and June. The hatched elvers then move into freshwater as well as into tidal and estuarine waters, and remain there anywhere from five to twenty years. In the fall, mature adults move down river systems to begin their migration to the Sargasso Sea to spawn.[30]

The eel migrations in the spring and fall provided Antoine Tecouenemac's family with a reliable and productive food source during two crucial periods of the year. In the early spring, the migration of elvers upriver provided his family with a plentiful resource at the end of win-

ter, when they would have migrated inland to hunt for moose, woodland caribou, and beaver. Winter was a potentially difficult time of the
year, not only because of the cold weather, but also because of the scarcity of dependable wildlife. For this reason, the knowledge that eels
could be caught in great numbers at Ouikmakanan early in the spring
must have acted as a physical and psychological marker within Antoine's
conception of the world.

Eels were also harvested in the fall, but instead of the small elvers
which had been caught in the spring, families fished for the larger
mature adult eels migrating to the sea to spawn. Their migration provided the Mi'kmaq of Ouikmakanan with a plentiful food supply which
could be smoked and later eaten during the winter months when food
was less readily available.

Catching and cleaning the eels during the fall was a labour-intensive
process which would have involved the assistance of all able-bodied
adults and mature, single women and men. In 1801, Titus Smith, who
surveyed Nova Scotia for its government, wrote that the best place to
catch eels was where a stream emptied into a lake. There, the Mi'kmaq
would build a dam of stones interspliced with spruce or fir boughs. If
the stream had a muddy bottom, a weir was constructed 'by driving
stakes so close together that the Eels cannot pass between them.'[31] After
the eels were caught, they were deboned and then cut into thin shreds
before being smoked.

The labour involved in the catching and drying of eels likely meant
that Antoine, his older brother, and his father, would not have abandoned their family during the fall to defend Port Royal from the New
Englanders. By doing so, the Tecouenemac men would have placed
their own personal and familial survival in jeopardy. Their world was not
governed by French–British rivalry for control of the northeastern mainland, nor indeed by any necessity of defending Acadian farms from the
depredations of New England privateers. Rather, Antoine Tecouenemac's world was governed by a different way of life, regulated by the
migrations of the fish and wildlife upon which he and his family
depended. That life cycle did not exist in a vacuum, but rather was identified with a specific geographical area and with a world far different
from that inhabited by the soldiers and militiamen who confronted
each other at the head of the Annapolis Basin during the latter days of
September 1710.

This suggests that in 1710 Antoine and his family lived their lives outside the events and the documents which form the basis for understand-

ing the history of 'Acadia' and 'Nova Scotia.' The siege of Port Royal by
New England forces offers a revealing example. The story told of the
siege, and the relative importance that historians place on that event,
reflects a narrative pitting Great Britain against France. Significantly, the
demise of one colony, Acadia, and the creation of another, Nova Scotia,
occurs within the land where the Mi'kmaq had lived from before the
arrival of either British or French people into their midst. Despite
the presence of French and British, the Mi'kmaq continued to live in
their world, outside the sight of European officials and unrecorded by
their pens. The 'silences' of history represent their past and one that is
sometimes ignored.

That being said, it is also true that the British conquest of Port Royal
and the subsequent signing of the Treaty of Utrecht had momentous
consequences for Antoine Tecouenemac and for the Mi'kmaq generally, in that after 1713 their lives intersected with British and French settlers to a greater extent than before. The consequences are most readily
apparent in the treaty signed between the British and the Mi'kmaq during the summer of 1726. Among those Mi'kmaq signing the treaty were
Antoine, his father Paul, his brother Philippe, and other prominent
male members of the Cape Sable community. The treaty's signing was a
direct result of Utrecht.

The Treaty of Utrecht ushered in a new political configuration in the
history of the Mi'kmaq and in their relationships with France and Great
Britain. First, the treaty formalized the British garrison's occupation of
Annapolis Royal. In succeeding years, the British would attempt to
secure political control over lands occupied and used by Mi'kmaq communities. Second, British attempts to do so would occur within the context of an Abenaki–Massachusetts conflict which had been escalating
since King Philip's War of 1675–6, as New Englanders pushed further
and further eastward.[32] And finally, this conflict would itself be subsumed by an international struggle for control over North Atlantic
trade, pitting Europe's two most powerful trading states, Great Britain
and France, against each other.

At the edges of this emerging conflict stood the Mi'kmaq and their
Wulstukwiuk and Abenaki allies. After 1713, the region inhabited by
these communities became strategically important to France and Great
Britain for two reasons. First, the area was located adjacent to the North
Atlantic fish stocks, a plentiful and valuable commodity traded on the
open market in Europe but also used as a cheap food source to feed
enslaved Africans working on British and French sugar plantations in

the Caribbean. Second, the maritime region's geography added to its strategic value, as it lay directly between New England and access to the St Lawrence River, which cut deeply into Canada's hinterland and led directly to Quebec and Montreal. Both factors were influential in animating French relations with the Mi'kmaq, Wulstukwiuk, and Abenaki after 1713.

Indeed, beginning in 1719, the French governor of Île Royale, Joseph de Saint-Ovide, would meet annually with Mi'kmaq elders and sakamows to discuss their common economic and political interests. Such meetings were consistent with a general French strategy of forging direct relationships with neighbouring aboriginal peoples to enlist and solidify their support in France's conflict with Great Britain. Though this strategy had long been employed with the Abenaki, Huron, and Mohawk, the period after 1713 witnessed its intensification as France's own economic and political interest in the North Atlantic expanded. Saint-Ovide's yearly meetings with the Mi'kmaq reflected this new conjuncture in French–British relations. What had been a local conflict between struggling planter colonies escalated towards an international war engulfing many aboriginal communities, including the Mi'kmaq, the Wulstukwiuk, and the Abenaki. And so, the colonial officials of New France had an abiding interest not only in encouraging political and military cooperation among northeastern aboriginal people but also in ensuring that their political interests were firmly defined to include opposing New England's economic expansion into Abenaki and Mi'kmaq territory.

Yet the Mi'kmaq and their allies were no mere pawns of the French king, moving as they were told to protect the King's interests. To the contrary. They at times ignored the King's advice. This suggests that the Mi'kmaq and their allies were more than just an unruly group of 'savages,' and that they themselves decided how to react to the British claims of sovereignty in the Atlantic northeast after 1713. This independence of action is shown by the events of the 1720s, which would eventually result in the signing of the 1726 treaty.

The 1720s brought fundamental change in the military and political history of the Mi'kmaq and their Wabanaki neighbours. For the first and only time, they would fight the three northernmost British colonies – Massachusetts, New Hampshire, and Nova Scotia – on their own terms and for their own reasons and not principally to defend French imperial interests. The war lasted about three years, from 1722 to 1725, and occurred as a result of an expansion of New England settlements along the Kennebec River and of the movement of more New England fishermen into Nova Scotia waters. The Treaty of Utrecht had facilitated this expansion by giving more security to British settlers and fishermen. Utrecht, however, had been signed in Europe and had not involved either the Mi'kmaq or the Wabanaki. Neither had been consulted. Neither was amused. And neither reacted passively to New England's aggression.

The Wabanaki expressed their opposition to New England's expansion in a letter they sent to Governor Samuel Shute of Massachusetts in late July 1721.[33] The letter, written by the Jesuit missionary Pierre de La Chasse, expressed Wabanaki anger to New Englanders settling lands at the mouth of the Kennebec in violation of previous treaties signed between Massachusetts and the Abenaki in 1693, 1699, and 1713. The letter is significant not so much for what it said but for who signed it and how they did so. In the 1693, 1699, and 1713 treaties, the Abenaki had been represented by individual chiefs who had signed on behalf of their communities. Not so with the letter sent to Shute. In this case, individual villages and tribes identified themselves by their collective names and signed by affixing an animal totem. The letter was signed by eleven Wabanaki communities and seven allied peoples. The Wabanaki communities were Narantsouak (Norridgewock), Pentugouet, (Penobscot), Naurakamig (upper reaches of the Androscoggin), Anmesokkanti (on the Kennebec River), Muanbissek (along the Merrimac River), Pegouaki (on the upper reaches of the Saco River), Medoctec (St John River, below Woodstock), Aukpaque (St John River, near Fredericton), Pesmonkanti (Passamaquoddy), Arsikanteg (lower reaches of the Androscoggin), and the 8an8inak (unknown).[34] These villages encompassed the major river systems stretching from the Merrimac River in present-day New Hampshire to the St John River in central New Brunswick. The seven allied people signing the letter were the 'Iroquois du Saute' (Kahnewake), the 'Iroquois de la Montagne' (Kahnesetake), the Algonquins, the Hurons, the 'Mikemakes,' the 'Montagnes du costé du nord,' and the 'papinichois & autres nations voisines.'

Although the letter did not bring a halt to the Abenaki–British confrontation in the Kennebec region, it had a profound and threefold significance. First, it shows that by at least 1721, the political ramifications stemming from an extension of British sovereignty in the northeast had precipitated a coordinated political response from the region's principal aboriginal inhabitants, namely the Wabanaki and the Mi'kmaq. Second, the letter shows the close political relationship linking the

Wabanaki and the Mi'kmaq with other aboriginal people living along the St Lawrence River. And finally, the letter suggests that this political confederacy, linking the region's main aboriginal communities, operated to a large degree independently of French political authorities. In sum, the letter indicates the degree to which the Mi'kmaq had become entangled in French–British rivalry but still resisted French political manipulation.

This tension found further expression in the treaty of 1726, signed by the Tecouenemacs along with other Mi'kmaq. A total of seventy-seven aboriginal individuals signed the treaty.[35] Fifty of these people were Mi'kmaq, twenty-five were Wulstukwiuk (including Passamaquoddy delegates), and three others were from the Penobscot River. Signing on behalf of the British crown was the lieutenant-governor of Nova Scotia, Lawrence Armstrong.

The treaty ended the 1722–5 war and established some general laws regarding the relationship of 'Nova Scotia's' aboriginal inhabitants – namely the Mi'kmaq and Wulstukwiuk – with Great Britain. The terms of the agreement were first set down in written form in November and December of 1725, when four Abenaki delegates from the Penobscot River, acting on behalf of Wabanaki and Mi'kmaq communities, negotiated terms with Massachusetts officials.[36] Two separate treaties were negotiated at this time: one with those Abenaki communities living between the Saco and Penobscot rivers and another with the Wulstukwiuk and Mi'kmaq.[37] Both treaties were later ratified by each individual community: by the Abenaki during the summers of 1726 and 1727 at Casco Bay, and by the Mi'kmaq and Wulstukwiuk at Annapolis Royal between 1726 and 1728.

One important difference between the two treaties is that the Abenaki treaty made no mention of the Treaty of Utrecht but rather referred to past agreements made with the colony of Massachusetts. In contrast, the Mi'kmaq/Wulstukwiuk treaty referred to Utrecht:

> Whereas His Majesty King George by the Concession of the Most Christian King made att the Treaty of Utrecht is become ye Rightfull Possessor of the Province of Nova Scotia or Acadia According it its ancient Boundaries, wee the Said Chiefs & Representatives of ye Penobscott, Norridgewalk, St. Johns, Cape Sables & of the Other Indian Tribes Belonging to & Inhabiting within This His Majesties Province of Nova scotia Or Acadia & New England do for our Selves & the said Tribes Wee represent acknowledge His Said Majesty King George's Jurisdiction & Dominion Over The Territo-

ries of the said Province of Nova Scotia or Acadia & make our Submission to His said Majesty in as Ample a Manner as wee have formerly done to the Most Christian King.[38]

The difference between the two treaties is significant for two reasons. First, it suggests that prior to the signing of the treaty, Great Britain had not established a formal relationship with either the Mi'kmaq or the Wulstukwiuk. Informal talks had occurred between individual communities and British officials at Annapolis Royal, though without result, as had been true of discussions with Abenaki communities.[39] Second, and more important, the effort to get the Mi'kmaq and the Wulstukwiuk to sign a treaty in which they recognized British sovereignty over Nova Scotia 'according to its ancient limits' suggests British recognition that occupation of the region could only be accomplished with the acquiescence of the indigenous inhabitants. Indeed, the war of 1722–5 had demonstrated the difficulties Great Britain would encounter in the region if it did not treat with the Mi'kmaq and Wulstukwiuk.

Through their signatures on the treaty, Antoine, Paul, and Philippe Tecouenemac recognized the irrevocable manner in which their lives had changed since the British had conquered Port Royal almost sixteen years before. In 1710, the British presence at Port Royal had not significantly affected Antoine and his family, and therefore the conquest probably meant little to them at the time. By the mid-1720s, however, things had changed. Though there were still few British soldiers at Annapolis, a small fort had been built at Canso and the size of the New England fishery had increased substantially. With that increase had also come the threat of retaliation from Massachusetts in the event of conflict with local Mi'kmaq communities. On the other hand, the French presence in the region had also increased since 1710. Witness, for example, the decision to build a fortress at Louisbourg and Governor Saint-Ovide's decision to meet with community elders yearly. For Antoine and his family, disinterest in what either the French or the British were doing in Mi'kma'ki was no longer possible. Indeed, British–French rivalry forced them to choose how their community would interact with both nations.

The particular issues elaborated by the Treaty of 1726 have been extensively discussed elsewhere and therefore do not require elaboration here. However, in terms of evaluating the long-term consequences of Utrecht for the Mi'kmaq, it is important to note that by signing the 1726 treaty, Antoine, his family, and his community were explicitly accepting the fact that the Treaty of Utrecht had altered their world.

Henceforth, the British, not the French, would have jurisdiction over Europeans who entered Nova Scotia. Equally important, Antoine and his family accepted – as did other Mi'kmaq – that this new political conjuncture necessitated certain limitations on their own actions. For instance, the sixth clause of the treaty stated that in cases of dispute or misunderstanding between the Mi'kmaq and subjects of the British crown, the Mi'kmaq would not unilaterally take action but rather would apply to the crown's servants at Annapolis for redress. Similarly, Antoine and his family agreed that they would neither assist nor harbour British soldiers attempting to desert from their regiment but rather would do their utmost to return them to Annapolis.[40] However, the agreement was not entirely one-sided. The British also made promises to the Mi'kmaq, the most significant of which was that communities would not be molested in their hunting, fishing, gathering or other lawful activities.[41]

We can interpret the 1726 treaty as a conscious attempt by the Mi'kmaq and the Wulstukwiuk to negotiate the terms of an agreement with the British that would allow them to live side by side with each other by providing some guidelines for mediating their disputes. This attempt – though ultimately unsuccessful in avoiding future conflicts – marked a significant departure from the fall of 1710, when the British conquest of Port Royal seemed to have little impact on many Mi'kmaq communities. In 1710 Antoine Tecouenemac and his family had chosen – for familial reasons – not to assist the French in defending Port Royal. In 1726 the Tecouenemac family chose to sign a treaty with the British, and in so doing they signified their conscious understanding of how their world had changed since 1710.

6

Imperialism, Diplomacies, and the Conquest of Acadia

John G. Reid

In July 1720, Governor Richard Philipps of Nova Scotia reported to London that British authority was 'in a manner dispised and ridiculed' by both Acadian and native inhabitants. Two months later, Philipps was even more blunt: 'this has been hitherto no more than a mock Government. Its Authority haveing never yet extended beyond cannon reach of this ffort.'[1] To prove the point, in the interim, Mi'kmaq raiders had seized fish and other goods from New England vessels at Canso, and a New England merchant had been similarly used in the Minas Basin. Referring to both incidents, Antoine and Pierre Couaret, Mi'kmaq leaders from Minas, had remarked to Philipps that 'jamais Ceux de vostre Nation ayent eu aucune part avec nous pour les soufrir encore libres dans nostre Pays come vous le voulez.'[2] The governor's mortification – his own word to describe his frame of mind – contrasted with the expansiveness with which a British envoy to France had described seven and a half years earlier the resolution of the few outstanding matters delaying the British–French peace treaty at Utrecht. With a thirty-league fishing limit agreed for French vessels off the coast of Nova Scotia and the Acadians (and French inhabitants of other ceded territories) denied the right to sell their lands but assured of freedom of religion if they chose not to move, Matthew Prior assured the Lord Treasurer of the day, the Earl of Oxford, that these final issues were 'so well adjusted, that ... I may congratulate Your Lordship upon the Peace made.'[3]

That the realities of native control had by 1720 unmistakably caught up with the fanciful British assumptions of 1713 is not surprising in historical retrospect, although the surprise and embarrassment caused to the Nova Scotia governor at the time were obviously real. The comments made by Antoine and Pierre Couaret, like those of Philipps and Prior, stemmed from the changes flowing from the British conquest of 1710, but more particularly from the role of diplomacy in defining the extent of those changes. Prior in 1713 believed that diplomacy had done its work, and that the imperial and economic consequences of the confirmation of British rule in Nova Scotia would now follow in logical and predictable sequence. Philipps in 1720 was aware that something had gone badly awry, but was torn between an enforced recognition of the need for a new round of British–Mi'kmaq negotiations based on native protocols of gift-giving, and a desire for greater military force to be used to frustrate the French in Île Royale whom he assumed to be prompting 'the Savages ... to assert their Native Rights to this Country' and Acadians to show 'Marks of Contempt ... to my Authority.'[4]

The Couarets certainly showed scant regard for British military force, and offered no hint that even a further diplomatic process would consolidate the full extent of British gains in Nova Scotia agreed at Utrecht. Diplomacy, for all that, was envisaged by the chiefs as the key to British maintenance even of the limited ascendancy at Annapolis Royal: 'nous disputerons à tous les hommes qui voudroient l'habiter [notre pays] sans notre consentement.'[5] Yet a serious problem was that all sides, in the wake of the 1710 conquest, had a status quo to defend through diplomatic channels – and it was only through diplomacy that the necessary negotiated relationships could be stabilized to facilitate future coexistence – but it was not the same status quo. Also promising future conflict was the existence of differing and multilayered approaches to diplomacy – formal and informal, native and non-native – that were difficult or impossible to reconcile.

The conquest of 1710 first entered into British–French negotiations in the following year, though it was not mentioned explicitly. Early British proposals, in secret exchanges during the spring and summer of 1711, included cession by France of all its claims in Newfoundland and Hudson Bay and the retention by either side of 'all such places in North America, as each shall be in possession of at the Publication of the Ratifications of the Treaty in that Part of the World.' The French response, embodied in preliminary articles signed by both sides in the early autumn, was to acknowledge the existence of the British demands, reserve specifically the fishing and drying rights of French vessels on the Newfoundland coast, and refer all other North American issues to the general peace conference that eventually opened in Utrecht in early

1712.[6] The reference to the peace conference was disingenuous. Although North American affairs were discussed at Utrecht, and some important details of the eventual treaty terms were hammered out there, the real negotiation was handled by special envoys, whose dealings were not immediately known to the formal plenipotentiaries. At one crucial point in the discussions over Newfoundland, the British envoy Prior observed from Paris that at Utrecht 'the Plenipotentiaries on both sides are at this moment fighting in the Dark.'[7] As early as March 1712, just a few weeks after the conference had begun, the French plenipotentiaries had complained to Louis XIV that both sides had firm enough instructions to avoid concessions on the question of Acadia/Nova Scotia to ensure that the matter was generating only 'disputes perpetuelles entre les parties.'[8] Concessions would eventually follow, but they did not originate around the bargaining tables of Utrecht.

In reality, the issues surrounding the disputes over Acadia/Nova Scotia and the other North American questions were complex, by no means unimportant in the general scheme of the peace negotiations, and well known in advance of the Utrecht conference. Aside from the matter of Hudson Bay – important to both sides for trade purposes, and also territorially significant to France because of the possibility of overland access to Canada, but only loosely connected with the east coast questions – there were two preeminent issues. Both had been discussed by Prior and the French secretary for foreign affairs, the Marquis de Torcy, in July 1711. One, not surprisingly, was the control of the North Atlantic fisheries. 'Say whatever you please for Newfoundland,' Prior recalled Torcy informing him, 'we can say the same and more; it is the nursery for our seamen ... and for the fish we have more need of it than you.'[9] The fate of Acadia/Nova Scotia was relevant to this in two ways: as a bargaining counter for possible concessions in Newfoundland, and for the fisheries off its own shores now largely exploited by New England. The other major issue was strategic and territorial. Torcy, citing Louis XIV's personal reaction to the preliminary British demands, observed to Prior in 1711 that 'you ask in America all that which [with] our sweat and our blood we have been endeavouring for a hundred years to acquire.'[10] Should the British take control of Newfoundland, Acadia, and Cape Breton, observed a French briefing document in March 1712, 'ils seroient aussy les maistres de l'entrée de la Rivière de St Laurent' and Canada itself would be in jeopardy. The British, however, had the security of New England to consider, and the French plenipotentiaries at Utrecht were soon left in no doubt that Nova Scotia was seen in Lon-

don as 'un ancien Domaine qui faisoit la communication de leurs prin-
cipales Colonies d'Amerique.'[11]

The initial exchange of demands at Utrecht confirmed the areas of
active dispute in North America between Great Britain and France.
While the British claimed full territorial control of Newfoundland,
'comme aussi l'Acadie avec la ville de Port Royal, autrement appellée
Annapolis Royale, et ce qui en depend du dit Pais,' the French offered
only to cede Newfoundland if Plaisance were excluded from the cession
and if French fisheries on the Newfoundland coast were left as they had
been before the war. France did agree to other cessions demanded by
the British, of the Caribbean island of St Christopher and of Hudson
Bay, but only on condition that Acadia be restored.[12] In reality, the
French position was the more flexible. A passage written in cipher in a
French document of late March 1712 set out a series of fall-back positions, beginning with the possibility of agreeing to cede Acadia without
Cape Breton, thus retaining for France some degree of control over the
navigation routes to Canada. If the peace were still threatened by this
issue, a more extreme concession would be to allow Great Britain to
choose between Cape Breton and mainland Acadia. The last resort
would be to cede both of these territories, along with Newfoundland,
though this would buy peace at the expense of serious damage to
French fisheries and the isolation of Canada.[13]

The limits of the French resolve, however, were never tested. Although the French plenipotentiaries were pessimistic by early April
about any possibility of gaining restitution of Acadia, reporting that
their British counterparts 'nous ont protesté cent fois quils avoient
ordre exprés de tout rompre' sooner than to make concessions either
here or on Newfoundland, a new British proposal in May offered some
further basis for negotiation. While continuing to press for cession both
of Acadia and Newfoundland, and seeking to limit French fishing on
the Newfoundland coast to the Petit Nord, the British demand for Acadia 'selon ses Limites anciennes' was qualified by the proposal that the
two powers should share Cape Breton on condition that neither be
allowed fortifications there.[14] The French response refused to concede
or share Cape Breton in any circumstances, or to give up the right to
fortify the island, but did set out two alternatives for the balance of the
Acadian and Newfoundland disputes. France would agree to relinquish
any territorial claim in Newfoundland – including Placentia, but not
adjacent islands and without any concession on fisheries – and would
surrender mainland Acadia. Alternatively, France would additionally

cede the islands adjacent to Newfoundland, as well as two others off St
Christopher, and would agree to give up all of its fishing and drying
rights on the Newfoundland coast – but only if Great Britain restored
Acadia with the boundary (as, the French maintained, it had always
been defined by the British) at the St George River.[15]

Although it was predictable enough that neither alternative would
lead to immediate agreement, there was scope for future discussion.
Here matters rested for several months. When the British secretary of
state, Viscount Bolingbroke, visited France in August 1712 to renew a
temporary armistice, he professed chagrin to find that the North American issues – along with contentious aspects of the commercial treaty
concurrently being negotiated – were not even under active consideration.[16] A month later, under political pressure to show results from the
Tory ministry's peace strategy, Bolingbroke wrote privately to Prior on
the need now to cut short any further idle debate, and instead to find 'a
Scheme of the lowest Expedient which we can admit of on the Subject
of North America.' What this meant was to make as many concessions as
British trade interests could bear, and then issue an ultimatum accordingly.[17] By mid-December, another special British envoy was en route to
the French court, and one politically and socially more prestigious than
Matthew Prior. The instructions issued to the Duke of Shrewsbury noted
that 'the most essential dispute that remains between Us and the French
Court in the Project for a Treaty of Peace ... consists in fixing the
Bounds of their fishing and drying their Fish on the Coast of Newfoundland, and in the Possession of Cape Breton.' Shrewsbury's task, at least
as set out in the instructions, was simple. The French must choose
between their Newfoundland fishing rights and the possession of Cape
Breton. If they insisted on continuing their Newfoundland fishery,
Shrewsbury was to 'show them, that we likewise look'd upon Cape Bre-
ton to belong to Us, and reckoned that Island as part of our Ancient
Territory of Nova Scotia which is by this Treaty restored to us.'[18]

As a contribution to the reaching of a settlement, Shrewsbury's mission had an uncertain beginning. Torcy – who, reported Prior, was 'in
the last concern to find the Duke's instructions so strict' – declared that
France would never accept having to relinquish either Cape Breton or a
fishery that was 'absolutely necessary' for the French economy.[19]
According to Bolingbroke some days later, however, the real British aim
was not so drastic. 'What we see we may obtain when we shall please to
come to it,' wrote the Secretary of State to Prior, was the limitation of
the French fishery to the Petit Nord in exchange for sole French posses-

sion of Cape Breton. In a more private letter, Bolingbroke impressed on Prior the political dangers to the Tory ministry that would accompany a breakdown in the negotiations: 'we stand indeed on the brink of a precipice, but the French stand there too.' To Torcy, he urged that 'nos contestations a l'egard de Terreneuve ne seront point la pierre d'achopement.'[20] In reality, a solution to the apparent impasse on Cape Breton and Newfoundland was already available, although not yet fully acknowledged by either side. In late December, Prior – who considered the French claim to Cape Breton to be only 'too well founded' – had reached agreement with Torcy to recommend a proposal by which France would retain Cape Breton while Great Britain would be ceded Acadia 'avec tous les Droits et prerogatives dont les Francois ont jouy.' The French fishery in Newfoundland, meanwhile, would extend from Bonavista to Pointe Riche, taking in the Petit Nord and more besides – though not as much as the French had originally claimed.[21]

For the time being, Bolingbroke held out on Newfoundland in order to exert pressure for compromise on the commercial treaty, while Louis XIV instructed the French plenipotentiaries to hold Prior's proposal in reserve as a minimum demand pending efforts to wring further concessions from the British at Utrecht.[22] By the second week in February, however, both the king and Shrewsbury had agreed to accept Prior's article, while Torcy busied himself writing to the French plenipotentiaries on the need to accommodate Tory political interests by bringing the peace negotiations to a rapid and successful conclusion.[23] There were flurries of disagreement still to come over the thirty-league limit on French fishing off Nova Scotia and over whether departing Acadians (or French colonists in Newfoundland or the Hudson Bay settlements) would have the right to sell their lands. In early March, France conceded on these matters – although British royal orders were unilaterally given some weeks later to allow Acadians and French Newfoundland residents to sell or retain their lands – and the treaty was signed in April. The text concerning Acadia/Nova Scotia in Article XII was by no means free of ambiguities, notably over just what were the 'anciennes limites' by which the colony was vaguely defined. Nevertheless, to all appearances the diplomacy surrounding the treaty negotiations had transformed the seizure of Port Royal in 1710 into a genuine advance for Great Britain in North America.[24]

Acadia/Nova Scotia had been no mere pawn in the hands of the Utrecht negotiators, to be moved around or traded away as expediency dictated. While North American considerations did not head the list of *casus belli* in the same sense as did the Spanish succession or other major western European issues, neither control of the Gulf of St Lawrence nor what Torcy defined as 'the Subsistance of the Maritime Provinces of West France where thousands of Family's would be reduced to Beggary in case ... [the Newfoundland] Fishery be taken from them' was apt to be taken lightly by either France or Great Britain.[25] Thus the removal of negotiation on these issues away from Utrecht and into the hands of the ministers and their direct envoys, and thus also the ability of these issues to delay and at times to imperil the conclusion of the peace. Seriously as North America was taken in these respects, however, the negotiations were also characterized by crucially untested assumptions. The most significant of these was, quite simply, the existence of defensible colonial empires in northeastern North America. When French–British discussion centred on the Newfoundland fisheries or those in offshore reaches elsewhere in the North Atlantic, it was (to use an inappropriate metaphor) on firm enough ground. Those fisheries had long been integrated into western European economies and by 1713 it was well within the power of France and Great Britain, subject only to environmental constraints, to agree or disagree on the allocation of fishing grounds and the manner of their exploitation. The New England inshore fishery on the coasts of Acadia/Nova Scotia, though, was a different case, and for reasons that also cast doubt on the entire treatment of strategic and territorial issues in the negotiations leading to the Treaty of Utrecht. Control of the territory of Acadia/Nova Scotia – whether for the tangential needs of fishing vessels, for other economic uses, or for settlement – was far beyond the reach of either European power. Thus, while claims of sovereignty were easy to make, the Treaty of Utrecht offered scant prospect of their legitimation in the face of aboriginal scepticism.

With some modification, this principle could be extended even to Canada or New England. While extensive settlement of those areas gave an air of solidity, worthwhile questions could be raised about their military defensibility and whether, in the light of those questions, the solidity was real or apparent. The Earl of Bellomont, governor at the time of both Massachusetts and New York, had warned the British Board of Trade in 1700 that 'if ... there should be a general defection of the Indians, the English in a moneth's time would be forc'd on all the Continent of America to take refuge in their Towns, where I am most Certain they Could not subsist Two moneths, for the Indians would not Leave 'em any sort of Cattle or Corn.' When the intendant of New France heard of the Utrecht settlement, and considered whether the ancient

limits assigned to Acadia implied that French influence was to be relinquished on the coastline from the St George River to Beaubassin,
Michel Bégon's concern was the mirror image of that of Bellomont.
Seduced by British blandishments, the Abenaki might turn to 'piller et
détruire les habitations de la costé du sud du fleuve de St. Laurent et
même de tout le canada ce qui leur seroit facile, ces sauvages connois-
sant parfaitement toutes les habitations de la nouvelle France.'[26] If these
insecurities were current in the more heavily settled colonial areas of
northeastern North America, the ability of French and British negotiators to arbitrate the strategic or imperial status of Acadia/Nova Scotia,
where the carving out even of European spheres of influence had been
a notoriously arduous and fickle business, was doubtful indeed. Not that
the existence of limits to imperial sway had gone entirely unnoticed at
Utrecht. Article XV of the treaty sought to safeguard the security of the
native 'Sujets ou amis' of either European power, as well as to open up
mutual trading arrangements, but it had little effect in view of the
absence in future years of the planned consideration by commissioners
as to exactly 'quels sont ceux qui seront ou devront être censez Sujets &
amis de la France, ou de la G.B.'[27]

There was, however, another framework for the recognition and par-
tial resolution of such dilemmas. It was the practice of a double diplomacy, by which territorial dispositions arrived at in western Europe
would inform the exchanges between colonial administrators and imperial authorities, while a secondary and largely oral form of diplomacy
would characterize the relations between the administrators and indigenous peoples. The era of the Treaty of Utrecht, in which the independent power of aboriginal peoples had been necessarily identified by
colonial officials during a quarter-century of intermittent warfare, created a fertile environment for this approach. Precedents existed: both
immediate, and chronologically or geographically distant from Acadia/
Nova Scotia in this period. The image of the Janus-faced relationships of
the French with Algonkian allies, invoked by such historians as W.J.
Eccles and Richard White, stemmed from similar imperatives further
north and west.[28] In Acadia itself a temporarily successful double approach, though not one involving aboriginal inhabitants, had been
practised during the 1640s by Governor Charles de Menou d'Aulnay
Charnisay. While maintaining a negotiated peace with New England
from 1644 until his death six years later, d'Aulnay had reported consistently to France on the vigour of his efforts to displace the 'Religion-
nayres estrangers' whose settlements in Massachusetts encroached with-

in Acadia's claimed boundaries.[29] The most recent examples in a neighbouring territory to Acadia/Nova Scotia, however, came from the New
England relationship with the Abenaki.

On 13 July 1713, Governor Joseph Dudley of Massachusetts and New
Hampshire summarized for the benefit of assembled Abenaki and
Mi'kmaq representatives at Portsmouth, New Hampshire, the North
American provisions of the Treaty of Utrecht:

> In fformer Warrs twenty or thirty years ago what Lands and ffortifications
> wee then took from the ffrench King wee returned them againe, but now
> all that wee have got from him, wee hold it, And alsoe some things wee
> demanded of Him which wee had not taken And those he has surrendered
> to Her Majestie. We have taken Port Royal and we keep it. Wee demanded
> Menis [Minas] and Senectica [Chignecto] and all Cape Sables and he hath
> given it us, and all the Settlements of Placentia and St Peters on New
> ffound Land is ours and our Soldjers are now Entring in and takeing pos-
> session thereof. Noe more ffrench are to live in those places unles they
> becom Subjects to the Crown of Great Brittaine.[30]

The tone of Dudley's pronouncement, as reflected in the official record
of the proceedings that led eventually to the Abenaki–British treaty of
1713, was uncompromising. So, the record also indicated, was the governor's blame for the Abenaki as the aggressors in the recent warfare, and
insistence that they submit to the authority of the British crown. The
nature of his description of the Treaty of Utrecht is corroborated in the
criticisms levelled at it during a further meeting held immediately afterwards at Casco Bay, at which a larger native gathering met with New
England commissioners to receive and comment on the news of the
Portsmouth conference. Abenaki and Wulstukwiuk leaders followed a
polite expression of pleasure at the conclusion of peace between France
and Great Britain with a seemingly innocuous question as to how it
came about that so much territory had been surrendered from one
crown to the other. Receiving a patronizing answer about the superiority of British arms, Moxus of the Kennebec Abenaki and the other saga-
mores came to the nub of their concern: 'the French never said any
Thing to us about it and wee wonder how they could give it away without
asking us, God having att first placed us there and They having nothing
to do to give it away.'[31] Both native and British views of the Treaty of
Utrecht were stated, therefore, without agreement between them.

When it came to other salient elements of the Abenaki–British treaty, the evidence reveals further differences of understanding between the two sides. By contrast with Dudley's portrayal of the treaty as a submission, the Abenaki leaders at Casco Bay made clear that they took it to be an agreement that was both reciprocal and conditional. 'If the Queen att home makes this Peace contained in these Articles as strong and durable as the Earth,' remarked Moxus and his colleagues, 'Wee for our Parts shall endeavour to make it as strong and firm here.'[32] Where the text of the treaty asserted the right of English colonists to repossess the areas of the old province of Maine where settlements had been displaced, another Abenaki account of the discussions – summarized by the Jesuit missionary Sébastien Rale, who was not a neutral observer but whose account is consistent with the Abenaki positions taken at Casco and recorded elsewhere – recalled the Abenaki view of this matter to have been prefaced by yet another expression of scepticism regarding the ability of the French to give away native territory. This document is ambiguous as to whether the statement was made at Portsmouth or at Casco. It can be read to imply a direct response to Dudley, which would have been necessarily at Portsmouth, but its citation of the presence of 358 assembled natives (including forty Wulstukwiuk and twenty Mi'kmaq) is more consistent with the meeting at Casco. The statement itself was not ambiguous in the least: 'J'ay ma terre que je n'ai donnée a personne et que je ne donnerai pas. Je en veux tousjours etre le maistre, j'en courrois les limites et quand quelqu'un y voudra habiter il payera.'[33]

That there would be different understandings of the treaty and related discussions is not surprising, given the complexities of cross-cultural negotiation. The Abenaki accounts, however, indicate a marked discrepancy between the tone and the substance of the remarks made by Dudley for, respectively, British and native consumption. The preceding forty years had seen a number of agreements made between English and Abenaki. All of them had reflected the English need for a negotiated relationship, and the treaty of 1678 that had ended the northeastern hostilities associated with the so-called King Philip's War had explicitly provided for English payment of a tribute in recognition of their use of Abenaki land: the principle to which the Abenaki speaker in 1713 had returned.[34] The treaty of 1693 negotiated by Sir William Phips, governor of Massachusetts at the time, had introduced the language of sovereignty and submission, but in a context that cast doubt on any likelihood that any common understanding of such terminology had been reached.[35] At the beginning of the eighteenth century, however, New England negotiators – including the newly appointed Joseph Dudley –

dropped the language of submission in favour of that of friendship and coexistence, and adopted such protocols of native diplomacy as reciprocal gift-giving.[36] The resumption of hostilities in 1703 led to English condemnation of the Abenaki as 'bloody Rebells,' and public statements by Dudley up until the early stages of the Portsmouth conference reflected this view.[37] More privately, according to reports of Dudley's intermittent efforts to neutralize the Abenaki, the governor's statements were altogether different. Governor Vaudreuil of New France reported in 1710 that 'Monsieur dudley ... na rien negligé cette année' to win over the Abenaki; the effort had even extended to an offer of gifts to a group that had recently raided a New England settlement, 'leurs temoignant le chagrin quils [the British] avoient d'estre en guerre avec ceux' and offering trade on favourable terms.[38] The Abenaki account of the 1713 discussions, as relayed by Rale, was consistent with this form of approach. It had Dudley allowing for Abenaki wishes as to whether the English settlements should be resettled, requesting – 'je te prie' – that any returning settlers not be disturbed in their fishing, hunting, or cutting of timber, and again offering a favourable trade.[39] The double style of diplomacy, at least in the short term, had prevailed.

The inherent tendency of this diplomatic technique was for it to collapse under the weight of its own contradictions. Though outright duplicity was likely the exception rather than the rule, it was identified by one Boston merchant in 1715. 'I have been present,' observed Thomas Bannister to the Board of Trade, 'when an Article of the Peace has run in one Sence in the English, and quite contrarie in the Indian, by the Governours express order.'[40] In 1717, at a further major British–Abenaki conference held on Arrowsic Island, the Kennebec speaker Wiwurna clashed repeatedly with a new Massachusetts governor, Samuel Shute, on matters that ranged from Wiwurna's insistence that 'other Governours have said to us that we are under no other Government than our own' to the existence of a guarantee orally made by the New England commissioners at the Casco meeting of 1713 that no more British forts would be built in Abenaki territory.[41] Such tensions, focusing notably on continuing colonial encroachments in the Kennebec and Androscoggin valley, led eventually to the reigniting of hostilities in 1722. Nevertheless, it was diplomacy of this nature that framed initially the relationship between native peoples, of the area claimed by Great Britain as its colony of Nova Scotia, and the Annapolis Royal regime following the Treaty of Utrecht. Earlier exchanges had been inconclusive, despite the Mi'kmaq initiatives of early 1711, and had been eclipsed by the intermittent hostilities that had subsequently persisted. Governor Samuel Vetch, optimistic over the arrival of a Mohawk company at Annapolis Royal in 1712, signalled to London his expectation that the new force would 'in a litle time ... Either wholly Banish our Troublesome Indians, or Oblidge them to submitt themselves to her Majesties Government.'[42] The weak and isolated military status of the Annapolis Royal garrison, however, hardly justified his hopes. More consistent with reality was the letter sent by the missionary Antoine Gaulin to Dudley in July 1713. Gaulin, a *Canadien* and a participant in Mi'kmaq military actions following the conquest, warned that failure to release Cape Sable Mi'kmaq captives who had been held in Boston – and who were now, unknown as yet to Gaulin, in the process of being returned – would result in ship seizures and the capture of officers from the Annapolis Royal garrison, to be used as bargaining counters.[43]

The presence of Mi'kmaq representatives at the Portsmouth–Casco meetings in August 1713, and Dudley's announcement of the release of the prisoners – some twenty-one 'men of your Tribes' – put matters on a different trajectory.[44] Also by this time, Francis Nicholson had succeeded in wresting the governorship of Nova Scotia from Samuel Vetch after a period of deteriorating relations between the two. For the next year, until the roles were reversed following the death of Queen Anne and the Hanoverian succession, Nicholson was a regular attendee at conferences held between Dudley and the Abenaki. His presence reflected the location of the Penobscot Abenaki within the claimed boundaries of Nova Scotia, and also the more general recognition of Dudley that – as the Massachusetts governor commented to the colony's general court in February 1714 – the government of Nova Scotia 'must be equally concerned [with Massachusetts] in the Trade with the Indians.'[45] No doubt Thomas Caulfeild, the British officer who commanded at Annapolis Royal during the frequent absences of both Nicholson and Vetch, would have agreed with Dudley's principle. In practice, Caulfeild was not optimistic: 'the chiefest trade with the Indians,' he reported to Nicholson, 'is upon the Coast and most partly followed by those from Boston who affording their Commoditys att much Cheaper rates than our Merchants here Cann ... and unless there be a method found to put a stop to that way of management wee never shall have any Correspondence with them [natives], who seldom or never Come here but when Necessity or Want of provisions drives them.'[46]

The ensuing nine years saw a series of wary and largely unproductive initiatives on both sides. At Annapolis Royal, Caulfeild received instructions from Nicholson in the summer of 1714 to draw the attention of neighbouring native leaders to the recent British–Abenaki conferences inaugurated through the treaty of Portsmouth as examples of imperial benevolence.[47] Consistently enough with the British text of that treaty, though not with the native side of the diplomacies that had surrounded it, Caulfeild seized on the news of the accession of King George I to send commissioners to both Aboriginal and Acadian inhabitants of the territory claimed as Nova Scotia to demand an oath of allegiance. From a British viewpoint, little success was achieved. The visitors to the Penobscot, for example, were informed politely but firmly that, while trade would be acceptable, 'je ne proclame point de roy Etranger dans mon pays.'[48] A few weeks later came a complementary Mi'kmaq statement, in the context of a brief though intense period of ship seizures off Cape Sable that were apparently prompted by rumours of renewed war between France and Great Britain over the claims of James Stuart as a rival to George I.[49] On at least one occasion, the Mi'kmaq captors had asserted their right to apprehend a vessel and its crew pending the payment of £30 for its release by declaring – as quoted by aggrieved Boston merchants – that 'the Lands are theirs and they can make Warr and peace when they please.'[50]

A further result of the seizures was for Caulfeild to appoint Peter Capon, commissary at Annapolis Royal, to sail around the coast to Louisbourg, visiting ports en route to inquire into the causes of the outbreaks. On three occasions during his return voyage, Capon became the intermediary for overtures made by Mi'kmaq groups to Annapolis Royal. At Port Maltais (Port Medway), he reported,

> I went ashoar to theire Wigwamms, and told them the dammage the Indians had done to the English, which they seemed sorry for, and desired me to meet them in the Spring on the Coast, being sent by theire Chiefe to tell me, that all theire Chiefs and Indians would meet me, and desired Articles then to be drawn relating to trade and other affairs at that Conference, and the Articles then agreed upon, they would signe and faithfully perform, and pressed me hard to promise to meet them, I answered them if I had the Governors orders soe to doe, I should willingly obey them.[51]

While there is no evidence that further meetings arose out of the invitations extended to Capon, his discussions of 1715 illustrated both the Mi'kmaq receptiveness to a diplomatic approach and the concurrent native concerns regarding the activities of irregular and unscrupulous New England traders on the coast. 'The Indians are very Cross,' a letter from Annapolis Royal had noted earlier in 1715: 'They say the English Cheats them.'[52] Increasingly, the stability of the market for furs at Louisbourg, and the regular gift-giving of French officials, became a potent attraction. As a member of the Nova Scotia council, William Shirreff, informed the Board of Trade, the avarice of Boston traders in the region 'hath Caused the Indeans ... [to] Complain and Retire from Thence with their furrs and other Marchandize to Cape Breton, where all manner of Necessarys are furnished them att reasonable Rates (if not by the Marchants) out of the King's Magazine keept There for supplying both Officers and Soldiers, and for the Encouragement of the Savages and others to Trade to that Place.'[53]

Shirreff's suggestion was to establish a similar magazine at Annapolis Royal, and it was endorsed by Caulfeild in a lengthy report to the Board of Trade in November 1715, advocating an effort to win over the Aboriginal inhabitants by favourable terms of trade and 'by kindly using of them, on which foundation their friendshipp is wholy founded.'[54] This, along with Shirreff's assertion earlier in 1715 of the successful results for the French of intermarriage between colonists and Aboriginal inhabitants, proved intriguing to the British Board of Trade as it grappled with North American questions.[55] Its instructions of 1719 to Richard Philipps as the new governor of Nova Scotia contained a strong endorsement of a gradual and diplomatic approach. Philipps was instructed to 'cultivate and maintain a strict friendship and good Correspondence with the Indian Nations inhabiting within the precincts of Your Government, that they may be reduc'd by Degrees not only to be good Neighbours to His Majesty's Subjects, but likewise themselves become good Subjects to His Majesty.' The means specified were through the distribution of presents, and through financial incentives for intermarriage. Any British man or woman who married a native spouse would receive £10 in cash and a land grant of fifty acres.[56] A more general statement followed from the Board of Trade some two years later, in a lengthy report on the trade and government of all the British colonies in North America. It identified three general areas that were essential to British interests in America: to curb French expansion, to improve colonial governance, and to cultivate 'a good understanding with the Native Indians.' On British–Aboriginal relations, the Board skirted the question of subjection by concentrating on ways of establishing and solidifying relationships with Aboriginal peoples on what it supposed to be the French model. The Nova Scotia instruction regarding intermarriage 'should be extended to all the other British Colonies.' Presents should be regularly distributed and put on a secure budgetary footing. British missionaries should be dispatched among 'those poor Infidels.' Trade should be developed as an instrument of state policy. Finally, the report argued, 'the Several Governors of Your Majesty's Plantations should endeavor to make Treaties and Alliances of Friendship with as many Indian Nations as they can,' and the unity of British colonies and native allies should be promoted at all times.[57]

As the British imperial approach to native diplomacy evolved, however, Mi'kmaq and Wulstukwiuk leaders had more immediate concerns. One of them was the failure of the Annapolis Royal regime to follow due diplomatic protocols. A new lieutenant-governor, John Doucett, reported in early 1718 that 'some of the Cheifs of the Indian's have been with me to tell me, that if wee Expected them to continue our Freind's, they Expected Presents Yearly from His Majesty, as they allway's receiv'd when this country was in the hand's of the French King.' Doucett's recommendation was that gifts be given, and he repeated it in a more urgent context four months later. Blaming the incitement of the missionaries, he observed that 'Some of the Indian's ... pretend that the Country belongs only to them, and that neither the English or French have any thing to doe here, and have Insulted and used the Like Argument's to some of our Traders on the Coast, but yett are very Civill when they are in reach of our Country.'[58] Richard Philipps, as governor, arrived convinced of the need for gifts to be distributed but with slender resources for doing so. 'I heare nothing of the presents,' Philipps complained from Boston, while on his way to Annapolis in 1720, 'that were ordered for the Indians, and would be very apropos at my arrival among them.'[59] During the following spring and summer, Philipps finally met formally with both Mi'kmaq and Wulstukwiuk chiefs. A group of Mi'kmaq sakamows visited Philipps, he reported in May, to ask 'if the French were to leave the country whether the Two Crownes, were in Allyance, whether I intended to debarr them of their Religion, or disturb them in their Traffick, to all which Querys, I answered to sattisfaction, and sent them away in good Humour, promising they would be very peaceable while the Union lasted between the two Crownes.' Philipps admitted that he was delaying meeting with the Wulstukwiuk because of his lack of presents. Eventually, he issued an invitation to a conference in late July, at which he apologized for having no better gifts to offer than those provided from funds voted the previous day by the council at Annapolis Royal. For all that, the meeting was friendly, with the Wulstukwiuk representatives addressing Philipps respectfully though not submissively as 'Notre Perre,' while complaining that British governors and merchants had reneged on promises of trade.[60]

Then came the raids of August 1720, at Canso and at Minas, and tensions on the coastline that increased with the concurrent deterioration of Abenaki–British relations further to the southwest.[61] Philipps's perplexity at the obvious inability of his Annapolis Royal garrison to deter such events was deepened rather than relieved when in November he received messages from Wulstukwiuk groups in the Wulstukw valley and on Passamaquoddy Bay, disavowing the Mi'kmaq actions at Canso and Minas. 'Nous sommes vos amis,' read the Wulstukw letter, 'et ... nous esperons pareilment de vous.' Philipps's mystification showed in his assurance to the British Board of Ordnance of his good relations with most native inhabitants of the region and immediate confession that even those most friendly to him would commit themselves only so long as peace was maintained between Britain and France.[62] Although poorly understood by Philipps, there were two related processes at work. First, the effective confinement of the British regime to Annapolis Royal was clearly recognized by those native leaders who wished for whatever reason to enter into diplomatic contacts. Diplomacy meant that respect, formality, and protocol must be maintained, but it did not demand that native representatives be drawn into the fiction that 'Nova Scotia' was British territory. The more absurd of British pretensions could thus be politely ignored. Where outright denials of British authority were made, they came from a somewhat different source.

For an extended period, going far back into the previous century, New England fishing and trading vessels had enjoyed an informal Mi'kmaq tolerance, except at times when – because of war, trade irregularities, or other sources of tension – it was withheld and ship seizures resulted. The assertion of the British claim to 'Nova Scotia,' however, together with the abandonment in 1714 of efforts by Massachusetts to restrict trade with the Abenaki to government-operated truckhouses, brought more New England vessels to the northeastern coasts than ever before.[63] Mi'kmaq chiefs had expressed their disquiet to the French governor of Cape Breton both in 1715 and in 1720, and the conspicuous New England fishing presence at Canso and equally noticeable trading activities at Minas were obvious examples of what was taking place.[64] By contrast with the essential compatibility of Acadian settlement with Mi'kmaq activities, the New England traders posed difficulties that had been foreseen by Governor Dudley when he had argued in vain for government-regulated trade: 'a Trade managed by private Persons will be liable to be corrupted by extorted Prices and selling them Drink.'[65] One Mi'kmaq option was to demand a tribute, thus in effect regulating the trade for themselves; another was to attempt by force to loosen the New England grip. Such tensions, combined with those affecting the British–Abenaki relationship, were fully capable of undermining whatever rudimentary diplomatic relationship might be emerging, and even the report in a Boston newspaper in late 1722 of a treaty signed at Annapolis with local Mi'kmaq residents ended with the telling observation that 'all the English inhabitants are fortifying their Houses, resolving never to trust such perfidious, blood-thirsty Enemies.'[66] Armed conflict followed and diplomacy, for the time being at least, had failed.

Throughout the earliest years of the Annapolis Royal regime, however, there was a further relationship that was essentially diplomatic in nature, though not formally so. Superior Acadian numbers, and the ability of Acadians to withhold necessary supplies or labour from the fort, had been sources of frustration for the British garrison from the time of the conquest. The Treaty of Utrecht removed some elements of uncertainty by determining that, however the boundaries of Nova Scotia might be defined or controverted, the British province would include most of the existing Acadian settlements. Whether Acadians would still be occupying those areas, however, remained to be clarified. Early British talk of deporting the Acadians had subsided in the absence of a settler population to replace them. Samuel Vetch, in January 1711, had been eager for imperial permission to dispatch the Acadians – except for those who might become Protestants – to Martinique and Plaisance. By November, with the notion of expulsion unencouraged from London and contradicted by the efforts of the commanders of the Canada expedition to induce Acadians to stay and swear allegiance to the British crown, Vetch's pleas for Protestant settlers and dire warnings on the presence of 'no Inhabitants in the Country save Roman Catholicks and savages yett more biggott than they,' were offered – however reluctantly – in a different context.[67] Vetch claimed to have succeeded in persuading some Acadians to take an oath of allegiance, although the accounts of others invariably portrayed his relationship with them as sour and troubled. An officer of the garrison, George Vane, reported in May 1712 that Vetch's absence in Boston had improved matters noticeably and that 'the [Acadian] people dread him to that degree that now he talkes of comming back ... theres a perfect cloud in Every face, and Ime informed severall of the Inhabitants, talke of abandoning ther habitations; if he be not changed before next winter.'[68]

The prospect of Acadians' quitting their settlements was an issue that went far beyond the personal failings of Vetch. Following from the terms of the Treaty of Utrecht, two French officers arrived from Cape Breton in August 1714 to supervise the arrangements for those Acadians who wished to remove to the new colony of Île Royale. A series of meetings followed, at which Acadians were invited to declare their intentions in the presence of the two envoys and of Nicholson and Caulfeild. The sessions were eventful. At Annapolis Royal, Acadians demanded compensation for their hardships under the earlier British regime. Here and in the other major settlements, most of the assembled Acadians opted to move to Cape Breton. Any thought that this would be straightforwardly accomplished was soon disproved, however, when Nicholson made difficulties both regarding the treaty provision for the Acadians to take with them their movable effects and the later royal order to permit them to sell their lands. Both of these, Nicholson ruled with the support of the Nova Scotia council, must be referred to London.[69] Later allegations had Nicholson not only putting obstacles in the way of Acadian removal, but also harassing any who seemed determined to leave by cutting them off from trade with the Annapolis Royal garrison. The net result, according to two officers of the garrison, was to incline Acadian inhabitants further towards leaving. Nicholson himself cited reports during the summer of 1715 that 'the ffrench here [at Annapolis Royal] and at Minas have built ... forty or fifty sloops in order to carry them to Cape Breton. Severall of them Slips away dayly.'[70] Yet there was also evidence of Acadian reluctance to depart and, by the fall of 1715, of some who had returned from Cape Breton disillusioned by poor lands and shortage of supplies. In all, during the twenty-one years following the Treaty of Utrecht, only some sixty-seven Acadian families moved there to stay.[71] That the large majority elected to remain in their existing communities prevented an immediate economic crisis for the British regime to contend with, but also represented a source of renewed frustration for British officials. Philipps and his officers complained in 1720 that 'the ffrench Inhabitants unanimously refuse to sweare Allegiance to the Crowne of Great Brittain ... That notwithstanding this, they do not seem to entertain much thoughts of quitting their Habitations.'[72] Some months earlier, the lieutenant-governor John Doucett had rightly noted that French colonial officials had urged Acadians not to take the oath. An exasperated Doucett had speculated that soon the French 'will Claim every thing to within Cannon Shott of this Fort, which has been often the Topick of the Inhabitants discourse.'[73]

The reality was more complex. By the time Doucett wrote, the British regime was well embarked on the lengthy and tortuous process of establishing a negotiated relationship with Acadian inhabitants, even though the uncompromising terminology of the British claims that proceeded from the Treaty of Utrecht prevented the discussions from being recognized as the diplomatic exchanges that they essentially were. It was true that Acadians had generally refused to take an oath of allegiance to the British crown. Nevertheless, a number of more circumscribed commitments had been offered. Acadian declarations in early 1715 – the subscribers including the influential Prudent Robichaud of Annapolis Royal – had promised peaceable conduct, and even a temporary form of allegiance to the British crown, until the expected removal to Cape Breton.[74] Later communications to Doucett put the often-repeated argument that swearing the oath would jeopardize both the Catholicism of the jurors and their relationship with Mi'kmaq neighbours, but that a less formal understanding or even an oath not to take up arms for either France or Great Britain would surely suffice.[75] By the spring of 1720, declarations carrying substantial numbers of signatures – 136 from Annapolis River Acadians, and 179 from those of Minas – refused again the oath of allegiance, renewed the question of migration to Île Royale, but also promised to keep the peace in the meantime and hinted at the possibility of a longer-term understanding.[76]

While such declarations must be interpreted in the context of the existence of other Acadian factions that took a more thoroughly pro-British or pro-French position, the repeated promises of limited cooperation with the Annapolis Royal regime revealed an approach to negotiation that was accurately informed by the weakness of the British bargaining position. In the absence of other colonists, as Samuel Vetch reflected in 1715, a general removal of Acadians 'will wholly Strip and Ruine Nova Scotia so it will att once make Cape Brittoun a populous and well stocked Colony which many years, and great Expence Could not have done directly from france.'[77] Variations on this theme ranged from Caulfeild's fear later in 1715 that the loss of Acadian settlement would remove a buffer against the hostility of the Mi'kmaq, 'the worst of Enemys,' to the argument advanced by a group of Annapolis Royal merchants in 1718 that employment of Acadian fishers was indispensable to their operations.[78] More generally, the lack of an institutional framework for Acadian governance that was recognizable to British civil or military officials forced on the new authorities an unwelcome need to improvise. Their only option in the existing circumstances was to work uneasily with Acadian leaders such as

Robichaud or the seigneurial landholder Agathe de Saint-Étienne de La Tour, and otherwise to govern, as Thomas G. Barnes has argued, 'by rule of thumb.'[79]

While Philipps and his officers might argue from time to time for a military solution to their dilemma regarding the Acadian presence – additional troops to expel or subdue the Acadians, followed by British settlement – expense and the lack of an obvious source of new immigration were decisive obstacles.[80] The British Board of Trade, however, had another expedient to prescribe, in the form of a double diplomacy originating – unlike that practised vis-à-vis the Abenaki by governors who found it unnecessary to report their approach to London – in imperial directives. In a submission to the crown dated 30 May 1718, the Board of Trade reviewed the difficulties facing the Annapolis Royal regime. One of its less likely solutions was to encourage British residents of Newfoundland to move to Nova Scotia. The recalcitrance of Acadians regarding the oath of allegiance, however, would have to be dealt with in the context of the precarious British hold on Nova Scotia: 'it might be adviseable at least, till more British Inhabitants shall be settled there, and the Indians brought over intirely to Your Majesty's Interest, that the French should not be treated in the manner they deserve for so undutiful a behaviour.' At the governor's discretion, efforts might be made to impose economic penalties for refusal to take the oath, such as exclusion from fisheries, but the starker ultimatum of a choice between the oath and departure would have to await the strengthening of the British regime.[81] Soon after Philipps's arrival at Annapolis Royal, Philipps summoned Acadians to send deputies 'de traiter entre moy, ou ceux que je deputerai et les ... Habitans,' and signalled in a report to London his intention 'for the sake of gaining time and keeping all things quiet ... to send home the Deputys, with smooth Words, and promise of enlargement of time, whilst I transmitt their Case home and receive his Majestys farther direction therein.'[82]

The Board of Trade approved. 'As to the French Inhabitants of Nova Scotia,' it informed Philipps,

who appear so Wavering in their Inclinations, We are apprehensive they will never become good Subjects to His Majesty whilst the French Governors and their Priests retain so great an Influence over them: For which reason we are of Opinion they ought to be removed so soon as the Forces which We have proposed to be sent to you shall arrive in Nova Scotia ... but as you are not to attempt their removal without His Majesty's possitive

Orders for that purpose, you will do well in the mean while to continue the same prudent and cautious towards them.[83]

British actions were not always so cautious. When naval force could be brought effectively to bear, as in the disputed fishing ports of the Canso area from which French inhabitants were 'dislodged' by force in September 1718, the opportunity would be taken. Reviewing this action, the Board of Trade admitted that 'a gentler method might possibly have been more adviseable' but held that any criticism on this ground was outweighed by the 'very laudable Zeal' that had been shown.[84] Where French or Acadians were concerned, the implication went, the question was one of tactics only. The Treaty of Utrecht had established the legitimacy of the British position. What remained was to ensure that principle was carried satisfactorily into practice. Viewed in that deceptive light, the British–Acadian relationship was not a diplomatic one at all.

The unstated imperial context, however, argued otherwise. Even within the areas of established British settlement in North America, imperial authority – as Jack P. Greene has shown – was a matter for negotiation between colonists and the inherently unsystematic institutions of the early modern state.[85] In an eighteenth-century empire that increasingly sought to bring non-British peoples within its geographical and economic bounds, but lacked the theoretical or institutional infrastructure to do so, the complexities were greater and ambivalence became a recurring characteristic of the resulting relationships. In some cases, quasi-autonomous corporations such as the Hudson's Bay Company and the East India Company could act as intermediaries for the state. Existing non-British institutional frameworks also had an established role, even in English law, in providing a clothing of legitimacy for imperial claims.[86] Yet Nova Scotia presented unusual complications that were resolved by none of the obvious available parallels. In Jamaica in 1655, English settlers in substantial numbers soon erased the Spanish character of the population. English settlement of New York had also followed the conquest of 1664, and the Protestants of the former New Netherland quickly assimilated in an institutional context even while remaining linguistically distinct. Minorca, taken by the British in 1708, had a highly systematized institutional structure that was left virtually intact despite the misgivings of the first British governor.[87] Indigenous structures for the ordering of native and Acadian affairs already existed in Nova Scotia, but in forms largely unrecognizable to the incoming British. Meanwhile, the independence and pragmatism of Acadian leaders combined with the economic dependence of the colony upon their continuing presence to ensure that the need for a negotiated relationship could not be ignored even by the most reluctant of imperial officials. Similarly, the military potency of the Mi'kmaq and Wulstukwiuk, and the articulacy with which excessive colonial demands were rebuffed by native diplomats, demanded that negotiation be a continuing process even though it had not proved successful by 1722.

Nova Scotia after the conquest of 1710 was characterized by tensions that, in the broadest imperial sense, were normal results of the attempt to incorporate and accommodate non-British peoples. Nova Scotia also presented, in the forms these tensions assumed, complexities that at the time were unique. Far from ending the diplomatic history of the conquest of Port Royal, the Treaty of Utrecht had been only the launching point for the diplomatic activity that involved those whose lack of representation at Utrecht was an inaccurate reflection of their power to influence events in the world of reality that underlay the notional extensions of empire. Not that the French–British agreements at Utrecht were unimportant. They too exerted an influence after 1713, for they created the status quo of putative control of Nova Scotia that British officials were obliged henceforth to defend as best they could, as well as the status quo of continuing strength in the Gulf of St Lawrence and in the North Atlantic fisheries that was more solidly asserted by France. The status quo defended by native diplomats, however, was one in which any imperial presence was peripheral, while that of Acadians was framed by the majority rejection of removal to Île Royale and the continuing existence of communities that now faced both imperial and native pressures.

If the existence of these competing understandings endangered the ability to resolve future disputes without resort to violence, matters were further confounded by the uneasy coexistence of diverse and inherently unstable diplomacies. The ambiguities of the Treaty of Utrecht on the boundaries of the British and French claims to Acadia/Nova Scotia had remained unresolved after futile attempts at negotiation in 1714 and 1719–20.[88] Mi'kmaq–British negotiation had ended for the time being in 1722, as had Abenaki–British contacts further southwest, and the prospect for resumption after hostilities ended was in the context of the double diplomacy that had produced agreement on certain issues at Portsmouth in 1713 but also carried significant risks of contradictory understandings. Double diplomacy in a somewhat different form had emerged as the favoured British approach towards the Acadians. While the notion that the British–Acadian relationship was a diplomatic one would have been denied by British officials, it had been carried on as such. That the aim was ultimately to replace negotiation with coercion was not disclosed for the time being. The future of a long-term alternative to violent conflict rested, therefore, on diplomacies of which none was yet conclusively discredited but each in its own way was compromised. What would result from their interaction was ominously unclear by the early 1720s. Richard Philipps, however, had clearly grasped the essence of what little was obvious as he remarked to the Board of Trade in September 1720 that '[I] tell you plainely that I find this Countrey in no likelyhood of being setled under the King's Obedience upon the footing it is.'[89]

PART FOUR: TRANSITIONS

7

Making a British Nova Scotia

Barry Moody

When on 4 October 1710 (N.S.) the French fleur-de-lis was lowered at
the fort at Port Royal, and the union flag of England and Scotland was
raised to the top of the pole, it was more a symbol of expectation than of
actual accomplishment. Similar acts of victory had taken place on several occasions over the past seventy-five years, only to have the French
flag, and a French presence, reinstated shortly thereafter. If 1710 was to
be any different, if it was to signal the beginning of a permanent British
occupation of the region, the will of politicians and bureaucrats across
the Atlantic would have to be engaged and brought to bear on the colony. Resurrecting the old term 'Nova Scotia' for the region, and giving
the newly captured town the name Annapolis Royal to replace Port
Royal were simple matters: whether these names could be made to stick,
and have some real meaning, would be something else entirely. The
next few decades would be crucial in determining the fate and nature of
a British colony in the region.

   With the surrender of the garrison by Subercase, it is clear that a number of important changes had taken place. A British administration, controlled by British politics and politicians, replaced the traditional French
structure, with consequences not yet apparent. Annapolis Royal had
become, somewhat precariously, a British town, in name at least, with a
motley British garrison to replace the equally disreputable French one.
Trade between the region and the nearby New England colonies, a constant in the colony's economic past, would no longer take place outside
the law, while the rich fishery seemed more open than ever before to
English colonial exploitation. Much remained to be done, however. The

defences of the new acquisition would have to be secured, a British, or at least Protestant, population acquired, and a new governmental structure built if Nova Scotia were to be cemented firmly into the British empire in North America, safe from future French efforts to reassert their supremacy in the region. Beyond that, of course, would be the crucial decision of what *kind* of British colony would be created; the very nature of the society could be determined in this formative period. In the heady days of victory in the fall of 1710, all of this, and more, might be thought possible. The next three decades would bring another kind of reality, as an aggressive Boston and a lethargic London would leave the colony undeveloped and at times virtually defenceless. The foundations of a British Nova Scotia would indeed be laid in the decades immediately after the conquest, but the result would fall far short of initial expectations. Nova Scotia would remain precariously positioned at the very edge of the British empire in North America.

In spite of efforts to modify the interpretation, the basic framework within which this period was viewed in the twentieth century was established by the historian John Bartlet Brebner, writing in the 1920s. The title of his book reveals the main thrust of his argument: *New England's Outpost: Acadia before the Conquest of Canada.*[1] Even the major challenge to the thesis, by George Rawlyk, saw the new colony as essentially the creature of its more powerful English neighbours, especially Massachusetts.[2] While recognizing the important, and ever-present, New England influence, there are other significant aspects of this period that both authors recognized even if they chose not to emphasize them. More than an economic, political, and military outpost of Massachusetts developed, even if the reality did not always measure up to expectations. In the end, Nova Scotia did not turn out to be Massachusetts writ small in the wilderness, not merely the outer frontier of New England, even if some greatly desired it to be so.

The terms of capitulation signed by Subercase in 1710 formally surrendered only the fort and town of Port Royal. The rest of the colony of Acadia could not be termed officially British until after the Treaty of Utrecht ended the War of the Spanish Succession in 1713. Port Royal/Annapolis Royal would thus see the first and most significant impact of the presence of the victors. Almost overnight the town was transformed from a French community into an English one, an English island in the midst of a sea of French and Mi'kmaq. The fate of Annapolis Royal during the next thirty years reveals much about the nature and consequence of this particular conquest.

In spite of the uncertainty concerning future British control of the region, some of the conquerors wasted no time in putting down roots in the community, making Annapolis Royal English in more than mere name. This process was facilitated by the determination of many of the French inhabitants of the town not to live under direct British control. Some of the civilians withdrew with the evacuation of the French troops in the fall of 1710, while over the next few years others left for Île Royale. In fact, 71 per cent of those who chose that option came from the Annapolis area.[3] Others, and these apparently mostly Acadians who had lived within Port Royal, chose to dispose of their properties and move into the countryside. In the town itself, there were those among the conquerors, and their followers, who were ready to fill the vacuum.

The extent and nature of this change can be seen clearly in the transfer of properties within the town during the first few years after the conquest. Soldiers, traders, and speculators began buying up available lots and houses in the town, making what deals they could with the departing inhabitants, French and Acadian alike. Fortunately, the records of many of the land transactions have survived, allowing us to plot the fairly rapid shift in ownership and occupation of the properties within the town.[4]

The transfer of land and houses appears to have been orderly and peaceful, with no evidence of attempts to merely seize the property of the departing inhabitants, or to force the French out, however tempting that might have been. Fair prices seem to have been paid, as the amounts tended to rise very little in subsequent transactions among the British themselves. Two Bostonians who had taken part in the military events of 1710 played a key role in this transformation of Annapolis Royal. Sir Charles Hobby and John Adams appear to have acted in partnership, with Adams making the initial purchases, and then transferring most of the property to Hobby.[5] These two men were the major agents of the physical changes to Annapolis during this time. Of the two, the impact of Adams would be far more significant, as he committed most of the rest of his life to the new community. He would not finally leave the colony until 1740, after a failed bid for power following the sudden death of lieutenant-governor Lawrence Armstrong. Hobby's interest proved to be more transitory, and the collapse of his own financial affairs quickly sidetracked his initial interest in the future of the colony and town.

An important characteristic of the demography of this period is the almost complete separation of English and Acadian residents of the area. With the sale of most of the properties in the town proper, the Acadians of Port Royal itself either withdrew from the colony entirely or moved to the countryside; Annapolis Royal became a British enclave. The reverse was also true. During the period under discussion, there is not a single reference to any British acquisition of property immediately outside the town itself. No farms were acquired by the citizens of Annapolis, no attempts made to move into the countryside. A complete geographic division evolved, drawing a line sharply between the two communities; even in later years, until after the *grand dérangement,* few proved willing to cross that line.

Immediately after the conquest, it had seemed as if a melding of the two populations might take place over time. As has so often been the case in the history of warfare, some of the men among the 'conquerors' found the local women much to their liking, and some of the Acadian women saw no reason not to respond. There were a few marriages between the two groups, the most notable being Marie-Madeleine Maisonnat to William Winniett (1711),[6] and Agathe de Saint-Étienne de La Tour to Edmond Bradstreet (1714).[7] Such a practice, if continued, might well have made a significant difference in the evolution of Nova Scotia, but there appear to have been no such unions beyond the first decade after the conquest. There is no indication why such marriages stopped, although it is unlikely that the Roman Catholic Church was ever very enthusiastic about them, especially as the young Acadian women tended to be drawn into English society, and the children seem to have been raised as Protestants. Whatever the reason, bonds that might have knit the two groups together and produced a new Nova Scotian society failed to develop, and that gap between Acadian and British, Annapolis and countryside, persisted and widened. The world of the countryside continued to belong exclusively to the Acadians and the Mi'kmaq, while British Nova Scotia was an entirely 'urban' affair (if one can use such a term to describe Annapolis Royal.)

For all that, there was considerable intermingling on the streets of the town. Under the French, tiny Port Royal had often been a fairly cosmopolitan community, as soldiers, administrators, farmers, traders, native peoples, fishermen, adventurers, and more were attracted to the community for longer or shorter periods of time. Under the conquerors, this trend was accentuated. Acadians, Mi'kmaq, English, Irish, Maliseet, New Englanders, Scots, Mohawks, and others were to be found at times on the streets of Annapolis, while the variety of social class, religious denomination, and occupation was as great. No one element was strong enough to dominate the evolving community completely, and although English was the prevalent language, it was spoken with many accents. Unlike the usual seventeenth-century English colonial experience, the 'new' Nova Scotia would not be based on a narrow segment of England's population, but reflected instead Annapolis Royal's position as an international crossroads, a meeting place of many cultures, regardless of the smallness of the scale.

The physical appearance of Annapolis showed more continuity than change. The layout and configuration of the town remained much as it had been under the French. Streets, lot boundaries, and buildings would be largely unchanged as a result of the conquest. The fort still dominated the town from its position on a slight rise, with most of the houses and shops straggling down the hill and along the waterside. The only significant change was in the name of the main thoroughfare – from Rue Dauphin to St George Street – which ran from 'Land's End' to the cape. Most of the houses had survived the siege of 1710, and were utilized by the conquerors. In appearance and layout the town consequently more closely resembled an English or European medieval village than an eighteenth-century New England town.[8] Something of the medieval flavour of the community is given in a 1724 judgment of the governing Council concerning a fire that had recently destroyed a house in the town: 'Agree That Said Mrs. Rice Should pay five pounds for presuming to make a fire in a place where there was no funnel to Carry the fire or Smoke through the Thatch.'[9] In general appearance, at least, the town remained very much as the French had created it.

Appearances might, however, belie the extent and nature of the changes that were taking place within the community during the three decades after 1710. The foundations of a British community were being firmly laid, even if it did not eventually conform to what some of its planners had in mind. If the layout of the town, and the houses themselves, retained much of their seventeenth-century flavour, significant changes were taking place within those buildings, changes that clearly reflect the extent of outside influences on the community. What historian Richard L. Bushman has characterized as the 'refinement of America' was clearly at work at this British outpost, as at least parts of Annapolis Royal society were being transformed.[10] Developing beside the thatched houses with no chimneys were to be found the sophisticated households of individuals such as the well-to-do Samuel Douglass and the urbane Paul Mascarene. When Douglass died in 1744 the extensive inventory of his estate listed among other things such items as looking glasses, 'a Sett of China

[bed] Curtains,' table clothes and linen napkins, table forks, and a silver teapot and 'Tea Board' (tea-table).[11] For some, life in this frontier community was surprisingly sophisticated, exhibiting characteristics of the more urban centres of British North America.

Annapolis Royal was first and foremost a garrison town, in a way that probably no other English community in North America was during this time. Although the garrison was always small (usually 100 to 150), the civilian population was even smaller. Therefore, for good or ill, much of the economic and social life of the town revolved around the officers and men of the fort. Special holidays, days of thanksgiving or mourning, were proclaimed by the fort's commander, during which no 'Servil Labour' was to be done in the town. 'The Honourable Lt. Governor,' declared one such proclamation, 'upon the Good News that Arrived here in the printed Papers of his Majestys having Discovered a most Horrid Bloody Crule and most Barbarous Inhumain Conspiracy formed against his Sacred Person & Government proposed a Day of Publick Thanksgiving for that Great Mercy Vouchsafed to his Majesty.'[12] Such holidays proclaimed the 'Britishness' of the town, reinforcing the ties with both old England and new.

Although the general populace of the town remained very small during these three decades, some of the traits of an English (but not a New England) community began to appear. In spite of the important role played by Massachusetts in the capture of Port Royal, and the influence which some of its merchants would continue to exert, the prevailing religious influence was Anglican rather than Congregationalist. Immediately after the conquest, it was the Rev. Thomas Hesketh, Church of England chaplain to the marines, who was invited to preach the sermon of thanksgiving.[13] His *Divine Providence Asserted and Some Objections Answered. A Sermon Preach'd October the 10th 1710 (at Annapolis-Royal in America)* (Boston, 1710) must have been one of the first occasions on which the new name of the town appeared in print. The attempted connection here was important: Annapolis Royal's ties should lie with Anglican England, it was expected, not with Puritan Massachusetts.

The Anglican influence was intended to go far beyond an initial sermon or two. Immediately after the conquest, the Rev. John Harrison was appointed chaplain to the garrison and, by extension, to the community at large. Over the next ten years, whatever religious service the town enjoyed was provided by this Anglican divine. In spite of occasional scandal (in 1724 the then Anglican clergyman, the Rev. Robert Cuthbert, insisted on living with another man's wife), the Church of England filled important roles in the fledgling British community. The first English school was established under its jurisdiction, and by 1728 the minister-schoolmaster was able to boast fifty scholars (although he complained of a shortage of books and a low salary). By 1733 there were plans to build a parish church in the community, a design not carried out until much later.[14]

Nova Scotia might not possess an established church in law until after the founding of Halifax in 1749, but the Church of England was already functioning as such, with the full backing of the civil and military leadership. In 1720, Harrison was appointed to the first Council established to govern the colony, setting a precedent for later Anglican involvement.[15] A more tangible and, for Annapolis Royal, more significant move was made in 1732: the formal conveyance of the former glebe lands of the Roman Catholic Church in the community to the Church of England. The Council 'Agreed that As it hath always been Called the Church land that it Should Continue So to be, and that a Patent should be prepared to Secure the Same for the use of the Church for Ever.'[16] These glebe lands consisted in part of a significant block of land in the lower town, where, on a series of crooked little streets, those who could not afford to purchase land were able to rent it from the Church and there build their small houses, paying an annual 'ground rent' to the Church. For the next 135 years, the glebe lands in the midst of the town would serve as a visible reminder of the intended power and position of the Anglican Church in the community.

The Anglican influence, real and intended, was obvious in other ways as well. Not surprisingly, the overwhelming majority of the officers and men of the garrison were, officially at least, members of that denomination, giving the Church of England powerful support within such a small community. Until the troops were finally withdrawn from the fort, 144 years after their first arrival in 1710, their weekly presence at Anglican services was a constant reminder of the role that that church was expected to play in Annapolis Royal.

It was, however, not merely the military and civil officials who added strength to the Anglican position. Although the influence in Nova Scotia of Boston traders, merchants, and seamen has frequently been noted by historians, the strong Anglican nature of that influence has usually been overlooked. A remarkable number of those Bostonians most intimately involved in the affairs of their neighbour in the first half of the eighteenth century were active members of the growing Anglican community of that city. The walls of the Anglican King's Chapel and

Old North Meeting House in Boston contain numerous memorial plaques to men who frequently turn up in the records of nearby Nova Scotia. Sir Charles Hobby, Cyprian Southack, Arthur Savage, Gillam Phillips, Thomas Bennet, Christopher Kilby and others formed a solid Anglican Boston influence in the affairs of the colony. Clearly men such as Governor Richard Philipps, Lawrence Armstrong, and Paul Mascarene preferred to do business with, employ, and seek advice from men of a similar religious bent. The Church of England, the roots of whose power are to be found in this formative period, was to play an increasingly important and controversial role in the affairs of the colony over the next century and a half.

Another strongly English influence was injected into the colony in 1738 with the establishment in Annapolis Royal of the first Masonic Lodge in what is now English Canada.[17] As with so many of the developments in Annapolis Royal during this period, the arrival of this fraternal organization reflected the dual influence of both England and Massachusetts. As Brock Hanyan observes: 'Freemasonry by the late 1730s haphazardly made its way across the Atlantic [from England] to the American provinces, where seaboard mercantile and professional leaders used it as a vehicle through which they could publicly express their superiority, unity, and cosmopolitan ties to gentility and enlightenment.'[18] In 1737, the Massachusetts Provincial Grand Lodge, itself only recently established, admitted Erasmus James Philipps of Philipps's Regiment in Annapolis as a member. Within a year, the records indicate, the 'Rt Worshl Grand Master Granted a Deputation at ye Petition of sundry Brethren at Annapolis in Nova Scotia to hold a Lodge there,' with Philipps as Grand Master.[19] The Lodge encompassed most of the military officers of the garrison and the merchants of the town, and forged important links with Boston. However, Freemasonry also provided important ties within the British military, as many individual regiments, including the 40th (Philipps's), were soon to have lodges of their own. The small size of the English-speaking population and the perceived hostility of the surrounding countryside may well have made both of these links very important ones in the minds of many of the residents of Annapolis. The Masonic Lodge also provided a powerful unifying force drawing the civilian and military communities even more closely together.

However important the growth of an English Annapolis Royal might be, there was, of course, much more to the history of Nova Scotia than the story of that small enclave. In many respects, the two most important issues of this period were the Siamese twins of defence and settlement. Many of the studies of this period have focused almost exclusively on the position of the Acadians, perhaps with good reason, for the difficulties surrounding the oath of allegiance and Acadian loyalty were real and significant. However, if British authorities had dealt more effectively with the proper defence of the new colony, and pursued an efficient settlement program, the 'problem' of the Acadians would have taken on very different proportions.

Almost from the beginning of British occupation of the region, the proper defence of Nova Scotia had become a nearly insurmountable problem. There appears to have been little thought given to what would actually be done with the colony after its seizure, how Britain might capitalize on the capture of Port Royal. If the Walker Expedition against Canada had been successful in 1711, and the French presence removed from the continent then instead of in 1760, developments in North America, and Nova Scotia, would obviously have been very different, and the defence of the latter would have been of little consequence. However, the Walker Expedition was a dismal failure, and the repercussions of this would impact on Nova Scotia for many years to come. Nova Scotia was to remain for nearly fifty years the ragged outer edge of the British empire in North America, while Acadia survived as the phantom fringe of the French presence on the continent.

The extensive correspondence concerning Annapolis Royal during its first ten years reads as a long litany of troubles for the tiny garrison and fledgling community. Although the small number of troops that Britain was prepared to devote to the cause was certainly one difficulty, it was by no means the most serious one, as the fort was seldom under real threat of enemy seizure during this time. Far more dangerous to the welfare of the British presence in the region were the serious problems of supply, credit, and military pay.

At this late date, it is impossible to sort through the tangled knot of bills, credits, charges, and countercharges and make full sense of the confused financial affairs of the colony. Almost certainly both military governors of the time, Francis Nicholson and Samuel Vetch, were heavily implicated in the systematic fleecing of the garrison, while at the same time each making serious charges against the other's honour and integrity.[20] Officers had to advance considerable sums of money merely to ensure that their men were fed and clothed, while credit ran thin in Boston due to nonpayment of bills by the British government. As early as the fall of 1712, according to Samuel Vetch, the garrison was near mutiny due to failure to pay their wages, while Vetch's agent in Boston faced ruin because of the supplies that he had advanced to Annapolis, with no recompense from London.[21]

This neglect by the British government, and the constant quarrelling between Vetch and Nicholson, must be seen against the background of danger and uncertainty faced almost daily by the garrison at Annapolis. The successful native attack at Bloody Creek in 1711 resulted in the loss of over sixty men, and the subsequent Mi'kmaq siege of the fort itself kept the garrison virtual prisoners for much of the summer.[22] Similar threats, although not so serious, were made the following year.[23] Even the signing of the peace treaty in 1713 did not greatly enhance the security of tiny Annapolis.

It is difficult to determine what, if anything, was behind the neglect and mismanagement of the colony in these early, crucial years. It may have been merely a grossly inefficient bureaucracy and quarrelsome, self-seeking local officials at the bottom of the troubles, but a reading of the documents concerned makes it hard to avoid the conclusion that something more lay behind it all. It is possible, in our focus on the New World, and especially New England's involvement in Nova Scotian affairs, that insufficient attention has been given to the fact that the conquest itself was primarily a British venture, that these were British officials, that it would be a British treaty signed in 1713, and that the key decisions were being made, or avoided, by a British government. The period 1710 to 1715 was an unstable time in London, with deep divisions between Whig and Tory, between those who favoured a Protestant succession to the throne, and those who were determined to restore it to the Catholic Stuart line. Those divisions would leave their imprint on post-conquest Nova Scotia. Given its very weak state, the colony would be heavily dependent on the attitude and policy of the British government for the foreseeable future. One direct and immediate consequence of the conquest was that it was now caught up in the play of British politics, and its success or failure would be very much dependent upon the outcome of the political struggles in the mother country.

The other way in which the situation in Britain directly influenced events in Nova Scotia is found in an examination of the working of the governmental bureaucracy. In decision making and administration of the colony, an incredible number of agencies and individuals were involved, making decisive and rapid action regarding Nova Scotia's many problems highly unlikely if not completely impossible. Political interference, then, was not the only factor that prevented the efficient functioning of the colony. For Nova Scotia to move ahead quickly and decisively during this period would require that a bewildering array of agencies and levels of government work smoothly and efficiently together, with a common aim, a common direction, a common objective. Reality would dictate a very different outcome. London displayed far more efficiency in the conquest of the colony that it would in its administration.

Anything to do with the defence of the colony might fall under the jurisdiction of any one of a number of departments in London, or worse, under several. The Secretary at War was responsible for the recruitment, billeting, and supply of the army. However, the office of the Secretary of State controlled the planning of campaigns and the movement of troops. Soldiers' pay came under the Paymaster's Office, while the Board of Ordnance was responsible for military stores, fortifications, army engineers, and the artillery. If a naval vessel were required for support, as was often the case in Nova Scotia, then the Admiralty would have to be petitioned.[24] That the garrison at Fort Anne often languished, or went without pay or supplies or recruits is scarcely surprising, given the cross-purposes at which these agencies often worked.

In addition to the morass of military bureaucracy, governors and administrators of Nova Scotia had to deal with a bewildering array of officials in London in their handling of the civil affairs of the colony. The Board of Trade, the Secretary of State, the Cabinet, the Attorney General, the Solicitor General, and Surveyor General of the Woods might all be involved in the making of a fairly simple decision concerning Nova Scotia. There was a great deal of overlap in jurisdiction and much jealousy between the various departments, delaying action even more. Frequently, it would appear, it was easier simply to do nothing, and that was often what was done, to the great detriment of Britain's new acquisition; Nova Scotia would languish as a result.

The correspondence directed to London from Annapolis Royal during these decades reveals a very realistic and often perceptive grasp of the military situation in the colony and the necessary steps needed to place Nova Scotia on a safe footing. Richard Philipps, Lawrence Armstrong, John Doucett, Paul Mascarene, and others reported faithfully on the deplorable state of the fortifications, the deteriorating condition of the troops, and the precarious nature of the British occupation of the colony. Year after year reports, requests, petitions, suggestions went to London, seldom eliciting a positive response; frequently there was no response at all. The schizophrenic bureaucracy of London seemed unable to determine a plan or direction for the recent acquisition. No real purpose for holding the colony would develop until mid-century.

Much of the problem surrounding the fort, and consequently the defence of the colony, involved the Board of Ordnance's decision that attempts to repair the existing fortifications would be pointless; only an entirely new fort, with stone walls instead of the unstable earthenworks, would be adequate. Orders were therefore sent to its engineer on the spot that no efforts at repair should be made.[25] And yet, over the following years, the Board made no attempt to build the requisite replacement. Thus, Annapolis Royal ended up with the worst of both worlds. As the then lieutenant-governor and acting commander aptly phrased it in a letter to his engineer:

> I am putt under a very great dilemma, first by [it] being in so bad a condition that if any misfortune should happen to the Garrison, I should be condemn'd and suffer for what is out of my Power to remedy and to order you to putt everything into Repair I should be then lyable to the displeasure of the Honble Board for going directly opposite to their positive Commands.[26]

Even in the face of increased tension between British and Mi'kmaq in the colony, the Board could not be moved. Only by a direct contravention of the Board's orders was the fort finally put in a semblance of a defensive position, and even then it was almost a question of too little and too late.

The Board of Ordnance's neglect of the colony's defences probably had several causes. The end of the War of the Spanish Succession in 1713 ushered in a remarkably long period of peace, never a favourable situation for those who argue for major expenditures on imperial defence. Once Robert Walpole returned to office in 1721, those who wished for peace in Europe and smaller government expenditures had a powerful champion.[27] For as long as Walpole was in power, England would be at peace, a policy which might well serve the mother country, but which took no recognition of the reality of affairs in Nova Scotia. The paralysing bureaucracy of early Georgian England was almost certainly a contributing factor as well. On the odd occasion when the Board seemed willing to stir itself, the administrative structure proved unable to respond. In June 1722, the Board of Trade wrote optimistically to Governor Philipps that the Board of Ordnance was to send men and materials for the construction of a new fort, as soon as orders were received to proceed.[28] For reasons that are no longer apparent, the necessary orders were not forthcoming that year, or at any time in the future. In fact, the fort at Annapolis Royal was never rebuilt, and the earthenworks at the present National Historic Site are substantially the same ones about which the engineer and commanding officer complained so bitterly in the 1720s.

The failure of the British government to provide for the proper defence of its new colony had serious implications for the future. In spite of Mi'kmaq attacks in the 1720s, and French and Mi'kmaq assaults in the 1740s, the British managed to retain possession of their dilapidated fort – barely. However, for a period of nearly forty years, they presented an image of great weakness, a message that was not lost on Mi'kmaq, Acadian, or French, and all responded, in their own way, to the failure to provide for the adequate defence of the colony. In the end, this would cost the British many times the few thousand pounds that the parsimonious London government refused to expend in the years immediately after the conquest.

The other area of governmental failure is to be found in the issue of settlement of the new colony, and here also London, as well as the colonists of Nova Scotia, would pay dearly for the neglect. Writing 170 years ago, Nova Scotia's first historian, T.C. Haliburton, observed laconically but truthfully: 'The English did not display the same zeal in the settlement of the Country which they had manifested in its conquest.'[29] Brebner, while observing the deficiency, could find no explanation for it, writing: 'For reasons which are not entirely clear, none of the colonisation schemes brought before the Board [of Trade] was carried out by them.'[30] Certainly there was no want of proposals for settlement, with London receiving dozens of requests for land in the thirty years after the conquest. And yet, not a single scheme came to fruition, and only a handful of English settlers arrived on their own initiative to take up an uneasy residence at Annapolis Royal or Canso. An explanation for this is to be found in the procrastination and inefficiency of London, and in the machinations of nearby Massachusetts. Only a rigorous settlement scheme, coupled with an extensive plan of defence, could have provided Nova Scotia with the security so obviously needed during this period.

If one is looking for superficial explanations for the failure of settlement schemes during this period, they are not difficult to find. Nova Scotia was militarily unstable, with serious threats, real or perceived, emanating from the native peoples, the Acadians, and the French. Much of the best of the farmland was already occupied by the Acadians, and conflicting claims, both French and English, seemed to tie up most of the rest of it in impossible legal tangles. The colony also possessed an ill-disguised military government, with virtually no semblance of even incipient representative institutions. Trade seemed to be firmly in the hands of New Englanders, while the fishery, primarily controlled by them as well, was often imperilled by the French from Louisbourg. However, these are really more excuses than reasons for the lack of settlement in the colony during this crucial time period, and could certainly have been dealt with if there had been the will to do so.

The main reasons for English interest and involvement in Acadia/ Nova Scotia over the previous century had been military and economic. The objective was usually to preserve and protect what was already possessed (e.g., New England), rather than to acquire more extensive territories for settlement, although the latter on occasion played its part.[31] By 1710 there was as yet no real shortage of land for prospective settlers in British North America. In addition, Britain had traditionally played very little role in the actual peopling of its possessions in the New World, relying on individual initiative, or corporate action. In the seventeenth century, aside from issuing charters and granting huge blocks of land, the English government had usually been involved but little in the actual work of creating colonies and providing them with substantial populations. It was Acadia's fate to become a permanent British possession at a time when Britain was no longer prepared to treat its colonies in such an offhanded manner. The government resolutely refused to allow local authorities to make important decisions concerning settlement, while seeming unable or unwilling to take any firm action itself in such matters.

Settlement proposals followed quickly after the conquest. They came from governors, lieutenant-governors, individual merchants, professional settlement promoters, philanthropists, and speculators. As early as 1711, Samuel Vetch wrote to the Board of Trade, advocating the immediate settlement near Annapolis Royal of four to five hundred Protestant families. He suggested that they be given free transportation, tools, and food for a year as an added inducement, and that the able men be used as an adjunct to the garrison in times of emergency.[32] This proposal typified those from the military officers of the colony, who (rightly) saw settlement as an important aspect of defence. As long as Nova Scotia was inhabited largely by Acadians and Mi'kmaq, they argued, there could be no real security for the small English communities of Annapolis Royal and Canso, and no certainty of continued British control of the colony.

After the signing of the Treaty of Utrecht, when the future of Nova Scotia as a British colony seemed secure, there was considerable interest in settlement schemes, apparently almost everywhere except where it mattered most – among the bureaucrats and politicians in London. There were suggestions to send disbanded soldiers, a plan not carried into effect until 1749 with the founding of Halifax.[33] Surveyor and settlement promoter David Dunbar proposed bringing a large number of Scotch-Irish families, and other Protestants, to the region.[34] Andrew LeMercier, a French Protestant minister in Boston, put forward a number of proposals for the settlement of Huguenots in Nova Scotia, an idea much talked of but never acted upon by British authorities.[35] Thomas Coram, of London, wished to transport German-speaking Protestants to people the colony,[36] but this approach would not be adopted until 1750. In 1732, Lawrence Armstrong and the Council tried to entice New Englanders to Nova Scotia by advertising in the Boston papers, and sending an agent to the nearby colonies.[37] It would be nearly thirty years before that particular scheme would actually bring any settlers to the region. Nothing, however, seemed to bring the desired results, no grants of land were forthcoming, and no settlements were established. Some of the proposals seem to have been more than mere speculation. In 1730, Daniel Hintze, an agent for the recruitment of Germanic settlers for the British colonies, wrote to the Board of Trade to indicate that he had secured 450 families to go to Nova Scotia the following year.[38] Not even this promising approach brought a single additional settler to the colony.

The most persistent of the serious proponents of settlement in Nova Scotia was Thomas Coram. As early as the summer of 1713, Coram was actively promoting the settling of the colony, an interest that would last nearly thirty years.[39] Founder of the Foundling Hospital, Coram was a London philanthropist concerned with the plight of the poor, who saw settlement in the New World as a viable solution to the condition of some at least of the lower classes. In 1732, he joined other philanthropists such as James Edward Oglethorpe as a trustee for Georgia, a new colony with many parallels to Nova Scotia.[40] Certainly he possessed the contacts, the ongoing concerns, and the drive to assist in the extensive settlement of Nova Scotia, and yet not even he proved able to battle successfully the lethargy and inefficiency of the British government and the negative propaganda and obstruction emanating from Boston.

In the available documentation, there is no indication that the British government actually opposed the settlement of Nova Scotia, or was hostile to proposals from those who wished to undertake it. In fact, the instructions issued by London to Governor Richard Philipps in 1719 seemed to indicate that the peopling of the colony was imminent. Few of the requests for grants and the proposals for settlement were rejected outright by the government at any level. However, each proposal seemed to be shunted from department to department until it disappeared from view. Even when London was inclined to act, nothing happened. For example, in 1731, an order-in-council was issued by the Privy Council ordering the Board of Trade to prepare instructions to govern the manner of the settling of lands in Nova Scotia. This the Board of Trade did, and the results were duly approved by cabinet and ordered to be transmitted to Philipps. There, however, the process seems to have stopped; nothing concrete ever came of this initiative.[41]

At least part of the problem centred on the need for an adequate survey of the lands available for distribution to prospective settlers. The growing demands by the British navy that timber suitable for its purposes be reserved for the crown before any grants were made greatly slowed the process of settlement along parts of the Atlantic coast of North America, and was especially acute in a newly acquired area such as Acadia/Nova Scotia. Lands could not be granted until a proper survey of the timber resources of the area was made, and in spite of repeated requests that this be done, London seemed unable to devote the necessary energy to accomplish the task in a reasonable time. As early as 1721 Governor Philipps petitioned the Board of Trade to move quickly on this matter. He had had several offers from prospective settlers, he argued, but could accept none until the survey was completed. Could there not be a blanket reserve of all suitable naval timber in a given area, he asked, so that settlement could begin forthwith? No action from London was forthcoming.[42] Nearly ten years later, Philipps was still complaining that his hands remained tied until a survey of the entire colony was completed.[43]

Inefficiency and indifference in London regarding surveys and naval stores accounted for some of the problems in the settlement of Nova Scotia in the aftermath of the conquest, but the situation was also greatly complicated by the large number of claims to the territory that kept the colony in a legal tangle for years. Nova Scotia was not really a 'new' British colony in 1710, but really a reacquired one, for English and Scottish claims to the region went back at least to the early seventeenth century, if not before.[44] Over the years, the 'ownership' of the land had become unbelievably tangled, making new grants difficult from a legal point of view. Aside from the legal aspect, there was also a political dimension, as the main heir of Sir Thomas Temple, one of the principal seventeenth-century claimants, was the influential Sir Richard Temple, Viscount Cobham, one of Walpole's chief political foes.[45]

Added to the British claims, there was no lack of French titles to be extinguished before settlement could take place. Did the Acadians who remained in the colony after the signing of the Treaty of Utrecht, and who may or may not have taken the oath of allegiance, retain any rights to the land? And what about the seigneurial rights of some of the prominent families such as the de Saint Étienne de La Tours and the Le Borgnes de Belle-Isle, who had long claimed much of peninsular Nova Scotia?[46] As Armstrong pointed out to the Board of Trade in 1731, in asking for a clarification of the extent of seigneurial rights in the colony,

> If they [seigneurs] are to enjoy without a limitation of certain conditions, the Country will in a great measure remain a wilderness and there will be scarce one acre left, especially in this place [Annapolis], to be granted to protestant subjects, who are much desired, and for whom room might be found here, if these Seigniors did not thus pretend a right to the greatest part, if not the whole Province.[47]

The only concrete action taken by the British government to clarify the status of the French seigneurial claims was to purchase the rights of Agathe Campbell, a grand-daughter of Charles de Saint-Étienne de La Tour who insisted that she alone possessed all of the family rights in the colony.[48] In spite of the dubious nature of her claims, and the opposition of some of those who were most familiar with the colony, the Board of Trade chose to recognize her rights and extinguish the seigneurial system in Nova Scotia by purchase.[49] It was done, the secretary to the Board of Trade wrote, because 'it will remain a doubt whether without this Purchase, His Majesty can grant any Land in Nova Scotia.'[50] Not even this action, however, led to the granting of land in the colony; government inertia, not seigneurial claims, was the main stumbling block to English settlement.

While the British government must shoulder much of the blame for the complete ineffectiveness of settlement initiatives during this period, Boston itself must share part of the responsibility. Although it was usually in the best interest of Massachusetts that nearby Acadia not be in the hands of a hostile France, it did not necessarily serve its purpose that a strong and separate British colony be erected there.[51] Massachusetts saw the lands to the east as essentially its sphere of influence, perhaps to be annexed when the time was ripe. Certainly control of that region (present-day New Hampshire, Maine, New Brunswick, and Nova Scotia) best suited many of the politicians, merchants, and land speculators of Massachusetts.

The historian Alan Taylor has examined the role of Massachusetts in obstructing the early settlement of Maine, the objectives of the great proprietors, and the important part that land to the east played in Massachusetts politics. Although Taylor does not deal directly with the lands even further east, his work does raise interesting questions concerning the failure of settlement in Nova Scotia at the same time. Massachusetts claimed jurisdiction over an indeterminate amount of land, and would brook no opposition to its claims. The efforts of David Dunbar, surveyor and colonizer, to establish settlements in Maine and thereby create a new colony were effectively blocked by Massachusetts influence, and Dunbar would be destroyed.[52] There is considerable evidence that Nova Scotia was dealt with in much the same fashion. Certainly those involved in the proprietary claims of Maine would also exert great influence on Nova Scotia as well. Men such as Jonathan Belcher, Samuel Waldo, William Pepperrell, and especially Waldo's London lawyer, William Shirley, would all play significant roles in Nova Scotia's future, usually with more than the interests of the British empire in mind.

A frustrated David Dunbar summed up the attitude of many in Boston when he reported in 1729: 'Some New England agents who attended the Council yesterday and heard of my success the night before have boasted of the Disappointment as many of 'em have lately taken possession of great tracts [in Maine] where I proposed to fix the Irish familys.' The following year, Philipps made a similar charge against Massachusetts, stating that settlers sent to Boston bound for Nova Scotia were induced to go to the Carolinas instead, thus preventing the settling of the lands to the east.[53] The private correspondence of then-governor Jonathan Belcher lends substance to these complaints. Belcher was clearly using what influence he had in London to prevent, directly and indirectly, the settlement of his neighbouring colony. Writing to Thomas Coram, who for years had advanced various schemes for the settlement of Nova Scotia, Belcher did his best to denigrate the colony, pointing out its deficiencies of government and agricultural lands:

It is above 26 years since the Reduction of Nova Scotia to the Obedience of the Crown of Great Britain, and it yet remains an uncultivated Wilderness, (even as at the Creation) and so it doubtless will to the End of all things, if it be kept in its present Situation, and to compare the Difference ... between this Province and Nova Scotia, must make Princes, and all Mankind, in love with lawful Reasonable Liberty ... arbitrary Despotick Government will never bring forward new Colonies; and as to Nova Scotia, in which you seem to be pretty warmly engag'd, I must observe to you, that, by the strictest Enquiry of those acquainted, the Soil is none of the best.

Belcher then proceeded to reveal his real objective: the further settlement of eastern Massachusetts and the establishment of a new colony to the east, the latter to be added to Belcher's other responsibilities as governor of Massachusetts and New Hampshire. Coram was urged to communicate this proposal secretly to Walpole and his colleagues for their consideration. Other settlement schemes for Maine or Nova Scotia did not suit the personal agenda of Belcher, and many of the great owners of the eastern lands. At the same time, Belcher seldom missed an opportunity to assure officials in Nova Scotia of his great interest in and concern for that colony, and his willingness to do anything in his power to advance its interests. Having done his best to prevent the settlement of the colony, he wrote solicitously to Armstrong in 1734 that he found 'that your Province should be belonging to the Crown of Gt Britain now 24 years and be Still an unpeopled wilderness is Strange, while I Suppose this Province is increas'd in Number 30 to 40 Thousand.'[54] With friends like this, Nova Scotia scarcely needed the many open enemies it already possessed.[55]

Legally, politically, and bureaucratically, Nova Scotia had become stuck in a quagmire from which no one seemed inclined to extricate it. Decisive government action could have cleared away many of the impediments to settlement, and allowed for the early peopling of the colony with a British, or at least Protestant, population, but no such action was undertaken, and the events of the 1740s and 1750s would unfold in a very different manner as a result. Much has been made by historians of the failure of the British to extract an oath of allegiance from the Acadians during this period; the real failure was the inability to acquire a population that would have strengthened the British position. If 20,000–30,000 Protestants had settled in Nova Scotia between 1710 and 1750, the attitude and action of the Acadians would have been of little consequence in the thinking of British officials. Instead, Nova Scotia was hampered by a British government that would neither act decisively nor allow its men on the spot to do so, and by a nearby colony which did its best to manipulate and control development in the best interests of a few individuals. Even so, some beginnings were made in establishing the colony's governing institutions.

At first glance, one could be forgiven for concluding that little of significance in this area occurred during the first three decades of British rule. Brebner, with little good secondary work to rely on, and attempting to examine a period of 150 years, not surprisingly saw British efforts as largely 'phantom rule' and 'Government by Analogy and Rule of Thumb.'[56] J. Murray Beck, following Brebner's lead, concluded that, 'All in all the scheme of government between 1710 and 1749 amounted to little more than a makeshift *modus vivendi*,'[57] and devoted little time to this period. Certainly there is much to justify such conclusions, especially during the first decade of what passed loosely for British control. However, something of a permanent nature was being created, the solid base on which more important structures could be built; faced with the spectacular failures of the British in Nova Scotia, it is not surprising that the quiet gains have often gone largely unnoticed. To be sure, the first decade after 1710 was characterized by greed, bitter infighting, and serious abuses of power. The struggle between Vetch and Nicholson for power, the animosities created by the Jacobite–Whig divisions, the inability of British authorities to make crucial decisions concerning the government of the new colony, and the failure to establish any sense of respect for the new government seriously jeopardized the conquerors' ability to govern effectively in the years to come. With usually absentee governors, administrators with no money and less authority, and apparent indifference on the part of the British authorities, it is not surprising that Nova Scotia continued to have little effective government.[58]

It was not until 1717 that Richard Philipps was appointed governor of Nova Scotia, with a new mandate and new instructions. A man of solid if unexceptional Whig background, Philipps was already approaching the age when most men were considering a quiet retirement (he was born c. 1661). Nevertheless, he undertook his governorship of thirty-two years with considerable energy, and it was he who pointed out to the authorities the necessity of establishing some form of civil government for the colony. The model on which the government of Nova Scotia was to be based was that of Virginia, rather than the by now highly suspect colonies of New England. This provided the colony with the framework and philosophy of government that would have profound implications for the future. It would ultimately be the Virginian system of secondary election, rather than New England's primary election, that would shape governmental development in Nova Scotia. As a first step, a Council of twelve was to be established and the election of a house of assembly was provided for, although the British government made no effort over the years to ensure that the colony would receive the Protestant population that would have made such a branch of government possible.[59]

As with so many other things, Nova Scotia would have to wait many years for the elected assembly, which was not called until 1758.[60] However, shortly after his arrival in Annapolis Royal, Philipps named his Council of twelve; with governor and Council the colony was thus provided with two of the three branches of government which would mould and shape it for over 200 years. For the next thirty years the Council would be composed of a mixture of civilians and officers from the garrison, the latter included because there were never sufficient civilian males in the capital to fill even the modest ranks of the Council.[61]

Clearly, the presence of so many officers in the Council over the years, and the fact that the governor himself (1717–1749) and almost all the presidents of the Council were officers in the regiment, lent much credence to the claims of Nova Scotia's detractors that it had an ill-disguised military government. Belcher, never one to miss an opportunity to denigrate his neighbour, wrote in 1733 with considerable exaggeration that 'The Government of the Paultry Province of Nova Scotia has been but one constant Scene of Tyranny. I believe it may be Something easier at present, But God deliver me & mine from the Government of Soldiers. They are good & proper in their places, but not to be at the head of a Civil Polity.'[62] In fact, in spite of the preponderance of military personnel, considerable progress was made in laying the foundations of English government in the colony. Few historians of this period have taken the time to analyse carefully either the workings of government by Council or the abilities and personality of those who struggled with the leadership against considerable odds. The repeated failure to govern the Acadians effectively, and especially the inability to extract an acceptable unqualified oath of allegiance from the old residents of the colony has tended to obscure the real gains that were being made by this 'phantom' government. In the relevant chapter in a recent general history of the Atlantic provinces, the author does not even mention the creation of the Council, let alone any productive results that might have come from it.[63]

Although the scale of the accomplishments tended to remain rather small, given the size of the community, nonetheless Richard Philipps and especially Lawrence Armstrong worked hard to create an essential framework of government. The latter made very effective use of the Council during his long tenure as lieutenant-governor, although he has received scant credit from most historians.[64] Both men attempted to put in place the necessary structure for the administration of a British colony, although they, and the British government itself, were ill-equipped to deal with the non-English, Roman Catholic majority they were required to govern. Given the usual predilections of military men, that they even made the effort to establish the forms of civil government is rather surprising.

In the early 1720s, aside from the Council, other aspects of civil administration were established. A collector of customs was appointed, as well as constables, a provincial secretary, and justices of the peace. The latter were of particular importance in attempting to govern distant Canso, and the introduction of this very English office into Nova Scotia shows a fair understanding by Philipps and Armstrong of governmental developments in England itself.[65] In reprimanding the senior military officer at Canso, Armstrong clearly stated his intent that the justices of the peace should be the real force in governing that fishing community. He wrote:

> I would not have you in the least (in your Military Capacity) to Interrupt the Justices of the peace ... in the legal Execution of their duty ... least by your So Doing you frighten or Discourage the Settling of that place, the least Appearance of a Civil Government being much more agreeable to Inhabitants than that of a Martial [one].[66]

Armstrong also urged that an assembly be called. Given the scarcity of qualified voters in the colony, he advocated that at least the first one be appointed, for without an assembly, he argued, 'the best man on Earth cannot Manage and Govrn' the fishermen of Canso. Surprisingly enough, he even proposed creating an assembly which would include the Acadians, as the best way of involving them in government, and thereby making them more responsive to its demands. In these, as in virtually all other matters, Armstrong elicited little or no response from London. In spite of such efforts, Nova Scotia would see no assembly during this period, and the failure to establish representative government certainly added to the difficulties in the way of attracting a new British population. Even the Board of Trade recognized the dilemma faced when it wrote: 'The way to people the Province is to form a civil government, but that cannot be done till there is population enough to compose an Assembly.'[67]

The government that the colony did possess often failed to run smoothly. Proceedings were sometimes disrupted by bitter quarrels over position and precedence, exacerbated by the prolonged absence of the governor and the small family compact that grew up around the Philipps–Cosby–Winniett relationship.[68] Yet these struggles, with all their pettiness, should not be allowed to obscure the solid work the Council accomplished as its members struggled along year after year, unpaid and unappreciated. In 1721, the Council established a Court of Judicature, to fill a longstanding need for the administration of justice in the colony.[69] This measure introduced an English approach to justice to Nova Scotia, which, in spite of the lack of legal training of those involved, worked surprisingly well. In addition to their other responsibilities, the councillors now also sat as a court of justice, before which both Acadians and British appeared in civil as well as criminal cases. Thomas Barnes has argued that the court achieved 'remarkable' success, given the difficulties under which it laboured. Justice was administered 'with exceptional even-handedness ... [T]he council's record indicates an admirable constancy in maintaining procedural correctness and substantive probity, and raises no suspicion of corruptness or partiality.' Justice was done, and seen to be done.[70]

That the court did not prove as effective a tool in imposing British control over the Acadian population is scarcely surprising, although that was held to be one of the court's more obvious failures. It did manage to impose a semblance of order on the British population and, given time, might well have proved an effective vehicle for gradually attracting the Acadians to the British position. After 1749, more elaborate structures of British justice would be constructed in the colony, but the foundations at least had already been laid.

Annapolis Royal was not, of course, the sole English community in Nova Scotia during this period. Canso's development was very different from that of the European settlements focused on the Bay of Fundy, French and English alike. While the latter represented comparative stability and continuity, Canso could be seen as the tumultuous outer edge of the French, British, and New England experience in North America, and its development casts a different light on this period. British officials in Annapolis Royal frequently found it next to impossible to control and regulate events in their own backyard; in distant Canso it was all the more difficult. There the New England influence was both more direct and more forceful; there too the clash between English and French would be much more open.

Although Canseau/Canso had been a centre for the European fisheries off the coast of Nova Scotia for longer than the French had actually
been settled in the New World, by the time of the conquest there was little that could be seen as permanent about its existence.[71] The events of
1710, and the treaty of 1713, had a significant impact on that fishing station, and subsequent years would see dramatic growth and then sudden
decline in its fortunes. Until near the end of the first decade of British
ownership, French and New England fishermen appear to have harvested the seas in relative harmony. The conflict which then broke out
reflected the growing New England interest in the fishery, an increasing
French presence on Île Royale, and the vagaries of the Treaty of Utrecht. French possession of the region would be crucial in the control of
clandestine trade between the Acadians of Nova Scotia and Louisbourg,
of increasing importance in the provisioning of that fortress.[72] Canso
also proved to be a conveniently situated port for illicit trade between
the French from Louisbourg and New Englanders.[73]

Evicting the French from the region would be one thing (and as it
transpired a fairly simple one) but the establishment of a viable, thriv-
ing, and permanent English community would be quite something else.
Certainly the early years appeared to augur well for Canso's future. The
independent initiative by Boston in 1718 underscored the extent to
which Massachusetts looked upon Canso as its own, and was prepared to
bypass Annapolis Royal completely. As Donald Chard has observed,
Massachusetts's action helped to establish the boundary between the
English and French empires in North America, but this was in reality 'a
calculated effort by New Englanders to formulate imperial policy for
their own ends.'[74] It would be the job of the recently appointed governor of Nova Scotia, Richard Philipps, to attempt to establish a strong
British, rather than New England, presence there. In spite of the lack of
support from London, and the meagreness of their own resources, it
would be Philipps and his lieutenant-governor, Armstrong, who would
make and keep Canso British, not an erratic Massachusetts or an indifferent London.

Philipps had not yet taken up his command in Nova Scotia at the time
of the Smart expedition, but he was present in the colony when the
Mi'kmaq retaliated in 1720 and, for once, took decisive action. The
attack, in early August, at the height of the fishing season, had resulted
in the death of three fishermen and the reputed loss of goods, equipment, and fish to the value of £18,000.[75] When news of the attack
reached Annapolis, Philipps and his new Council began the process of

extending the government's authority to distant Canso, establishing a local militia there, and appointing the first of a number of justices of the peace, to regulate and govern the fishing community.[76] A more important step was taken that fall when Armstrong and troops from Annapolis were dispatched to Canso, to take possession of the fort that the fishermen were erecting and extend the protection of the British army to the shore fishery.[77] Some of the New Englanders were not enthusiastic about Philipps's action, perhaps seeing a stronger official presence as detrimental to their activities.[78] The extension of authority over the fishermen, rather than their protection from the French, may well have been Philipps' main objective, for Armstrong was sent with instructions to apportion to the fishermen shore lots and garden plots, and in general to begin the regulation of the fishing community ashore.[79]

Philipps's plans to make Canso a strong and secure centre for the British fishery were often thwarted by the lethargy and inaction of the British government. Although London appreciated the importance of the cod fishery, it proved incapable of taking decisive action to secure its safety. Philipps argued forcefully that Canso was 'the place of greatest consequence in all these parts, not only in respect to the fishery which will exceed every thing of that kind that has been known but as the best prospect of settling the Province,'[80] but, as with the defence of Annapolis Royal, London proved unable or unwilling to respond. The few steps taken for Canso's defence had to defy the Board of Ordnance's instructions that no new fortifications were to be erected in the colony until it had developed an overall plan. Philipps collected contributions from the fishermen, and used the money to erect temporary and, as it later proved totally inadequate, fortifications.[81] Canso survived until its seizure by the French in 1744, but this was entirely the result of local initiative and the long passivity of the French.

In the 1720s hopes ran high for a bright future for Canso. In spite of fears of Mi'kmaq attacks, discouragement over lack of decisive British actions,[82] and even the seizure of 20 fishing vessels by the Mi'kmaq along the south coast of Nova Scotia in 1722,[83] the fisheries grew significantly during the decade.[84] By 1723, eighty-three vessels were engaged in the fishery, and sent a reported 33,000 quintals of fish to market.[85] Six years later, the number of vessels had risen to 235, with 51,749 quintals of fish reported.[86] The flourishing of the fishery, and the more convenient location of Canso, led most Nova Scotia officials at one time or another to propose that it replace Annapolis Royal as the capital of the colony. Philipps spent the winter of 1721–2 there, busying himself with

plans for the community's defence.[87] In 1725, Armstrong, by then lieutenant-governor of the colony, made Canso his capital, and held several
council meetings there,[88] but, lacking permission from London, by the
following year he had returned the seat of government to Annapolis.

Even including the small garrison posted there, the year-round population of Canso remained small; few of the fishermen and merchants
who frequented it during the summer could be enticed to spend the
winter. In 1729, it was reported that only three families made their
homes there, along with the Irish servants who spent their time repair-
ing and building flakes.[89] By 1736, there was indeed a school with fifty
pupils, a chapel and chaplain,[90] but Canso remained, for the most part,
a transitory community, composed largely of those who flooded into the
region in the spring of each year to exploit the riches of the sea; few
were willing to put down roots in the area.

Edward How proved one of the exceptions, and his career in Canso
was important and revealing. From 1722 to the early 1740s, How was
Canso's most prominent citizen and most successful merchant. It was
How who really kept Canso alive during the years of imperial neglect,
building a barracks and guardhouse at his own expense in 1728, and
paying for garrison storehouses in 1737 and repairs to the barracks in
1739. He served as justice of the peace, sheriff, and captain of the militia, and frequently carried out commissions for the government.[91] Much
additional light has been shed on the life and activities of How through
recent excavations of How's home and warehouses at Canso, along with
a number of other related sites. The rich archaeological evidence provides important insights into life in Canso during this period, suggesting
a more sophisticated and varied existence, and greater comfort, than
the transient nature of a rough fishing station might suggest. There was,
for example, among the recovered shards of ceramic vessels a very high
percentage of Chinese porcelain, primarily teaware, indicating both the
impact of international trade on this outpost and the acceptance of the
newly popular social custom of tea drinking.[92] For some at least, life in
Canso took on a sense of permanency and comfort, with expectations
for the future reflected in the houses they built.[93] But the Edward Hows
proved few in number, and in general Canso's development was still
determined by the spring arrival of the fishing fleets, a small one from
old England and a much larger one from New England.

Throughout the 1730s, year after year, Armstrong lectured London
on the importance of the Nova Scotia fisheries, and of Canso, which
made those fisheries possible; year after year London ignored him, and

the neglect of the outpost continued.[94] Armstrong's grim determination helped keep the community going, soothing the ruffled feathers of Canso merchants, removing a high-handed commanding officer, attempting to assure the fishermen of adequate defence against the French and Mi'kmaq.[95] No amount of effort on the part of Armstrong, however, could compensate for British neglect; by 1739, in the face of renewed French encroachment, and fear of French attack, the fishery lay largely in ruins.[96]

Cod was not the only source of profit in Canso, for Louisbourg lay practically on its doorstep. While smuggling might be dangerous, it was also extremely lucrative. Seldom was this illicit trade mentioned in official documents, but no officer of the government in Nova Scotia could have been unaware of its existence.[97] Indeed, many of them appear to have been actively involved in it, at least as middlemen. This was especially true of the officers of Philipps's Regiment stationed at Canso. John Bradstreet, with relatives through his mother living in Louisbourg, was undoubtedly a major participant;[98] even so upright an individual as Paul Mascarene served as an intermediary in the trade in which his friend Governor Jonathan Belcher of Massachusetts and Governor Joseph de Mombeton de Brouillan of Île Royale were involved.[99] The extent of the trade which flowed through Canso is impossible to determine, but aside from providing some welcome extra income for the notoriously underpaid officers, it made little real difference in the economic life of Canso or of Nova Scotia. The illicit trade, along with the cod fishery, would be destroyed by the resumption of hostilities between France and Britain in the 1740s.

In all aspects, the hopes and expectations for the establishment of a strong English Nova Scotia were met with frustration and disappointment in the years immediately after 1710. British indifference and New England hostility guaranteed that the colony had little chance of solid growth. The real failures of this period were to be seen in the stagnant economy, the ineffective defences, and the small size of the British population. These weaknesses meant that in the future the relationship with the Acadians would loom larger than should have been necessary, eventually leading officials, in frustration and fear, to decisions that might not otherwise have been contemplated.

In the end, the period 1710 to 1744 proved to be one of transition, rather than dramatic new beginning. If the colony was not quite yet a British Nova Scotia, it was no longer exactly French Acadie. It is revealing that many of the British government documents during this time continued to refer to the colony as 'Nova Scotia or Acadia,' recognizing the essential duality of the situation. However, the continuing weakness of the English position, and the growing size of the Acadian population, should not obscure the fact that important foundations were being laid for a future British colony during this period. On the eve of war in 1744, Nova Scotia was certainly not the colony it had been more than thirty years before, but in large measure 'Nova Scotia' remained confined to the two small English communities which were the sole sign of a British presence. And for the time being, Annapolis Royal and Canso remained English islands in a sea of uncertainty.

8

The Third Acadia:
Political Adaptation and Societal Change

Maurice Basque

In October 1710, Governor Daniel Auger de Subercase of Acadia was not able to ward off English troops as the French had done earlier in 1707 when Port Royal was attacked. The reaction of the Acadians to the imposing invading forces of 1710 did not please Subercase when he learned that most of them had fled to the woods. Nevertheless, many Acadians did fight alongside the French soldiers and the few native allied troops.[1] The Acadian elders of Port Royal were accustomed to seeing French troops defeated in their small colonial town, and the raising of the Union flag must have been a reminder of Phips's capture of the town in 1690. This time, though, new and disturbing elements came into play. The British soldiers were not going away, and, even after the French troops had departed for France, Abenaki forces continued to roam the region, attacking isolated British detachments. Acadian political culture, which had experienced the discourse of neutrality since the 1690s, would now see it transformed into a conscious policy, even though many leading individuals and ordinary farmers inside the Acadian community did not espouse the neutrality stand of their neighbours. This chapter proposes to examine the dynamics surrounding the evolution of the acceptance by the majority of Acadians of this neutrality discourse in the years following the surrender of Port Royal in the fall of 1710. It also deals with those Acadian individuals who refused neutrality, thus shedding new light on the complexities of Acadian political culture before the *grand dérangement.*

The first year following the conquest was a very troubled one for Acadians. Article 5 of the capitulation of the fort of Port Royal signed by

Francis Nicholson and French governor Subercase gave the inhabitants 'within cannon shot of Port Royal' two options: if they wanted to stay in the colony, they must swear allegiance to Queen Anne, or else they had two years to sell their possessions and move.[2] Acadians, especially those of the Annapolis area, were by now no strangers to taking oaths to the British crown. This time, though, the oath appeared to be more explicit and could have required them to take up arms against the natives. The British clearly wanted to cut off the Acadians from their perceived native allies. They had learned the hard way in the two unsuccessful raids on Port Royal in the summer of 1707 how native warriors could be effective in guerrilla warfare with the active or tacit participation of Acadians. A few days following the capitulation, Nicholson issued a proclamation stating that Annapolis Royal, 'with the Circumjacent teritorys to which her Majesty hath an undoubted Right of Inheritance as well as Conquest,' was now a British possession and that no inhabitant could trade or even correspond with the French or the natives. All trade was to be carried on at Annapolis Royal. According to Nichoslon, disobedience warranted the death penalty.[3]

In the absence of the French colonial authorities, who had left the country following the capitulation, the principal Acadian inhabitants of Annapolis Royal met in early November 1710 and decided to send a messenger to Quebec with a letter for the governor general of New France, the Marquis de Vaudreuil. In it, they stated that, having the misfortune of being captured by the English, they begged for his help so that they could leave and settle in the St Lawrence Valley.[4] The capture of Port Royal had reminded the Acadians that Acadia was a part of New France, even though they had had little contact with Quebec in the preceding years. Nevertheless, many Acadians of Port Royal did take the oath and in November 1710, fifty-seven heads of families had done so.[5] Some Acadians had already started doing business with the English at the fort. This was the case of Prudent Robichaud, an Acadian-born inhabitant of Port Royal whose extensive family ties with leading local families, including his uncle, merchant Abraham Boudrot, must have been very useful in his dealings with the British. A relative of Robichaud, Marie-Madeleine Baptiste, daughter of French privateer Pierre Maisonnat dit Baptiste and Acadian Madeleine Bourg, even wed a former British officer of the Annapolis Royal garrison, William Winniett, around 1711. Winniett, a Huguenot (the French spelling of his name was Guillaume Ouinet), was an influential merchant in Nova Scotia. His family relations with many Acadian groups profited his business.[6]

The articles of capitulation of 1710 did not include the other Acadian settlements. For the new governor of Nova Scotia, Samuel Vetch, the settlers of Minas Basin, Beaubassin, Cobeguid, and other villages were, as he wrote in early November 1710, 'prisoners at discretion and ... both their persons and Effects are absolutely at the Disposal of the Conquerours.' Vetch ordered the French-speaking Huguenot officer Paul Mascarene to visit Minas so as to officially inform the inhabitants of the fall of Port Royal. Furthermore, Vetch ordered the Acadians of Minas and Chignecto to contribute the sum of 6,000 livres in money or in furs, and an additional 20 pistoles per month. Five Acadians were chosen as receivers of those contributions. They were Pierre Melanson, Alexandre Bourg, Antoine LeBlanc, Jean Landry, and Pierre Landry. At the inhabitants' request, Mascarene accepted that eight of them be chosen as their representatives to deal with the British. Among the eight, Pierre Melanson was again selected, his leadership in Grand Pré having survived the French defeat. Mascarene reported that Minas inhabitants complained that the sum expected from them exceeded their means, but they paid it in part in the ensuing months.[7] Again, accommodation by leading inhabitants was the initial response to the new British presence.

By early 1711, the British conquest of Acadia was still far from certain. The fort of Annapolis Royal was in dire need of repair and morale was low among the British garrison as illness and the fear of native attacks loomed over them. The Acadians at Annapolis Royal were not unaware of the garrison's vulnerability. Wrote Samuel Vetch in May 1711:

As to the Civil State of affairs the Inhabitants in generall as well French as Indian continue still in great ferment and uneasiness those within the Banlieu (who are but a few) that have taken the oath of alegiance to her Majesty are threatened and made unsafe by all the others who call them trators and make them believe the french will soon recover the place and then they will be ruined the priests likewise who are numerous among them and whome I cannot catch (save one sent to Boston) threaten them with their eclesiasticall vengeance for their subjection to Heriticks.[8]

In fact, Vetch had arrested many Acadian leaders by now, including the Récollet Justinien Durand, the parish priest at Annapolis, whom he had sent to prison in Boston in January. Vetch was right about the actions of the priests: Durand, with his colleague Antoine Gaulin, parish priest at Minas, was discouraging the Acadians from taking the oath and, in Gaulin's case, encouraging them to take up arms against the British.

Durand and Gaulin's behaviour was a far cry from that of the former Port Royal parish priest, Louis Petit, who had informed Boston authorities of French ships in the 1690s. Durand had devised a clever strategy to remove the Acadians from British allegiance by urging them to leave the three-mile radius around the fort, the cannon-shot region of Article 5 of the capitulation, and to resettle in the upper region of the Annapolis River; as it turned out, though, very few actually made the move.[9] When Lieutenant Peter Capon ventured upriver, he was captured and ransomed by a group of Acadians and natives; according to Paul Mascarene, only the Acadian Pierre LeBlanc's intervention saved Capon from being sent as a hostage to Canada.[10] Without a doubt, many ordinary Acadian farmers did not share the Port Royal elite's overtures to the new British masters.

However, a more severe threat was looming. The Marquis de Vaudreuil had responded to the departure of the French garrison and administrative elite by naming, in January 1711, the young Baron Bernard Anselme d'Abbadie de Saint-Castin as French commander in Acadia, who was at that time in Quebec City. Under Saint-Castin's command, Abenaki warriors established a blockade of the fort at Annapolis Royal, supported by a few hundred Acadians who had rejected the oath of allegiance to the British in the fall of 1710. In the early fall of 1711, military enforcement from New York strengthened the British garrison at Annapolis Royal and convinced Saint-Castin to lift his blockade.[11]

The Annapolis Royal 'uprising' of 1711 meant that the Acadians involved were far from being French neutrals. In the Minas Basin region, the same Alexandre Bourg, who had been chosen by the inhabitants to be one of their representatives to negotiate with British officer Paul Mascarene, was named in July 1711 by the intendant of New France, Jacques Raudot, to be judge, notary public, and surveyor of Minas Basin.[12] As an Acadian leader, Bourg, a son-in-law of the former militia captain Pierre Melanson, was playing the same political game after the conquest as his predecessors had played beforehand, that of waving both French and British flags. It should not come as a surprise that Alexandre Bourg had inherited his uncle Abraham Boudrot's ability of befriending arch-rivals. His cousin Prudent Robichaud of Annapolis Royal was manifesting the same behaviour while supplying the British garrison. In that regard, Acadian elders must have thought that little had changed in the political nature of their society since the time of Villebon in the 1690s. But times were different still. As already stated, French authorities and military officials had all left the country, British soldiers had no intention of leaving, and news that a peace treaty was signed in the little-known Dutch town of Utrecht in the spring of 1713 confirmed that these changes would be permanent.

John Bartlet Brebner wrote that there were two Acadias: one that existed in the minds of diplomats and governors, and another created by the Acadians themselves. A closer examination of Acadian responses to the years leading up to the 1710 conquest leads us to believe that there was a third Acadia; it consisted of a small world of influential families and individuals who utilized – sometimes very cleverly – accommodation, neutrality, and/or open support for French or British crowns as a means to promote and protect their own interests. In doing this, these elite families were not inventing new political behaviour, but probably calling upon older European traditions in dealing with troubled times. Their actions could sometimes mean that ordinary Acadian farmers would follow their lead if they wanted privileged access to New England commerce. One can imagine that Prudent Robichaud alone could not supply the British garrison of Annapolis Royal with greatly needed foodstuff and wood. Other Acadian farmers, probably members of Robichaud's extended family network, would have participated in these transactions, knowingly helping the British enhance their footing in Acadia. But their actions could also be contested as in the months following the October conquest of Port Royal in 1710, when certain collaborating Acadians were branded traitors. Nevertheless, their role as lead actors in the formative stages of Acadian political culture would mould the nascent Acadian identity, which evolved with the discourse of neutrality after Utrecht. The conquest of Port Royal had given them a new stage to play on.

Thus, following Francis Nicholson's conquest of Port Royal in 1710, immediate Acadian responses were not always accommodating to the new British presence. In the spring and summer of 1711, the Baron de Saint-Castin's blockade of the Annapolis fort had the effective military support of many of the local Acadians. But by late summer, the failure of this blockade was apparent when Saint-Castin had to flee to Minas Basin to be sheltered by the missionary priest Félix Pain. In the meantime, British forces had pillaged his dwelling at Pentagouet.[13] Witnesses to this turning of the tide, the Annapolis Royal Acadians adopted a more pragmatic attitude towards the British. In August 1711, they sent a letter to Saint-Castin by former militia captain Pierre LeBlanc informing the French commander that they had no choice but to be accommodating with the British authorities at Annapolis Royal. Saint-Castin, frustrated by this approach, replied angrily that the Acadians would be exposing themselves to Abenaki attacks.[14] Despite Saint-Castin's anger, there is evidence that the French settlers of Annapolis Royal and Minas Basin were less than hostile to the British presence; however, for some observers, this did not mean resignation. In November 1711, the governor of New France, the Marquis de Vaudreuil, wrote to the minister of the Marine at Versailles that the Acadians showed accommodating sentiments because they wanted to harvest their crops peacefully and because they were out of munitions. Vaudreuil was persuaded that the Acadians remained consistently loyal to the French crown.[15]

Acadian allegiance to the French King would be put to a severe test by the Treaty of Utrecht in 1713. According to this document, Britain was now in possession of 'all Nova Scotia or Acadia, with its ancient boundaries, as also the city of Port Royal, now called Annapolis Royal, and all other things in those parts, which depend on the said lands and islands.'[16] Article 14 of the treaty was of particular significance to the Acadians, stating that they had a one-year grace period to remove themselves from Nova Scotia; otherwise they would be required to swear an oath of allegiance to the British crown. Queen Anne's letter, in which she gave permission to the Acadians to sell their lands and estates before moving, supplemented Article 14 and was annexed to the treaty. In June 1713, the monarch wrote a letter to Nova Scotia governor Francis Nicholson informing him of her decision.[17]

Before Acadians got wind of this decision, British and French administrators thought that they had already decided their fate. At Versailles, the minister of the Marine, Louis Phélipeaux, comte de Pontchartrain, boasted to the Marquis de Vaudreuil that he was convinced that the Acadians would not swear allegiance to Queen Anne and that they would happily remove to Cape Breton.[18] The Acadians would thus continue to serve French interests by moving to and strengthening the neighbouring colony of Île Royale. Pontchartrain's enthusiasm did not take into account recent events in Acadian history in which the inhabitants of Port Royal had pledged, forcibly it is true, their allegiance to the English crown. Notwithstanding Article 14 of the peace treaty and Queen Anne's letter, the British colonial authorities of Nova Scotia understood what this exodus meant for the rebirth of French influence and power in the region. In December 1713, Samuel Vetch had already expressed his concerns to the Board of Trade and had, for the time being, no intention of letting them leave.[19]

If the great majority of French settlers of Placentia in Newfoundland rapidly decided to move to Île Royale after 1713, the same cannot be said of the Acadians. French historian Robert Rumilly simply but accurately described the situation: 'Le déménagement est plus facile aux pêcheurs de Terre-Neuve qu'aux cultivateurs acadiens. On peut transporter sa barque et ses agrès et non pas sa terre.'[20] Initial reactions among Acadians, recorded by French missionaries Antoine Gaulin and Félix Pain during the winter of 1713–14, were far from sharing the comte de Pontchartrain's enthusiasm about moving, even though the minister of the Marine had assured them that the region of Port Dauphin which was reserved for them possessed good lands and the most beautiful forests in the world.[21] At the time, French officials such as Governor General Vaudreuil of New France, knew that the Acadians would have preferred the more fertile lands of Île Saint-Jean, even though Vaudreuil was against this move because of the island's vulnerability to English attacks.[22] France had wasted little time in trying to transform Île Royale into a real colony with settlers and an administrative infrastructure partly made up of military officers, troops, and civil officials who had been at Port Royal before the conquest. Hence, by 1714, in the new settlement of Louisbourg, Acadians, especially from Port Royal, could have been greeted by familiar faces and family members. Acadia's former *lieutenant civil et criminel*, Mathieu de Goutin, had been appointed Île Royale's first *écrivain du Roi* in 1714. His marriage, around 1689, to Jeanne Thibodeau, daughter of Acadian pioneer and leader Pierre Thibodeau, meant that he had dozens of relatives living in Nova Scotia.[23] The same was true of Jean-Chrysostôme Loppinot, former notary public at Port Royal, who, thanks to his Acadian wife Jeanne Doucet, had a *trâlée* of in-laws in Acadia, stretching from Annapolis Royal to Beaubassin.[24]

However, it was the military officers of Louisbourg with whom the Acadians had the strongest family ties. By 1714, Acadian-born Lieutenant Charles de Saint-Étienne de La Tour was living in Île Royale while his cousins and in-laws ranked among the higher-status Acadian families, namely the Le Borgnes de Bélisle, the d'Entremonts, and the Melansons. And then there were the brothers Dupont: Captain François Dupont Duvivier had wed Marie Mius d'Entremont, while his younger brother Lieutenant Louis Dupont Duchambon had married her sister Jeanne.[25] Acadian historian Bernard Pothier has found that 'in all, eleven of the seventeen officers of the 1710 garrison of Acadia, and two officers of the civil administration, served in Île Royale after 1713.'[26] One must also keep in mind that numerous Acadians of the Annapolis

area had French military or civil officers as a godparents even though
further research is needed to measure the real significance of this spiri-
tual kinship. Added to these familiar faces was a small group of lesser
officials and artisans who had left Annapolis Royal in 1713–14 and
moved to Île Royale.[27] They were privateer Pierre Morpain, canoneer
Thomas Jacquot, sergeant Louis Lachaume, baker Nicholas Pugnant dit
Destouches, blacksmith Pierre Part dit Laforest, and Marie-Anne Maisonnat dit Baptiste, widow of merchant Christophe Cahouet. The latter
was the half-sister of Marie-Madeleine Maisonnat, wife of Annapolis
Royal merchant William Winniett. Most had Acadian spouses and, consequently, an extended family network in Nova Scotia.

Perhaps clouded by Louisbourg's famous fog, few historians have
noticed that in 1714, a large number of Nova Scotia Acadians had at
least one blood relative or an in-law living in Cape Breton. If we agree
with Naomi Griffiths's interpretation of the importance of family ties for
colonial Acadians, Île Royale was not then the terra incognita so often
portrayed. In what appears to have been a well-coordinated mission on
behalf of Acadian leaders, emissaries were sent from the principal settlements of Nova Scotia to visit Cape Breton in 1714. Among them were
men of high status in Acadian society and members of notable families
whose leadership was established prior to the conquest of 1710. Such
was the case of Michel Haché dit Gallant, a former militia captain of
Beaubassin, who had been the right-hand man of seigneur Michel Le
Neuf de La Vallière in the 1680s.[28] Others included the brothers Charles
and François Arseneau (also of Beaubassin, sons of Acadian trader
Pierre Arseneau),[29] François Amireau dit Tourangeau and navigator
François Coste of Port Royal, and Jacques LeBlanc of Grand Pré.[30]
Some, like Jean Pitre of Beaubassin, made this trip a family venture;
Pitre brought with him his wife Françoise Babin and their children so
that they could see for themselves the new lands of Île Royale.[31] Most of
them were unimpressed by what they saw and even the presence of high-
status family members in Louisbourg did not sway them. For the
moment, the Acadians waited, seemingly pondering who among British
and French authorities offered the better conditions.

Meanwhile, more Acadians were establishing contacts with the British
garrison at Annapolis Royal. As his younger brothers Charles and
François were assessing the potential of Cape Breton farmlands, Pierre
Arseneau set off on a trading expedition in a birch canoe during the
spring and summer of 1714. His voyage brought him to the Gaspé peninsula, back to Beaubassin, and then off to Île Royale. In September of

that same year, he arrived at Annapolis Royal, and in the presence of Francis Nicholson and other British officials, he signed a sworn deposition in which he described in detail his journey, even informing Nicholson that in Louisbourg harbour, he had seen a French ship unloading canons from Placentia, five or six merchant ships involved in the cod fisheries, and two English sloops loaded with salt and planks, among other things.[32] The reasons why this Acadian from Beaubassin, a region which was still outside of British control at the time, relayed this information remain obscure. A trader like his father, he might have regarded the British of Annapolis Royal as a potential market. A few French inhabitants of the Nova Scotia capital were already doing business with the English by supplying them with wood for the reconstruction of the fort. Among those who now figured among the suppliers in the garrison ledger of 1714 were Prudent Robichaud, René Martin, Antoine Thibodeau, Abraham Bourg, and Charles Melanson, eldest son and namesake of one of the more anglophile settlers of Port Royal in the 1690s.[33] British Annapolis Royal merchant William Winniett's marriage to Acadian Marie-Madeleine Maisonnat dit Baptiste around 1711 also helped in establishing these commercial ties. Until the *grand dérangement* of 1755, Annapolis Royal's military garrison and small community of English settlers were an interesting market for many Acadian farmers who could exchange their agricultural surpluses with them for much-needed products. Again, the Robichaud family of Port Royal figured prominently in this group, Prudent's example being followed by his brother François and his sons Prudent and Louis, who were known to have privileged access to the Annapolis Royal garrison.[34]

By the spring of 1714, Acadian reluctance to resettle in Cape Breton had lessened somewhat, with even some of those Annapolis inhabitants who had sold wood to the garrison now willing to move. In August of that year, Francis Nicholson wrote to the Board of Trade that up to fifty small vessels had been built by the Acadians of Annapolis Royal and Minas Basin in anticipation of a move to Île Royale, and that some Acadians had already relocated.[35] At the same time, French colonial authorities at Île Royale had sent a small mission to Nova Scotia consisting of captains Louis Denys de La Ronde and Jacques d'Espiet de Pensens to obtain formally from Nicholson an undertaking to respect the terms of Queen Anne's letter concerning the removal of the Acadians, and to orchestrate the removal.[36] De La Ronde and Pensens, formerly officers of the French garrison in Port Royal, met with Acadians in Annapolis Royal, Minas Basin, and Cobeguid in August and compiled a list of the

Acadian households in these settlements. Of the 355 *chefs de famille* enumerated by the two officers, an overwhelming majority of 302 signed documents indicating that they wanted to move.[37] To persuade the Acadians, de La Ronde and Pensens, without consulting their superiors, promised those who would move one year's ration to help them resettle in Cape Breton or even on the Île Saint-Jean.[38]

What a year 1714 must have been for the Acadians: busy building sloops; inquiring about the quality of land at Île Royale; meeting with de La Ronde and Pensens; being interrogated by the missionary Félix Pain, who by late October had compiled censuses for the Annapolis, Minas Basin, Beaubassin, and Cobeguid regions; and, moreover, witnessing the departure of friends and family who boarded three small French ships in late August and left for Cape Breton. At first glance, the mission of de La Ronde and Pensens appeared to be a success, judging by the number of heads of families agreeing to move and Nicholson's approval of the first departures in August.[39] The gloomy descriptions of rocky Île Royale given by Acadian emissaries had not yet sunk into the collective Acadian mind. Abraham Bourg of Annapolis Royal, the same who had sold wood to the British garrison, was one who embarked on the French King's ship *La Marie Joseph* in late August en route for Cape Breton. He would return to Annapolis; nevertheless, his sons Pierre, Michel, and Charles, and his sons-in-law Pierre Broussard and Jean Fougère remained in Cape Breton.[40] Joseph Mirande and his wife Marie Gaudet of Beaubassin also left in 1714. For them, there was no turning back. They remained in Île Royale, as did their children, three of whom married there in the 1730s and 1740s.[41]

However, Joseph Mirande's family was not representative of the majority of Acadian families. If 302 French settlers of Nova Scotia had declared to de La Ronde and Pensens their intent to relocate, only eight families arrived in Île Royale in September of 1714. By as late as 1734, a total of sixty-seven families had left Acadia to settle in the neighbouring island of Île Royale. A greater number of families had emigrated, but many returned to Acadia, as did Annapolis Royal's Abraham Bourg, judging that they were better off in Acadia. The French crown wanted to attract farmers to their new colony, but the Acadians who settled there were mostly shipbuilders, carpenters, coasters, and some needy individuals who were enticed by the free rations.[42] The grand plan of the comte de Pontchartrain had failed, as the vast majority of Acadians remained in Acadia. By 1715, British colonial authorities in Nova Scotia started vigorously to oppose Acadian departures while French colonial authorities provided little assistance for the removal of the Acadians. However, according to Bernard Pothier, 'it was the Acadians themselves who were the real determinant in bringing about the virtual failure of the immigration scheme' because 'their affection for Acadia and the bountiful ease of the Bay of Fundy marshlands was stronger than their hatred of England and Protestantism, and their love for France and its institutions.'[43]

History cannot be rewritten in the conditional tense, but what if the farmlands at Île Royale had been as fertile as those of the Bay of Fundy? The Acadian urge to move away, which is recorded in both French and English documents of the spring and summer of 1714, casts some doubt on their affection for their lands and extended families. Were the 302 heads of families panic-stricken when they expressed a will to emigrate or did their intention represent a coordinated strategy spread from Annapolis Royal to Minas Basin? And why were so many fact-finding Acadian emissaries sent to Île Royale in 1714 if the Acadian community was firmly settled in its ways on the shore of the Bay of Fundy? What remains certain is that after the 1710 conquest family members engaged in heated debates about whether to stay or go. This question would be formulated again and again until 1755 – Annapolis Royal Acadians debating if they should move to Grand Pré, Beaubassin settlers asking themselves if they should cross the Misaguash River into French Acadia (present-day New Brunswick), young Cobeguid couples arguing whether they should relocate to Île Saint-Jean, and Pisiguid siblings wanting to start over on the banks of the Petitcodiac, Memramcook, or St John Rivers. Debate of this kind had already existed before the conquest of 1710. The pioneer settlers who left Port Royal to establish the newer settlements of Beaubassin, Grand Pré, Cobeguid, Pisiguid, and Chipoudie did not leave overnight. The question of moving and starting over again, even in a frontier society, even in a world of marshlands where farmers reportedly worked less than their *Canadien* counterparts, could certainly not be taken lightly. Moreover, families did not necessarily share the same aims and goals. The Acadian carpenters, shipbuilders, and mariners who left Acadia to settle in Île Royale in the years following the conquest appear to have been more concerned with economic gain than with community values. Family was not a synonym for community.[44]

One of the major issues, if not the most important one, influencing these internal and external migrations was the debate over the oath of allegiance. As discussed in chapter 3, swearing the oath of allegiance in Acadian communities prior to the conquest did not seem to provoke the same animated debate which was recorded in Acadian settlements after

1710. But then, after 1710, the oath to the British crown would mean, if taken literally, that Acadians could be called as militiamen to fight alongside British troops in the event of a colonial war. The presence of important groups of Mi'kmaq warriors posed an increasing threat to Acadians who would openly take up arms alongside the British. In the years preceding the tragic events of 1755, a majority of Acadians would not agree with Mi'kmaq warfare against the British. It is easy then to imagine the moral dilemmas that could arise from such an oath. Approximately one month after the capitulation of Port Royal, fifty-seven heads of families swore an oath to Queen Anne, rapidly becoming targets of threats by Acadians who had refused to take the oath. Samuel Vetch wrote that they were seen as traitors.[45]

Queen Anne's death in 1714 revived the problematic issue. As was customary in Europe or elsewhere in colonial North America, new subjects could be called upon to renew their oath when a new sovereign, in this case George I of Great Britain, ascended the throne.[46] In the winter of 1715, Nova Scotia's new lieutenant-governor, Thomas Caulfeild, sent emissaries to the major Acadian settlements asking them to take the oath. Closest to the British garrison, the Acadians of Annapolis Royal were the first to respond. On 22 January, thirty-six heads of family swore only to remain loyal to King George for as long as they resided in Acadia. Furthermore, the heads of family declared that they could leave with all of their belongings whenever they wanted and go wherever they wanted.[47] The oath that these thirty-six Acadians pledged appears to have been a simple one, promising loyalty to the crown and containing no reference to the supremacy of the Protestant faith or abjuration.[48] Of course, the clause relating to the possibility of their leaving Acadia was intimately linked to the major debate of that year. Even though British authorities believed that the delay given to the Acadians by Queen Anne in her 1713 letter had by now expired, they nonetheless accepted this January 1715 oath.

That the Acadian community of Annapolis Royal was divided on the allegiance question is revealed by the absence of the signatures of many adult males from the document. According to the 1714 census taken by Récollet missionary priest Félix Pain, the greater Annapolis area counted at least 120 adult males who were heads of families. The thirty-six who signed the January oath did not even constitute the majority. Among them were familiar names such as the brothers Claude, Pierre, and Charles Melanson, the sons of the pro-English Annapolis Royal settler of the 1690s Pierre Melanson, who seemingly followed their father's political stand. New Acadian leaders were now making their appearance in Annapolis Royal, for the departure of French administrators and military elites in the fall of 1710 had created a vacuum that some individuals were eager to fill. A good case in point was that of the now-well-known Robichaud family of Annapolis Royal, who demonstrated pro-English behaviour until 1755. In fact, the prominent Robichaud family member, Prudent, was the first man to sign the January 1715 oath, a clear indication of his leadership role.[49] His family network linked him to British officers of the garrison: he was a cousin of William Winniett's wife, Marie-Madeleine Maisonnat. However, the Annapolis Robichauds had an even closer tie to the English. Around 1712, Prudent Robichaud's younger brother Alexandre's step-daughter, Agathe de Sainte-Étienne de La Tour, married Lieutenant Edmond Bradstreet of the British garrison of Annapolis Royal. Widowed in 1718, Agathe remarried another British officer, Hugh Campbell. Agathe Bradstreet Campbell would go down in Acadian history as the last *seigneuresse* of Acadia, having fraudulently sold the property titles of Acadian seigneuries to the British crown in 1734.[50]

The Robichaud family's aims were apparently centred more on developing a relationship with the small English community of Annapolis Royal than on conciliating the majority of Acadians who had refused the oath. Nevertheless, the Robichaud brothers were not all of the same mind, their family being a microcosm of Acadian politics at the time. The eldest, Charles, did not sign the January 1715 oath even though he was in the Annapolis area at the time. A few years later, he moved to Cobeguid, where many of his wife's family members had already settled.[51] Charles Robichaud did not have favourable experiences with either the French or the British in Port Royal. In 1705, French engineer Jean Delabat, in his reconstruction scheme of the Port Royal fort, ordered the demolition of nearby houses because they were obstructing fortifications.[52] Charles Robichaud's house was one of the dwellings that had to be torn down. And then, in June 1707, during Colonel John March's raid against Port Royal, Robichaud's new house was burned down.[53] Robichaud's move to Cobeguid after 1714 can be seen as a search for a peaceful retreat. However, the houses of his younger brothers, Prudent and François, were also destroyed during March's raid. In spite of this, they remained in Annapolis Royal and kept relatively good ties with the English. Given these different responses to the British regime, the winter of 1715 was not one of harmony for the Acadian community at Annapolis Royal.

By contrast with the Acadians of Annapolis Royal, who were divided over the oath question, those in Minas Basin and Beaubassin appeared to share the same political views when they met with lieutenant-governor Caulfeild's emissaries: they refused the oath. At Grand Pré, the principal Acadian settlement of the Minas Basin area, Acadian family heads, including widows, held a meeting in early March 1715 that was attended by the majority of the settlers. Alexandre Bourg, in his capacity as notary public,[54] drew up a list of inhabitants who attended the meeting. The attendees chose sixteen delegates to deliver to the British authorities the Minas Basin response to the demand for the oath.[55] The response was negative, even though it recognized King George I as the legitimate monarch of Great Britain. Probably stretching the truth a bit, the Minas inhabitants professed that they would be happy to remain in Nova Scotia under such a fine ruler as George I, but that they had already decided the previous summer to settle in Île Royale, on lands ruled by the King of France.[56] As it turned out, though, only eleven families left Minas Basin for Cape Breton between 1713 and 1734.[57] In Beaubassin, Acadians also held a meeting that March, which took note of a proclamation announcing George I's accession to the British throne. Parish priest Félix Pain, like Bourg at Minas, made up a list of Acadians who attended the meeting, and seven representatives, known as *arbitres*, were chosen to write the community's response to the requirement for the oath. The Beaubassin inhabitants declared that they could not take the oath of allegiance to King George because they were waiting for answers from French authorities as to the approach that they should take. Furthermore, when asked by Capon and Button, Caulfeild's emissaries, for supplies for the garrison of Annapolis Royal, the *arbitres* answered that because it was winter they could not comply. They would be more than willing, the *arbitres* added, to provide supplies the next year, depending on a good harvest.[58]

In 1717, Nova Scotia acquired a new governor, Colonel Richard Philipps, who, remaining in London, sent a lieutenant-governor in his place, Captain John Doucett. As most British administrators would do upon their arrival in Nova Scotia, Doucett ordered the Annapolis Royal Acadians to swear an oath of allegiance to King George. Doucett used sterner words than had Caulfeild in 1715: should the Acadians refuse the oath, he would not let their ships sail past the fort to go fishing or trading.[59] This time, the Acadian community of Annapolis, in an attempt to delay their response, asked Doucett to convene deputies from other Acadian villages so they could adopt a common standpoint. When pressured, the representatives of the Annapolis Acadians proposed a bargain of sorts to Doucett. If British soldiers would protect them from native attacks, they would take the oath but would abstain from using arms against the British or the French, or any of their subjects or allies.[60] Doucett was not amused, and while writing to the secretary of state, gave his interpretation of the Acadians' refusal: 'Many would sign rather than lose the fishing season, if it were not for the priests, who, seeing the plight of the garrison and weakness of the fort, tell their people that the Pretender will soon be settled in England and the province handed back to France.'[61]

The idea of neutrality thus became formulated in an Acadian document for the first time. The concept of neutrality was not unprecedented in the region; it had been around for many decades in the northeastern colonial world of North America, as seen for example in the failed treaty of neutrality that was signed at Whitehall in 1686 between Louis XIV of France and James II of England.[62] During the last quarter of the seventeenth century and the first decades of the eighteenth, French and British colonial administrators and high-ranking civil servants in London and Versailles had repeatedly contemplated the possibilities of neutralizing colonial North America.[63] Neutrality was also a political concept familiar to many of the native peoples who were in contact with French and British imperial forces. For instance, the peoples of the Iroquois League knew of this strategy.[64] The neutrality of the entire Iroquois League and of other native nations was a hotly debated issue at the many conferences that led to the signing of the Grande Paix de Montréal in 1701.[65] So neutrality was hardly a new idea when the Acadian leadership of Annapolis Royal proposed it to Doucett in 1717. What made this kind of Acadian neutrality politically unique, though, was the fact that they made it a condition of their membership in the British realm. Since the 1690s, many Acadians had adopted what could be labelled a neutral political behaviour. As defined by political scientist Donald Desserud,

> political neutrality, refers to that neutrality when the neutral party can and must maintain communications with both sides, and must behave in such a manner as to avoid helping one side at the expense of the other, or helps and hinders each in an equitable fashion, but cannot avoid being actively involved in the dispute. Political neutrality, further, would seem to require considerable political skill to be successful, a skill which would require a sound understanding of the issues at hand, and the character of the combatants.[66]

Thus, the Acadian trader Abraham Boudrot, in his dealing with Boston merchants and Acadian governor Robinau de Villebon in the 1690s, would have been politically neutral according to Desserud's definition. However, Port Royal settler Charles Melanson's anglophile behaviour could not be considered neutral, nor could that of his francophile brother Pierre Melanson of Grand Pré.

If the Annapolis Royal Acadians of 1717 were the first recorded Euramerican settlers to try to negotiate their new status as British subjects with representatives of the British crown in the colonial world, they were not the first group in the region to declare that they did not want to take arms against the French or the English. In fact, the Abenaki people had sought neutrality in their diplomatic relations with both New France and New England in the last quarter of the seventeenth century. At a conference in Boston in December 1701, Abenaki leaders had declared to their English hosts that 'if there should happen to be war between England and France, we would have all calm and quiet in this Land ... [and] not have it affect us.'[67] In Abenaki society, there appears to have been a consensual will to live in peace with their new European neighbours, buying goods from English traders from New England, while keeping cultural and religious ties with the Catholic missionaries, especially the Jesuits of New France. But as in the case of the Iroquois League, analysed by Richter, there were also powerful and influential groups within the Abenaki world who did not adopt neutrality, choosing rather the anglophile or the francophile camp.[68]

Both borderland societies, Abenaki and Acadian, were trying to establish in the beginning of the eighteenth century a political culture that had neutrality as its core but certainly not as its only politically discussed option. One might observe Abenaki similarities and influences in Acadian politics, especially considering that Acadians had deep-rooted cultural, family, and religious links to the French of Île Royale but did most of their business with New England merchants and traders since the middle of the seventeenth century. Many Acadians had regular contacts with the Abenaki, particularly in the war years that preceded the conquest of Port Royal, most notably the influential Saint-Castin family, who managed easily to bridge the Abenaki and Acadian worlds. With all those links to Abenaki society, there is a good possibility that the Acadian proposal of neutrality in 1717, which became the standard request of Acadian settlements by 1726–30, was an Abenaki idea even though Acadian leaders did not say so in the numerous documents sent to French and British officials.

When John Doucett ordered the Minas Basin Acadians to take the oath of allegiance in 1717, their reply was also negative, although the neutrality clause was not included in their answer. Minas Basin inhabitants' first reaction to Doucett's order was similar to that of Annapolis Royal: they requested a meeting of all Acadians of the region to discuss the matter, although inclement weather rendered this gathering impossible.[69] Their final response, however, was very different from that of Annapolis. First of all, as Naomi Griffiths points out, the representatives of Minas regarded Doucett's order as an offer presenting the proposals and advantages that were made to them by King George rather than as a direct order.[70] It is almost as though these Acadians considered themselves to be in a grey area, between the imperial realms of France and Britain, and to be shopping for the better offer between the two.[71] According to the Acadians of the Grand Pré region, three major obstacles prevented them from taking the oath: first they believed the oath was not clear enough when it came to their free practice of religion; second, they feared that they would be exposed to attacks from natives; and third, their ancestors, when living under British rule, had never had to pledge allegiance to the crown. Minas Basin used the same rhetoric as Port Royal on the potentiality of a native attack, but differed from the older settlement when referring to the free practice of their Roman Catholicism, invoking the 1690s, a time when taking an oath had seemed less difficult. Although there is no known document to indicate whether Doucett sent emissaries to Beaubassin, it is clear from the Annapolis Royal and Minas evidence that Acadian responses to his order lacked consensus. Only in 1730 would Acadians from Annapolis Royal, Minas Basin, and Beaubassin finally accept and pledge the same oath. It would take an additional thirteen years of heated political debate between British and French imperial administrators and Acadians, and among the Acadians themselves, to arrive at such a consensus, after which time the Acadians would be labelled the French Neutrals of Nova Scotia.

In a move similar to that of Doucett, Governor Richard Philipps, upon his arrival in Annapolis Royal in April 1720, presented two options to the Acadians: take the oath, or leave the province.[72] The local parish priest Justinien Durand – whom Samuel Vetch had sent to a Boston prison in the months following the conquest – was the first notable to react to Philipps's order. In a report to London, Philipps wrote that the priest had told him that the Acadians were afraid of native attacks and that they could not pledge an oath of allegiance to King George because they were still subjects of the King of France. Also, under Governor Francis Nichol-son's rule, they had agreed to move to Île Royale.[73] Durand made no reference to the neutrality clause which appeared in the Annapolis Royal petition of 1717. Hence, Philipps's first attempt at resolving the oath question was a failure. Almost ten years after the conquest, Acadian spokesmen were still making tactical use of the removal clause guaranteed in Queen Anne's letter, even though it had expired by 1720. And yet, very few Acadians were relocating their families to Cape Breton. Governor Philipps had a near-prophetic vision in 1719 when he wrote that Acadians would never swear the oath of allegiance and would never leave the province.[74]

Acadian emissaries, including Annapolis Royal notable Prudent Robichaud, were sent to Louisbourg in 1720 to meet with Île Royale's governor, Joseph Mombeton de Brouillan de Saint-Ovide. In a letter signed by deputies of the inhabitants of Annapolis, Minas Basin, and Beaubassin, they assured the French governor that they refused to take the oath to the British crown because they were good and loyal subjects of French King Louis XV, and asked him for advice on how they should react to the repeated demands of British authorities at Annapolis Royal that they take the oath.[75] Saint-Ovide wrote back, strongly suggesting that the Acadians claim that the British had not been true to their word and had restricted their removal from Acadia as guaranteed in 1713. He told them to give the same negative answer that they gave Nicholson in 1710. Even further, the Île Royale governor instructed Acadian representatives to state clearly, when questioned by British officials, that nothing in the world would make them abandon their Catholic faith and that they would always remain subjects of the King of France.[76]

Saint-Ovide was right when he wrote that Acadians would not abandon their Roman Catholic faith, and yet the question of their remaining subjects of the French King was not that easily resolved. It appears as though the Acadian delegates were buying time when they solicited the advice of the French colonial authorities in Louisbourg. If Acadian families truly wanted to move to Île Royale, very few obstacles were in their way. Even the British authorities at Annapolis Royal conceded that they had very little influence beyond the immediate surroundings of the small colonial town. One must also keep in mind that by 1720, Acadians had many blood relatives and in-laws living in Cape Breton, especially with the military and merchant families of Louisbourg. Former Île Royale governor Philippe Pastour de Costebelle had even married an Acadian, Anne Mius de Pombomcoup, in 1716.[77]

By 1727, the three major Acadian settlements proposed to the British authorities that they would swear the oath with a series of qualifying clauses. The timing was good, as in that same year George II ascended the throne of Great Britain. The year before, after much discussion, 133 Acadians of Annapolis Royal had signed an oath of allegiance with a clause indicating that they were not obliged to carry arms.[78] When Lieutenant-Governor Lawrence Armstrong sent a young ensign, Robert Wroth, to Beaubassin and Minas Basin in the fall of 1727, Acadian leaders were waiting for him. Acadians recognized and swore that they would be loyal and would faithfully obey King George II, provided that they could freely exercise their Roman Catholic faith, that they would be able to leave Nova Scotia whenever they desired with the right to sell their dwellings beforehand, that the right to own land in the province would be recognized for themselves and their heirs, and that they would be granted the right to never bear arms in any conflict.[79] Wroth agreed, although his concessions to the Acadians were not well received by the authorities in Annapolis Royal, where the Council declared them null and void. Returning to the province in 1729, Governor Richard Philipps revived the allegiance debate. When he left Nova Scotia the following year, he reported to the Board of Trade that the oath question was resolved and that most of the Acadians had pledged allegiance to George II. However, as Naomi Griffiths explains, 'There is no official British document that confirms the contention of the Acadians, at the time and later on, that this oath was sworn on the understanding that they had been granted the right to bear arms.'[80]

By early September 1730, the Acadians of Annapolis Royal, Minas Basin, Beaubassin, Cobeguid, and Pisiguid had, in their majority, accepted the oath. Even the small Acadian settlements on the St John River sent delegates to Armstrong in September 1732 to swear allegiance to King George II. Nonetheless, these settlements maintained contacts with French officials of New France in Quebec City, ties that would be strengthened in the years preceding 1755; in 1749, an Acadian settler of the village of Sainte-Anne des Pays-Bas on the St John River, Joseph Bellefontaine dit Beauséjour, was named commander of all the region's militias by the governor general of New France, the Marquis de la Galissonière.[81]

However, the compromise obtained by Acadian leaders did not sit well with all. Some Acadians publicly expressed their reservations about the oath, as noted by ensign Wroth when he was in Beaubassin. While talking with some Acadians of that settlement, Wroth was confronted by

Jean-Baptiste Vécot, a one-time *notaire royal* of Beaubassin before 1710, who was opposed to pledging allegiance to the British crown. True to his opposition, Vécot moved his family to Port St-Pierre on Île Saint-Jean in 1728, the year following the Beaubassin pledge of allegiance conducted by Robert Wroth.[82] Vécot's removal to a neighbouring French colony was not exceptional, for in the 1730s at least six families from Beaubassin left for Cape Breton or Île Saint-Jean.[83] Departures were also noted in the Minas Basin region, where a few couples – some with children, others newly married – and some young bachelors decided to settle the fertile marshlands of the Petitcodiac River. There, they founded a small village, Le Coude (present-day Moncton). News that the British military authorities of Annapolis Royal wanted to construct a blockhouse at Grand Pré, combined with the 1730 oath, might have persuaded these Acadians to start again in a region that France still considered hers.[84] However, these examples of geographically mobile individuals are not fully representative of Acadian society in the 1730s. The troubled decade of the 1740s would convince hundreds of Acadians that resettlement in regions free from the passage of military troops had become a necessity.

For the great majority of Acadians who remained in Nova Scotia, choosing to honour the pledge of loyalty to the British crown meant that they would not have to bear arms in the event of war. Many documents produced by Acadian leaders prior to the *grand dérangement* of 1755 directly referred to their understanding of the 1730 oath. When Governor Edward Cornwallis arrived in Nova Scotia in 1749 and ordered the Acadians to swear a more explicit oath of allegiance and fidelity to the British crown, the deputies from the different Acadian districts of Nova Scotia presented him with a petition signed by one thousand Acadians, stating: 'The inhabitants in general, Sir, over the whole extent of this country, have resolved not to take the oath which Your Excellency requires of us; but if Your Excellency will grant us our old oath which was given at Mines to Mr. Richard Philipps, with an exemption for ourselves and our heirs from taking up arms.'[85] Again, during the fateful summer of 1755, 103 inhabitants of Pisiguid wrote to Lieutenant-Governor Charles Lawrence that they had taken an oath of fidelity 'to His Britannic Majesty, with all the circumstances and reservation granted to us, in the name of the King, by Mr. Richard Philipps, Commander in Chief in the said province.' That same July, 203 inhabitants of Minas and Rivière-aux-Canards also sent a petition to Lawrence referring to the Philipps oath.[86]

The Annapolis Royal administrators, despite their scepticism concerning the clauses added to the oath by Wroth, attempted during the 1730s to draw Acadians into the British realm by integrating their leaders into the administrative infrastructure of Nova Scotia. Already, since 1720, Governor Richard Philipps had put in place a system of Acadian deputies to represent the different settlements of the colony. These deputies would receive more responsibilities in the years following the oaths of 1726–30. In 1727, Lieutenant-Governor Armstrong had named four Annapolis Royal Acadians to low-ranking positions. Jean Duon, a former notary public during the French regime, became clerk of the justices of the peace; Réné Martin, constable; François Richard, high constable; and Prudent Robichaud, the most prestigious position, justice of the peace.[87] Even Alexandre Bourg of Minas Basin, who still had his commission as a New France notary public, would take the same role by order of the British authorities. Too often portrayed as local elders, these deputies were mainly men in their late thirties and early forties, men of good standing and healthy enough to undertake numerous journeys between Annapolis Royal and their respective villages.[88] In the Annapolis region, of the twenty-eight Acadians known to have been chosen as deputies between 1720 and 1749, five were Robichaud men (Prudent, his sons Prudent, Louis, and Joseph, and the elder Prudent's brother Alexandre), while nine others were nephews, brothers-in-law, or first cousins of these Robichauds. In fact, half of Annapolis Royal's deputies belonged to the Robichaud family network.[89] The political scene in the village of Cobequid also included many Robichaud men serving as deputies up to 1755.[90] Many of these deputies were merchants, mill owners, ship captains, or prosperous farmers. Such occupations also predominated among the known Acadian deputies of Grand Pré.[91]

British authorities not only relied on deputies to integrate Acadians in the English imperial realm; they also tried to convince the Acadians to bring any legal disputes to the General Court at Annapolis Royal rather than have them resolved among themselves or by their priests. Over time, the number of such cases heard at Annapolis Royal increased.[92] Furthermore, the British recognized the Acadian seigneurial families who had been respectful of English rule by ordering the inhabitants to pay their seigneurial dues. In 1734, for example, the widowed *seigneuresse* Marie de Saint-Étienne de La Tour benefited from such payments.[93]

These overtures by British authorities with regard to Acadian leaders and the population as a whole certainly did not mean that the 1730s were without friction among the Acadians themselves. In 1731, eighty-seven

Acadian landowners of Annapolis Royal sent a petition to Lieutenant-Governor Armstrong stating that they did not want their properties to be surveyed as the British had planned. Many prominent Acadians did not sign the petition, although, remarkably, nearly all of the adult males of the influential Robichaud clan did. The anglophile Robichauds of Annapolis Royal may not have wanted to frustrate the British authorities, and yet even Prudent Robichaud's son Louis signed the petition.[94] Other signs of discontent also must have divided the Acadian community, such as a 1736 petition supported by thirty-eight signatories and addressed to the 'Bien Aimé' himself, King Louis XV of France, asking for his intervention in favour of missionary priests de Saint-Poncy and Chauvreulx, whom Armstrong had ordered out of Nova Scotia.[95] The small number of signatures on this petition meant that most Annapolis Acadians probably did not favour such a provocation to British rule. In the same year, 107 heads of families of the Annapolis river appealed directly to Armstrong by way of a petition requesting the return of de Saint-Poncy.[96] Evidently, the grande famille acadienne was far from being united. Another example of friction among the Acadians occurred when Grand Pré settler René LeBlanc, a local deputy, made a commercial trip to the St John River on behalf of the Annapolis Royal merchants Donelle and Winniett in the early 1730s. Upon his return, he went to Annapolis Royal and signed a sworn deposition to Armstrong in which he informed him of the number of Frenchmen on the St John River who could bear arms. He also criticized Alexandre Bourg for collaborating with the French, but was scorned by Bourg's son-in-law Joseph Godin dit Châtillon dit Préville for being an ally of the British. LeBlanc lamented that he was scorned when he threatened some French inhabitants of the St John River with a legal suit before 'la Justice d'Annapolis Royalle.'[97] LeBlanc would eventually push Bourg aside when he replaced Bourg as notary public at Grand Pré in the 1740s. A legendary figure in Longfellow's famous poem Evangeline, LeBlanc paid dearly for his penchant for the British, as the abbé Le Loutre had him kidnapped by the Mi'kmaq in the late 1740s and sent for almost two years to be a virtual prisoner in the home of francophile Acadian leader Joseph Broussard dit Beausoleil at Le Coude on the banks of the Petitcodiac River.[98]

The oath compromise of 1726–30 would last until the next decade, when war pitted France against Britain and Nova Scotia again became a battlefield. Again, the Acadian population would be pressured by British, French, Canadien, and native military forces to take sides in the War of the Austrian Succession during the 1740s. The 1730s, however, witnessed relative peace as one of the most important problems resulting from the conquest of 1710 had been resolved, at least from an Acadian point of view. Acadians had recognized George II as their sovereign. In return, they could freely practise their religion, freely own land and bequeath it to their children, remove to French territory (though very few did in the 1730s); they were now known and recognized as neutral French. The decade of the 1730s constitutes a turning point, marking the end of the conquest era for the Acadian population. The following decade, the 1740s – with its several unsuccessful invasions of Nova Scotia by French and *Canadien* troops, with the effective military participation of numerous Acadians in these campaigns, and with the founding of Halifax – heralded a more troubled time for the French inhabitants of Acadia, leading to the Expulsion years.

In a first reading, the conquest legacy from 1710 to the 1730s would appear to consist of years of debate, at times tumultuous, among the French, the British, and the Acadian delegates, to arrive at a *modus vivendi* represented by the oaths of allegiance administered by Lieutenant-Governor Lawrence Armstrong, ensign Robert Wroth, and Governor Richard Philipps between 1726 and 1730. Indeed, before the conflicted years of the 1740s, most Acadians were neutral, if neutrality meant that they had not taken arms in military activities.[99] However, the nature of neutrality in Acadian Nova Scotia was more of a political neutrality, which meant, as explained by Donald Desserud, that the French neutrals were directly involved in the rivalry between British and French interests in Acadia. As was the case in 1710, there were three Acadias in the 1730s. The first was the Acadia/Nova Scotia of the imperial powers. The second was the ever-growing Acadian population who were building and expanding in the period that Naomi Griffiths has labelled the golden years.[100] But a less-examined third Acadia consisted of those Acadians who were building ties with the French or British camps. These linkages would become more public and more compromising for some leading Acadians in the 1740s. The rhetoric of neutrality, with its loosely defined borders, almost encouraged rival anglophile and francophile camps to try to benefit from Acadian Nova Scotia's particular position, sitting as it did on the border of two colonial empires. Thus, neutrality was an important legacy of the conquest, but a legacy that was not treasured by all Acadians. Victor Hugo wrote that in time of revolution, he who is neutral is powerless. He was right. When the dramatic turmoil of 1755 hit Acadians, they realized too late that neutrality could also be a poisoned gift.

9

Imperial Transitions

Elizabeth Mancke

In 1713 Louis XIV, ostensibly at the request of the British government, released French Protestants who had been imprisoned on naval galleys. To match this French show of benevolence, Queen Anne sent a letter to Francis Nicholson, governor of Nova Scotia, informing him that Acadians who were 'willing to Continue our Subjects [were] to retain and Enjoy their said Lands and Tenements without any Lett or Molestation.' Those who chose to relocate into French territory could sell their property. Beyond showing herself to be as magnanimous a monarch as Louis XIV, Queen Anne's letter was a personal gesture to her new 'subjects' that symbolized Britain's sovereignty over Nova Scotia.[1]

Such displays of royal benevolence anticipated a complementary show of fealty from the recipients, in the case of the Acadians an oath of allegiance. As is well known, they demurred. By declining, Acadians implicitly, though whether willfully is unclear, challenged British sovereignty in Nova Scotia. The internationally negotiated transfer of Acadia from French to British sovereignty needed acceptance and legitimation on the ground by the Acadians, if not the natives as well. The absence of clear acceptance and legitimation raised a number of problems. If Acadians did not swear an oath of allegiance, could they still own their property as Queen Anne had promised, and practise Catholicism as stipulated in the Treaty of Utrecht? Were they entitled to the crown's protection? Did the refusal to swear the oath mean that Acadians did not acknowledge the territorial transfer of Acadia from France to Britain? How was the crown's responsibility to establish civilian government to be expressed if the local population refused the crown's sovereignty?

Technically not subjects or denizens, were the Acadians to be treated as friendly aliens or enemy aliens? In short, how was civilian government to be established in Nova Scotia, and what kind of government would it be?

No colony in British America offered clear precedents. In all earlier British colonial ventures, the settlement of large numbers of English subjects meant that governmental authority and sovereignty were negotiated and legitimated within a common cultural matrix that included notions about law, property holding, governmental authority, the appropriate relations between the governed and their governors, and who was friend and who foe.[2] As well, these colonies developed creole colonial elites defined not just by their social and economic power, but also by political power. Even the conquered colonies of Jamaica and New York (with New Jersey carved off the latter) did not offer precedents. After the English conquest of Jamaica in 1655, most Spanish residents fled the island for Spanish territory, thereby obviating the problem of incorporating Spanish-speaking, Catholic residents into the English world.[3] In New York, conquered in 1664, most of the Dutch residents of the former colony of New Netherland had stayed; predominantly Protestants, most were naturalized by legislation or allowed resident status by executive patents.[4] In both Jamaica and New York, the arrival of English settlers soon consolidated English control.

In neither Jamaica nor New York did colonial officials suffer chronic fear that the Spanish or the Dutch would try to retake their former colonies. While Spain had other large colonies near Jamaica, in particular Cuba and Hispaniola, neither posed a threat of the magnitude that the French presence in Île Royale and Canada posed for Nova Scotia. New Netherland had been the only Dutch colony on mainland North America. After its loss, the Dutch evinced no serious interest in temperate climate colonies, concentrating their expansionist energies on colonies in tropical zones. Jamaica had no remaining native peoples, though it had a large maroon population living in the island's interior who challenged British control of the island through the eighteenth century.[5] New York had large numbers of natives, in particular the Houdenasaunee (Iroquois), and the English built on the trade and military alliances the Dutch had established. Nova Scotia's native peoples, by contrast, asserted their autonomy, intermittently resisted the British, and maintained diplomatic relations with the French.[6]

In Nova Scotia, none of the above characteristics existed. Political elites, as represented by metropolitan officials, had few ties to social and economic elites among the Acadians.[7] The dominant residential populations were Acadian and native. Acadians were Catholic and the natives at least nominally so, thus perpetuating ties to New France through the ministration of French priests. While the British acknowledged native groups as self-governing, Acadians were to be within the pale of day-to-day British government. Yet under the English Test Act of 1673, their Catholicism made them ineligible to hold public office or sit on juries, even if they did swear an oath of allegiance. How was Nova Scotia to be governed when, by law, the majority of the European population could not participate in government? And if Acadians could not participate, who would? The near-absence of Protestant settlers in Nova Scotia before 1749 meant that under existing laws there were not enough people to establish the full apparatus of British government that had become conventional in other colonies: an assembly that would vote taxes to run the colony, county and/or town government for local administration, a land office and registry of deeds, and a judicial system.

New legislation on naval stores further complicated the recruitment of settlers for Nova Scotia, as well as reflected a piecemeal interest by the metropolitan government in the potential of new colonial resources. During the War of the Spanish Succession (1702–13), the Board of Trade persuaded Parliament to pass the Naval Stores Act (1705) to encourage the North American colonies to produce tar, pitch, rosin, turpentine, hemp, masts, yards, and bowsprits for use by the Royal Navy. To reserve the woods for naval stores, the legislation prohibited the cutting of 'Pitch, Pine, or Tar Trees,' under twelve inches in diameter on ungranted land, a clause which applied to land from New Jersey north. The 1691 charter of Massachusetts had already reserved trees over twenty-four inches in diameter for use as masts for the navy. Both the 1705 legislation and the Massachusetts charter were interpreted to extend to Nova Scotia, and thus land could not be granted to new settlers without being surveyed for naval stores. As written, the legislation implicitly required colonies to bear the cost of the surveys, and in Nova Scotia there simply was no money for such expenses.[8]

With its garrisoned, English-speaking, Protestant officials, and its dispersed native and French Catholic communities, Nova Scotia was not representative of early-eighteenth-century British America. However, officials who governed Nova Scotia had the untenable charge 'to establish a form of Government consonant to that of the other Plantations in America.'[9] For nearly half a century, they struggled unsuccessfully to find the combination and sequence of conditions, short of deporting the Acadians, to pull the colony within the normative range of colonial governance. Their failure to craft and legitimate a new definition of colonial subject and an appropriate system of government that was acceptable in both Nova Scotia and Britain is testimony both to the profoundly English political and constitutional legacy of seventeenth-century colonial development and to how wrenching would be the accommodation of a more ethnically and constitutionally polyglot empire in the eighteenth century.[10]

In this sense, Nova Scotia's history is central to understanding the constitutional and political reconfiguration and redefinition of the British empire over the eighteenth century. The Acadians' refusal to swear an oath of allegiance after the Treaty of Utrecht made variable what had become normative and interdependent elements of British colonial governments. The maintenance of colonies depended on populations that acknowledged themselves subject to the British monarch, that staffed the civilian governments established on an English model, and that voted taxes to pay the expenses of running a colony. The absence of these three critical elements of colonial governments – a natural-born or naturalized subject population, a civilian government, and locally generated financial resources – stymied the men sent to govern Nova Scotia. Unable to act within established conventions, officials articulated a wide range of values about the fundamentals of colonial governance in order to explain why they were obliged to govern outside those norms. Their quandary makes the official record of post-conquest Nova Scotia an extended discussion about the nature of British colonial government.

Ironically, the severe limitations of Nova Scotia laid bare the skeleton of colonial governance that the success of other colonies obscured. Using the official record from 1710 to 1749, this chapter analyses what the political history of Nova Scotia can tell us about the nature of British colonial government in the early modern era. The chapter is divided into four sections: the first deals with the establishment of civilian government; the second considers the necessity of a civilian population of subjects; the third examines the problem of financing colonies; and the final section assesses the impact of shifting metropolitan policies after 1748. Within this analysis there are three important chronological periods. The first period, from 1710, the year of the conquest, to 1720, when Governor Richard Philipps arrived in the colony, was characterized by enormous ambiguity over the long-term status of the colony and its Acadian and native residents. The second period, 1720–30, saw the establishment of an executive council as the institutional cornerstone for the colony's civilian government. But as Philipps soon discovered, until the Acadians swore an oath of allegiance, the government would lack civilian subjects and thus the personnel to establish collateral institutions. In the late 1720s the Acadians swore qualified oaths of allegiance, giving the colony a civilian population of subjects, albeit Catholic and of suspect loyalty. In the third period, 1730–48, the colony's government began the process of surveying and registering Acadian lands and collecting quitrents, but it still could not call an assembly that could vote the taxes so necessary for financing colonies. The colony's financial straits ended in 1748 when Parliament appropriated monies to build Halifax as a north Atlantic naval port and new capital of Nova Scotia. Suddenly the colony had abundant financial resources, unprecedented both in the history of Nova Scotia and the history of British America, a shift, as it were, from colonial to imperial government.

Richard Philipps, appointed governor general of Nova Scotia in 1717, found upon his arrival in the colony in April 1720 that there 'has been hitherto no more than a Mock Government.' He recognized that without the Acadians swearing an oath of allegiance 'the British Government canot [sic] be said to be Established,' unless the government supplied resources to coax or coerce the Acadians into fidelity or to settle 'Natural born Subjects' in the colony.[11] The Acadians' unwillingness to swear an oath of allegiance compelled him to tell the Board of Trade that the effective extension of British sovereignty to Nova Scotia depended not just on the conquest and the subsequent Treaty of Utrecht, but also on the ongoing appearance and substance of a British presence in the colony. Quite simply, 'it is necessary that the Government at home exert itself a little and be at some extraordinary expence.' So appalled was Philipps at the state of the colony and the lack of resources for governing that he argued it would be better to give the territory back to the French than to 'be contented with the name only of Government.'[12]

Philipps's frustration, a decade after the 1710 conquest, is indicative of how incomprehensible conditions in Nova Scotia were from the perspective of the metropole. Much of the two years between the issuing of his original commission in 1717 and his arrival in Nova Scotia, Philipps had spent in London negotiating with officials for instructions and powers that fitted the known problems of the colony. Since the conquest, metropolitan policy for governing this new acquisition was ill-defined. A garrison command under successive governors or their deputies had nominally governed the colony, and many of the concerns they commu-

nicated back to Britain dealt with the abysmal state of the finances for
maintaining troops stationed at Annapolis Royal and the financial and
psychological wounds sustained by everyone in the open antagonism
that developed among the officers, especially between Francis Nicholson and Samuel Vetch.[13]

Various of Philipps's predecessors who had found themselves responsible for the colony had made hesitant moves to separate military and
civilian governance, but like efforts to resolve other problems, their
efforts fell victim to metropolitan indifference and internal squabbling.
The winter after the conquest, four British army officers and two Acadians convened a court to adjudicate disputes.[14] After the Treaty of Utrecht, Thomas Caulfeild, lieutenant-governor under Nicholson and then
Vetch, tried to establish courts suitable to the Acadians and the British,
but Nicholson challenged his authority to do so. In reporting the incident to the Board of Trade, Caulfeild said that he had told Nicholson
that as the highest civilian officer resident in the colony, he 'Should allways endeavour to Cultivate as good an Understanding amongst the
People as possible believeing the same Essential for his Majesties Service.' Given the choice of establishing a court without a commission or
holding 'myselfe blamable to Suffer Injustice to be done before Me
without taking Notice thereof,' he chose the former.[15]

The decision of the French to build Louisbourg, combined with the
death of Caulfeild in 1717, forced even indifferent metropolitan officials
to acknowledge the colony's needs. The British crown formed a new
regiment of foot, under the command of Colonel Richard Philipps, as a
permanent part of His Majesty's land forces. Philipps was also appointed
governor general of Nova Scotia, and his military commission would pay
his gubernatorial salary. Philipps quickly recognized that his military
commission did not include sufficient powers or instructions to manage
Nova Scotia's known problems, much less its unknown ones. In particular, he was concerned that he have the authority to establish a civilian
government. Staying in London until 1719, he negotiated with the
Board of Trade and Board of Ordnance for more resources, power, and
a new commission, without realizing how utterly inadequate these preparations would still be.[16]

The royal instructions to Philipps in 1719, and subsequent instructions drafted until 1749, included the injunction that until Nova Scotia's
government was established the governor would receive 'a copy of the
instructions given by his Majesty to the governor of Virginia, by which
you will conduct yourself till his Majesty's further pleasure shall be

known.'[17] John Bartlet Brebner labelled this government by analogy, which it was, but he overdrew the comparison to Virginia and underestimated the larger colonial context.[18] Since the Restoration, the Privy Council had slowly been regularizing and routinizing basic communications with colonies, and dispatches to one colony were often used as the template for instructions to other colonies.[19]

Similarities among colonies had emerged less from metropolitan design than from an English commitment to 'such devices as trial by jury, habeas corpus, due process of law, and representative government.'[20] An increasingly integrated British Atlantic economy depended on shared legal protections of property, thus encouraging compatible judicial systems throughout British America. Colonial charters, and then instructions to governors after many colonies were royalized, emphasized that no laws were to be passed that were inconsistent with English law. The Treasury expected colonies to be self-financing, and throughout the Americas this financial imperative encouraged the establishment of colonial assemblies, based on the model of the House of Commons and the principle that elected representatives should determine taxation.

By the end of the seventeenth century, from an imperial perspective, the problem with colonial governments lay not so much in their weaknesses, but stemmed rather from too much unchecked and undisciplined vitality and autonomy. Little in the 106 years between the founding of Virginia (1607) and the French cession of Acadia (1713) would lead metropolitan officials to believe that Nova Scotia would not develop a similarly vital government. And because much of metropolitan practice for governing far-flung territories had developed reactively rather than proactively, there was no bureaucratic practice of designing a colonial government.[21]

From within the colony, however, it was blindingly and frustratingly obvious that configuring Nova Scotia's government to the colonial standard would be a daunting, if not impossible, task. As Philipps noted, without people willing to acknowledge themselves subject to the British crown, the home government had to spend money to make manifest British sovereignty among a non-British people. If the merits of British government were not culturally internalized, as with natural-born subjects, or consciously accepted, as with naturalized subjects, then they had to be intentionally externalized, displayed, and made tangibly attractive. The presence of the governor general and the establishment of civilian government were two such manifestations. Philipps believed, perhaps arrogantly, that the Acadians were surprised to find that he, and not just a deputy, had come to Nova Scotia. Gauging the symbolism of leadership, the Acadians had concluded, he believed, that if the British did not send a high-ranking official to the colony, then they did not consider it important and they might well return the colony to the French.[22]

Philipps promptly set about to establish the foundation for a civilian government. He issued a proclamation to the Acadians reminding them of their duty to swear an oath of allegiance that would protect their rights to 'le libre Excercise de leur Religion,' as well as allow them 'de Droits et Privileges Civils comme S'ils estoint Anglois.'[23] On 25 April, his fifth day at Annapolis Royal, he convened a civilian council. Lacking a full complement of twelve Protestant civilians who could serve on the Council, he chose by rank three military officers.[24] A year later, on 19 April 1721, Philipps also constituted the Council as a 'Court of Judicature,' despite the absence of conditions necessary to establish courts 'according to the Lawes of Great Britain.' The Virginia instructions, however, did allow the governor and Council to sit as a court of justice, and given the large number of 'Memorialls, Petition[s], and Complaints' submitted to Philipps for his assessment, he thought it best to have them decided by the Council sitting in a judicial capacity.[25] Initially the Council planned court days for the first Tuesdays in May, August, November, and February, but in practice it heard cases throughout the year as they occurred. The Council secretaries never wrote separate minutes for executive and judicial business, and in many sittings the Council shifted back and forth between its two roles. Only by reading the text of the minutes can one discern distinctions in the Council's exercise of its two functions.

The seeming blending of executive and judicial functions was largely a consequence of limited personnel rather than a disregard of appropriate judicial procedure. In an analysis of Nova Scotia's justice system circa 1710–50, Thomas Barnes has argued persuasively that over time 'the council became less summary and more procedure-bound,' particularly after 1730, when the number of cases heard by the council increased. Lawrence Armstrong, who served as lieutenant-governor during most of the 1730s, and Paul Mascarene, who became Council president upon Armstrong's death in 1739, were staunch advocates of due process.[26] The rising number of civil cases in the 1730s prompted Armstrong to issue a memo to the Acadians that emphasized the injustice of attempts at 'Hurried' and 'Impatient' litigation that did not give people

'Due time to prepare and make Answer to Such Complaints & Petitions as have been often Lodged & Exhibited against them.' Haste also resulted in 'many frivolous and undigested Complaints' being brought to the Council. To curb the problems, Armstrong reinstated four terms in which the Council would sit as a court.[27]

The other major component of civilian government in early Nova Scotia was the system of Acadian deputies. On 29 April 1720 the Council, working beyond the letter of its instructions, voted to authorize the French inhabitants in the settlements on the Annapolis River to choose six deputies to represent their interests to the governor and Council. Within a few weeks the communities at Minas and Cobequid had also elected deputies.[28] While the system of deputies remained until the deportation of the Acadians beginning in 1755, their role in the government of Nova Scotia shifted considerably, especially after the oath taking in the late 1720s and 1730.[29]

In the early 1720s, the deputies had quasi-diplomatic functions. They were the spokespeople when the Acadians declined to swear an oath of allegiance in 1720. The Council consulted them for witnesses or evidence in both criminal and civil cases. During the hostilities between the natives and the British from 1722 until the signing of a peace treaty in 1725, the deputies were consulted about the presence of natives in their communities. Once peace obviated their quasi-diplomatic role, the importance of deputies temporarily declined. The council contacted them very few times between 1725 and 1729 and their selection, or non-selection, became haphazard. On 21 November 1729, one day after arriving back in Annapolis Royal after an eight-year absence, Philipps notified the Council that he had appointed new deputies for the Annapolis River settlements and had increased their number from four to eight.[30] Philipps's unilateral decision to appoint deputies is indicative of how irregular their selection had become and how infrequently the Council had consulted them in the previous years. In 1732, after Philipps had returned to Britain and Lawrence Armstrong was the chief governing officer, the deputies complained that Philipps had appointed them rather then letting them be elected by the people they represented.[31]

One of the primary reasons for Philipps's 1729 return to Nova Scotia was to get the Acadians to swear an oath of allegiance, a new push that had been started in 1726 by Lawrence Armstrong after a five-year hiatus on the issue during which the peace had been negotiated with the natives. In Philipps's oath-taking negotiations with the Acadians, he promised them in the name of George II that their religious and property rights would be honoured, provided they surveyed and registered claims to the latter.[32] As he explained to the Board of Trade, the collection of quitrents would 'contribute towards the Support of Government.'[33] Informing the council on December 7, 1730, that he had obtained oaths from all the Acadians, he also noted that he had appointed Alexander Bourg, former procurator general under the French regime, as collector of rents. Philipps instructed him to report on 'what Homage and Duties they paid to the [French] Crown,' as the basis for establishing quitrents, one of the few instances of the British harkening back to practices of the French regime.[34]

The decision to survey and register Acadian lands and to charge quitrents generated a whole new set of administrative tasks that reinvigorated the role of the deputies, created new offices such as the farmers of rents, and fostered disputes over land boundaries that sent dozens of litigants to the Council for dispute resolution. It became common for deputies to ascertain the nature of land disagreements, to order inhabitants to mark property lines, and to organize inhabitants to clear roads and keep dikes in good repair.[35] The enhanced importance of deputies to the administration of local government also brought about the regularization of their election. On 11 September 1732, the council decided, in consultation with lieutenant-governor Armstrong and the Annapolis River deputies, that annual elections for deputies would be held on 11 October, provided it was not a Sunday and 'then it Shall be on the Munday following.' Significantly, the chosen date commemorated the reduction of Port Royal.[36]

After Paul Mascarene became president of the council after the death of Armstrong in 1739, he wrote a memorial that codified the role of the deputies. They were to be men of property and good sense who had the interest of the community at heart. They had the power to consult among themselves and to convene meetings of the residents they represented. They were to monitor the maintenance of fences and the control of livestock, oversee the upkeep of bridges and roads, and find people to farm the king's rents.[37] In addition to the responsibilities of the deputies after 1730, the rent farmers were to record all land transactions, as well as wills and testaments, tasks associated with registrars of deeds and probate in other British colonies.

Administratively, most of the functions of local government common in British colonies had been institutionalized in Nova Scotia during the 1730s, largely through the office of the deputies, and they would remain critical to local administration until the deportation. Mascarene, in particular, described the nature of local government in Nova Scotia to the Board of Trade, noting that the needs of government were great enough to warrant allowing the Acadians to hold local offices.[38] Operational within the colony, the deputies had no legal standing under British law, which prohibited Catholics from holding public office, and virtually no acknowledgment outside the colony. Significantly, when the Acadians were deported, beginning in 1755, deputies who had faithfully served the British government were treated no differently from Acadians who had supported the French.

What is striking about Nova Scotia's early-eighteenth-century record is how assiduously officials worked to create and maintain a government that honoured 'the rights of Englishmen,' including the minimization of military rule. The first four decades of British governance in Nova Scotia, despite the preponderance of members of the government with military commissions, is testimony to Jack Greene's argument that the single most defining characteristic of English, and then British, identity in the early modern Atlantic world was a commitment to English liberty.[39] If any place in seventeenth- or eighteenth-century British America had a government run on military principles, it would have been Nova Scotia, as some people at the time, and some historians, believed was true.[40] The chief pieces of evidence for this contention were the military officers and a government that deviated from other British colonial governments. Neither individually nor together do they make the case.[41]

First, we cannot assume that all men in the British army eschewed the English commitment to liberty. When outsiders charged that the officers stationed at Annapolis Royal were attempting to create a military government, ten of them protested that they served merely 'for want of other Brittish Subjects.' They acted 'with a due regard to the Liberty and Property of the Subject and the Peace and well being of his Majesty's Province,' and had 'never had any advantage or Salary.'[42] Men inclined to abuse their military power were likely to be checked, either by a superior officer or the council. After the death of lieutenant-governor Armstrong in 1739, the relationship between the civilian Council and the garrison command became a matter of contention. Alexander Cosby, lieutenant-colonel of the 40th regiment and Paul Mascarene's superior officer in the army, questioned the propriety of Mascarene, rather than he, serving as Council president. A Board of Trade ruling, however, had stated that in the absence of both the governor and lieutenant-governor, the most senior councillor would serve as council president, not the most senior military officer. Cosby tried to remove Mascarene from Annapolis Royal by ordering him to Canso to serve in the garrison there, but Mascarene refused to go. He reported to the Board of Trade that 'I am firmly persuaded if I had remov'd from hence, the Civil Government would have been of no use, and disorder would naturally have issued.' Despite endless slights from Cosby, Mascarene believed that he had preserved 'the good effects of the Civil Government administred ... over the French Inhabitants of this Province.'[43]

In the settlement of Canso, inhabited largely by New Englanders engaged in the fishery, Governor Philipps had first appointed justices of the peace in 1720. In 1729, during his brief sojourn there, four residents petitioned Philipps to appoint a 'Civil Magistracy' that could sit in Canso and adjudicate 'the many Petty Differences & Cases which Daily Arise in this Fishery that Call for a determination too tedious & Triball to trouble Your Excellency with,' which he did.[44] In 1732 Edward How, one of Canso's justices of the peace, complained to Armstrong that Captain Christopher Aldridge, the highest-commanding officer at Canso, divested the 'Justices of the Peace and Civil Magistrates of all Authority.' Armstrong sent Aldridge a strong reprimand for having 'taken upon your Self the entire Management of the Civil as well as the Military affairs.' Apparently, Aldridge had told the angry JPs that he arrogated no more power than Philipps or Armstrong had as the chief authority in Annapolis. Armstrong corrected Aldridge's claim, noting that 'you assume a much Greater power than Either his Excellency or my self Ever pretended to and in making Either of us your precedent in such Respects; I must say ... that you do us injustice.' Aldridge was not to conflate his military authority as the highest-ranking officer at Canso with his civilian authority as the president of the Council there, in which latter capacity he had to heed the advice and decisions of all civilian officers.[45]

Armstrong's strong defence of civilian government against usurpation by military men is ironic when framed against his pay. In 1728 or 1729, Armstrong petitioned the Board of Trade to receive a portion of Philipps's salary, based on the Virginia proviso that if the governor was not resident in the colony then the lieutenant-governor should receive a portion of the governor's salary. Armstrong pointed out that he, and not Philipps, had been serving as governor in Nova Scotia. The Board of Trade referred Armstrong's petition to the entire Privy Council, which concluded that it had no discretion over Philipps's salary. Virginia, which paid its governor from an export duty of two shillings per hogs-

head of tobacco, was the only mainland colony with a permanent revenue for the governor's salary, or the lieutenant-governor's in the
former's absence. Philipps's salary, like the governors' salaries in Bermuda and South Carolina, came from the captaincy of an independent
company of foot, and it was 'Founded on the Establishment of Your Majestys Land Forces ... and not within the Jurisdiction of Your Majestys
Privy Councill.'[46] Without an assembly to raise taxes for the governor or
lieutenant-governor's salary, the men who served in Nova Scotia were
entirely dependent on their military pay. Armstrong received some justice when in 1731 the British government ordered him to return to Nova
Scotia with orders for Philipps's recall to answer charges that he had not
paid the officers in his company. Upon resuming control of the government as lieutenant-governor, Armstrong would receive the governor's
salary.[47]

The problem of how to pay officials of the crown serving in the colonies indicates that the appointment of men with military commissions to
overseas postings had less to do with a desire to militarize the empire
than a desire to run the empire parsimoniously. Commissioned officers
had a salaried, bureaucratic relationship to the metropolitan government, whether they were stationed in London, Hanover, Gibraltar, or
Annapolis Royal. Given the lack of Protestant subjects to serve in an
assembly and vote taxes to pay a governor, and given an absence of metropolitan monies to pay a civilian to be governor, a British colonial government in early-eighteenth-century Nova Scotia would have been
inconceivable without men who were also military officers. The ideological and pecuniary biases in favour of Protestant and self-financing overseas dependencies exaggerated the role of military men in Nova Scotia,
and the men appointed to govern the colony understood the negative
prejudice of that bias. Philipps, Armstrong, and Mascarene were all
acutely aware that the perception that 'martial law prevails here' discouraged settlers from moving to the colony. Despite the hardships of a
shortage of subjects, a monetary deficit, and some military officers who
would have abused their power had they not been checked, the government of Nova Scotia from 1720 to 1749 was more civilian than military in
its ethos and execution.[48]

The problems engendered by the Acadians' refusal to swear an oath
of allegiance have generally been interpreted as ones of security; they
were 'Snakes in [our] Bosoms,' to use Lawrence Armstrong's graphic
phrase.[49] The problem was, however, more fundamental. The lack of
subjects impeded the day-to-day governing of the colony, and in the

minds of most British officials, civil governance was a symbiotic and dia-
letical relationship between the governed and their governors. So long
as Acadians did not swear an oath of allegiance, and so long as they
remained on Nova Scotian soil that could not be granted to Protestant
settlers, a 'proper' civilian government with officials drawn from the
local population could not be established. Land could not be granted or
deeded. Taxes could not be assessed, except for minimal charges. The
Navigation Acts made Acadian trade illegal. And, as Philipps noted, the
presence of subjects in a colony legitimated claims of sovereignty in ways
that treaties and soldiers could not.

The question was, who might become these Nova Scotian subjects?
And how might they be cajoled or, if need be, coerced into this role? In
the minds of British officials, two different groups were possible. The
Acadians could swear an oath of allegiance, which, as noted above, did
make possible the deeding of land. Legally they could not hold public
office, but extra-legally, given the exigencies of the colony, they did.
Protestants, either British or foreign, were preferable, because there
were no legal bars on their participation in government. But they
needed to be persuaded to move to the colony, and the legal and financial constraints on land grants needed to be removed. The Mi'kmaq and
Wulstukwiuk were never mentioned as possible subjects for the purposes of establishing English-style civilian government. In the first
instance, the British wished to achieve amity, in lieu of the open emnity,
with them, with occasional and unresolved discussion about whether
they were 'Friends or Subjects.'[50]

The terms of the Treaty of Utrecht, followed by Queen Anne's letter
to Nicholson, obliged the British government to look first to the Acadians as potential subjects. Since the signing of the terms of capitulation
in 1710, the British had made intermittent attempts to persuade the
Acadians to swear an oath of allegiance. The Acadians, for their part,
became adept equivocators, supported in some measure by the terms of
the capitulation, their treaty rights, Queen Anne's letter, the weakness
of colonial government, and the volatile geopolitics of the northeast.
The first systematic attempt to persuade the Acadians to swear an oath
of allegiance began in 1717, when John Doucett, the new lieutenant-governor under Richard Philipps, arrived in Nova Scotia. Doucett soon
heard the range of Acadian explanations for why they would not swear
an oath of allegiance. The foremost plea was that they were still considering relocating. Some Acadians thought they could move across the
Bay of Fundy to the Passamaquoddy area 'where they Fancy themselves

secure and that there no notice would be taken of them, tho it is still in his Majesty's Dominions.' Doucett, like other officials, looked on these protestations about moving with a jaundiced eye, noting that 'this has been their declaration every Winter for Five or Six Years Past so that wee do not give much Creditt to it.'[51]

Acadians also argued that if they swore an oath of allegiance to the British monarch, they would invite the wrath of the natives. This excuse elicited little sympathy; Doucett noted that if an Indian acts 'insolent in their Houses,' they do not hesitate to throw out the person. Doucett did not know of cases of Mi'kmaq taking revenge on Acadians.[52] On this matter, his scepticism was probably unfounded, given the ongoing tensions between the natives and the British that would not slacken until the mid-1720s. The British believed that the natives were tools of the French, and resisted understanding natives as agents independent of the French and negotiating their own issues. The Acadian response probably does represent their recognition of native autonomy, from the French government and from themselves, despite a long history of trade relations, intermarriage, and at times military alliances.

Rumours, reputedly started by the French priests, provided new rationales for procrastination. After the accession of George I in 1714, a priest working in Nova Scotia reputedly received a letter from France claiming that the 'Pretender was Again Landed in Scotland.' In response to the threat George I had 'sent for Ten thousand French' troops to drive back the Stuart pretender. Upon landing in England, the French troops 'all declared for the Pretender [and] ... Establisht him on the Throne of Great Brittain.' In gratitude, he 'intended to give to the French, all they should ask,' which presumably included Acadia. Doucett rebutted this rumour, telling Peter Mellanson of Minas that 'King George ... is, God be Praise'd, as firm & fixt in the Throne of Great Brittain as Ever Lewis the 14th was in the French Throne.'[53]

In recounting this story to the Board of Trade, Doucett hoped it would not find him 'impertinent,' but wanted to use the incident to ask it to find 'Some Method to Convince these People that their Priests are Fallible.' The story was not entirely far-fetched. Queen Anne had died in 1714, and there had been some uncertainty over her successor. But it was far-fetched that George I, a German prince, would ask the French for military support against the Stuart pretender they had been sheltering since the flight of James II in 1688.[54] A more plausible rumour was that the Acadian right to worship as Catholics and have French priests was a ploy by the British. Their priests reminded them that the British in

Ireland did not allow Catholic priests and also dispossessed Catholic landowners of their real property. This rumour cast doubt on the promise of Queen Anne that the Catholic Acadians could continue to practise their religion and retain their property.

Both sides, Acadian and British, played a waiting game. For the Acadians, if the past were any measure, British governance might well be fleeting. In the first decade after the conquest, governors tried coercion, backed not by force, but by inflated rhetoric and a willingness to let British residents suffer a penalty worse than the one they meted on the Acadians. Nicholson, in his frustration with Acadian obstinacy, banned trade with them, which caused serious deprivation among the troops, who had few alternative sources for most food supplies.[55] Meanwhile the Acadians ate well and smuggled their surpluses to the French in Cape Breton. In the fall of 1717, Doucett, appealing to the Navigation Acts, banned Annapolis River Acadians from trading and fishing. He calculated that by spring and the start of the fishing season, these Acadians would abandon their obdurate position and would swear the oath of allegiance. They did not weaken. These threats depended on some ability to enforce them. With no government vessels to patrol the waters near Annapolis Royal, much less up the Bay of Fundy to Minas Basin or Cobequid, Doucett's pronouncements to the Acadians that it was 'Dangerous ... to Triffle with so Great a Monarch [as George I],' were little more than bluster, and the Acadians surely understood as much.[56]

Richard Philipps's decision, pursuant to his arrival in April 1720, to have the Acadians elect deputies was to give him representatives with whom he could negotiate taking the oath of allegiance. By September, the Acadians had proved 'insolent' rather than compliant, obliging the Council to address the problem 'of the most effectuall way of setling this his Majestys Province.' It recommended telling the metropolitan government that 'more regular fforces [be] sent over here to curb the Insolency's of the present ffrench Inhabitants, and Indians,' a vain request until 1749. More reasonably and immediately, it decided that the five communities of Acadians be allowed to continue to elect deputies who would report to the governor and Council.[57]

Governor Philipps and the Council wrote the King on 27 September 1720 asking for guidance on how to proceed with the problem of making the Acadians subjects, noting that the French priests had told them that their allegiance to France was 'indissoluble,' an interpretation of the bonds of allegiance that was not inconsistent with some legal thought. After rehearsing the impunity with which the Acadians acted, largely because the King's authority scarcely extended beyond firing range of the fort, the governor and council asked for additional troops and matériel, as well as naval vessels for service in Nova Scotian waters.[58]

This letter, in the minds of the governor and council, shifted the responsibility for determining how to proceed in getting the Acadians to become British subjects to the King and his ministers. The following spring (1721) the Acadians living on the Annapolis River petitioned Philipps for permission to sow their fields or leave for Cape Breton. Philipps responded that he was extending the time allowed for them to submit to the British King, that he had written him, and until he had an answer the issue of the oath of allegiance was deferred. This deferral, unless he heard otherwise, protected their property rights.[59] In February 1723, after Philipps had returned to England, the Acadian deputies from Annapolis River presented Doucett with a memorial, along with Philipps's 1721 letter to them, requesting permission to plant their fields. Doucett and the council determined that until they had further notice Philipps's decision stood, and they too would await a royal response.[60]

For the next three years, the issue of the Acadians swearing an oath of allegiance or leaving the colony was moot. The Board of Trade did not respond to Philipps's and the Council's 1720 letter. Peace in Europe, and especially amity with the French, had made the King's ministers complacent about colonial affairs. Relocating the Acadians posed as much of a problem for the British as it did a solution. After the signing of the Treaty of Utrecht, the French began resettling fishers from Placentia, Newfoundland, to Cape Breton. In 1717 they began the building of Louisbourg as a major administrative centre, commercial entrepôt, and naval base. The British recognized that the departure of seasoned French settlers to Cape Breton would be a gift to the French, who had a difficult time recruiting people to go to the colonies. Nova Scotian officials were also concerned that if the Acadians left the colony their lands would have to be quickly resettled and the dikes maintained so that the sea not reclaim its due.

Ongoing tensions with the natives also made peace the most pressing need in the colony, and the governor and Council dealt with little else in the early 1720s. Consequently, concern about an Acadian oath of allegiance receded. Only after 1725 did the question of establishing a civilian population of subjects re-emerge as a regular policy issue for the governor and Council, although by that time the reality of a long-term Anglo–French peace muted the immediate security concerns that the

Acadians had earlier posed. A new campaign to persuade them to swear an oath of allegiance began in 1725 with the appointment of Lawrence Armstrong as lieutenant-governor, who more generally attempted to implement policies that would bring the colony into greater conformity with practices of British colonial governance elsewhere.[61]

When Armstrong arrived back in Annapolis Royal, he began his efforts at getting the Acadians to swear an oath of allegiance with the people living along the Annapolis River. In the 1710s, the Acadians' two main concerns about swearing a British oath of allegiance had been whether they would relocate out of the colony and whether they would invite the retaliation of the natives; both issues had receded by 1726. Their new and persisting concern would be whether they would have to bear arms in future conflicts with the French or natives. Armstrong told them that as Catholics they were prohibited by law from military service so that the issue was irrelevant.[62] But the concern with military service was not so easily dismissed. Armstrong and the Council tried to circumvent the issue by having the Annapolis River Acadians swear an oath of allegiance with the exemption from military service noted in the margin of the French translation, neither part of the oath nor a formal addendum. The governor and council decided on this allowance as a device 'to gett them over by Degrees.'[63]

To administer an oath to the Acadians outside the Annapolis area, Armstrong commissioned Captain Joseph Bennett and Ensign Eramus James Philipps to undertake the task. They reported back in the spring of 1727 that the Acadians had refused to swear the oath of allegiance. A priest, Joseph Ignace, told Philipps that the French and English were at peace and that 'the English Ought not to Trouble and Importune a Parcel of Inhabitants that would live quietly and pay the Taxes Justly required without takeing any Oath.' One Acadian, Baptist Veco, told Philipps that the people at Annapolis River were treated worse than before they had taken the oath, 'their Oxen being worked on the Kings Account Without being paid for them.'[64] The governor and council decided to write 'a Civil Letter' inviting 'them once more' to swear the oath of allegiance. When the Acadians declined the invitation to become subjects of the King of England, the governor and Council decided to bar trade up the bay, though the Annapolis River Acadians were exempted because of the oath they had sworn the previous fall.[65]

The death of George I and the accession of George II precipitated a second attempt in September 1727 to elicit an oath. Armstrong sent orders to the Annapolis River deputies to meet with him to consult on the matter. He discovered that the concessions he had made the previous year had not succeeded in winning them 'over by Degrees.' Rather they requested not just an exemption from military service but more priests besides, a presumption which briefly landed four deputies in jail and which prompted an extension of the trade ban to include them.[66] Armstrong and the Council hired a vessel for £100 and sent Ensign Robert Wroth and a detachment up the Bay of Fundy to proclaim the new king and ask the Acadians and natives to swear an oath of allegiance.[67] The Acadians found Wroth an obliging negotiator, who acceded in writing to their request for an exemption from military service. When he reported back to the Council, it found his concessions 'unwarrantable and dishonourable to His Majestys authority and Government and Consequently Null and Void.' At the same meeting, the Council voted that the Acadians' acknowledgment of George II's 'Title and Authority to and over this Province,' their qualifications notwithstanding, made them eligible for 'the Libertys and Privileges of English Subjects.' In particular, the trade ban that Armstrong had imposed on the Acadians would be lifted and trade between the Acadians and British was once again legal. It was yet another illustration of how difficult it was for the government to sustain any form of coercion.[68]

When Richard Philipps returned to Nova Scotia in 1729, he turned his hand to persuading the Acadians to swear an oath of allegiance that was not prejudiced by concessions. In May 1730 he informed the Council of the 'Submission of the Inhabitants of this Province,' save for 'about Seventeen of those of Chignictou who persist in their obstinancy in refusing to Conform to his Majestys Orders.'[69] Philipps might have made concessions to the Acadians to persuade them to swear an oath of allegiance, but there is no written record if he did. As governor he did not have to report in detail to the council, as had Robert Wroth, Joseph Bennett, and Erasmus James Philipps. The Acadians claimed he had made an oral promise that they would not have to bear arms, a contention that became a serious disagreement after 1749 with the establishment of Halifax and the appointment of a new colonial government.[70] During the 1730s and 1740s, however, officials in Nova Scotia treated the oaths as sufficient for beginning a more systematic, although still unconventional, development of British civilian government.

The lack of an oath had precluded much taxation of the Acadians, leaving the skeletal staff of British officials without funds to run the colony. From the conquest in 1710 to Parliament's 1748 decision to fund the building of Halifax, Nova Scotia's officials pleaded with London to finance the most basic needs of colonial government. The lack of a vessel to survey the coast, communicate with other communities, regulate trade, and protect the fishery meant that 'a Governor can be accountable for no more then [*sic*] the spott he happens to reside on.'[71] By the mid-1720s the ramparts at the fort at Annapolis Royal lay 'level with the Ground in Breaches sufficiently wide for fifty men to enter a breast.'[72] Without an assembly to vote taxes there was no way to raise money in an emergency 'tho' it were but a Shilling and its safety depended on it.'[73] The metropolitan government wanted British settlers in Nova Scotia, but before a governor could grant land the woods had to be surveyed 'for the Preservation of the Woods, which are necessary for the Service of the Royal Navy.'[74] Board of Trade missives that impressed upon Nova Scotia officials the need to preserve naval stores and to settle British subjects elicited responses that stated the obvious: without money to pay a surveyor, the land would remain unused by the navy and ungranted to British settlers.[75]

The unwillingness of the metropolitan government to fund the Nova Scotian government lent urgency to the swearing of an oath by the Acadians. Acadian acceptance of British subjecthood would allow some taxation and hopefully greater Acadian participation in government. Lawrence Armstrong recommended in 1728 that plans for persuading the Acadians to swear an oath of allegiance include posting a garrison on the isthmus. It would allow some oversight of communications between natives in the eastern and western portions of the colony and allow the regulation of the trade throughout the Bay of Fundy. A small garrison, Armstrong reckoned, would not cost more than £1000, 'which those Inhabitants (when subjected) are rich. enough to make good.'[76] This infrastructure, however, required an initial investment by the metropolitan government, without which the revenues from the Acadians could not be collected.

Governor Philipps and his lieutenant-governors repeatedly enjoined the Board of Trade to invest in the colony's infrastructure, arguing that the enhanced collection of trade revenues would justify the expense. Among Philipps's initial critiques of Nova Scotia in 1720 was that New Englanders nearly monopolized the trade, but paid no impost towards the maintenance of the government. Upon returning to Nova Scotia in 1729, he recommended fortifying Canso and levying duties on the fish trade, which, he predicted, would generate a colonial revenue second only to the duties collected on the export of tobacco from Virginia, and would exceed the expense of fortifying Canso. The safety of the province, he reminded the Board of Trade, depended on continued peace with France, without which Annapolis Royal and Canso were extremely vulnerable. To recover those settlements if lost would be far more than the outlay for proper regulation and taxing of the fish trade.[77] Colonial officials cautioned the Board of Trade against putting too much emphasis on the collection of quitrents and not on the collection of duties from trade. Quitrents, they believed, would only generate limited revenues; rents collected in the 1730s produced between £10 and £15 annually.[78] Armstrong told the Board of Trade that a quitrent of a penny per acre per annum was too high for the quality of the land, particularly in comparison with neighbouring colonies, and would discourage British or foreign Protestant settlers from moving into the colony.[79]

Reports to Whitehall also emphasized how the financial weaknesses of Nova Scotia's government encouraged the violation of the crown's normal prerogative, particularly by New Englanders. In 1720, Philipps reported that New Englanders regularly took coal from the upper part of the Bay of Fundy, and he was powerless to regulate it in any way.[80] New England traders were frequently cited as agitators among the Acadians. Armstrong reported that William Gamble of Boston, formerly a lieutenant in the army, had told the Acadians not to take the oath of allegiance. In this instance, the issue seemed to have been a power struggle between Alexander Cosby and Armstrong, with Gamble telling the Acadians that Cosby would soon replace Armstrong as lieutenant-governor.[81] As Armstrong tried to explain to the Board of Trade, 'if His Majesty's British Subjects are Suffered to treat his Council with such Indignity and Contempt what can we expect from the French?'[82] The lack of financial resources meant that New Englanders, Acadians, and natives could flout with impunity the authority of the royal government sitting in Annapolis Royal.

Colonial officials believed that the underfunding of government kept the Acadians from swearing an oath of allegiance. Armstrong noted that the 'Lenity' of government encouraged Acadians to stall. Under his commission, he could inflict few penalties. He could prohibit them from fishing, but the Acadians were willing to bear the losses 'in hopes of some Speedy Revolution or Change of Government.'[83] In July 1727 Armstrong barred trade up the Bay of Fundy, on the basis that the Acadians were not subjects and therefore any trade with them was in violation of the Navigation Acts. His proclamation prohibited 'English' subjects from trading with the 'French,' which incensed New Englanders. Thomas Lechmere, Britain's surveyor general for North America, wrote the Board of Trade complaining about the prohibition and asking it to override Armstrong and reopen the trade.[84]

Lack of funds also jeopardized attempts to stabilize relations with natives. Beginning in the 1710s, officials in Nova Scotia repeatedly told the Board of Trade that gift-giving in negotiations with the natives was not discretionary. John Doucett informed the Board of Trade in 1718 that gifts were necessary if the natives were to remain friends of the English. He believed that 'the Generality of the Indians would be Sway'd more by the benefitts they receive in this World then trust to all Benefitts their Priests can tell them they will receive in the [next].'[85] Philipps, in contrast, was 'convinced that a hundred thousand [pounds] will not buy them from the French Interest while their priests are among them.' Nevertheless, gift-giving could not be avoided and Philipps had spent £150 on sundry presents that he had distributed in his negotiations with the natives in 1720.[86] When finalizing treaties with the Natives in the mid-1720s, Doucett spent £300 of his own money on gifts.[87] Despite abundant evidence that could demonstrate that regular gift-giving was both important and cost-effective in establishing British–native relations, it never became routinely funded.

From the perspective of Nova Scotia, Parliament's 1748 decision to fund the building of a northern American naval port on Chebucto Bay was almost too much government and too much money too late. The establishment of Halifax was only tangentially related to the colony's internal needs. Rather it spatially represented the convergence of a number of structural stresses in the empire that had been building over the eighteenth century and metropolitan strategies for handling them. The longstanding problems of Nova Scotia were subsumed under new imperial-level policy, but that meant that the solutions were not necessarily tailored to specific colony-level needs. At the end of the War of the Austrian Succession, Britain faced the problem of how to address the circumstances that had produced its desultory military performance in the war. Both the Ministry and Parliament believed that the Treaty of Aix-la-Chapelle (1748) had created a hiatus in fighting, rather than long-term peace, and it would be but a few years before unresolved problems in both Europe and the extra-European world would produce armed conflict. The British were already planning that in the next war territorial objectives would assume an importance that they had not had in the War of the Austrian Succession (1740–8) when commercial objectives had been paramount. Nova Scotia was just one of many points of territorial tension with other imperial powers: Canada, Rupert's Land, the trans-Appalachian West, Florida, the Caribbean, and Central America were all sites of actual or potential conflict. The building of Halifax was to prepare for hemisphere-wide conflict, a northern extension of naval bases that stretched from Jamaica to Antigua to Bermuda to Nova Scotia.[88]

For nearly four decades, British officials in Nova Scotia had attempted to make the Board of Trade understand that the poor articulation between metropolitan policy and colonial conditions posed serious long-term problems and had to be rectified. Within the colony, officials recognized that resolving local problems would also resolve imperial problems. A better infrastructure would have allowed for the generation of more revenue and allowed a more systematic surveying of the land for both naval stores and grants to settlers. More government presence might have convinced the Acadians that the British were serious about keeping the colony. As well, it might have made Nova Scotia more attractive for British settlers. Colonial officials knew that the undetermined boundaries between France and British territory, whether on the west side of the Bay of Fundy or along the Canso Strait, would eventually become volatile if not addressed in peacetime. But as Richard Philipps told the Board of Trade in a 1730 communique, 'I am only the Watchman to call and Point out the danger, tis with Your Lordships to get it prevented.'[89]

The building of Halifax did not resolve the problem of the articulation between colonial needs and metropolitan policy, but in an immediate sense made the situation worse, particularly for the Acadians and natives. The escalation of Anglo–French competition privileged imperial needs at the expense of colonial needs. By shifting the seat of the government from Annapolis Royal to Halifax and appointing a new cohort of colonial officials, the metropolitan government eliminated, albeit unwittingly, the internal articulation between British officials, Acadians, and natives, both Mi'kmaq and Wulstukwiuk, that the old regime had crafted over the decades. In so doing, it destroyed an ambiguous but nonetheless shared past, and thus exacerbated the conflict between British officials, Acadians, and natives over the relationship between the past, present, and the future of Nova Scotia and their respective places in it.

The persistent endeavours by the French government to press its interest in Nova Scotia accelerated after 1748. Capitalizing on the ambiguity of the boundary between Nova Scotia and Canada, the French built Fort Beauséjour on the Isthmus of Chignecto. They encouraged –

or forced, in some cases – Acadians to move across the Missaguash River, which the French had asserted was their eastern boundary. To resolve the dispute state-to-state the French and British convened a commission to determine the boundary, while in North America, British officials in Nova Scotia built Fort Lawrence just east of the Missaguash and stepped up their pressure on the Acadians to swear an unqualified oath of allegiance. In the meantime, the Mi'kmaq protested the British decision to establish settlements and forts without consulting the people whose land it was. They attempted to resolve their differences through both face-to-face meetings with British officials and with attacks on new settlements in Chebucto Bay, Mahone Bay, and Minas Basin. British officials in Nova Scotia had little intention of negotiating with native peoples whom they deemed to be subjects in rebellion against the crown rather than autonomous nations. Instead, the governor accelerated tensions by authorizing attacks on the Mi'kmaq and offering bounties for their scalps.[90]

In 1755, British troops attacked and seized Fort Beauséjour and in its aftermath began deporting the Acadians, a policy that would continue until 1762. With an unprecedented deployment of soldiers and sailors, the British took Louisbourg in 1758 before moving down the St Lawrence River to defeat the French at Quebec (1759) and Montreal (1760). With the deportation of the Acadians and the defeat of the French at Louisbourg, British officials again recruited Protestant settlers for Nova Scotia. In October 1758, the governor of Nova Scotia, Charles Lawrence, issued a proclamation inviting New Englanders to move to the colony, a decision that further provoked the Mi'kmaq on whose lands these new settlers would plant themselves. When New England agents visited potential town sites they found themselves confronted by militant Mi'kmaq, whose objections delayed the arrival of settlers from 1759 to 1760 and forced the British into another round of treaty negotiations that allowed for settlements on the west side of peninsular Nova Scotia.

With the end of the Seven Years' War and the Treaty of Paris in 1763, the Anglo–French imperial struggle in North America came to an end. The problems of the British empire, however, did not. To some extent, the tortuous process of accommodation that had characterized Nova Scotia since the conquest of Port Royal had left a legacy of newly crafted methods for adapting to the multiethnic empire that now existed on an even larger scale and demanded constitutional accommodation.[91] This was seen in such specific contexts as the adoption of the exact wording of Philipps's 1719 instructions regarding British–native relations – hitherto unique to Nova Scotia, and renewed in instructions to all subsequent Nova Scotia governors until 1773 – to the new Province of Quebec. Quebec governors (and those of East Florida, West Florida, and, with alterations, Grenada) were now enjoined to maintain with native inhabitants 'a strict friendship and good correspondence, so that they may be induced by degrees not only to be good neighbors to our subjects but likewise themselves to become good subjects to us.'[92] More generally, the metropolitan government realized that in its new colonies it could not pretend that they would soon have a natural subject population, English institutions of government, and locally generated financial resources to fund the government. Rather, resources had to be provided to facilitate the transition to a more accommodating form of British government, a logic that eventually found explicit parliamentary expression in the Quebec Act of 1774.

Yet, in other contexts, the problem of weak articulation between metropolitan policy and North American conditions persisted. Again, this administrative disjunction was specifically seen in such situations as General Jeffery Amherst's ill-judged decision in 1760 to eliminate further gift-giving to First Nations, contributing directly to Pontiac's insurgency in 1763. More generally, this same disjunction led frustrated British officials in the Thirteen Colonies to attempt to use coercion to resolve problems. Civil war was the result, and it is well known that the second Treaty of Paris in 1783 left British North America a much smaller place. The experience of Nova Scotia during the four decades following the conquest of Port Royal was not enough to equip contemporaries to salvage very much of the First British Empire. In enabling historians to delineate the empire's difficulties more than two centuries too late, however, the Nova Scotia experience is just the right diagnostic.

Conclusion

John G. Reid, Maurice Basque, Elizabeth Mancke,
Barry Moody, Geoffrey Plank, and William Wicken

The conquest of Acadia is an intensely revealing episode in the early modern history of northeastern North America. When viewed from appropriate perspectives, it emerges as an event with complexities that fall into identifiable patterns of interaction among imperial, colonial, and native interests.

The conquest was no simple event, although at a certain level it can be seen as such. Nicholson's marines trudging through the marsh mud; the Union flag raised at the fort; Subercase's gallant *au revoir:* these are valid images in the construction of the conquest as a military incident within the well-known imperial struggle between France and Great Britain in North America. By extension, the conquest can also be regarded – as historians of the twentieth century so often did – as a precursor of subsequent developments. The Acadian expulsion and the conquest of Canada followed several decades later. Depending on one's perspective, it can be argued with reasonable conviction either that the conquest of Acadia was significant primarily as a steppingstone to the even greater transfigurations of the mid-eighteenth century, or that the conquest and the Treaty of Utrecht combined to form the seminal event that allowed these important but essentially derivative later changes to occur.

Yet this study is not primarily designed to address these arguments. Since the book is predicated in part on the belief that the conquest of Acadia as a geopolitical event has not received its fair share of historical recognition, the event and its place in broader geopolitical currents inevitably receive attention from time to time. The authors' main preoccupation, however, is with delineating – through the historical lens the conquest provides – societal conflicts and crosscurrents that were characteristic of the troubled human experience of the northeast in this era.

Even when considered as an event in an apparently straightforward geopolitical context, the conquest defies simplistic interpretation. It was, of course, an episode in a lengthy war and an even lengthier imperial struggle between rival powers in western Europe. For New Englanders, it was also a satisfying chastisement of the treacherous nest of raiders and privateers that Port Royal represented for them. For the Acadian colonial population, the conquest could readily be incorporated into the pragmatic though untidy strategies that already informed the actions of leading families, and had done so with especial urgency since the raid by Sir William Phips's New England forces in 1690. For the Mi'kmaq, it continued an unsurprising series of European reversals at Port Royal, significant enough to warrant diplomatic overtures to the newcomers as winter set in, but in the meantime hardly sufficient to divert the attention of Antoine Tecouenamac and others from the harvesting and preservation of essential food supplies. There was no single narrative of the unfolding of the autumn of 1710 in Mi'kma'ki/Acadia/Nova Scotia, but there were different ones of equal validity to the respective contemporaries who recounted them.

In historical perspective, the conquest of Acadia created a delicate equilibrium. Translated through the European diplomacy that created the Treaty of Utrecht and then through more localized processes of negotiation, it offered a framework within which Mi'kma'ki, Acadia, and Nova Scotia might coexist. Within the territories that are central to this study, a crucial degree of geographical separation prevailed. Most territory remained the preserve of the Mi'kmaq. They supplemented their fishing and hunting economy by trade relations with both Acadians and New Englanders. Acadian settlements fronted on portions of the Bay of Fundy, with its inlets and marshlands. The agricultural and population expansion that Naomi Griffiths has defined as the Acadian 'Golden Age'[1] formed the backdrop not only for the murkier currents of French–British tension but also for the 'third Acadia' of familial manoeuvring for position. The British Nova Scotia that had begun tentatively in 1710 was built around, and partially in opposition to, these two preexisting geographies. While the British presence at Canso depended on the arrival of summer fishing fleets more than on the small resident population, the British experience at Annapolis Royal in this period was essentially urban. The town's cosmopolitan daytime appearance, its streets characterized by ethnic and social diversity, denoted a trading centre. The leading officers of the garrison attempted, even though with limited success, to generate institutions that could provide civil rather than military government and offer at least dispute resolution to non-British inhabitants. Their physical separation from those inhabitants, however, was clear. Even in the immediate vicinity of Annapolis, the exodus of Acadians from the town proper had left it – by night at least – as a British enclave.

Until 1744, coexistence was largely though not continuously peaceful, and negotiation the favoured safeguard against destructive frictions. Negotiation governed the processes of adjustment that occupied the first decade following the conquest. After the British–Mi'kmaq hostilities of 1722–5, negotiations led to the series of treaties between 1725 and 1728 that reconciled the British crown and its colonies with northeastern aboriginal peoples. Negotiations translated the convoluted question of the Acadian oath of allegiance into an apparently promising modus vivendi by 1730.

Nevertheless, elements of these relationships remained actually or potentially destabilizing. One uncertainty concerned the future directions to be taken by the imperial powers. Following the conquest, the old patterns of elite co-option by which imperial authority in the region had been delegated during the seventeenth century were decisively swept away in an institutional sense. Direct imperial rule followed at both Annapolis Royal and Louisbourg. There were, however, mitigating forces. British neglect of Nova Scotia, and the colony's chronically tenuous financial status, severely limited the ability of colonial officials to behave in an aggressive or authoritarian manner vis-à-vis the non-British inhabitants of Nova Scotia's claimed territory. This handicap reflected, in part, the inherently unsystematic apparatus of the state, as well as the parsimony of Walpole's regime, although it was also in harmony with Philipps's clear instruction to use friendly persuasion to bring Mi'kmaq inhabitants within the British sphere. The recognition of Acadian deputies by Annapolis Royal officials represented, among other things, a localized form of elite co-option in the interests of circumventing the inherent difficulties of British governance of a Catholic and non-British population. In the short term, even the Board of Trade was willing to countenance a temperate approach towards the deputies and the Acadian communities they represented. For the French at Louisbourg, there were also limitations. For all the conflicting imperial interests of the British and French in North America that persisted despite the Treaty of Utrecht, the period from 1716 to 1731 was one of diplomatic reconciliation between the two powers,[2] and restraint was the order of the day.

The difficulty, of course, lay in the possibility that efforts at imperial expansion might at some point be resumed. The double diplomacy that preserved the understanding between British and Mi'kmaq had inbuilt ambiguities. Should British encroachment on Mi'kmaq territory be resumed, the ambiguities could easily break down into outright conflict. Following the conquest, the principal leaders and elders of the Mi'kmaq had necessarily sensitized themselves to the need for alliance as a measure of insurance against British expansion. No longer, as had been true even in the decade or so following the fall of Port Royal, could the Mi'kmaq assume that their denial of permission to encroach – backed up if necessary by a sharp rebuke – would keep the colonial presence within its proper limits. Their identification with Wabanaki allies, as in the context of the Kennebec confrontation of 1721, combined with increasing contacts with Governor Saint-Ovide to underline the Mi'kmaq ability to counter British territorial aspirations with more sustained and calculated force than in the past. Potential Acadian responses to British pressures, meanwhile, had their own elements of instability. The strategy of neutrality corresponded satisfactorily with the negotiating styles of Annapolis Royal officials of the 1720s, 1730s, and early 1740s. Acadian elders and deputies got along well enough with the likes of Wroth, Armstrong, Mascarene, and Philipps. The resumption of French–British warfare in 1744 and the militarization of the region that followed the peace of Aix-la-Chapelle in 1748, however, raised the possibility that the francophile and anglophile tendencies of substantial Acadian minorities, instead of being, as hitherto, the bookends of neutrality, would become powerful centrifugal forces. And throughout it all, the external influence of Massachusetts was another unpredictable force, capable of generating violent interventions in Nova Scotia and of fanning the flames of anti-British grievance among the non-British peoples.

Until 1748, there was room for real uncertainty as to the future patterns for Mi'kma'ki/Acadia/Nova Scotia. It was not clear whether the unorthodox, negotiated modus vivendi that had emerged after the conquest would prove to be the beginning of a long and evolutionary process or a mere short-term conjuncture. The uncertainty soon dissipated after the signing at Aix-la-Chapelle. French and British militarization, the armed (though contested) British occupation without Mi'kmaq assent of territory at Chebucto (Halifax, as imperial officials now insisted on calling it), and the *grand dérangement*: all indicated that the old coexistences had been displaced by an official culture of violence, just as surely as the Annapolis Royal regime had faded away with the retirement of its last senior figure, Paul Mascarene. For a time the Mi'kmaq retained the military capacity to take the initiative when necessary, outside of Halifax at least, even after the French alliance had succumbed to France's overall defeat in North America. As late as 1768, Lord William Campbell, as governor of Nova Scotia, reported to London from Halifax that the Mi'kmaq remained fully able to 'bring fire and Destruction to the very entrance of this Town.'[3] Hence the ability of the Mi'kmaq, and the Wulstukwiuk, repeatedly to bring the British to the treaty-making table throughout most of the eighteenth century. Yet the arrival of some 35,000 Loyalist refugees in 1783 and 1784 finally created an imbalance of population so great that encroachment on native lands increased exponentially, military resistance became impossible, and even treaty promises faded into eclipse for two centuries. In that perspective, the unusual balances of the postconquest era had indeed proved to be conjunctural.

Yet the conquest of Acadia, and the fragile equilibrium that followed it, do speak eloquently about deeper currents and more extended chronologies. As the twenty-first century begins, historiography has begun to move away from the tendency to view colonial settlement and imperial hegemony as normative in eighteenth-century northeastern North America prior to the Revolutionary era. Instead, as Alan Taylor has recently observed of Maine, geographical areas previously dismissed as peripheral can now emerge historiographically as 'more representative of a North American history reimagined in its diverse fluidity.'[4] Mi'kma'ki/Acadia/ Nova Scotia in the wake of the conquest accommodated three separate populations. Each had interconnections with the others, and each of the relationships was a negotiated one. In population terms, the British presence was by far the smallest. Paradoxically, the fiction of a British colony of Nova Scotia extending beyond Canso and Annapolis Royal had necessarily to be maintained through accommodations with Mi'kmaq and Acadians that effectively ensured that the real Nova Scotia could only be constructed on the basis of a tacitly observed nonencroachment outside of those enclaves. By the standards of southern New England or the lower Hudson Valley, it was an oddity indeed that non-British populations should collectively wield such power and influence. By the standards of the territory between the Penobscot and the Wulstukw rivers, or the Hudson Valley above Fort Albany, or (on a larger scale and in a French imperial context) the *pays d'en haut*, it was less so; and by the standards of European trade-driven enclaves in Africa and Asia, it was ordinary enough that nonencroachment and negotiated relationships should prevail – although in all of these contexts it was atypical that a colonial population of a third national origin should be involved.

By any standards at all, it was precisely the unusual elements of Mi'kma'ki/Acadia/Nova Scotia that made it a virtual laboratory for cultural and political realignment in the Atlantic world. It was not, of course, a laboratory in any sterile, scientific sense. This laboratory was created by the sweat, blood, and lost lives of people making their way as best they could. Yet the conquest of Acadia created, for almost four decades, a hybrid. The product of Mi'kmaq toleration, Acadian accommodation, and the haphazard extension of European state formation, none of its individual elements was unique in the history of the early modern world, or even of the early modern Atlantic world. In combination, however, they brought imperial goals into uncommon juxtaposition with native and colonial societies. Thus imperial officials were forced to grapple with first principles in their efforts to build a civil, Anglican society in an imperial context, but to do so in a daily climate where the fiction of British control and the double diplomacy that underwrote it created endless ambiguities in dealings with both Mi'kmaq and Acadians. Thus too the troubled legacy of Acadian leaders whose strategy of neutrality could never entirely bridge the divisions arising from the francophile or anglophile orientations of certain influential families – divisions which would assume even greater significance after 1748, as the Acadian borderland moved ever closer to becoming, to adopt the definition of Jeremy Adelman and Stephen Aron, a 'bordered land' with more rigid boundaries and allegiances.[5] Thus, finally and most influentially, the aboriginal nations negotiated alliances among themselves and adopted a specific treaty-making diplomacy, because the Mi'kmaq controlled most of the territory and much of the military power, partly – though far from exclusively – through French support from Louisbourg.

In the final analysis, the conquest of Acadia offers two salient general insights regarding early modern northeastern North America. The first is the bankruptcy of the notion that this period in history was the 'colonial' era. Colonies existed, but they existed in relationship to imperial and native worlds that interacted with each other as well as with colonial populations. Influences ran in multiple directions, making complex rather than simple patterns. Second, the experience of Mi'kma'ki/Acadia/Nova Scotia, by conforming neither with the accepted pattern of a colony of settlement nor with that of a 'middle ground,'[6] provides the historian with an intermediate model. Here, European settlement existed and so did imperial institutions of governance. The Acadian communities, however, represented a form of settlement that had become divorced from state formation and from formal imperial expansion. The institutions at Annapolis Royal, meanwhile, had limited importance beyond the town itself. As imperial, colonial, and native influences vied with one another in northeastern North America, the results could range from the extreme represented by the colony of settlement to the other extreme represented by the 'middle ground.' The differences, however, are best represented by a continuum, just as the differences between European commercial exploitation and colonization in North America in the seventeenth century should also be so portrayed. Thus, conjunctural as it was in a linear sense, the experience of Mi'kma'ki/Acadia/Nova Scotia in the wake of the conquest exposes a hitherto-underexplored dimension of northeastern North American history. It is one that becomes accessible to historians only when its different narratives are juxtaposed.

Notes

Introduction

1 During the eighteenth century, the Julian (Old Style) calendar was in force in Great Britain until 1752, when it was replaced by the Gregorian (New Style) calendar. The Gregorian calendar had been used in France since the sixteenth century. Thus, during the period with which this book principally deals, British and French dates were eleven days apart. The date of the capitulation of Port Royal was 5 October (O.S.) and 16 October (N.S.) In this study, dates are rendered in the style appropriate to the source cited, except in instances where confusion might be created, as in treatments of diplomatic interactions. In such cases, the Gregorian calendar dates will be used.

2 While population figures are notoriously difficult to gauge with accuracy, these estimates are based in part on Bock, 'Micmac,' 117; Erickson, 'Maliseet-Passamaquoddy,' 125–6; Snow, 'Eastern Abenaki,' 145. Also useful in estimating Mi'kmaq population is the somewhat later census count in Recensement fait les sauvages portant les armes, 1735, France, Archives des Colonies (hereafter AC), C11D, 9, 76.

3 Clark, *Acadia*, 129–30, 201–12.

4 See Rawlyk, '1720–1744: Cod, Louisbourg, and the Acadians,' 108.

5 Treaty of Utrecht, 11 April 1713, in Parry, ed., *Consolidated Treaty Series*, XXVII, 485. Authors' translations: 'Nova Scotia otherwise known as Acadia'; 'in its entirety, according to its ancient limits, as also ... the town of Port-Royal, now known as Annapolis Royal, and in general ... all that depends upon the said territories and islands of that country.'

6 Address of the Governor, Council, and Assembly of the Massachusetts Bay to

the Queen, 11 November 1710, Great Britain, Public Record Office (hereafter PRO), CO5/10, no. 138; Pontchartrain to François de Beauharnois de
la Chaussaye, 24 December 1710, AC, B, vol. 32, 508. Authors' translation:
'I think continually about ways in which this important post could be retaken
before the English are securely established there.'

7 See Braudel, *Écrits sur l'histoire*, esp. 112–15.
8 See Countryman, 'Indians, the Colonial Order, and the Social Significance
of the American Revolution'; Greene, *Negotiated Authorities*; Greene, *Peripheries and Center*; White, *The Middle Ground*.
9 Bayly, *Imperial Meridian*; Bosher, *The Canada Merchants*; Bowen, *Elites, Enterprise and the Making of the British Overseas Empire*; Bowen, 'British Conceptions
of Global Empire'; Canny, 'Writing Atlantic History'; Canny, ed., *The Origins
of Empire*; P.J. Marshall, 'Empire and Authority in the Later Eighteenth Century'; Marshall, ed., *The Eighteenth Century*.
10 See the bibliography, below, for relevant works by Basque, Mancke, Moody,
Plank, Reid, and Wicken.
11 Young and Dickinson, *A Short History of Quebec*, 56–8; Hautecoeur, *L'Acadie du
discours*, passim.
12 Samuel Vetch to Board of Trade, 27 July 1708, PRO, CO323/6, no. 64; see
also Alsop, 'Samuel Vetch's "Canada Survey'd."'
13 Osgood, *The American Colonies in the Eighteenth Century*, I, 437–9.
14 Frégault, 'L'Èmpire britannique et la conquête du Canada,' 164 and passim.
Authors' translation: 'a French colony had fallen into the hands of the
English empire, never to re-emerge.'
15 Frégault, 'La Déportation des Acadiens,' 309.
16 Bernard, *Histoire de l'Acadie*, 25. Authors' translation: 'the three essentials of
any durable society – religion, family, and property – existed in Acadia from
the beginning, and formed the basis of its ethnic development.'
17 Bernard, *Le drame acadien depuis 1604*, 245. Authors' translation: 'continued
to sustain the little French creation of Acadia.' While Bernard argued that
Acadians had no desire to leave their lands, an example of the case for British obstruction can be found in Casgrain, *Un pèlerinage au pays d'Évangéline*,
60, 112–13. See also Lauvrière, *La tragédie d'un peuple*, esp. I, 181–2. On the
relation of these portrayals to Longfellow's *Evangeline*, see Griffiths, 'Longfellow's *Evangeline*'; Taylor, *Promoters, Patriots, and Partisans*, 187–9.
18 Gipson, *The British Empire before the American Revolution*, V, 169; Clark, *Acadia*,
105, 138, 190.
19 Letter of Joseph Dudley, Samuel Vetch, and John Moody, 25 October 1709,
PRO, CO5/9, no. 33.
20 Hutchinson, *The History of the Colony and Province of Massachusetts Bay*, II,

137–8; Murdoch, *A History of Nova Scotia or Acadie*, II, 309, 320. For related accounts, see also Haliburton, *An Historical and Statistical Account of Nova-Scotia*, I, 91–2; Campbell, *Nova Scotia in Its Historical, Mercantile and Industrial Relations*, 72–4, 123–4. For a wider context, see Taylor, *Promoters, Patriots, and Partisans*, 44–83, 181–230.

21 Brebner, *New England's Outpost*, 56 and passim.

22 Lanctôt, 'L'Acadie et la Nouvelle-Angleterre, 1603–1763,' 352–3. Authors' translation: 'When all is said and done, in spite of the new flag and the new garrison, Acadia hardly changed at all.'

23 Ibid., 354. Authors' translation: 'a slight enough victory in economic and political terms.'

24 Brebner, *New England's Outpost*, 67.

25 Rawlyk, *Nova Scotia's Massachusetts*, xv–xvi and passim.

26 Chard, 'The Impact of French Privateering on New England, 1689–1713,' 162–5; see also Chard, '"Pagans," Privateers, and Propagandists.'

27 Chard, 'Canso, 1710–1721,' 72; see also Chard, 'The Impact of Île Royale on New England, 1713–1763.'

28 Steele, *Warpaths*, 158; Alsop, 'The Age of the Projectors,' 30–53; Alsop, 'Samuel Vetch's "Canada Survey'd,"' esp. 56–8.

29 Sauvageau, *Acadie*, 147–56, 165–70. Authors' translation: 'the hundred years' war of the French in America.' See also the review and related correspondence in La Société historique acadienne, *Les Cahiers* 19 (1988), 162–7; 20 (1989), 196–207; 21 (1990), 49–50.

30 Barnes, '"The Dayly Cry for Justice"'; see also Barnes, '"Twelve Apostles" or a Dozen Traitors?'

31 Daigle, 'Nos amis les ennemis,' 184–98 and passim.

32 Godfrey, *Pursuit of Profit and Preferment in Colonial North America*, 1–3.

33 Hynes, 'Some Aspects of the Demography of Port Royal.'

34 Choquette, *Frenchmen into Peasants*, esp. 21, 287–90.

35 Pothier, 'Acadian Emigration to Île Royale after the Conquest of Acadia.'

36 LaPlante, 'Pourquoi les Acadiens sont-ils demeurés en Acadie?'

37 Griffiths, *The Acadians: Creation of a People*, 19–23.

38 Griffiths, *The Contexts of Acadian History*, esp. 35–6; see also Griffiths, 'The Golden Age.'

39 Upton, *Micmacs and Colonists*, 31.

40 Dickason, 'Louisbourg and the Indians: A Study in Imperial Race Relations, 1713–1760,' 3–130 passim.

41 Dickason, *Canada's First Nations*, 106–12, 159–62; see also Dickason, 'La "guerre navale" des Micmacs contre les Britanniques, 1713–1763,' 233–48.

42 Paul, *We Were Not the Savages*, 63–7.

1 The 'Conquest' of Acadia: Narratives

1 Massachusetts Historical Society (hereafter MHS), Miscellaneous Bound, 1706–1713 [October 1710]. This translation was anonymously made from Samuel Sewall's Latin original. The original is in MHS, Sewall Papers, Letterbook, 1687–1737, 222:

ANNA Nicholsonum Bostonam visere jussit,
  Ne sit vicinis præda voranda suis.
Advolat extemplò, valida comitante caterva;
  Prodigus Is vitæ, prodigus æris erat.
Matthæaeus ceteris præcurrit claudere portum;
  Terribilis tandem bellica classis adit.
Quam bene Franciscus Francos depellit iniquos!
  Hinc Gallicinium cessat abesse malum.
Subercassus enim cecidit, moderamine cassus,
  Et leve festinat Suber adire domum.
Rectorem agnoscit proprium Nova Scotia Scotum,
  Vetchus et Hobbæus parta tuentur ibi.
Est decimus pariter septingentesimus Annus,
  Portum Regalem possidet ANNA suum.
[Oblinet Europa sosiales ANNA triumphos
  In partes illic lubrica fama fugit
Adjuvat Orbe Novo Franciscum nullus amicus
  Ut detur domine gloria tota suæ]
Semper opus firmum præestes, mitissime CHRISTE,
  Et tua sit pennis tecta columba tuis.

The bracketed portion was included in the version used for the translation (MHS, Miscellaneous Bound, 1706–1713 [October 1710]), the initials 'SS' indicating that Sewall was the author of the insertion as well as of the original version entered in his letterbook. The letterbook also contained a different translation that had reached Sewall in late November 1710, apparently from the hand of the prominent minister Simon Willard. MHS, Sewall Papers, Letterbook, 1687–1737, 226–7.

2 Sewall to Nicholson, 31 October 1710, MHS, Sewall Papers, Letterbook, 1686–1737, 222.

3 Ibid.

4 *The Diary of Samuel Sewall, 1674–1729*, II: *1709–1729*, 15 July 1710, 639–40; Letter of Francis Nicholson, 16 May 1710, Great Britain, Public Record Office (hereafter PRO), CO5/9, no. 59.

5 Instructions, 18 March 1710, in 'Journal of Colonel Nicholson at the Capture of Annapolis, 1710,' *Report and Collections of the Nova Scotia Historical Society, for the year 1878*, vol. I (Halifax, 1879; hereafter *NSHS Collections*, I), 60.

6 John Usher to Board of Trade [28 June 1708], PRO, CO5/864, no. 225. See also John Redknap to Board of Trade, 20 February 1708, ibid., no. 233; and An Account of the Expedition to Port Royal, May–June 1707, ibid., no. 225 (iii).

7 Joseph Dudley, Francis Nicholson, Samuel Vetch, and John Moody to the Earl of Sunderland, 24 October 1709, PRO, CO5/9, no. 32; Alsop, 'Samuel Vetch's "Canada Survey'd,"' 47–58.

8 Resolution of Massachusetts House of Representatives, 27 October 1709, PRO, CO5/9, no. 30.

9 Letter of Nicholson, 16 May 1710, PRO, CO5/9, no. 59; Muster Rolls, ibid., no. 61.

10 Vetch to [Sunderland], 15 May 1710, PRO, CO5/9, no. 54; Chard, 'The Impact of French Privateering on New England,' 160–2.

11 Black, 'Introduction,' in Black and Woodfine, eds., *The British Navy and the Use of Naval Power in the Eighteenth Century*, 8; also Baker and Reid, *The New England Knight*, ch. 5.

12 Minister to Subercase, 20 May 1710, AC, B, vol. 32, 354. Author's translation: 'it seems that you do not have much to fear from them.'

13 Subercase to the minister, 3 January 1710, AC, C11D, vol. 7, 42. Author's translation: 'I fear that the past may be a lesson to them for the future and that they may profit from their mistakes.'

14 Ibid., 50. See also Simon-Pierre Denys de Bonaventure to the minister, 24 December 1706, AC, C11D, vol. 5, 246; Subercase to the minister, 20 December 1708, ibid., vol. 6, 168–9.

15 Deposition of Simon Slocomb, 8 August 1710, Massachusetts Archives (hereafter MA), vol. 38A, 8–10.

16 Nicholson to [Dartmouth], 16 September 1710, PRO, CO5/9, no. 65; Increase Mather to Samuel Penhallow, 22 May 1710, MHS, Belknap Papers, vol. 1, no. 41.

17 Instructions to Viscount Shannon, 13 July 1710, PRO, CO5/9, no. 64; Dartmouth to Dudley, 31 August 1710, PRO, CO324/32, 20–1. See also Graham, ed., *The Walker Expedition to Quebec, 1711*, Introduction, 10.

18 'Journal of Colonel Nicholson at the Capture of Annapolis, 1710' (hereafter 'Journal'), *Boston News-Letter*, 342, 30 October–6 November 1710, 1. This special edition of the *Boston News-Letter* contained much more than a simple journal, including a large number of associated documents. It constitutes the major surviving source collection on the 1710 expedition and the surrender

of Port Royal. A transcription can be found in *NSHS Collections*, I, 64–104.
For the troop contingents and colonial quotas (which were defined in
Nicholson's instructions as being identical to the quotas established for the
cancelled Canada expedition of 1709), see Instructions to Samuel Vetch,
1 March 1709, PRO, CO5/9, no. 22; Joseph Dudley to William Popple,
16 August 1709, PRO, CO5/865, no. 20; Address of the Governor and Company of Connecticut, 7 August 1710, PRO, CO5/10, no. 223; Address of Governor, Council, and Assembly of Massachusetts Bay, 22 August 1710, PRO,
CO5/10, no. 137; Muster Rolls, 1710–11, MA, vol. 91, ff. 1–25.

19 'Journal,' 1.

20 Subercase to the minister, 1 October 1710, AC, C11D, vol. 7, 90. Author's
translation: 'But ultimately, Monseigneur, I ask you to believe that I cannot
do the impossible. It is as if I am in a prison where I can move nothing either
in or out, and the harvest has been very poor at Port-Royal; on top of which,
I am penniless and our credit is exhausted.'

21 'Journal,' 1.

22 Ibid.

23 The Case of Samuel Vetch [20 February 1707], PRO, CO5/864, no. 89 (i).

24 'Journal,' 1. The numbers cited in the account of the wreck of the *Caesar* in
'Journal' are not fully consistent with the muster roll, which listed fifty-three
officers, noncommissioned officers, and soldiers on active duty. See Muster
Rolls, Sir Charles Hobby's Regiment, Company of Lt Col. John Ballentine,
1710, MA, vol. 91, 1.

25 Robert Reading to Board of Trade [15 April 1715], PRO, CO217/1, no. 98;
Calnek, *History of the County of Annapolis*, 60–1.

26 'Journal,' 1–2. A military 'pace' was an indefinite measure of distance that
could mean approximately three or approximately five feet. See *Oxford
English Dictionary*, XI, 33.

27 'Journal,' 2–3.

28 Ibid., 3.

29 Ibid., 4.

30 Ibid., 3–5.

31 Articles of Capitulation, 2 October 1710, PRO, CO5/9, no. 66.

32 'Journal,' 5–6.

33 Ibid., 6.

34 Ibid.

35 Ibid., 6–9.

36 Ibid., 6–8.

37 Commission to Francis Nicholson, 18 March 1710, *NSHS Collections*, I, 59–60;
Instructions to Francis Nicholson, 18 March 1710, ibid., 60–2.

38 Proclamation to the Inhabitants, 12 October 1710, PRO, CO5/9, no. 73; Proclamation to British Subjects on the Continent of America, ibid., no. 74; Council of War to Queen Anne, 14 October 1710, ibid., no. 72. On New Scotland and the order, see Reid, *Acadia, Maine, and New Scotland*, 21–5.

39 Vetch to Dartmouth, 22 January 1711, PRO, CO5/9, no. 84.

40 On the significance and development of competing definitions of these terms, see chapter 2 below; also Reid, 'The Conquest of "Nova Scotia."'

41 Vetch to Dartmouth, 22 January 1710, PRO, CO5/9, no. 85.

42 Principal Inhabitants of Port Royal to Vaudreuil, 13 November 1710, AC, C11D, vol. 7, 98. Author's translation: 'the harsh manner in which Mr Vetch treats us.'

43 Vetch to Dartmouth, 14 June 1711, PRO, CO5/9, no. 98.

44 Vetch's Instructions to Mascarene, 1 November 1710, *NSHS Collections*, IV, 86.

45 Proclamation of Mascarene, 12 November 1712, ibid., 87; Mascarene's Commission to Sundries at Minas, 16 November 1710, ibid., 88; Memorial of Paul Mascarene, 6 November 1713, Nova Scotia Archives and Records Management (hereafter NSARM), RG1, vol. 9, 9–12.

46 Memorial of Mascarene, 15.

47 *Boston News-Letter*, 362, 19–26 March 1711, 1–2.

48 Vetch to Dartmouth, 14 June 1711, PRO, CO5/9, no. 98.

49 Ibid.

50 Philippe de Pastour de Costebelle to the minister, 6 November 1710, AC, C11C, vol. 7, 40. Author's translation: 'the deplorable news.'

51 Pontchartrain to Beauharnois, 24 December 1710, AC, C11D, vol. 7, 100; Pontchartrain to Beauharnois, 16 January 1711, AC, B, vol. 33, 237. Author's translation: 'You know ... how important it is to recapture this post before the enemy is securely established there; it is equally necessary for the conservation of all North America and for the sake of the trade in fish.'

52 Pontchartrain to Beauharnois, 24 January, 20, 27 February, 16, 30 March, 6 May 1711, AC, B, vol. 33, 241–2, 245–8, 249–50, 259–60, 262–3, 278.

53 Costebelle to [the minister], 24 July 1711, MA, vol. 2, 622–5. This document is an English translation of a dispatch that had been captured en route.

54 See Pontchartrain to Beauharnois, 16 January 1711, AC, B, vol. 33, 238–9.

55 Pontchartrain to Beauharnois, 16 January 1711, AC, B, vol. 33, 236–7; Louis XIV to Vaudreuil, 7 July 1711, ibid., 304–5.

56 Pontchartrain to Beauharnois, 3 July 1711, AC, B, vol. 33, 286. Author's translation: 'you must achieve the impossible in order to surmount whatever difficulties may arise.'

57 Commission to Saint-Castin, 1 January 1711, AC, C11D, vol. 7, 122; Instructions to Saint-Castin, 18 January 1711, ibid., 129–33; Georges Cerbelaud

Salagnac, 'Bernard-Anselme d'Abbadie de Saint-Castin,' in Brown et al., eds, *Dicionary of Canadian Biography* (hereafter DCB), II, 3–4; Salagnac, 'Jean-Vincent d'Abbadie de Saint-Castin,' DCB, II, 4–7; 'Journal,' 6.

58 Minister to Gaulin, 30 March 1711, AC, B, vol. 33, 268–9; on the nonarrival of the supplies, see David Lee, 'Antoine Gaulin,' DCB, II, 238.

59 For example, Vaudreuil to the minister, 3 November 1710, AC, C11A, vol. 31, 52–3; on the Houdenasaunee–French negotiations, see Miquelon, *New France, 1701–1744*, 19–25.

60 Vetch to Dartmouth, 14 June 1711, PRO, CO5/9, no. 98; Letter of Gaulin, 5 September 1711, AC, C11D, vol. 7, 177–80.

61 Vetch to Dartmouth, 18 June 1711, PRO, CO5/9, no. 99; Journal of Colonel Richard King, 25 June 1711, in Graham, ed., *Walker Expedition*, 318–19.

62 Letter of Gaulin, 5 September 1711, AC, C11D, vol. 7, 177–80; Journal of Paul Mascarene, NSARM, RG1, vol. 9, 28. Author's translation: 'This action has so strongly revived the courage of the French inhabitants and of the natives.'

63 Lawrence Armstrong to the Duke of Newcastle, 15 November 1732, NSARM, RG1, vol. 17, no. 20.

64 Graham, ed., *Walker Expedition*, Introduction, 23, 30.

65 King Journal, 14 July 1711, in Graham, ed., *Walker Expedition*, 323–4.

66 John Hill to Lord Dartmouth, 31 July 1711, PRO, CO5/9, no. 9; King Journal, 29 July 1711, in Graham, ed., *Walker Expedition*, 326.

67 Journal of Sir Hovenden Walker, 23, 24 August 1711, in Graham, ed., *Walker Expedition*, 137– 41; ibid., Introduction, 33–8. On the departure of the marines, see Vetch to Dartmouth, 16 November 1711, PRO, CO5/9, no. 103.

68 Hill to Dartmouth, 9 September 1711, PRO, CO5/9, no. 14; Vetch to Dartmouth, 16 November 1711, ibid., no. 103.

69 Vetch to Dartmouth, 3 January, 9 February 1712, PRO, CO5/9, nos. 104, 105; see also John David Krugler, 'John Livingston,' DCB, II, 436–8.

70 Blathwayt to Thomas Harley, 12 October 1711, Huntington Library, Blathwayt Papers, BL 127; for an example of Vetch's representations, see Vetch to Board of Trade, 26 November 1711, PRO, CO217/1, no. 1.

71 Letter of George Vane, 5 May 1712, PRO, CO217/31, no. 6.

72 Minister to Mathieu de Goutin, 10 August 1710, AC, B, vol. 32, 426–7. Author's translation: 'matters have reached a point where, should the English arrive, far from the inhabitants being ready to repel them, it is greatly to be feared that they will join with them.'

73 Vetch to Dartmouth, 16 November 1712, PRO, CO5/9, no. 103; on the complaints, see Mascarene Journal, NSARM, RG1, vol. 9, 10.

74 Letter of George Vane, 5 May 1712, PRO, CO217/31, no. 6. Vane was no friend of Vetch, and so was not a neutral observer, but the substance of his

comments had also been noted by others. See, for example, Richard King to Henry St John, 25 July 1711, CO5/898, no. 11; also F.J. Thorpe, 'George Vane,' DCB, II, 643–4.

75 Vetch to Dartmouth, 16 November 1711, PRO, CO5/9, no. 103.
76 See Circular Letter of Queen Anne [1711], PRO, SP105/266, 50.
77 Matthew Prior to Lord Bolingbroke, 8 January 1713, PRO, SP105/28, 68.
78 See Colley, *Britons*, 18–30; Hinderaker, 'The "Four Indian Kings" and the Imaginative Construction of the First British Empire.'
79 'Prior's Negotiation in France,' 23–5 July 1711, in Great Britain, Historical Manuscripts Commission, *Report on the Manuscripts of His Grace the Duke of Portland Preserved at Welbeck Abbey*, vol. 5, 36–7. Author's translation: *'Here again is another impossibility ... Newfoundland.'* On the geopolitical role of defence of the imperial status quo, see also J.D. Alsop, 'The Age of the Projectors,' esp. 51–2.
80 See Griffiths, 'The Golden Age,' 25–6.
81 Petition of Jean Martel and Abraham Boudrot, 6 May 1691, MA, vol. 37, 23.
82 For a stimulating recent discussion of historical narrative in cross-cultural perspective, see Ramirez, 'Clio in Words and Motion.'
83 Lescarbot, *The History of New France*, II, 528. Author's translation: 'The winter having arrived, the natives of the country converged at Port-Royal from far away to trade their goods with the French.'
84 Relation of Richard Guthry, 1629, in Griffiths and Reid, 'New Evidence on New Scotland, 1629,' 506–8.
85 Sir Thomas Temple to [Thomas Povey] [1660], PRO, CO1/14, no. 64.

2 Elites, States, and the Imperial Contest for Acadia

1 We exclude for this purpose the initial Acadia grant of 1603, in which the French crown delineated a territory stretching from the 40th to the 46th degree of latitude, on the ground that this claim rapidly proved to bear no relation either to colonization or to the creation of any French sphere of influence covering such an extensive area.
2 Meneval au Ministre, 10 September 1688, AC, C11D, 2, 96–7. Authors' translation: 'This country is so imperfectly formed that one could say it is not formed at all, that it lacks virtually everything, and that except for the cod fishery there are few methods hitherto known that could improve it.'
3 William Blathwayt to Thomas Harley, 12 October 1711, Huntington Library, Blathwayt Papers, BL 127.
4 On the 1631 negotiations, see Reid, 'The Scots Crown and the Restitution of Port Royal, 1629–1632.'

5 On companies chartered for expansion and colonization see Scott, *The Constitution and Finance of English, Scottish and Irish Joint-Stock Companies to 1720*, vol. 2; and Biggar, *The Early Trading Companies of New France*.

6 On the English overseeing bodies, see Andrews, *British Committees, Commissions, and Councils of Trade and Plantations*; and Steele, *Politics of Colonial Policy*. On the French, see Miquelon, *Dugard of Rouen*, 4–11.

7 M.J. Braddick, 'The English Government, War, Trade, and Settlement, 1625–1688.' Unfortunately there is nothing similar for France that provides a closely argued and documented case for the growth of state involvement in the empire.

8 Baugh, 'Maritime Strength and Atlantic Commerce'; Ertman, *Birth of the Leviathan*, 90–223; Greene, '"A Posture of Hostility"'; Moogk, 'Ile Royale: The Other New France.' On earlier divergences as they affected Acadia, see Griffiths, '1600–1650: Fish, Fur, and Folk,' 40–6.

9 In the French case, the pattern is clear from such indicators as chapter headings; see Eccles, *France in America*, in which Chapter 2 is 'Merchants and Missionaries, 1632–1663,' and Chapter 3 is 'Colbert's Colonies, 1663–1685.' In the British case, historians write of the 'First' and 'Second' British empires, with the break coming with the end of either the Seven Years' War or the American Revolution. See Harlow, *The Founding of the Second British Empire*, and Bayly, *Imperial Meridian*. Fresh assessments of the relationship between the state and overseas expansion are emerging. See Mancke, 'Another British America,' and Braddick, 'The English Government, War, Trade, and Settlement, 1625–1688'; and, more generally, Greene, 'Negotiated Authorities.'

10 Brewer, *The Sinews of Power*; Tilly, *Coercion, Capital, and European States*, esp. 20–8; Ertman, *Birth of the Leviathan*, 1–19. For definitions of the state, see Tilly, 'Reflections on the History of European State-Making,' 70–1.

11 Greengrass, 'Introduction: Conquest and Coalescence,' 3–4; Greengrass, *France in the Age of Henri IV*, 236–42; Sahlins, *Boundaries*, 1–102.

12 Greengrass, *France in the Age of Henri IV*, 87, 101, 104–5.

13 See, for example, Ertman, *Birth of the Leviathan*. John Brewer acknowledged the problem in 'The Eighteenth-Century British State: Contexts and Issues,' 65–8, while David Armitage explored it in greater detail in 'Greater Britain: A Useful Category of Historical Analysis?' For a recent effort to analyse the relationship, see Braddick, *State Formation in Early Modern England*, 379–425; and Mancke, 'Empire and State.'

14 Braddick, 'The Early Modern English State and the Question of Differentiation'; Braddick, *State Formation in Early Modern England*, passim; Greengrass, 'Introduction: Conquest and Coalescence,' 6–7; Sahlins, *Boundaries*, 8–9.

15 Braddick, 'Elite Co-Option and State Formation in the British Atlantic
    World.'
16 Griffiths, '1600–1650: Fish, Fur, and Folk,' 52–3; Shammas, 'English Com-
    mercial Development and American Colonization,' 153.
17 See, for example, Lawson, *The East India Company*, 30–7; more generally,
    Carruthers, *City of Capital*; and Webb, *Lord Churchill's Coup*.
18 Pope, *The Many Landfalls of John Cabot*, 14.
19 Boucher, *Les nouvelles Frances: France in America, 1500–1815: An Imperial Per-
    spective*, 1–15. This book provides a useful, brief overview of early modern
    French expansion into the Americas.
20 Andrews, *Trade, Plunder and Settlement*; Davies, *The North Atlantic World in the
    Seventeenth Century*, 3–34; Pastore, 'The Sixteenth Century'; Trigger, *Natives
    and Newcomers*, 111–63; Turgeon, 'Pour redécouvrir notre 16e siècle'; Tur-
    geon, 'Basque–Amerindian Trade in the Saint Lawrence during the Six-
    teenth Century.'
21 Rabb, *Enterprise and Empire*, 19–101.
22 Reid, *Acadia, Maine, and New Scotland*, 14–18.
23 See Pagden, 'The Struggle for Legitimacy and the Image of Empire in the
    Atlantic to c. 1700,' 51–2.
24 Lounsbury, *The British Fishery at Newfoundland*, 113, 116–17, 125; Morgan,
    American Slavery, American Freedom: The Ordeal of Colonial Virginia, 196–7. Only
    in the early nineteenth century did a British colonial secretary, Lord Liver-
    pool, acknowledge begrudgingly that Newfoundland 'is become a sort of
    Colony, and in the end it will become so entirely.' Quoted in Head, *Eigh-
    teenth Century Newfoundland*, 231. See also, more generally, Cell, *English Enter-
    prise in Newfoundland*; Matthews, *Lectures on the History of Newfoundland*;
    Ommer, *From Outpost to Outport*; and Ryan, 'Fishery to Colony.'
25 For the ambivalence of traders to colonization see Andrews, *Trade, Plunder,
    and Settlement*, 356–64; and Trudel, *The Beginnings of New France*, 54–70. The
    quandary persisted throughout the seventeenth century; see Jean Daigle,
    '1650–1686: "Un pays qui n'est pas fait."'
26 Choquette, *Frenchmen into Peasants*, 249–50; Greengrass, *France in the Age of
    Henri IV*, 117–81; Reid, *Acadia, Maine, and New Scotland*, 14–16. Authors'
    translation: 'merchants of this town of Rouen, Saint-Malo, la Rochelle, and
    Saint-Jean-de Lux.'
27 In the early sixteenth century Francis I had challenged the exclusivity of
    Spanish and Portuguese possession of the Americas, by arguing that Europe-
    ans had to fix their claims with occupation. In areas without permanent set-
    tlements, trade would be open to all, and non-Iberians could plant colonies.
    See Eccles, *France in America*, 3.

28 Greengrass, *France in the Age of Henri IV*, 89–116. In the 1620s, the crown manipulated Catholic and Huguenot interests to make New France a colony of the Counter-Reformation and La Rochelle a Catholic rather than Huguenot port; see J.F. Bosher, 'The Political and Religious Origins of La Rochelle's Primacy in Trade with New France, 1627–1685.'

29 See Boulle, 'French Mercantilism, Commercial Companies, and Colonial Profitability'; Boucher, *Les nouvelles Frances*, 27–30.

30 See Cell, *English Enterprise in Newfoundland*, 53–80.

31 Brenner, *Merchants and Revolution*, 92–112.

32 Brenner in *Merchants and Revolution*, 99, qualifies Rabb's attribution of gentry investment as overestimated, but does not consider Puritan investments; see also Shammas, 'English Commercial Development,' 153. On investments in Puritan settlements, see Martin, *Profits in the Wilderness*, 7–128; on more general factors affecting English migration, see Canny, 'English Migration into and across the Atlantic During the Seventeenth and Eighteenth Centuries'; on the environmental implications of New England settlement, see Cronon, *Changes in the Land*.

33 Bottingheimer, 'Kingdom and Colony'; and Crosby, *Ecological Imperialism*, 70–103. For a qualification of the French situation, see Boucher, *Les nouvelles Frances*, 27; also Choquette, *Frenchmen into Peasants*, 181–99.

34 Bosher, 'The Imperial Environment of French Trade with Canada'; Bosher, 'Huguenot Merchants and the Protestant International in the Seventeenth Century.'

35 Thomas Gorges to Henry Gorges, 19 July 1640, in Moody, ed., *The Letters of Thomas Gorges*, 2.

36 This paragraph is largely based on Reid, *Acadia, Maine, and New Scotland*, 20–33, 136–7. For a fuller discussion of claims and boundaries, see Reid, 'The Conquest of "Nova Scotia."'

37 There are numerous accounts, of varying narrative description and analytic rigour, of this rivalry. Useful perspectives can be found in Bosher, 'The Lyon and Bordeaux Connections of Émmanuel Le Borgne'; Clark, *Acadia*, 90–107; MacDonald, *Fortune and La Tour*; Trudel, *The Beginnings of New France*, 192–209.

38 Reid, *Acadia, Maine, and New Scotland*, 145–6.

39 Ibid., 141.

40 Clark, *Acadia*, 99–108, 121–3; Hynes, 'Some Aspects of the Demography of Port Royal,' 4–6; Reid, *Acadia, Maine, and New Scotland*, 140–1.

41 See Winthrop, *Winthrop's Journal*, II, 43, 85, 88.

42 On d'Aulnay's relationships with native inhabitants, see Abraham Shurt to John Winthrop, 28 June 1636, *Winthrop Papers*, VI, 570–1; Mémoire of

d'Aulnay [c. 1643], France, Bibliothèque Nationale, Fonds français, 18593, 377. On other issues regarding d'Aulnay's role as a promoter, see Faulkner and Faulkner, *The French at Pentagoet*, 19; Reid, *Acadia, Maine, and New Scotland*, 109–10.

43 Quoted in MacDonald, *Fortune and La Tour*, 45. Authors' translation: 'Great sakamow of the Mi'kmaq, Etchemin, Penobscot, and Kennebec.'

44 See Reid, *Acadia, Maine, and New Scotland*, 115–16.

45 For Plaisance, see Plaze, 'La colonie royale de Plaisance.'

46 See Davies, *The North Atlantic World in the Seventeenth Century*, 289–92.

47 Jean-Baptiste Colbert to Jean Talon, 11 February 1671, AC, B, 3, 23–4. Authors' translation: 'not only in a condition to sustain itself, but also to supply to the French West Indies some portion of the commodities which they need for the subsistence of the inhabitants there and for their other needs.'

48 Talon to Colbert, 11 November 1671, AC, C11A, 3, 184–5.

49 On population, see Clark, *Acadia*, 121–32. New England trade is examined in Daigle, 'Nos amis les ennemis: Relations commerciales de l'Acadie avec le Massachusetts'; and Johnson, *John Nelson, Merchant Adventurer*.

50 See Instructions to Grandfontaine, 5 March 1670, AC, B, 2, 57–61.

51 For the names of these governors, and their years of service, see Clark, *Acadia*, 111–12.

52 For more extended discussion of this and related points, see Mancke, 'Spaces of Power in the Early Modern Northeast.'

53 On the pre-1690 exceptions, see Baker, 'New Evidence on the French Involvement in King Philip's War.'

54 Richard Coote, Earl of Bellomont, to Board of Trade, 20 April 1700, PRO, CO5/861, No. 31. On developments of the 1680s in Acadia, see Reid, *Acadia, Maine, and New Scotland*, 176–81.

55 See Alsop, 'The Age of the Projectors,' 51–2.

56 Clark, *Acadia*, 125–8.

57 Report of Meneval, 1 September 1689, AC, C11D, 2, 126–34. Authors' translation: 'the daughter of a peasant.' See also Clement Cormier, 'Pierre Tibaudeau,' DCB, II, 629–30; and Bernard Pothier, 'Mathieu de Goutin,' ibid., II, 257–8.

58 Johnson, *John Nelson, Merchant Adventurer*, 27, 151n; Daigle, 'Acadian Marshland Settlement.'

59 Petition of Pierre Lanoue [1 December 1696], MA, 2, 582. On Phips's expedition, see Baker and Reid, *The New England Knight*, 86–94.

60 See Miller, 'Errand into the Wilderness.'

61 Greene, 'Political Mimesis: A Consideration of the Historical and Cultural

Roots of Legislative Behavior in the British Colonies during the Eighteenth Century.'

62 See Reid, *Acadia, Maine, and New Scotland*, for an extended analysis of the similarities between Acadia and Maine.

3 Family and Political Culture in Pre-Conquest Acadia

1 Daigle, 'Acadia from 1604 to 1763,' 19.
2 Reid, *Six Crucial Decades*, 30.
3 In the second half of the nineteenth century, French historian François-Edme Rameau de Saint-Père wrote a very influential work on Acadian history, *Une colonie féodale en Amérique*, which portrayed Acadian colonial society as an egalitarian one. This thesis had, and still has, a remarkable influence on the writing of Acadian colonial history. See Clarke, 'The Makers of Acadian History in the Nineteenth Century.' From the same author, see 'Rameau de Saint-Père, Moïse de l'Acadie.' In a recent work, Allan Greer espouses this 'Rameauesque' view of seventeenth- and eighteenth-century Acadia. See Greer, *The People of New France*, 95–7. Recent scholarship has challenged this traditional interpretation. See Griffiths, *The Contexts of Acadian History*; Brun, 'Marie de Saint-Étienne de La Tour'; Reid, '1686–1720: Imperial Intrusions'; Basque, *Des hommes de pouvoir*; Vanderlinden, *Se marier en Acadie française*; Tapie, 'Les structures socio-économiques de Grand Pré, communauté acadienne'; and Plank, *An Unsettled Conquest*.
4 Brebner, *New England's Outpost*, 75.
5 Rawlyk, *Nova Scotia's Massachusetts*. In one of his last publications, Rawlyk attempted to give more voice to Acadian actors of the first half of the eighteenth century: '1720–1744: Cod, Louisbourg, and the Acadians.'
6 Roy, *L'Acadie des origines à nos jours*, 94.
7 Griffiths, *The Contexts of Acadian History*, 40–5 See also Griffiths, 'Subjects and Citizens in the Eighteenth Century'; and Griffiths, 'The Formation of a Community and the Interpretation of Identity.'
8 Reid, *Six Crucial Decades*, 29–32; Reid, '1686–1720: Imperial Intrusions'; Barnes, '"Twelve Apostles" or a Dozen Traitors?'; Basque, *Des hommes de pouvoir*, 51–99; Basque and Brun, 'La neutralité à l'épreuve.' It also should be noted that historians Bernard Pothier and Robert Rumilly had already written about Acadians who were less than neutral. See Pothier, *Course à l'Accadie*, and Rumilly, *L'Acadie anglaise*.
9 Roy, 'Settlement and Population Growth in Acadia,' 138–40.
10 Reid, *Acadia, Maine and New Scotland*, 183.

11 Daigle, 'Nos amis les ennemis: Relations commerciales de l'Acadie avec le Massachusetts.'

12 Nagel, 'Empire and Interest'; Baker and Reid, *The New England Knight*, 75–85.

13 Recit de la prise de Port Royal par les habitants de Boston et de Salem commandes par William Phipps, le 21 mai 1690, in Doughty, *Rapport sur les travaux de la Division des Archives pour l'année 1912*, 68. This relatively small number of Acadian civilian militia exemplifies the Acadians' unwillingness from time to time to take up arms to protect French imperial interests. One should always keep in mind that Acadians were primarily farmers, not soldiers. As in most agrarian societies, farmers were not fond of abandoning their wheat fields for the battlefields. French historian Robert Sauvageau seemingly exaggerates the number of Acadian militia present at the fort in Port Royal in 1690 when he writes that there were 180. See Sauvageau, *Acadie*, 55.

14 'Account of my voyage to Acadia in the ship Union and all that took place in the country during my visit,' Villebon to the Marquis de Chevry, quoted in Webster, *Acadia at the End of the 17th Century*, 24. The late W.J. Eccles erroneously placed this raid in the autumn of 1689 and wrote about churches that were desecrated. See W.J. Eccles, *The French in North America, 1500–1783*, 107.

15 Baker and Reid, *The New England Knight*, 92–3.

16 Émery LeBlanc, 'Vincent Saccardy,' DCB, I, 586–7; Baker and Reid, *The New England Knight*, 87–8. French fortification in Port Royal was always a problem in the last quarter of the seventeenth century and at the turn of the eighteenth century. See Barrieau, 'L'évolution du paysage colonial d'un établissement colonial.'

17 Recit de la prise de Port Royal, 70. Author's translation: 'And having taken all of the inhabitants' names, they led them into the church and closed the doors; they told them that they had to swear allegiance to the Prince of Orange and to Mary of England as King and Queen of England, or that they would be taken as prisoners of war and have their houses burned down.'

18 Rawlyk, *Nova Scotia's Massachusetts*, 68.

19 Recit de la prise de Port Royal, 71.

20 White, *Dictionnaire généalogique*, II, 1145–6. Melanson's father-in-law, Abraham Dugas, was an armourer at Port Royal and had reportedly occupied the function of *lieutenant général civil et criminel*. See Vanderlinden, *Se marier en Acadie française*, 27.

21 Webster, *Acadia at the End of the Seventeenth Century*, 23. Some historians have confused Charles Melanson with his brother Pierre. See Baker and Reid, *The New England Knight*, 88. Villebon's account of Phips's raid states that Sir

William Phips sent David Basset ashore to get his father-in-law. See Webster, *Acadia at the End of the Seventeenth Century*, 23. Basset's wife, Marie Melanson dit Laverdure, was the daughter of Charles Melanson and Marie Dugas of Port Royal. See White, *Dictionnaire généalogique*, I, 78–9. Charles Melanson's brother Pierre was living at Grand Pré at the time. See the Acadian census taken by New France intendant Jacques DeMeulles in 1686: Recensement des habitans de la Baye des Mines, AC, G.

22 M.C. Rosenfield, 'David Basset,' DCB, II, 46–7; White, *Dictionnaire généalogique*, I, 78–80.

23 Charles Melanson's correspondence with Massachusetts lieutenant-governor William Stoughton indicates that he was able to write in standard seventeenth-century English. See Ebacher, 'Charles Mellanson Letters,' 314–15; Babitch, 'The English of Acadians in the Seventeenth Century.' A good command of the English language and of the local native tongues permitted some Acadians to become interpreters, giving them elite status within the community. See Ringuet, 'Les stratégies de mobilité sociale des interprètes en Nouvelle-Écosse et à l'Île Royale.'

24 Mill owner Louis Allain of Port Royal had many contacts in Massachusetts, even owning land in present-day Maine. See Kelly, 'Louis Allain in Acadia and New England.'

25 White, *Dictionnaire généalogique*, I, 23–4; Daigle, 'Nos amis les ennemis: Relations commerciales de l'Acadie avec le Massachusetts,' 100–1.

26 White, *Dictionnaire généalogique*, II, 1430–9; Vanderlinden, *Se marier en Acadie française*; MacDonald, *Fortune and La Tour;* Reid, *Acadia, Maine and New Scotland*; Brun, 'Marie de Saint-Étienne de La Tour'; Daigle, 'Nos amis les ennemis: Relations commerciales de l'Acadie avec le Massachusetts,' 91; d'Entremont, *Histoire du Cap-Sable de l'an mil au traité de Paris, 1763*, vol. 3.

27 Daigle, 'Nos amis les ennemis: Relations commerciales de l'Acadie avec le Massachusetts,' 75–198; Jacques Vanderlinden, 'À la rencontre de l'histoire du droit en Acadie avant le dérangement,' 65. Michel Boudrot's presence in Acadia is first attested in a document dated 21 September 1639, in which he is mentioned as one of the *syndics* of Port Royal. See Massignon, 'La seigneurie de Charles de Menou d'Aulnay, gouverneur de l'Acadie, 1635–1650,' 484; White, *Dictionnaire généalogique*, I, 184–6; Basque, *Des hommes de pouvoir*, 24–48.

28 Tapie, 'Les structures socio-économiques,' 99; White, *Dictionnaire généalogique*, II, 1148–50. In the 1686 census of Grand Pré, Pierre Melanson's holdings included 31 head of cattle, 8 sheep, 27 swine, and 50 acres of cultivated land. He also had 12 guns in his house, a clear indication that his role as a military leader was not only a symbolic one. See Recensement des habi-

tans de la Baye des Mines, AC, G. See also Rouet, 'L'Acadie, du comptoir à la colonie. Migration et colonisation du bassin des Mines,' 49–50; Coleman, *The Acadians at Grand Pré*, 6.

29 This assembly was known as 'The Council established at Port Royal for the preservation of peace at Port Royal, Acadia and Nova Scotia'. See Webster, *Acadia at the End of the Seventeenth Century*, 29.

30 Council members were Charles Chevalier dit La Tourasse, sergeant of the French garrison at Port Royal, president; Mathieu de Goutin, *lieutenant civil et criminel* of Acadia; *sieur* Alexandre Le Borgne de Bélisle, seigneur of Port Royal; Pierre Chênet, *sieur* Dubreuil, *procureur du roi* in Acadia; and two of the most prosperous farmers of Port Royal, René Landry and Daniel LeBlanc. See Webster, *Acadia at the End of the Seventeenth Century*, 29.

31 Ibid., 30.

32 MacDonald, *Fortune and La Tour*; Reid, *Acadia, Maine and New Scotland*. See also Couillard-Després, *Charles de Saint-Étienne de la Tour*, and Lauvrière, *Deux traitres d'Acadie et leur victime*.

33 Clark, *Acadia*, 107–8; Griffiths, *The Contexts of Acadian History*, 9.

34 White, *Dictionnaire généalogique*, I, 184–6, 251–3; II, 1536–7.

35 Recit de la prise de Port Royal, 70. Author's translation: 'That they did this with great pain and they asked that a document be drawn for posterity which would be then deposited in the Port Royal archives and that a copy should be sent to the French court and one to Monsieur the Comte de Frontenac, and that they begged His Majesty not to abandon them and that they would be ready to give their lives for their dear homeland and not let them be forced to abandon their religion and to embrace the Anglican faith.'

36 Villebon was right about the vulnerability of Port Royal. In June of the same year, crews from New York warships attacked Port Royal, burning more houses and even killing inhabitants. See Reid, '1686–1720: Imperial Intrusions,' 82; Rawlyk, *Nova Scotia's Massachusetts*, 71.

37 Baker and Reid, *The New England Knight*, 94; Webster, *Acadia at the End of the Seventeenth Century*, 24, 41.

38 Ibid., 44–7; C. Bruce Fergusson (in collaboration), 'Charles La Tourasse,' DCB, II, 426–7. In 1694, Chevalier became an ensign in the company of French marine officer Claude-Sébastien Le Bassier de Villieu. In the fall of 1696, he was killed in an ambush by English soldiers under the command of Benjamin Church.

39 Webster, *Acadia at the End of the Seventeenth Century*, 45; White, *Dictionnaire généalogique*, I, 345.

40 Baker and Reid, *The New England Knight*, 160. On 20 August 1694, Villebon wrote the French minister of Marine, the Comte de Pontchartrain: 'Abra-

ham Boudrot, of Port Royal, who sails to and from Boston with the approval of Count Frontenac and myself, has come from there within six weeks. Having twice been inside Fort Pemaquid, he assures me that he examined it carefully; it is four-sided, with four bastions, each curtain, as far as he could judge, being 160 feet in length.' Webster, *Acadia at the End of the Seventeenth Century*, 68.

41 Émery LeBlanc (in collaboration), 'Joseph Robinau de Villebon,' DCB, I, 576.

42 Good examples of shifting allegiances by local elites and villagers in time of armed conflict are provided by Daniel Hickey, *The Coming of French Absolutism*; Theibault, *German Villages in Crisis*.

43 See Kettering, *Patrons, Brokers, and Clients in Seventeenth-Century France*, and Béguin, *Les princes de Condé*.

44 Baker and Reid, *The New England Knight*, 228–9. The *sieur* de La Tour could not always benefit from such protection, as in 1696 when his boat *Le Saint-Jacob* was seized by the English. The affair went all the way to the Supreme Court of Massachusetts, where La Tour lost his appeal. See Daigle, 'Un Acadien devant la cour suprême du Massachusetts,' 106–8.

45 Coleman, *The Acadians at Grand Pré*, 8–9.

46 Rawlyk, *Nova Scotia's Massachusetts*, 74–5; Webster, *Acadia at the End of the Seventeenth Century*, 200. This was to be Tyng's last appointment. After a brief visit to Port Royal, he was captured by the French and died in captivity in France.

47 Rawlyk, *Nova Scotia's Massachusetts*, 73.

48 Baker and Reid, *The New England Knight*, 158.

49 Ebacher, 'Charles Mellanson Letters,' 316.

50 Daigle, 'Nos amis les ennemis: Relations commerciales de l'Acadie avec le Massachusetts,' 147–8.

51 Ibid., 151; Reid, '1686–1720: Imperial Intrusions,' 83. Another Minas Basin settler, René LeBlanc, also kept Villebon informed on the whereabouts of English ships. Ironically, his father Daniel LeBlanc was a member of the Nova Scotia Council that Phips established in 1690. See Webster, *Acadia at the End of the Seventeenth Century*, 46–7; and White, *Dictionnaire généalogique*, II, 985–9.

52 W. Austin Squires, 'Pierre Maisonnat dit Baptiste,' DCB, II, 449–50; Squires, 'François Guion,' DCB, II, 271; White, *Dictionnaire généalogique*, II, 1114. In the fall of 1693, the Acadian settlers at Port Royal paid dearly for having such an ominous character living in their community. The crew of an English frigate searching for Baptiste landed in Port Royal and, according to Villebon's journal, burned one dozen houses. The fact that the inhabitants had raised

the British flag did not protect them. See Webster, *Acadia at the End of the Seventeenth Century*, 53–4.

53 Reid, '1686–1720: Imperial Intrusions,' 83.

54 Daigle, 'Nos amis les ennemis: Relations commerciales de l'Acadie avec le Massachusetts,' 149; White, *Dictionnaire généalogique*, I, 255, 256, 562; Webster, *Acadia at the End of the Seventeenth Century*, 17.

55 Daigle, 'Nos amis les ennemis: Relations commerciales de l'Acadie avec le Massachusetts,' 149. Again, one can assume that the Beaubassin settlers whose houses had been destroyed by Church's men would have been more than frustrated when looking at Bourgeois's spared house. In the *grande famille acadienne* that was Beaubassin at the time, Church's raid clearly indicated that some settlers had a privileged status. See Samantha Rompillon, 'La migration à Beaubassin, village acadien'; and Marsaud, 'L'étranger qui dérange.'

56 Naomi Griffiths has written that colonial Acadians were 'a clan, a body of people united by blood ties, common beliefs and common aims for the group as a whole.' *The Acadians: Creation of a People*, 18. This interpretation, though, does not take into account individual aims in a society, compared with family aims. See Lynch, 'The Family and the History of Public Life.'

57 Barrieau, 'L'évolution du paysage colonial,' 20–1. Like Saccardy's fort, Brouillan's was never completed.

58 Coleman, *The Acadians at Grand Pré*, 10.

59 Webster, *Acadia at the End of the Seventeenth Century*, 41, 46, 55, 104, 109, 129, 148; Coleman, *The Acadians at Grand Pré*, 8.

60 Coleman, ibid., 10.

61 Ibid., 12.

62 Coleman, *The Acadians at Port-Royal*, 31–4. Brouillan was irritated by what he considered to be an Acadian lack of martial prowess. See Miquelon, *New France 1701–1744*, 29; Sauvageau, *Acadie*, 119.

63 Coleman, *The Acadians at Port-Royal*, 35, 37–8. Rameau de Saint-Père indicates that many native troops were present and that the d'Entremonts had come from Cap Sable with both their French and Mi'kmaq men to defend the fort. See *Une colonie féodale en Amérique*, I, 334.

64 Sauvageau, *Acadie*, 133. Laurent Granger had abandoned his Protestant faith when he married an Acadian, Marie Landry, in Port Royal around 1667. See White, *Dictionnaire généalogique*, I, 761–2.

65 Ibid., I, 473; II, 891, 1149, 1204, 1435.

66 Rumilly, *L'Acadie française*, 205.

67 White, *Dictionnaire généalogique*, II, 1114, 1233. Governor Subercase himself played an important role in these matrimonial strategies, seeing them as a

means for French officers and privateers to remain in Port Royal. The marriage of Bernard Anselme d'Abbadie de Saint-Castin, son of the well-known Baron of Pentagouet, to Marie Charlotte d'Amours de Chauffours in 1707 was reportedly of Subercase's devising. See Sauvageau, *Acadie*, 138.

68 Chard, '"Pagans," Privateers, and Propagandists,' 82–3. Canadian-born officer Simon Pierre Denys de Bonaventure complained to the minister of the Marine in 1705 that almost half of the soldiers of the French garrison at Port Royal were not in good health. Fifty-two of them were placed with Acadian families until they recovered. In all likelihood, these families were annoyed with their unwelcomed guests.

69 Rouet, 'L'Acadie, du comptoir à la colonie'; Rompillon, 'La migration à Beaubassin, village acadien,' 110–48.

70 Ibid., 109. Author's translation: 'the country is stripped of everything; there is no trade.'

4 New England and the Conquest

1 For a discussion of Mi'kmaq maritime activities, see Martijn, ed., *Les Micmacs et la mer*. Scholars debate when the Mi'kmaq first began visiting Newfoundland regularly. See Bartels and Janzen, 'Micmac Migration to Western Newfoundland'; Marshall, 'Beothuk and Micmac.' For the overland trail, see Prins, 'Tribulations of a Border Tribe.'

2 For an accessible overview of early Acadian history see Griffiths, *The Contexts of Acadian History*. See also Daigle, ed., *Acadia of the Maritimes*.

3 The best account of the life of a provincial office holder in the early years is Moody, '"A Just and Disinterested Man": The Nova Scotia Career of Paul Mascarene.'

4 See McCusker and Menard, *The Economy of British America*, 103.

5 Though the present-day town of Canso is situated on the mainland of Nova Scotia, in seventeenth-and eighteenth-century usage the place name 'Canso' referred to an offshore island, now known as 'Grassy Island.' See generally Flemming, *The Canso Islands*.

6 Daigle, 'Nos amis les ennemis: Relations commerciales de l'Acadie avec le Massachusetts.'

7 See Chard, 'The Impact of French Privateering on New England.'

8 See generally, Dickason, 'La guerre navale des Micmacs contre les Britanniques'; Rawlyk, *Nova Scotia's Massachusetts*, 59; see also Gyles, *Memoirs and Odd Adventures*, 12. Even after the outbreak of Anglo–French warfare in 1689, the fighting between Mi'kmaq warriors and New England fishermen was sporadic, ebbing and flowing according to a pattern established by local

conditions rather than imperial politics. On several occasions the various groups of New Englanders and Mi'kmaq reached temporary accommodations, but by 1713 almost all their agreements had been broken, and it proved very difficult for either group to regain the other's trust. For evidence of a temporary local armistice in 1706 around the island of Canso, see Samuel Vetch, 'The Case of Samuel Vetch,' 1707, in *Calendar of State Papers, Colonial Series, America and West Indies* (hereafter CSP), XXIII, 380–1.

9 See, for example, Philopolites [Cotton Mather], *A Memorial of the Present Deplorable State of New England*, 31, in which Cotton Mather reports on the state of mind of the fishermen in 1689. For its attribution to Mather, see Silverman, *The Life and Times of Cotton Mather*, 213–14.

10 For an analysis of Algonkian styles of warfare in the seventeenth century, see Malone, *The Skulking Way of War*.

11 Hirsche, 'The Collision of Military Cultures in Seventeenth-Century New England'; Johnson, 'The Search for a Usable Indian.'

12 See Baker, 'New Evidence on the French Involvement in King Philip's War.'

13 See Buffinton, 'The Puritan View of War.' See also George, 'War and Peace in the Puritan Tradition'; Johnson, *Ideology, Reason, and the Limitation of War*, Walzer, *The Revolution of the Saints*.

14 For information on the Deerfield massacre, see Williams, *The Redeemed Captive*, 15, 172; Church, *Entertaining Passages Relating to Philip's War*, 99; Stephen Williams's autobiography, 31 January 1769, Boston Public Library, ms. 1000. See also Demos, *The Unredeemed Captive*, 11–25; Rawlyk, *Nova Scotia's Massachusetts*, 93. For an account of the pressure for retaliation, see Douglass, *A Summary, Historical and Political, of the First Planting, Progressive Improvements, and Present State of the British Settlements in North America*, I, 307.

15 Church, *Entertaining Passages Relating to Philip's War*, 105.

16 *Boston News-Letter*, 5 June, 7, 21 August 1704; 'Memorial on the English Expedition in Acadia, 1704,' Nova Scotia Archives and Records Management (hereafter NSARM), RG1, vol. 3, doc. 22; Church, *Entertaining Passages Relating to Philip's War*, 114–16; Penhallow, *The History of the Wars of New England with the Eastern Indians*, 18.

17 See Vetch's essay, 'Canada Survey'd,' which he wrote for Charles Spencer, Earl of Sunderland, Britain's Secretary of State for the Southern Department, in 1708. The full text of the essay can be found in Samuel Vetch's Letter-Book, 46–60, in the collections of the Museum of the City of New York. Excerpts from 'Canada Survey'd' can be found in CSP, XXIV, 41–51, 147–150. For scholarly discussions of the essay, see Waller, *Samuel Vetch*, 106–9; Bond, *Queen Anne's American Kings*, 22–4; and Alsop, 'Samuel Vetch's "Canada Survey'd,"' 39–58; see also Alsop, 'The Age of the Projectors,' 43–4.

18 Philopolites [Mather], *A Memorial of the Present Deplorable State of New England*, 3. For Dudley s response to this pamphlet, see Dudley, *A Modest Inquiry into the Grounds and Occasions of a Late Pamphlet.*

19 Waller, *Samuel Vetch*, 79–89. Vetch was tried before the Massachusetts General Court; he could have faced capital charges for his crime, but Dudley exercised sufficient control over the proceedings to shield Vetch from the worst. He was found guilty of a misdemeanour and fined. Abstract of Joseph Dudley to Board of Trade, 8 October 1706, in CSP, XXIII, 258–9; Dudley to William Popple, 21 October 1706, ibid., 278; Petition of Samuel Vetch and others, 1707, ibid., 379; Vetch, 'The Case of Samuel Vetch,' ibid., 379–82; Philopolites [Mather], *A Memorial of the Present Deplorable State of New England*, 16.

20 For background information on Dudley, see Olson, *Making the Empire Work*, 82–6. See also Kimball, *The Public Life of Joseph Dudley.*

21 Philopolites [Mather], *A Memorial of the Present Deplorable State of New England*. See also Mather, *The Deplorable State of New England.*

22 In the fall of 1706 Dudley wrote the Board of Trade to ask for assistance in a campaign against Acadia and Quebec. Dudley to Board of Trade, 2 October 1706, Huntington Library, HM 9916.

23 See Alison Olson, 'Sir Charles Hobby,' DCB, II, 288–90.

24 Philopolites [Mather], *A Memorial of the Present Deplorable State of New England*, 9.

25 See Rawlyk, *Nova Scotia's Massachusetts*, 110; Barnard, 'Autobiography,' 192–6; Penhallow, *The History of the Wars of New England with the Eastern Indians*, 42; Mather, *The Deplorable State of New England*, 33–4; Bonaventure Mason to ?, 5 July 1707, NSARM, RG1, vol. 3, doc. 32; Dudley to Charles Spencer, Earl of Sunderland, 5 March 1708, Huntington Library, HM 22287; Dudley to Sunderland, 30 November 1708, ibid., HM 22271.

26 On the recruitment of Nicholson, see Alsop, 'Samuel Vetch's "Canada Survey'd,"' 43; see also Waller, *Samuel Vetch*, 121–3; Alsop, 'The Age of the Projectors,' 45. For background information on Nicholson, see McCully, 'Governor Francis Nicholson'; Webb, 'The Strange Career of Francis Nicholson.' For indications of Nicholson's way of promoting the 1710 Acadia expedition, see Bond, *Queen Anne's American Kings*; Hinderaker, 'The "Four Indian Kings" and the Imaginative Construction of the First British Empire'; Garratt, *The Four Indian Kings*, 3–17.

27 *Instructions for Samuel Vetch.*

28 For a list of the eleven officers assigned to serve under Vetch, see Alsop, 'The Distribution of British Officers in the Colonial Militia for the Canada Expedition of 1709,' 120–1.

29 Abstract of Dudley to Sunderland, 2 October 1709, Huntington Library, HM 1368; see generally Waller, *Samuel Vetch*, 121–41.

30 See ibid., 135–8; Representation of the Lieutenant Governor and Council of New Jersey, countersigned by Vetch and Francis Nicholson, received in London 3 September 1709, Huntington Library, HM 1393; Minutes of a conference at Rehoboth, Massachusetts, 14 October 1709, Museum of the City of New York, Samuel Vetch Letter-Book, 89.

31 Memorial of Richard Ingoldsby, Vetch and Francis Nicholson, 1709, Huntington Library, HM 1373; Nicholson and Vetch to Dudley, 13 May 1709, Museum of the City of New York, Samuel Vetch Letter-Book, 14.

32 Waller, *Samuel Vetch*, 142–57.

33 Dudley to Samuel Vetch, 8 September 1709, Museum of the City of New York, Samuel Vetch Letter-Book, 64. The letter indicates that the province hired chaplains to serve the 1709 expedition. It does not say who they were, but it is likely that they were New Englanders, because the British forces that were expected to join in the expedition never arrived. That is not conclusive evidence that the chaplains were Congregationalist, however. In 1710 the governor found an Anglican clergyman to travel with the troops.

34 Petition of John Scander, et al., 19 October 1710, Library of Congress, Peter Force Collection, Series 8D/6.

35 Journal of John Livingston, 15 October 1710–23 February 1711, PRO, CO217/31, no 1.

36 Address of Nicholson and a Council of War, 14 October 1710, CSP, XXV, 229.

37 For an example of Whig policy toward French colonists in another context (Newfoundland), see Instructions for James Stanhope, received 9 May 1715, PRO, CO194/5, no. 334.

38 Instructions for Richard, Viscount Shannon, 13 July 1710, CSP, XXV, 135. Shannon was directed to relay these instructions to Vetch and Nicholson. See also Nicholson and a Council of War to Board of Trade, October 1710, ibid., 245–7.

39 Francis Nicholson, 'Journal of Colonel Nicholson at the Capture of Annapolis, 1710,' 82.

40 Petition of Hobby, et al., 13 October 1710, Library of Congress, Peter Force Collection, Series 8D/6; Minutes of a council of war, 13 October 1710, ibid.; Petition of John Scander, et al., 19 October 1710, ibid.; Memorial of a Council of War, n.d., Museum of the City of New York, Samuel Vetch Letter-Book, 129; Proposal of disbanded soldiers, 29 June 1713, PRO, CO217/1, no. 45; Board of Trade to ?, 13 July 1713, ibid., no. 39; Disbanded soldiers to Board of Trade, [13 August 1713], ibid., no. 43.

41 Declaration of George Vane, et al., 31 May 1714, ibid., no. 187.

42 Samuel Vetch's Answers to Queries put by the Board of Trade, 1714, ibid., no. 97.

43 Petition of Hobby to the King in Council [14 January 1715], ibid., no. 167.

44 Ibid.

45 See, for example, Vetch to William Legge, Lord Dartmouth, May 1711, ibid, no. 122.

46 Vetch to Dartmouth, 14 June 1711, MHS, Gay Papers, Nova Scotia; Vetch to Dartmouth, 8 August 1712, British Library (hereafter BL), Sloane MSS, 3607, doc. 19; Samuel Vetch, 'The Case of Samuel Vetch,' 1714, PRO, CO217/1, no. 105. See also Johnston, *Control and Order in French Colonial Louisbourg*, 21.

47 *Boston News-Letter*, 6 November 1710.

48 Mascarene to Nicholson, 6 November 1713, in *Nova Scotia Historical Society Collections*, 4 (1884), 73–4.

49 Vetch to Dartmouth, 14 June 1711, MHS, Gay Papers, Nova Scotia, vol. 1, doc. 100.

50 Christopher Cahonet to ?, 20 July 1711, NSARM, RG1, vol. 3, doc. 51; Antoine Gaulin to ?, 5 September 1711, ibid., doc. 48.

51 Minutes of a council of war, 15 June 1711, PRO, CO217/1, no.124.

52 Vetch to Dartmouth, 6 November 1711, BL, Sloane MSS, 3607, doc. 9.

53 Thanks to the expansion of the press during the first four decades of the eighteenth century, we have much better documentation on the response of New Englanders to the diseases that struck the garrison in Louisbourg in 1745. It was common then for New Englanders to conclude that moving to the maritime region would be unhealthy for them. See Douglass, *Summary*, I, 175, 235; see also *Boston Evening Post*, 14 December 1747; *Independent Advertiser*, 28 February 1748.

54 See Rawlyk, *Yankees at Louisbourg*, xvi–xvii; Chard, 'Canso, 1710–1721,' 56–7.

55 Chard, 'Canso 1710–1721,' 60; Flemming, 'The Canso Islands,' 10.

56 See, for example, Appleton, *The Origin of War Examined and Applied*; Williams, *Martial Wisdom Recommended*.

57 Consider, for example, the set of biblical analogies informing the captivity narrative of John Williams, *The Redeemed Captive Returning to Zion*.

58 See Vetch to Privy Council, 16 October 1712, BL, Sloane MSS, 3607, 23; Vetch to Peter Mason, 22 May 1713, PRO, CO217/31, no. 35; Thomas Caulfeild to Nicholson, 5 November 1713, PRO, CO217/1, no. 64; Petition of Vetch, Winter 1714, ibid., no.104; Samuel Vetch, 'The Case of Colonel Vetch' (1714), ibid., no. 105. See also Chard, 'Canso, 1710–1721,' 55–6.

59 *The Diary of Samuel Sewall*, II, 652.

60 For evidence of Nicholson's support in New England, at least among

Boston's Anglicans, see *To the Honourable The Society for Propagating the Gospel in Foreign Parts.*

61 See Petition of Hobby to the King in council [14 January 1715], PRO, CO217/1, no. 167.

62 For the difficulty of communication, see Mascarene to William Douglass, 28 November 1741, MHS, Mascarene Family Papers; Mascarene to William Shirley, 22 September 1744, BL, Additional MSS, 19,071, doc. 54.

63 See Donald F. Chard, 'Cyprian Southack,' DCB, III, 596–7.

64 Instructions for Cyprian Southack, 11 March 1713, PRO, CO217/2, no 244; Southack to Samuel Shute, 22 January 1719, ibid., no. 252.

65 Abstract of a memorial of Southack, 9 December 1713, CSP, XXVII, 258; Instructions for Southack, 11 March 1713, PRO, CO217/2, no. 244. See also Samuel Vetch, 'Some Reasons and Proposals Humbly Offered for Settling the Main [Atlantic] Coast of Nova Scotia with All Imaginable Speed,' 1714, PRO, CO217/1, no. 100.

66 For a reference to Tourangeau, see 'Recensement general,' 1708, Newberry Library, Ayer MSS, 751, 40.

67 Dudley to Southack, 8 April 1715, PRO, CO217/2, no. 245; Southack to Shute, 4 November 1718, PRO, Admi/2452; Southack to Shute, 22 January 1719, CO217/2, no. 252.

68 David Jeffries and Charles Shepreve to Robert Mears, 6 July 1715, PRO, CO217/2, no 5; Jean Loyard to Caulfeild, 1715, ibid., no. 55; Caulfeild to the Cape Sable Indians, 1715, ibid., no. 56; Abstract of Instructions for Peter Capoon, 16 August 1715, in MacMechan, ed., *A Calendar of Two Letter-Books and One Commission-Book*, 21; Abstract of Caulfeild to Board of Trade, 14 December 1715, ibid., 35; *Boston News-Letter*, 25 July, 1, 8 August 1715; Reid, 'Mission to the Micmac.' See also Chard, 'Canso, 1710–1721.'

69 Chard, 'Canso, 1710–1721,' 59; Flemming, *The Canso Islands*, 4.

70 Flemming, *The Canso Islands*, 6.

71 In the preceding summer, according to the account that Southack received, there had been no English-speaking fishermen using the island that season. Cyprian Southack, 'Memorandum,' PRO, CO217/2, no. 249.

72 Southack went on board as a representative of the council of Massachusetts. Flemming, *The Canso Islands*, 12–13; Chard, 'Canso, 1710–1721,' 62.

73 Anon, *Some Considerations on the Consequences of the French Settling Colonies on the Mississippi*, 32–3; Cyprian Southack, 'Journal,' 13 January 1719, PRO, CO217/2, No. 250.

74 See Savelle, *The Diplomatic History of the Canadian Boundary*, 7–8.

75 Anon., *Some Considerations on the Consequences of the French Settling Colonies on the Mississippi*, 34. See also Little, *The State of Trade in the Northern Colonies*

Considered, 83; Journal of Paul Mascarene, beginning 17 August 1721, BL, Additional MSS, 19,071, doc. 18.

76 Chard, 'Canso, 1710–1721,' 68.

77 See Flemming, *The Canso Islands*, 16; George Rawlyk, '1720–1744: Cod, Louisbourg, and the Acadians,' 113–15; John Doucette to Board of Trade, 15 May 1718, PRO, CO217/2, no. 217; Abstract of Richard Philipps to Board of Trade, 3 November 1719, PRO, CO217/30, 7; Abstract of Philipps to Board of Trade, 3 January 1720, PRO, ibid., 8–9; Philipps to James Cragg, 26 September 1720, PRO, CO217/4, no. 51; Paul Mascarene, 'Description of Nova Scotia,' in Akins, ed., *Selections from the Public Documents of the Province of Nova Scotia*, 48; Anon., *Some Considerations on the Consequences of the French Settling Colonies on the Mississippi*, 31.

78 Philipps to Board of Trade, 3 January 1720, in Akins, ed, *Selections from the Public Documents of the Province of Nova Scotia*, 16–17.

79 Petition of twenty-four inhabitants of Annapolis Royal and twenty-seven 'officers civil and military, together with the inhabitants [of Canso]' to the Board of Trade, 1 August 1734, PRO, CO217/39, no. 120; Paul Mascarene to Board of Trade, 1 December 1743, BL, Additional MSS, 19,071, doc. 41.

80 The phrase, of course, is from the title of John Bartlet Brebner's *New England's Outpost*. For the historiographic significance of Brebner's work, see the Preface above. For an analysis of the ties between Canso and New England, see Robison, 'Maritime Frontiers.'

81 For accounts of the war and the treaties that ended it, see Upton, *Micmacs and Colonists*, 40–5; Morrison, *The Embattled Northeast*, 185–90; Dickason, 'Amerindians between French and English in Nova Scotia,' 39–41; Dickason, 'La guerre navale des Micmacs contre les Britanniques,' 244; Wicken, 'The Mi'kmaq and Wuastukwiuk Treaties.' To place the war in a broader Native American context, see Walker, Conkling, and Buesing, 'A Chronological Account of the Wabanaki Confederacy'; Speck, 'The Eastern Algonkian Wabanaki Confederacy.'

82 Dickason, 'Louisbourg and the Indians,' 77; Dickason, 'La guerre navale des Micmacs contre les Britanniques,' 244.

83 Wicken, *Mi'kmaq Treaties on Trial*, contains a close analysis of these agreements.

84 See Johnston, *Control and Order in French Colonial Louisbourg*, 67.

5 Mi'kmaq Decisions: Antoine Tecouenemac, the Conquest, and the Treaty of Utrecht

1 For instance, Expedition faites par les anglois de la Nouvelle Angleterre au Port Royal, Les Mines et Beaubassin à L'accadie, AC, C11D, 5, ff. 27–9.

2 Recensement générale fait au mois de novembre mille Sept cent huit de tous les sauvages de l'Acadie, 1708 (hereafter 1708 census), Newberry Library, Edward E. Ayer MSS, IV, no. 751.

3 Subercase au ministre, 20 décembre 1708, AC, C11D, 6, f. 184.

4 Recensement fait cette presente année du nombre des sauvages, 1735, AC, G1466, no. 71.

5 M. Delabat to M. De Villermont, 20 Nov. 1703, in Morse, ed., *Acadiensa Nova*, II, 1–12.

6 Mémoire concernant l'acadie, 9 décembre 1698, AC, C11D, 3, ff. 320, 324.

7 Thury au ministre, 11 octobre 1698, AC, C11D, 3, f. 309.

8 Ministre à Thury, 15 avril 1699, AC, B, 20, ff. 167–8.

9 Brouillan au ministre, 25 novembre 1703, AC, C11D, 4, f. 277; Mémoire de M. de Brouillan qui concerne le Fort Royal de l'Acadie, 5 mars 1705, AC, C11D, 5, f. 71.

10 Conseil de la Marine, 3 mai 1718, AC, C11B, 3, f. 42. In the correspondence regarding the mission, it is called 'Chedabouctou,' which is located adjacent to the Strait of Fronsac and separates the Acadian peninsula from Cape Breton. However, in discussing the proposed mission in 1705, Subercase said that it was at the head of 'Naspatagan Bay.' He stated that the mission was located only three to four hours from La Hève. Mémoire de M. de Brouillan qui concerne le Fort Royal de l'Acadie, 5 mars 1705, AC, C11D, 5, f. 71. According to a survey of Nova Scotia completed in 1764, 'Aspotagoen' refers to the high land which separates Saint Margaret's and Mahone Bay. See 'Miscellaneous Remarks and Observations on Nova Scotia, New Brunswick and Cape Breton,' in *Collections of the Massachusetts Historical Society for the Year 1794*, First Series, vol. III (New York, Johnson Reprint Company), 96. This would suggest that in transcribing correspondence, French officials in Versailles had written 'Chedabouctou' instead of 'Chebouctou.' Royal approval for the change of location is in Ministre à Subercase, 24 août 1707, AC, B, 29, f. 47.

11 Gaulin au ministre, 20 décembre 1708, AC, C11D, 6, ff. 250–1.

12 Gaulin au ministre, 23 décembre 1708, AC, C11D, 6, f. 263.

13 Bonaventure au ministre, 24 septembre 1706, AC, C11D, 5, f. 246.

14 Patterson, 'Indian–White Relations in Nova Scotia,' 24–6.

15 'Cap de Sable' is the term used by Gaulin in the 1708 census. This region was called Cape Sable by the British during the same time period.

16 Recensement générale, 1708 census, Newberry Library, Ayer MSS, IV, no. 751; Recensement des sauvages, 27 décembre 1721, AC, C11B, 6, f. 74; Recensement fait cette presente année du nombre des sauvages, 1735, AC, G1466, no. 71.

17 Deposition of John Curtiss Senior of Marblehead, 14 June 1706, PRO, CO5/ 864, 160.

18 A Journal of a Voyage to Cape Briton on the King's Acct. by Mr. Peter Capoon,' 1715, MA, 38A, 11, 15.

19 Paul Mascarene, 'Journal of a Voyage from Annapolis Royal to Canso, 1721,' NSARM, RG1, 9, 113.

20 The following analysis relies upon Miller, 'The Micmac: A Maritime Woodland Group,' 326–31; Nietfeld, 'Determinants of Aboriginal Micmac Political Organization,' 306–84.

21 The Examination of Charles D'Entremont of Pobomcoup in his Majesty's Province of Nova Scotia, 11 May 1736, PRO, CO217/7, ff. 182–5.

22 Mémoire des costes de L'acadie, 12 octobre 1701, AC, C11D, 4, f. 85.

23 Sur L'Acadie, 1748, AC, C11D, 10, n.p.; J.R. Campbell, *A History of the County of Yarmouth*, 20.

24 Commission of Governor William Campbell to Francis Alexis, Chief of the Tribe of Cape Sable Indians, 22 June 1771, NSARM, RG1, 168, 155.

25 Report of the Reservations for the Indians by the Surveyor General, 7 May 1820, NSARM, Miscellaneous: Indians, Land Documents.

26 Ricker, *Historical Sketches of Glenwood and the Argyles*, 4.

27 Mémoire de Bonaventure, 1701, AC, C11D, 4, f. 85.

28 Mémoire et Description de l'Acadie par de Cadillac, 1692, AC, C11D, 2, f. 195.

29 Prest, 'Edible Wild Plants of Nova Scotia,' 404–5.

30 Eales, *The Eel Fisheries of Eastern Canada*, 3–5.

31 Smith, 'Survey of Western Nova Scotia,' 1801, NSARM, RG1, 380A.

32 Morrison, 'The Bias of Colonial Law'; Baker and Reid, *The New England Knight*, 156–177.

33 Eastern Indians' Letter to the Governour, 27–8 July 1721, in *Collections of the Massachusetts Historical Society*, ser. 2, VIII, 259–63. The letter has been translated into English, in *Maine Historical Society Quarterly*, 13:3 (1974), 179–84.

34 The location of individual villages is given in Sévigny, *Les Abénaquis*.

35 The 1726 treaty is examined in detail in Wicken, *Mi'kmaq Treaties on Trial*, 25–159.

36 For a summary of the discussions, see PRO, CO5/898, ff. 178–188.

37 Submission and Agreement of the Delegates of the Eastern Indians, 15 December 1725, PRO, CO5/898, ff. 173–4.

38 Articles of Peace and Agreement, 4 June 1726, PRO, CO217/5, f. 3.

39 These talks are discussed in Wicken, *Mi'kmaq Treaties on Trial*, 107–9.

40 Articles of Peace and Agreement, 4 June 1726, PRO, CO217/5, f.3.

41 Promises of John Doucett, 4 June 1726, PRO, CO217/4, f. 321.

6 Imperialism, Diplomacies, and the Conquest of Acadia

1 Richard Philipps to James Craggs, July 1720, NSARM, RG1, vol. 14, 32; Philipps to Board of Trade, 27 September 1720, PRO, CO217/3, no. 18.

2 Memorial of John Henshaw et al. [29 August 1720], PRO, CO217/3, no. 18 (i); Deposition of John Alden, 14 September 1720, ibid., no. 18 (xii); Antoine Couaret and Pierre Couaret to Philipps, 2 October 1720 [N.S.], ibid., no. 18 (xiv). Author's translation: 'Those of your nation have never had leave from us to allow you the freedom of our country, as you would like to have.'

3 Matthew Prior to Oxford, 7 March 1713, PRO, SP105/28, 97; Louis XIV to French Plenipotentiaries, 7 March 1713, PRO, SP103/102, 314; Memoir of Duke of Shrewsbury, 7 March 1713, ibid., 320.

4 Philipps to St Ovide, 14 May 1720, NSARM, RG1, vol. 14, 16.

5 Antoine Couaret and Pierre Couaret to Philipps, 2 October 1720, PRO, CO217/3, no. 18 (xiv). Author's translation: 'we will quarrel with any and all of those who wish to inhabit our country without our consent.'

6 French Proposal of Peace, 22 April 1711, PRO, SP105/266, 4; British Demands, n.d., ibid., 8; Preliminary Articles, 27 September 1711 [8 Oct., N.S.], ibid., 27–33. For general discussion of the context of the negotiations, see the pro-Whig but informative account in George Macaulay Trevelyan, *England under Queen Anne*, vol. 3: *The Peace and the Protestant Succession*. More recent and specialized treatments of the negotiations regarding North America can be found in Hiller, 'Utrecht Revisited'; Laplante, 'Le traité d'Utrecht et la question des limites territoriales de l'Acadie'; Miquelon, *New France, 1701–1744*, 49–53.

7 Prior to Oxford, 29 December 1712, PRO, SP105/266, 246.

8 Plenipotentiaries to Louis XIV, 21 March 1712, PRO, SP103/98, 380–3. Author's translation: 'unending disputes between the parties.'

9 Prior's Negotiation in France, 23–5 July 1711, in Great Britain, Historical Manuscripts Commission, *Report on the Manuscripts of His Grace the Duke of Portland Preserved at Welbeck Abbey*, vol. 5, 36.

10 Ibid., 37.

11 French Response to English Demands, 20 March 1712, PRO, SP103/98, 343–5; [French Plenipotentiaries] to Louis XIV, 9 March 1712, ibid., 286. Author's translations: 'they would also be the masters of the entry to the Gulf of St Lawrence'; 'an ancient domain which preserved communications among their main North American colonies.'

12 French Offers [12 February 1712], PRO, SP105/266, 60; Demands of Great Britain, n.d., ibid., 62–4. Author's translation: 'as also Acadia with the town

of Port Royal, otherwise known as Annapolis Royal, and whatever depends on the said country.'

13 French Response, 20 March 1712, PRO, SP103/98, 343–5.

14 [French Plenipotentiaries] to Louis XIV, 3 April 1712, PRO, SP103/99, 26; [Henry St John], Mémoire touchant l'Amerique Septentrionale, 24 May 1712, PRO, SP105/266, 71–2. Author's translations: 'have protested to us a hundred times that they have express orders to break off [negotiations] entirely'; 'according to its ancient limits.'

15 Mémoire of Torcy, 10 June 1712, PRO, SP78/154, 300–3; French Responses [13 June 1712], PRO, SP103/99, 317–20.

16 Bolingbroke to Prior, 27 August 1713, PRO, SP105/266, 87.

17 Bolingbroke to Prior, 29 September 1712, PRO, SP105/266, 150–1.

18 Instructions to Shrewsbury, 11 December 1712, PRO, CO105/266, 212–13.

19 Prior to Bolingbroke, 19 January 1713, PRO, SP105/266, 304; Mémoire of Torcy, 14, 17 January 1713, PRO, CO105/27, 21. See also Relation de la Conference de M. de Torcy avec M. Prior, 19 December 1712, France, Affaires étrangères, Correspondance politique, Angleterre (hereafter CPA), vol. 240, 264–8.

20 Bolingbroke to Prior, 19 January 1713, PRO, SP105/266, 315–19; Bolingbroke to Prior, 19 January 1713, ibid., 321; Bolingbroke to Torcy, 20 January 1713, France, CPA, vol. 243, 131–5. Author's translation: 'our disagreements over Newfoundland should not be the stumbling block.'

21 Prior to Bolingbroke, 28 December 1712, PRO, SP105/266, 225–6; Proposition Concerted with Prior, 29 December 1712, PRO, SP105/27, 13; see also the analysis in Hiller, 'Utrecht Revisited,' 30–1. Author's translation: 'with all the rights and prerogatives that the French have enjoyed.'

22 Louis XIV to Plenipotentiaries, 23 December 1712, PRO, SP103/101, 278–9.

23 Louis XIV to Plenipotentiaries, 9 February 1713, PRO, SP103/102, 140; Proposal Concerted with Prior, Note, 10 February 1713, PRO, SP105/27, 13; Torcy to Plenipotentiaries, 9 February 1713, PRO, SP103/102, 158.

24 Louis XIV to Plenipotentiaries, 7 March 1713, PRO, SP103/102, 314; Dartmouth to Francis Nicholson, 20 May 1713, PRO, CO324/32, 218; Warrant to Francis Nicholson, 23 June 1713, PRO, CO217/1, no. 19; Treaty of Peace and Friendship, 11 April 1713, in Parry, ed., *The Consolidated Treaty Series*, XXVII, 485. An original Latin text of the treaty is in PRO, SP108/72.

25 Mémoire of Torcy, 14, 17 January 1713, PRO, SP105/27, 21.

26 Bellomont to Board of Trade, 20 April 1700, PRO, CO5/861, no. 31; Mémoire of Bégon [8 November 1718], Massachusetts Historical Society (hereafter MHS), Parkman Papers, vol. 9, 18. Author's translation: 'to pillage and destroy the habitations on the south shore of the St Lawrence River, and

even of all of Canada, which would be easy for them, these natives knowing perfectly all the settlements of New France.'

27 Treaty of Peace and Friendship, 11 April 1713, in Parry, ed., *The Consolidated Treaty Series*, XXVII, 486–7. Author's translations: 'subjects or friends.'; 'which are those who shall or ought to be counted as subjects and friends of France, or of Great Britain.'

28 Eccles, 'Sovereignty-Association, 1500–1783,' 485; White, *The Middle Ground*, 142.

29 D'Aulnay to Pierre Séguier, 10 September 1647, France, Bibiothèque Nationale, Fonds français, 17387, no. 21, 218; see also Reid, *Acadia, Maine, and New Scotland*, 97–8. Author's translation: 'Protestant foreigners.'

30 Proceedings of Portsmouth Conference, 13 July 1713, MA, vol. 29, 11.

31 Proceedings of Casco Conference, 15–18 July 1713, ibid., 19.

32 Ibid.

33 Letter of [Sébastien] Rale, 9 September 1713, MHS, Parkman Papers, vol. 31, 129–31; see also Submission and Agreement of the Eastern Indians, 13 July 1713, PRO, CO5/931, no. 10. Author's translation: 'I have my territory, which I have not given, and shall not give, to anyone. I wish always to be its master; I move throughout it, and when anyone wishes live there he will pay.'

34 No original text of the 1678 treaty has survived, but its terms were summarized in Williamson, *The History of the State of Maine*, II, 552–3.

35 See Baker and Reid, *The New England Knight*, 167–9.

36 See, for examples, Heads and Propositions, 3 June 1701, PRO, CO5/862, no. 101 (i); Memorial of Sagadahoc Conference, 27 July 1702, ibid., no. 125 (ii).

37 Council and Assembly of Massachusetts Bay, 12 July 1704, PRO, CO5/863, no. 105.

38 Vaudreuil to the Minister, 3 November 1710, AC, C11A, vol. 31, 52. Author's translations: 'Monsieur Dudley ... has spared no effort this year'; 'expressing to them the regret they feel at being in a state of war with them.'

39 Letter of [Sébastien] Rale, 9 September 1713, MHS, Parkman Papers, vol. 31, 129–31. Author's translation: 'I beg you.'

40 Thomas Bannister to Board of Trade, 15 July 1715, PRO, CO5/866, no. 53.

41 Proceedings of the Arrowsic Conference, 9–12 August 1717, PRO, CO5/868, 197–8.

42 Vetch to Dartmouth, 24 June 1712, PRO, CO5/9, no. 108.

43 Gaulin to Dudley, 8 July 1713, MA, vol. 51, 265–7.

44 Proceedings of Portsmouth conference, 11 July 1713, MA, vol. 29, 7.

45 Minutes of Massachusetts General Court, 10 February 1714, MA, General Court Records, vol. 9, 345–7.

46 Caulfeild to Nicholson [1713?], NSARM, RG1, vol. 15, 1.

47 Nicholson to Caulfeild, 3 July 1714, NSARM, RG1, vol. 15, 9–12.

48 Answer of the Penobscot [April 1713], PRO, CO217/1, no. 125 (iii). Author's translation: 'I proclaim no foreign king in my country.'

49 Dudley to Board of Trade, 31 July 1715, PRO, CO5/866, no. 69; Journal of Peter Capon, 31 August 1715, MA, vol. 38A, 11.

50 David Jeffries and Charles Shepreve to Robert Mears, 6 July 1715, PRO, CO217/2, no. 2 (1).

51 Journal of Peter Capon, 29 October 1715, MA, vol. 38A, 15.

52 Letter of Christopher Aldridge, 24 May 1715, quoted in Francis Nicholson to William Popple, 16 August 1715, PRO, CO217/2, no. 3.

53 Shirreff to Board of Trade, 24 May 1715, PRO, CO217/1, no. 120.

54 Caulfeild to Board of Trade, 1 November 1715, PRO, CO217/2, no. 8.

55 [Shirreff] to Board of Trade, 18 March 1715, PRO, CO217/1, no. 96.

56 Instructions to Philipps, 14 July 1719, PRO, CO5/189, 427–8.

57 Board of Trade to George I, 8 September 1721, PRO, CO324/10, 412–18.

58 Doucett to Board of Trade, 10 February, 20 June 1718, PRO, CO217/2, nos. 51, 54.

59 Philipps to Board of Trade, 3 January 1720, PRO, CO217/3, no. 5.

60 Philipps to the Lords Justices, 26 May 1720, PRO, CO217/3, no. 6; Speech of the St John's Indians, 26 July 1720, ibid., no. 18 (x); Speech of Philipps, 27 July 1720, ibid., no. 18 (xi); Minutes of Nova Scotia Council, 26 July 1720, in MacMechan, ed., *Nova Scotia Archives III*, 11. Author's translation: 'our father.'

61 See Wicken, '26 August 1726,' 16–18.

62 Speech of François de Salle, 10 November 1720, PRO, CO217/3, no. 19 (ii); Speech of Passamaquoddy, 10 November 1720, ibid., no. 19 (i); Philipps to Board of Ordnance, 28 December 1720, NSARM, RG1, vol. 14, 65. Author's translation: 'We are your friends, and ... we hope for the same of you.'

63 On Massachusetts trade deregulation, see Minutes of General Court, 27 May, 18 June 1714, MA, General Court Records, 9, 373–5, 398–9.

64 Wicken, '26 August 1726,' 13–17.

65 Minutes of General Court, 27 May 1714, MA, General Court Records, 9, 375.

66 *Boston Courant*, 31 December 1722–7 January 1723.

67 Vetch to Dartmouth, 22 January 1711, PRO, CO5/9, no. 85; Vetch to Board of Trade, 26 November 1711, PRO, CO217/1, no. 1.

68 Letter of George Vane, 5 May 1712, PRO, CO217/31, no. 6. See also Principal Inhabitants of Port Royal to Vaudreuil, 13 November 1710, AC C11D, vol. 7, 98–9; Journal of Richard King, 25 June 1711, PRO, CO5/898, no. 11 (i); Geoffrey Plank, 'Samuel Vetch's Imaginary Canada,' paper delivered to American Society for Eighteenth-Century Studies, Nashville, April 1997.

69 Undertaking of Annapolis Royal Inhabitants, August 1714, PRO, CO217/1, no. 56; Proceedings at Annapolis Royal, 19–20 August 1714, ibid., no. 67; Nova Scotia Council Record, 20 August 1714, ibid., no. 68; Proceedings at Minas, 27 August 1714, ibid., no. 72; Undertaking of Minas and Cobequid Inhabitants, 9, 17 September 1714; Pontchartrain to d'Iberville, 24 April 1715, PRO, CO194/5, no. 93 (iii).

70 Francis Spelman and Andrew Simpson to Board of Trade, 2 September 1715, PRO, CO217/2, no. 6; Nicholson to Popple, 16 August 1715, ibid., no. 3; see also Samuel Vetch to Board of Trade, 2 September 1715, ibid., no. 5.

71 [William Shirreff] to Board of Trade, 18 March 1715, PRO, CO217/1, no. 96; Caulfeild to Board of Trade, 23 November 1715, PRO, CO217/2, no. 14; John Doucett to Board of Trade, 20 June 1718, ibid., no. 54. See also Griffiths, *The Acadians: Creation of a People*, 25; Pothier, 'Acadian Emigration to Île Royale after the Conquest of Acadia.'

72 Representation of Governor and Officers [1720], PRO, CO217/3, no. 18 (xviii).

73 Doucett to Philipps, 13 December 1718, PRO, CO217/2, no. 64.

74 Declaration of French Inhabitants of Nova Scotia, 13 January 1715, PRO, CO217/1, no. 124 (xiii); Declaration of French Inhabitants of Nova Scotia, 22 January 1715, ibid., no. 124 (xii). See also Basque, *Des hommes de pouvoir*, 60–1.

75 French Inhabitants to Doucett, [1717], PRO, CO217/2, no. 47 (ii); French Inhabitants of Les Mines to Doucett, 10 February 1718, ibid., no. 51 (iv). See also Griffiths, *The Acadians: Creation of a People*, 23.

76 French Inhabitants of the River to Philipps, [1720], PRO, CO217/3, no. 6 (v); French Inhabitants of Minas to Philipps, [1720], ibid., no. 6 (xv); see also John Adams to Philipps, 14 May 1720, ibid., no. 6 (xvi).

77 Vetch to Board of Trade, 9 March 1715, PRO, CO217/1, no. 93; see also Sir Charles Hobby to Board of Trade, ibid., no. 94.

78 Caulfeild to Board of Trade, 1 November 1715, PRO, CO217/2, no. 8; Address of Inhabitants and Merchants of Annapolis Royal, 5 February 1718, ibid., no. 49 (ii).

79 Barnes, '"The Dayly Cry for Justice,"' 16.

80 See Paul Mascarene, Description of Nova Scotia, 1720, PRO, CO217/3, no. 18 (xx); Philipps to Board of Trade, 27 September 1720, ibid., no. 18.

81 Board of Trade to George I, 30 May 1718, PRO, CO218/1, 369–70.

82 Philipps to French Inhabitants of Annapolis River, 30 April 1720, PRO, CO217/3, no. 6 (vii); Philipps to Lords Justices, 26 May 1720, ibid., no. 6 (i). Author's translation: 'to treat between me, or those whom I may depute, and the ... inhabitants.'

83 Board of Trade to Philipps, 28 December 1720, PRO, CO218/1, 496–7.
84 Board of Trade to James Craggs, 18 March 1719, PRO, CO5/915, 263–4;
Board of Trade to Lords Justices, 5 June 1719, PRO, CO218/1, 411–15.
85 Greene, 'Negotiated Authorities.'
86 Mancke, 'Colonial Corporations and the Emergence of the British Imperial
State'; Walters, '*Mohegan Indians v. Connecticut*,' esp. 789–803. See Baker and
Reid, *The New England Knight*, 253–4.
87 See Plank, 'The Culture of Conquest,' 84–5.
88 See J.A. Murray and Joseph Martin to Bolingbroke, 27 July 1714, PRO,
SP103/16; Letter of Martin Bladen, 29 December 1732, ibid.
89 Philipps to Board of Trade, 27 September 1720, PRO, CO217/3, no. 18.

7 Making a British Nova Scotia

1 Brebner, *New England's Outpost.*
2 Rawlyk, *Nova Scotia's Massachusetts.*
3 Reid, '1686–1720: Imperial Intrusions,' 98.
4 Most of these transactions are to be found in Deed Book 1, Nova Scotia
Department of Lands and Forest, Dartmouth, NS (microfilm copy at
NSARM) and in BL, Sloane MSS, vol. 3607 (microfilm copy at National
Archives of Canada [hereafter NAC]). Matters concerning land ownership
in the town frequently came before the Council after its establishment in
1720. See MacMechan, ed., *Original Minutes of His Majesty's Council at Annapolis Royal, 1720–1739.*
5 Alison Olson, 'Sir Charles Hobby,' DCB, II, 288–90; Barry M. Moody, 'John
Adams,' DCB, III, 3–4. The extent of the activities of the partnership is
revealed in the deeds cited above.
6 Hector H. Hébert, 'Marie-Madeleine Maisonnat,' DCB, III, 421–2; Charles
Bruce Fergusson, 'William Winniett,' DCB, III, 665–6; Calnek, *History of the
County of Annapolis*, 631–2.
7 Clarence J. d'Entremont, 'Agathe de Saint-Étienne de La Tour,' DCB, II,
590–1; Godfrey, *Pursuit of Profit and Preferment in Colonial North America*, 3–5.
8 With the exception of the disappearance of the large block of glebe land in
the lower town, Annapolis Royal's basic design and layout have not changed
significantly since the seventeenth century. Although somewhat altered in
appearance, some of the buildings of this period, and earlier, still stand,
most of wattle and daub construction.
9 MacMechan, ed., *Original Minutes of His Majesty's Council at Annapolis Royal
Council, 1720–1739*, 54.
10 Bushman, *The Refinement of America*, xii, 74–8, 184.

11 Shortt, ed., *Documents Relating to Currency, Exchange and Finance in Nova Scotia*, 225–7.

12 MacMechan, ed., *Original Minutes of His Majesty's Council at Annapolis Royal, 1720–1739*, 44.

13 Rawlyk, *Nova Scotia's Massachusetts*, 121.

14 Charles Bruce Fergusson, 'John Harrison,' DCB, II, 274–5; MacMechan, ed., *Original Minutes of His Majesty's Council at Annapolis Royal, 1720–1739*, 74–5; Richard Watts to Bishop of London, 31 May 1728, NSARM, Society for the Propagation of the Gospel in Foreign Parts, vol. 21, doc. 408; Proclamation by Lawrence Armstrong, 25 April 1733, in Shortt, ed., *Documents Relating to Currency, Exchange and Finance in Nova Scotia*, 192.

15 Fergusson, 'John Harrison,' DCB, II, 274–5.

16 MacMechan, ed., *Original Minutes of His Majesty's Council at Annapolis Royal, 1720– 1739*, 236.

17 The actual beginnings of Freemasonry in Canada are obscure, owing to the scarcity of records and the difficulty of access to them. There are some indications that the society was established in Acadia as early as 1606, but the evidence is scanty, and open to various interpretations. *History of the Ancient and Honourable Fraternity of Free and Accepted Masons*, 439–42.

18 Craig Hanyan, H-AMREL review of Steven C. Bullock, *Revolutionary Brotherhood: Freemasonry and the Transformation of the American Social Order, 1730–1840* (Chapel Hill: University of North Carolina Press, 1996).

19 Quoted from the records of the Grand Lodge of Massachusetts A.F. & A.M., Masonic Temple, Boston, in James M. Sherman [Historian of the Lodge] to Alfred E. Harrington, 6 May 1983. Letter in possession of the author. The earliest history of freemasonry in Nova Scotia begins with the establishment of the Halifax Lodge, but mentions that Philipps at that time was already Provincial Grand Master. *Charges and Regulations, of the Ancient and Honourable Society of Free and Accepted Masons*, viii.

20 Bruce T. McCully, 'Francis Nicholson,' DCB, II, 496–9; G.M. Waller, 'Samuel Vetch,' DCB, II, 650–2; Waller, *Samuel Vetch*; NAC, MG11, NSA, vol 4, contains many documents concerning an inquiry Nicholson conducted into Vetch's handling of garrison accounts.

21 Samuel Vetch to Henry St John, 20 November 1712, NAC, MG11, NSA, vol 4.

22 Col. King's Journal [25 June 1711], MHS, Parkman Papers, vol. 37; Minutes of Council of War, 15 June 1711, NAC, MG11, NSA, vol. 3; Vetch to [Secretary of State?], 18 June 1711, ibid.

23 Vetch to Dartmouth, 27 July 1712, NSARM, RG1, vol. 5.

24 Marshall, *Eighteenth-Century England*, 47.

25 Paul Mascarene to Richard Philipps, 23 April 1720, NAC, MG 11, NSA, 11.

26 John Doucett to Paul Mascarene, 18 April 1723, NAC, NSA, 15.

27 Speck, *Stability and Strife*, 196–9, 233; Willcox and Arnstein, *The Age of Aristocracy*, 84, 96–7.

28 Board of Trade to Philipps, 6 June 1722, *Report on Canadian Archives, 1894*, 52.

29 Haliburton, *An Historical and Statistical Account of Nova-Scotia*, I, 92.

30 Brebner, *New England's Outpost*, 72.

31 The best summaries of the colony's growth and the interplay of French and English/Scottish designs for the area are to be found in Brebner, *New England's Outpost*, Rawlyk, *Nova Scotia's Massachusetts*, and Reid, *Acadia, Maine, and New Scotland*.

32 Vetch to Board of Trade, 26 November 1711, *Report on Canadian Archives, 1894*, 14.

33 Memorial [1714; read by Board of Trade 10 January 1715], ibid., 21.

34 Secretary of State Newcastle to Board of Trade, 17 March 1729, ibid., 68; Board of Trade to Newcastle, 21 March 1729, ibid.

35 Proposal for settling a colony of French Protestants in Nova Scotia [1729], ibid., 70.

36 Proposal of Thomas Coram [10 November 1729], ibid., 70.

37 Minutes, 26 August 1732, MacMechan, ed., *Original Minutes of His Majesty's Council at Annapolis Royal, 1720–1739*, 251; Minutes, 11 September 1732, ibid., 254.

38 Hintze to Board of Trade, 25 September 1730, *Report on Canadian Archives, 1894*, 74.

39 Harley to Board of Trade, 20 August 1713, including Thomas Coram's memorial, *Report on Canadian Archives, 1894*, 18.

40 Williams, *The Whig Supremacy*, 309.

41 Instructions for Richard Philipps, 19 June 1719, NAC, MG 11, Supplemental; Order-in-Council, 30 March 1731, *Report on Canadian Archives, 1894*, 77; Board of Trade to Privy Council, 22 April 1731, ibid.; Order-in-Council approving new instructions for Philipps, 11 May 1731, ibid.

42 Richard Philipps to Board of Trade, 1 October 1721, NSARM, RG1, vol. 7.

43 Richard Philipps to Secretary of State Newcastle, 3 January 1730, *Report on Canadian Archives, 1894*, 71.

44 The best overview of the conflicting claims to this region is to be found in Reid, *Acadia, Maine, and New Scotland*.

45 Letter of David Dunbar, 4 June 1731, in Shortt, ed., *Documents Relating to Currency, Exchange and Finance in Nova Scotia*, 182–3; Sir Richard Temple, Viscount Cobham, to Francis Nicholson, 18 August 1719, Houghton Library, Harvard University, bMS Am 1249; Williams, *The Whig Supremacy*, 204, 238.

46 Mason Wade, 'Emmanuel Le Borgne,' DCB, I, 433–6; George MacBeath, 'Charles de Saint-Étienne de La Tour,' DCB, I, 592–6.

47 Lawrence Armstrong to Board of Trade, 5 October 1731, in Akins, ed., *Selections from the Public Documents of the Province of Nova Scotia*, 91.

48 D'Entremont, 'Agathe de Saint-Étienne de La Tour,' DCB, II, 590–1; Godfrey, *Pursuit of Profit and Preferment in Colonial North America*, 4–5.

49 Petition of Agathe Campbell [2 April 1733], *Report on Canadian Archives, 1894*, 82; A. Popple to John Scrope, 22 March 1734, in Shortt, ed., *Documents Relating to Currency, Exchange and Finance in Nova Scotia*, 197; A. Popple to Nicholas Paxton, 2 October 1734, ibid., 201.

50 A. Popple to John Scrope, 22 March 1734, in Shortt, ed., *Documents Relating to Currency, Exchange and Finance in Nova Scotia*, 197.

51 It is this theme that, in their differing ways, Brebner and Rawlyk have explored. Brebner, *New England's Outpost*, and Rawlyk, *Nova Scotia's Massachusetts*.

52 Taylor, *Liberty Men and Great Proprietors*, 11, 31–2; Rolde, *Sir William Pepperrell of Colonial New England*, 39–41.

53 David Dunbar to A. Popple, 16 May 1729, *Report on Canadian Archives, 1894*, 68–9; Philipps to Board of Trade, 26 November 1730, ibid., 75.

54 Belcher to Thomas Coram, 27 November 1736, MHS, Belcher Papers, vol. 5, 60–2; Belcher to Lawrence Armstrong, 27 June 1734, ibid., vol. 4, 181–2.

55 For a more complete discussion of Belcher's interest and activities in the lands to the east of Massachusetts, see Batinski, *Jonathan Belcher*, 70–1.

56 Brebner, *New England's Outpost*, 134.

57 Beck, *The Government of Nova Scotia*, 5. A similar view is expressed in Beck's more recent *Politics of Nova Scotia, Vol I*.

58 Brebner, *New England's Outpost*, 62–3; DCB II, 122–3, 198–9, 288–90, 496–9, 643–4, 650–2.

59 Maxwell Sutherland, 'Richard Philipps,' DCB, III, 515; Brebner, *New England's Outpost*, 135.

60 Beck, *Politics of Nova Scotia*, 22–3.

61 Most of the minutes of the council meetings between 1720 and 1749, though not all, survived to be published in two volumes by the Public Archives of Nova Scotia: MacMechan, ed., *Original Minutes of His Majesty's Council at Annapolis Royal, 1720–1739* and Fergusson, ed., *Minutes of His Majesty's Council at Annapolis Royal 1736–1749*.

62 Belcher to Capt. Coram, 6 October 1733, MHS, Belcher Letterbooks, III.

63 Rawlyk, '1720–1744: Cod, Louisbourg, and the Acadians.' For further discussion of the relationship between the council and Acadian communities and their deputies, see chapters 8 and 9 below.

64 A major reassessment of Armstrong certainly seems warranted. Most historians are content to follow Brebner's lead, without reexamining the evidence. Brebner, *New England's Outpost*, 86–7. Rawlyk, on no evidence at all, concludes that he was 'probably insane for much of the time between 1731 and 1739': '1720–1744: Cod, Louisbourg, and the Acadians,' 113. Even Armstrong's suspicious 'suicide' in 1739 requires a second look. The most evenhanded assessment is Maxwell Sutherland, 'Lawrence Armstrong,' DCB, II, 21–4.

65 Philipps appointed a number of justices during his brief sojourns in Nova Scotia, and Armstrong appointed additional ones after he assumed control of the government in 1725. MacMechan, ed., *A Calendar of Two Letter-Books and One Commission-Book*, 169–72.

66 Armstrong to Christopher Aldridge, 15 November 1732, NSARM, RG1, vol. 14.

67 Armstrong to Alured Popple, 5 September 1725, in Shortt, ed., *Documents Relating to Currency, Exchange and Finance in Nova Scotia*, 160; Armstrong to Board of Trade, 25 September 1725, *Report on Canadian Archives, 1894*, 58; Armstrong to Board of Trade, 5 October 1731, ibid., 78; Armstrong to Secretary of State Newcastle, 15 November 1732, ibid., 81; Board of Trade to Armstrong, 18 September 1735, ibid., 87.

68 See especially the struggles of 1730–2 over the presidency of the Council. MacMechan, ed., *Minutes of His Majesty's Council at Annapolis Royal, 1720–1739*, 171–219; Board of Trade to Armstrong, 2 November 1732, *Report of Canadian Archives, 1894*, 80.

69 Barnes, '"The Dayly Cry for Justice,"' 17; MacMechan, ed., *Minutes of His Majesty's Council at Annapolis Royal, 1720–1739*, 28–9.

70 Barnes, '"The Dayly Cry for Justice,"' 33.

71 Pastore, 'The Sixteenth Century: Aboriginal Peoples and European Contact,' 34; Griffiths, '1600–1650: Fur, Fish, and Folk,' 50; Rawlyk, *Nova Scotia's Massachusetts*, 125–6.

72 John Doucett to Richard Philipps, 1 November 1718, *Report on Canadian Archives, 1894*, 33–4.

73 Chard, 'Canso, 1710–1721,' 60–1; McNeill, *Atlantic Empires of France and Spain: Louisbourg and Havana, 1700–1763*, 187.

74 Chard, 'Canso, 1710–1721,' 72.

75 McLennan, *Louisbourg from Its Foundation to Its Fall, 1713–1758*, 68–9.

76 MacMechan, ed., *Original Minutes of His Majesty's Council at Annapolis Royal, 1720–1739*, 12–13.

77 Richard Philipps to the Fishery at Canso, 22 October 1720, in MacMechan, ed., *A Calendar of Two Letter-Books and One Commission-Book*, 69.

78 Philipps to Secretary Craggs, 26 September 1720, Akins, *Selections from the Public Documents of Nova Scotia*, 50.

79 Philipps to the Fishery at Canso, 22 October 1720, MacMechan, ed., *A Calendar of Two Letter-Books and a Commission-Book*, 69.

80 Philipps to Board of Trade, 1 October 1721, NSARM, RG1, vol. 7.

81 Philipps to Paul Mascarene, September 1721, MHS, Belcher Papers, 61.A.96.

82 Philipps to Board of Trade, 19 September 1722, Akins, ed., *Selections from the Public Documents of Nova Scotia*, 61–2.

83 Paul Mascarene and John Washington to the Board of Ordnance, 20 September 1722, BL, Additional MSS, 19070.

84 See Balcom, *The Cod Fishery of Isle Royale*, 14–19, for the development of the cod fishery by the French during this time.

85 List of vessels to the port of Canso in 1723, *Report on Canadian Archives, 1894*, 56.

86 Report of John Weller, 1729, Shortt, ed., *Documents Relating to Currency, Exchange, and Finance in Nova Scotia*, 174–5.

87 Philipps to Board of Trade, 16 August 1721, NSARM, RG1, vol. 7; [Mascarene] to [Board of Ordnance], 16 August 1721, NAC, NSA, vol. 14; Philipps to Mascarene 26 September 1721, MHS, Belknap Papers, 61.A.98.

88 Armstrong to Newcastle, 5 September 1725, *Report on Canadian Archives, 1894*, 57; Armstrong to Lords of Trade, 25 September 1725, ibid., 58.

89 Report of John Weller, 1729, Shortt, ed., *Documents Relating to Currency, Exchange and Finance in Nova Scotia*, 175.

90 Petition of Edward How, 15 April 1736, Papers of Society for the Propagation of the Gospel in Foreign Parts, vol. 26, NSARM microfilm; Orders [Paul Mascarene], Canso, 18 April 1736, NAC, MG 11, NSA, vol. 23.

91 C. Alexander Pincombe, 'Edward How,' DCB, III, 297–8.

92 Hansen, *Eighteenth Century Fine Earthenwares from Grassy Island*, 2–3.

93 Ferguson et al., *Report on the 1979 Field Season at Grassy Island, Nova Scotia*; Campbell, 'The How Household,' 54–7.

94 Armstrong to the King [8 July 1736], Shortt., ed., *Documents Relating to Currency, Exchange, and Finance in Nova Scotia*, 206–7. In the same year, Armstrong even sent Edward How to London to plead the case of Canso. Armstrong to Board of Trade, 9 September 1736, MacMechan, ed., *A Calendar of Two Letter-Books and a Commission-Book*, 109–10.

95 For examples, see Armstrong to Christopher Aldridge, 15 November 1732, ibid., 86–7; Armstrong to Justices of the Peace at Canso, 16 November 1732, ibid., 87; Armstrong to Board of Trade, 9 September 1736, ibid., 109–10; Armstrong to Board of Trade, 27 September 1735, NAC, MG 11, NSA, vol. 23.

96 Admiralty to Board of Trade, 6 September 1739, *Report on Canadian Archives, 1894*, 92.

97 One of the few times it surfaces in official correspondences occurs when several masters of British vessels which frequented Canso complained bitterly to the Board of Trade about the unfair competition of the French traders. Representation of Matthew Maugir, Richard Homens & Bodman for themselves & several other Masters of Ships & the fishing Trade at Cansoe in General [8 February 1732], Shortt, ed., *Documents Relating to Currency, Exchange and Finance in Nova Scotia*, 184.

98 Godfrey, *Pursuit of Profit and Preferment in Colonial North America*, 15–19.

99 Belcher to Brouillan, 1 March 1737, MHS, Belcher Papers; Belcher to Mascarene, 1 March 1737, ibid. For Brouillan's involvement in illicit trade, see Bernard Pothier, 'Joseph de Monbeton de Brouillan,' DCB, III, 456.

8 The Third Acadia: Political Adaptation and Societal Change

1 Coleman, *The Acadians at Port Royal*, 39; Sauvageau, *Acadie*, 148–51.

2 Murdoch, *A History of Nova Scotia*, I, 318.

3 Shortt, ed., *Documents Relating to Currency, Exchange and Finance in Nova Scotia*, 18.

4 Rumilly, *L'Acadie française*, 223–4.

5 Basque, *Des hommes de pouvoir*, 59.

6 See White, *Dictionnaire généalogique*, II, 1588–90; Basque, *Des hommes de pouvoir*, 75–9.

7 Shortt, ed., *Documents Relating to Currency, Exchange and Finance in Nova Scotia*, 19–21.

8 *Collection de documents inédits sur le Canada et l'Amérique, tome premier*, 151–2.

9 Micheline D. Johnson, 'Justinien Durand,' DCB, III, 207; see also David Lee, 'Antoine Gaulin,' DCB, II, 238.

10 Shortt, ed., *Documents Relating to Currency, Exchange and Finance in Nova Scotia*, 23.

11 Murdoch, *A History of Nova Scotia*, I, 324–5.

12 Rumilly, *L'Acadie française*, 231.

13 Ibid., 234.

14 Ibid.

15 Ibid.

16 Coleman, *The Acadians at Port Royal*, 42; Akins, ed., *Acadia and Nova Scotia*, 14.

17 Pothier, 'Acadian Emigration to Île Royale after the Conquest of Acadia,' 118.

18 Rumilly, *L'Acadie française*, 241.

19 Pothier, 'Acadian Settlement on Île-Royale, 1713–1734,' 9.
20 Rumilly, *L'Acadie anglaise*, 22. Author's translation: 'Moving is easier for Newfoundland fishermen than Acadian cultivators. One can bring his boat and equipment, but not his land.'
21 Pothier, 'Acadian Emigration to Île Royale after the Conquest of Acadia,' 119.
22 Rumilly, *L'Acadie anglaise*, 23–4.
23 White, *Dictionnaire généalogique*, I, 756–9. See also Bernard Pothier, 'Mathieu de Goutin,' DCB, II, 257–8; Clément Cormier, 'Pierre Thibaudeau,' DCB, II, 629–30.
24 White, *Dictionnaire généalogique*, I, 530–1; II, 1099–1100. See also Pothier, 'Acadian Emigration to Île Royale after the Conquest of Acadia,' 121.
25 The Dupont clan was certainly the most influential military family in Louisbourg and their blood ties with Acadians, especially Acadian traders, gave them quite an advantage over their competitors. Crowley, 'Government and Interests.'
26 Pothier, 'Acadian Emigration to Île Royale after the Conquest of Acadia,' 120.
27 Ibid., 123; White, *Dictionnaire généalogique*, I, 304.
28 Ibid., II, 791–4. See also Daigle, 'Michel Le Neuf de La Vallière, seigneur de Beaubassin.'
29 White, *Dictionnaire généalogique*, I, 23–31. Accompanying the Arseneaus was Abraham Gaudet, the same settler who had participated in the attempted kidnapping of lieutenant Peter Capon in 1711. See Shortt, ed., *Documents Relating to Currency, Exchange and Finance in Nova Scotia*, 23, and White, *Dictionnaire généalogique*, I, 681.
30 Ibid., I, 19, 418–20; II, 996–8.
31 Ibid., II, 1323.
32 Déclaration et Journal du Voyage de Pierre Arceneau, habitant de Beauséjour s'en allant de ladite place pour faire le négoce jusqu'au Cap Gaspé le 28 mai 1714 dans un canot d'écorce, Université de Moncton, Centre d'études acadiennes, Fonds Auguste Daigle, 19.1–5.
33 PRO, War Office 55, no. 1: 1765, 2372; Université de Moncton, Centre d'études acadiennes, *Inventaire général des sources documentaires sur les Acadiens, premier tome*, 427. In Charles Melanson's case, living next to the fort, *'Proche le Fort'*, as stated in the 1714 census of Port-Royal, must have been practical for establishing ties with the British. See White, *Dictionnaire généalogique*, II, 1156.
34 Basque, *Des hommes de pouvoir*, 78–84, 95.
35 Coleman, *The Acadians at Port Royal*, 43.

36 Pothier, 'Acadian Settlement on Île Royale, 1713–1734,' 10; Rumilly, *L'Acadie anglaise*, 23.
37 Coleman, *The Acadians at Grand Pré*, 16.
38 Rumilly, *L'Acadie anglaise*, 24.
39 Pothier, 'Acadian Settlement on Île Royale, 1713–1734,' 11.
40 White, *Dictionnaire généalogique*, I, 231.
41 Ibid., II, 1200–1. The departures from Beaubassin have been examined in a detailed recent study. See Rompillon, 'La migration à Beaubassin, village acadien.'
42 Pothier, 'Acadian Emigration to Île Royale after the Conquest of Acadia.'
43 Pothier, 'Acadian Settlement on Île Royale, 1713–1734,' 19.
44 Naomi Griffiths has been one of the strongest proponents of this family-based interpretation of Acadian colonial society. The first two chapters of her *Contexts of Acadian History* provide numerous examples of this interpretation. Griffiths, *Contexts of Acadian History*, 4–61.
45 Basque, *Des hommes de pouvoir*, 59–60.
46 See Durand, *Les solidarités dans les sociétés humaines*, 197–202. See also Griffiths, 'Subjects and Citizens in the Eighteenth Century,' 23–33.
47 PRO, Colonial Records, Board of Trade – Nova Scotia, vol. 1, in *Collection de documents inédits sur le Canada et l'Amérique, tome premier*, 110–11.
48 Griffiths, 'Subjects and Citizens,' 27–9. This new interpretation by Naomi Griffiths is groundbreaking because up until now, almost all historians had linked the oath of allegiance question in pre-1755 Acadia to religion. For a good example of this approach, see Rumilly, *L'Acadie anglaise*, 28.
49 Basque, *Des hommes de pouvoir*, 69.
50 Ibid., 63; Delaney, 'The Husbands and Children of Agathe de La Tour.' See also Godfrey, *Pursuit of Profit and Preferment in Colonial North America*, 3. Around 1700, Alexandre Robichaud had married Anne Melanson, widow of Jacques de Saint-Étienne de La Tour. Agathe was approximately ten years old at the time. This matrimonial union added new prestige to the Robichaud clan. See Vanderlinden, *Se marier en Acadie*.
51 Basque, *Des hommes de pouvoir*, 61. One of the pioneers of Cobeguid, Martin Bourg, was the uncle of Marie Bourg, Charles Robichaud's wife. See Campbell, 'The Acadian Seigneury of St-Mathieu at Cobeguid,' 79. In the 1740s, while his Robichaud cousins in Annapolis Royal were allies of the English, Charles Robichaud's son Joseph was being accused of giving hospitality to the arch rival of the British, *abbé* Jean-Louis Le Loutre. See Robichaud, *Les Robichaud, histoire et généalogie*, 24. The Robichauds, with their pro-French and pro-British factions, are reminiscent of the brothers Charles and Pierre Melanson in the 1690s.

52 Rameau de Saint-Père, *Une colonie féodale en Amérique*, 344–5; Barrieau, 'L'évolution du paysage ,' 21.

53 Basque, *Des hommes de pouvoir*, 45–6.

54 See Rumilly, *L'Acadie française*, 231.

55 PRO, Col. Records – Nova Scotia, vol. 1, in *Collection de documents inédits sur le Canada et l'Amérique, tome premier*, 161–2; see also 111–12.

56 Ibid., 112.

57 Pothier, 'Acadian Emigration to Île Royale after the Conquest of Acadia,' 128.

58 PRO, Col. Records – Nova Scotia, vol. 1, in *Collection de documents inédits sur le Canada et l'Amérique, tome premier*, 113.

59 Rumilly, *L'Acadie anglaise*, 39.

60 MacMechan, ed., *A Calendar of Two Letter-Books and One Commission-Book*, 53.

61 Ibid., 51. Doucett's interpretation clearly indicates that the Catholic priests present in Nova Scotia were well aware of the possibility of the return of the Stuart dynasty to the British throne. They used the Pretender's possible return as a strategic tool in their offensive against the oath.

62 Griffiths, *The Contexts of Acadian History*, 11–12.

63 Miquelon, *New France 1701–1744*, 26–7.

64 See Richter, *The Ordeal of the Longhouse*.

65 For a thoroughly researched and penetrating analysis of the 1701 Peace of Montreal, see Havard, *La Grande Paix de Montréal de 1701*.

66 Desserud, 'Nova Scotia and the American Revolution,' 97–8.

67 Morrison, 'The People of the Dawn,' 273; Miquelon, *New France 1701–1744*, 26. See also Morrison, *The Embattled Northeast*, 133–64.

68 Richter, *The Ordeal of the Longhouse*; Calloway, 'The Abenakis and the Anglo–French Borderlands.'

69 Griffiths, 'Subjects and Citizens,' 29–30.

70 Ibid., 29; PRO, Col. Records – Nova Scotia, vol. 2, in *Collection de documents inédits sur le Canada et l'Amérique, tome premier*, 170.

71 Legal historian Jacques Vanderlinden arrived at the same conclusion when researching Acadian judicial behaviour in the first part of the eighteenth century, demonstrating that they chose either French or British law, whichever offered them a better outcome. See Vanderlinden, 'À la rencontre de l'histoire du droit en Acadie avant le Dérangement.'

72 Rumilly, *L'Acadie anglaise*, 49.

73 MacMechan, ed., *A Calendar of Two Letter-Books and One Commission-Book*, 60.

74 Griffiths, 'Subjects and Citizens,' 30.

75 Extrait d'une lettre des habitans du port Royal, des Mines, de Beaubassin,

envoyée a Mr de St-Ovide par des habitans députés de Leurs part, in *Collection de documents inédits sur le Canada et l'Amérique, tome premier,* 128.

76 Demandes que l'on suppose qui seront faites aux Des habitans avec les réponses envoyez par Mr de St Ovide aux missionnres pour être communiqués aux plus fidèles au cas de besoin, ibid., 129.

77 White, *Dictionnaire généalogique,* II, 1272–5.

78 MacMechan, ed., *Original Minutes of His Majesty's Council at Annapolis Royal, 1720–1739,* 130.

79 Griffiths, 'Subjects and Citizens,' 30–1.

80 Ibid., 32.

81 Pitre and Pelletier, *Les Pays-Bas,* 108, 114.

82 Ensn Wroth Proceedings up the Bay, in *Collection de documents inédits sur le Canada et l'Amérique, tome premier,* 182–4 ; White, *Dictionnaire généalogique,* II, 1558–60.

83 Rompillon, 'La migration à Beaubassin, village acadien,' 126. Acadian migration to Île Saint-Jean took place mostly in the late 1740s in the aftermath of the War of the Austrian Succession. Before that time, French colonial administrators of Louisbourg had tried, without much success, to attract Acadian settlers on Île Saint-Jean by naming Louis Dupont Duchambon *Lieutenant du roi.* This French military officer was married to Acadian Jeanne Mius d'Entremont and was reportedly very popular among the Acadians. See Arsenault, *Les Acadiens de l'Île,* 28–9.

84 Surette, *Petcoudiac, Colonisation et destruction,* 16. See also Surette, *Atlas de l'établissement des Acadiens aux trois rivières du Chignectou.*

85 Akins, ed., *Acadia and Nova Scotia,* 173. See also LeBlanc, 'Neutralité des Acadiens.'

86 Akins, ed., *Acadia and Nova Scotia,* 263, 265.

87 MacMechan, ed., *A Calendar of Two Letter-Books and One Commission-Book,* 171–2. For Jean Duon, this position meant a change of heart, for in 1725, he had made a request to leave the province to settle elsewhere. See White, *Dictionnaire généalogique,* I, 584.

88 Basque, *Des hommes de pouvoir,* 90.

89 Ibid., 71.

90 Ibid.

91 Tapie, 'Les structures socio-économiques de Grand Pré.'

92 Barnes, '"The Dayly Cry for Justice."'

93 Brun, 'Marie de Saint-Étienne de La Tour,' 259.

94 Basque, *Des hommes de pouvoir,* 80, 89. The anglophile Prudent Robichaud still kept good contacts in Louisbourg, where he and his son Prudent, Jr, did business with an influential merchant, Guillaume Delort.

95 Centre d'études acadiennes, Fonds Placide Gaudet, boîte 50, dossier 12; Université de Moncton, Centre d'études acadiennes, *Inventaire général des sources documentaires sur les Acadiens, premier tome,* 430.

96 Fergusson, ed., *Minutes of his Majesty's Council at Annapolis Royal 1736–1749,* 10.

97 Pitre and Pelletier, *Les Pays-Bas,* 156–7.

98 White, *Dictionnaire généalogique,* II, 1012.

99 Recent studies have shown that Acadian neutrality in the 1740s was not strictly observed by all the Acadians. See Plank, *An Unsettled Conquest;* Barnes, ' "Twelve Apostles" or a Dozen Traitors?'; Basque, *Des hommes de pouvoir.* See also Pothier, *Course à l'Accadie.*

100 Desserud, 'Nova Scotia and the American Revolution,' 97–8. Griffiths, 'The Golden Age.'

9 Imperial Transitions

1 Queen Anne to Francis Nicholson, 1713, PRO, CO217/1, f. 95; and Brebner, *New England's Outpost,* 64–5.

2 Greene, 'Negotiated Authorities.'

3 Dunn, *Sugar and Slaves,* 152–3. A handful of Spaniards fled into the mountains and resisted the English conquest for five years before being driven out.

4 In the English system, the crown, or in the colonies the governor, could endenize aliens with a patent. Only Parliament could naturalize subjects; the rights of colonial assemblies to naturalize subjects was contested. See Salmond, 'Citizenship and Allegiance,' 270–82; and Kettner, *The Development of American Citizenship,* 3–6, 30, 65–105.

5 Patterson, 'Slavery and Slave Revolts.'

6 See William Wicken, chapter 5 in this volume.

7 See Maurice Basque, chapter 8 in this volume. Note exceptions, such as de Goutin.

8 Malone, *Pine Trees and Politics,* 10–27.

9 Paul Mascarene to Board of Trade, 16 August 1740, PRO, CO217/8, f. 72.

10 On the development of a distinctly English definition of seventeenth-century colonies in the Americas, see Canny, 'The Origins of Empire: An Introduction'; compare Griffiths, *The Contexts of Acadian History,* 39. For studies dealing with the increasingly polyglot nature of the empire, see Marshall, 'Empire and Authority in the Later Eighteenth Century'; Mancke, 'Another British America'; and Bowen, 'British Conceptions of Global Empire.'

11 Philipps to Board of Trade, 15 May 1727, PRO, CO217/4, ff. 373–4; Maxwell Sutherland, 'Richard Philipps,' DCB, III, 515–18.

12 Philipps to Board of Trade [1720], PRO, CO217/3, f. 104.

13 Bruce T. McCully, 'Francis Nicholson,' DCB, II, 96–8; and G.M. Waller, 'Samuel Vetch,' DCB, II, 650–2.

14 Brebner, *New England's Outpost*, 61.

15 Caulfeild to Board of Trade, 16 May 1716, in MacMechan, ed., *A Calendar of Two Letter-Books and One Commission-Book*, 38–9; Charles Bruce Fergusson, 'Thomas Caulfeild,' DCB, II, 122–3.

16 Maxwell Sutherland, 'Richard Philipps,' DCB, III, 515–18; *Journals of the House of Commons 1715–1751*, XVIII, 342, 483, 636; XIX,11, 17; XXVI, 16.

17 'Nova Scotia Governor to Follow Virginia Instructions,' in Labaree, ed., *Royal Instructions to British Colonial Governors*, I, 85.

18 Brebner, *New England's Outpost*, 73, 134, 138, 239. For an assessment see Barnes, '"The Dayly Cry for Justice,"' 14–16.

19 Labaree, ed., *Royal Instructions to British Colonial Governors*, vii–xvii.

20 Greene, 'Empire and Identity from the Glorious Revolution to the American Revolution,' 209.

21 Braddick, 'The English Government, War, Trade, and Settlement.'

22 Here, the English and French terms might have created some confusion, though one that Philipps worked to the best advantage he could with the Acadians and the Board of Trade. The governor general in New France was the top military official and resident in Quebec. Under him were governors in Trois-Rivières, Montreal, Île Royale, and Louisiana. The civilian counterpart to the governor general of New France was the intendant, with subordinates under him in each jurisdiction. In the British American colonies, each royal colony had a governor, with a lieutenant-governor who, in the absence of the governor, served in his stead. Only in some British colonies was there a governor general, that is, a military officer with a military command in addition to his civil commission as governor. André Vachon, 'The Administration of New France.'

23 Proclamation, 20 April 1720, PRO, CO217/3, f. 40. Author's translations: 'the free exercise of their religion;' and 'civil rights and privileges as if they were English.'

24 The highest-ranking civilian official in Nova Scotia, whether the governor, lieutenant-governor, or president of the Council, always had to justify the appointment of military officers to the Council. See, for example, Philipps to Board of Trade, 3 January 1729, PRO, CO217/5, ff. 190–6; Armstrong to Board of Trade, ibid., ff. 39–44; Mascarene to Board of Trade, 16 August 1740, PRO, CO217/8, f. 72; Mascarene to Board of Trade, 28 October 1742, ibid., ff. 177–8.

25 Council Minutes, 12 April 1721, in MacMechan, ed., *Original Minutes of His Majesty's Council at Annapolis Royal, 1720–1739*, 28–9.

26 Barnes, '"The Dayly Cry for Justice,"' 18.

27 Armstrong, 'Proclamation to the Inhabitants of Nova Scotia,' in Mac-Mechan, ed., *A Calendar of Two Letter-Books and One Commission-Book*, 177–8.

28 MacMechan, ed., *Original Minutes of His Majesty's Council at Annapolis Royal, 1720–1739*, 4; Philipps to Craggs, 26 May 1720, in MacMechan, ed., *A Calendar of Two Letter-Books and One Commission-Book*, 60.

29 The system of deputies is surprisingly underresearched. The standard scholarship treats the system as largely unchanging over the period c. 1710–55, which it was not. See Brebner, *New England's Outpost*, 149–52; and Griffiths, *The Contexts of Acadian History*, 41–5.

30 MacMechan, ed., *Original Minutes of His Majesty's Council at Annapolis Royal, 1720–1739*, 170.

31 Armstrong, 'Order for Choosing New Deputies,' 26 August 1732, in Mac-Mechan, ed., *A Calendar of Two Letter-Books and One Commission-Book*, 190.

32 Minutes, 7 December 1730, in MacMechan, ed., *Original Minutes of His Majesty's Council at Annapolis Royal, 1720–1739*, 172–3; Minutes, August 1731, ibid., 188–9.

33 Philipps to Board of Trade, 25 November 1729, PRO, CO217/5, ff. 176–8.

34 Minutes, 7 December 1730, in MacMechan, ed., *Original Minutes of His Majesty's Council at Annapolis Royal, 1720–1739*, 173.

35 On the changing responsibilities of deputies from 1731 to 1740 see Mac-Mechan, ed., *A Calendar of Two Letter-Books and One Commission-Book*, 187–247. On the appointment of rent farmers see ibid, 197, 212–13, 216–19, 226. On the increasing number of litigants, see Barnes, '"The Dayly Cry for Justice,"' 18–19.

36 Minutes, 11 September 1732, in MacMechan, ed., *Original Minutes of His Majesty's Council at Annapolis Royal, 1720–1739*, 255; and 'Order for the Election of Deputies,' 30 August 1733, 12 September 1734, and 14 September 1735, in MacMechan, ed., *A Calendar of Two Letter-Books and a Commission-Book*, 196, 200, 207–8. For whatever reason, the chosen date for commemorating the conquest did not conform to the actual anniversary.

37 Mémoire pour Monsieur [illegible], from Paul Mascarene, 27 May 1740, ibid., 241–2.

38 Mascarene to Board of Trade, 16 August 1740, PRO, CO217/8, f. 72.

39 Greene, 'Empire and Identity.'

40 Brebner, *New England's Outpost*, 137; Griffiths, *The Contexts of Acadian History*, 41; Barnes, '"Twelve Apostles" or a Dozen Traitors?'

41 See chapter 7 in this volume.

42 Council to Philipps, 10 June 1738, in MacMechan, ed., *A Calendar of Two Letter-Books and One Commission-Book*, 120–1.

43 Mascarene to Board of Trade, 28 October 1742, PRO, CO217/8, ff. 177–8; Maxwell Sutherland, 'Paul Mascarene,' DCB, III, 435–9.

44 MacMechan, ed., *A Calendar of Two Letter-Books and One Commission-Book*, 169; Petition of Joshua Peirce, Stephen Perkins, Elias Davis, and Thomas Kilby to Richard Philipps, 19 August 1729, PRO, CO217/5, f. 183.

45 Armstrong to Aldridge, 15 November 1732, PRO, CO217/7, ff. 6–6d; Armstrong to the Justices of the Peace at Canso, 15 November 1732, ibid., ff. 62–3.

46 Armstrong to Board of Trade, 24 November 1726, PRO, CO217/5, ff. 1–2; Extract of Instructions to Virginia, PRO, CO217/8, f. 184d; Court at St James, 10 March 1730, PRO, CO217/6, ff. 35–6; Labaree, *Royal Government in America*, 312–72; and Greene, *The Quest for Power*, 129–47.

47 MacMechan, ed., *A Calendar of Two Letter-Books and One Commission-Book*, 173–4.

48 Philipps to Secretary of State, 1721, ibid., 76; Armstrong to Aldridge, 15 November 1732, PRO, CO217/7, ff. 6–6d; and Mascarene to Board of Trade, 28 October 1742, PRO, CO217/8, ff. 177–8.

49 Armstrong to Board of Trade, 2 December 1725, PRO, CO217/4, f. 314.

50 Duke of Bedford to Board of Trade, 20 July 1749, PRO, CO217/9, f. 63.

51 Doucett to Board of Trade, 6 November 1717, PRO, CO217/2, ff. 175–6. For earlier attempts to have Acadians swear an oath of allegiance, see Brebner, *New England's Outpost*, 64, 75–6.

52 Doucett to Board of Trade, 6 November 1717, PRO, CO217/2, f. 175.

53 Doucett to Peter Mellanson, 5 December 1717, ibid., f. 197.

54 Doucett to Board of Trade, 6 November 1717, ibid., f. 176.

55 Caulfeild to Board of Trade, 1 November 1715, in MacMechan, ed., *A Calendar of Two Letter-Books and One Commission-Book*, 27; Caulfeild to Vetch [1715], ibid., 29.

56 Doucett to Board of Trade, 6 November 1717, PRO, CO217/2, f. 175.

57 Council Minutes, 24 September 1720, in MacMechan, ed., *Original Minutes of His Majesty's Council at Annapolis Royal, 1720–1739*, 15.

58 Philipps and Council to the King, 27 April 1720, PRO, CO217/3, f. 104; and MacMechan, ed., *A Calendar of Two Letter-Books and One Commission-Book*, 66–7.

59 Philipps to the Inhabitants at Annapolis River, 10 April 1721, ibid., 74.

60 Council Minutes, 11 February 1723, in MacMechan, ed., *Original Minutes of His Majesty's Council at Annapolis Royal, 1720–1739*, 43–4.

61 Maxwell Sutherland, 'Lawrence Armstrong,' DCB, II, 21–4.

62 Brebner, *New England's Outpost*, 88–9.

63 Minutes, 25 September 1726, in MacMechan, ed., *Original Minutes of His Majesty's Council at Annapolis Royal, 1720–1739*, 129–30.

64 Report by Erasmus James Philipps to Armstrong, 1727, PRO, CO217/5, ff. 31–2; Minutes, 23 May 1727, in MacMechan, ed., *Original Minutes of His Majesty's Council at Annapolis Royal, 1720–1739*, 144.

65 Minutes, 1 June 1727, ibid., 146; Minutes, 25 July 1727, ibid., 149–50.

66 Brebner, *New England's Outpost*, 89–91; and Sutherland, 'Lawrence Armstrong,' DCB, II, 23.

67 Minutes, 26–7 September 1727, in MacMechan, ed., *Original Minutes of His Majesty's Council at Annapolis Royal, 1720–1739*, 161–4; Instructions of Armstrong to Robert Wroth, PRO, CO217/5, ff. 49–50.

68 Minutes, 13 November 1727, in MacMechan, ed., *Original Minutes of His Majesty's Council at Annapolis Royal, 1720–1739*, 168.

69 Minutes, 16 May 1730, ibid., 171.

70 Brebner, *New England's Outpost*, 166–202.

71 Philipps to Board of Trade, 15 May 1727, PRO, CO217/4, ff. 373–4. For similar sentiments, see Report of Colonel Philipps on Newfoundland and Nova Scotia, 1718, PRO, CO217/2, ff. 171–2; Philipps to Board of Trade, 3 January 1719, PRO, CO217/3, f. 21; 'The State and Condition of His Majestys Province of Nova Scotia truely Represented,' 8 May 1728, PRO, CO217/5, ff. 17–18; David Dunbar to Board of Trade, PRO, CO217/8, ff. 107–8.

72 Philipps to Board of Trade, 15 May 1727, PRO, CO217/4, ff. 373–4.

73 'The State and Condition of His Majestys province of Nova Scotia truely Represented,' 8 May 1728, PRO, CO217/5, ff. 17–18.

74 Report of Privy Council Committee, 15 February 1726, PRO, CO217/4, f. 324.

75 Philipps to Board of Trade, 3 January 1719, PRO, CO217/3, f. 21.

76 The State and Condition of His Majestys province of Nova Scotia truely Represented, 8 May 1728, PRO, CO217/5, ff. 17–18.

77 Philipps to Board of Trade, 2 October 1729, ibid., ff. 170–1; Philipps to Board of Trade, 2 September 1730, ibid., ff. 225–9.

78 Paul Mascarene to Board of Trade, 16 August 1740, PRO, CO217/8, f. 72. See also, 'Representation of the State of His Majesties Province of Nova Scotia,' 8 November 1745, in Fergusson, ed., *Minutes of His Majesty's Council at Annapolis Royal, 1736–1749*, 83.

79 Armstrong to Board of Trade, 20 November 1733, PRO, CO217/7, ff. 49–50.

80 Philipps to Board of Trade [1720], PRO, CO217/3, f. 104.

81 Armstrong to Board of Trade, 30 April 1727, PRO, CO217/5, ff. 28–30.

82 Armstrong to Board of Trade, 17 November 1727, ibid., f. 41.

83 Armstrong to Board of Trade, 9 July 1728, ibid., ff. 116–17.

84 Proclamation of Lt. Gov. Lawrence Armstrong, 29 July 1727, ibid., f. 71; and Thomas Lechmere to Board of Trade, 20 September 1727, ibid., f. 76.

85 Doucett to Board of Trade, 10 February 1718, PRO, CO217/2, f. 194.

86 Philipps to Board of Trade [1720], PRO, CO 217/3, f. 119.

87 Doucett to Board of Trade, 16 August 1726, PRO, CO217/4, ff. 316–18.

88 Greene, '"A Posture of Hostility"'; Mancke, 'Negotiating an Empire.'

89 Philipps to Board of Trade, 2 September 1730, PRO, CO217/5, ff. 225–9.

90 Upton, *Micmacs and Colonists*, 48–60; and Paul, *We Were Not the Savages*, 86–148.

91 In recent years scholars have increasingly emphasized the multiethnic character of the North American colonies, particularly Pennsylvania, New York, New Jersey, and Delaware. But, as noted earlier, the cultural diversity in these colonies did not require serious political and constitutional adjustments on the scale of those required in early-eighteenth-century Nova Scotia and post-conquest Quebec. Indeed legal decisions have recognized that the Proclamation of 1763 and the Quebec Act of 1774 granted constitutional rights to *Canadiens* and First Nations in ways that are unparalleled in the constitutional history of the United States.

92 Labaree, ed., *Royal Instructions to British Colonial Governors*, II, 469, 478–9.

Conclusion

1 Griffiths, 'The Golden Age: Acadian Life, 1713–1748.' 21–34.

2 See Black, *British Foreign Policy in the Age of Walpole*, 2–11.

3 Lord William Campbell to Lord Hillsborough, 25 October 1768, PRO, CO217/45, no. 27.

4 Taylor, 'Centers and Peripheries: Locating Maine's History,' 14.

5 Adelman and Aron, 'From Borderlands to Borders: Empires, Nation States, and the Peoples in Between in North American History.'

6 See White, *The Middle Ground*.

Bibliography

Primary Sources

Manuscript Sources

Canada
National Archives of Canada.
　MG 11, NSA: 3, 4, 11, 14, 15, 23.
Nova Scotia Archives and Records Management.
　Miscellaneous: Indians, Land Documents.
　RG1: 3, 5, 7, 9, 10, 14, 15, 16, 32, 380A.
Nova Scotia Department of Lands and Forests.
　Deed Book 1.
Université de Moncton, Centre d'études acadiennes.
　Fonds Auguste-Daigle.
　Fonds Placide-Gaudet.

France
Archives du ministère des Affaires étrangères.
　Correspondance politique, Angleterre: 240, 243.
Archives Nationales, Archives des colonies.
　Séries B; C11A; C11B; C11C; C11D; G.
Bibliothèque Nationale.
　Fonds français: 17387, 18593.

Great Britain
British Library.
 Additional MSS, 19070, 19071.
 Sloane MSS, 3607.
Public Record Office.
 Series CO1; CO5; CO194; CO217; CO218; CO323; CO324; SP78; SP103,
 SP105; SP108.

United States
Boston Public Library.
 Autobiography of Stephen Williams.
Houghton Library, Harvard College.
 bMS Am 1249.
Huntington Library.
 BL 127.
 HM 1368; 1373; 1393; 9916; 22271; 22287.
Library of Congress.
 Peter Force Collection, Series 8D/6.
Massachusetts Historical Society.
 Belcher Papers.
 Belknap Papers.
 Gay Papers.
 Mascarene Family Papers.
 Miscellaneous Bound, 1706–1713.
 Parkman Papers.
 Sewall Papers.
Massachusetts State Archives.
 Massachusetts Archives: 2, 37, 38A, 51, 91.
 Records of the General Court: 9.
Museum of the City of New York.
 Letter-Book of Samuel Vetch.
Newberry Library.
 Edward E. Ayer MSS, IV.

Published Primary Sources

Akins, Thomas B., ed. *Selections from the Public Documents of the Province of Nova Scotia.* Halifax, 1869.
– *Acadia and Nova Scotia: Documents Relating to the Acadian French and the First British Colonization of the Province, 1714–1758.* Cottonport, LA, 1972.

Anon. *Some Considerations on the Consequences of the French Settling Colonies on the Mississippi.* London, 1720; reprinted Cincinnati, 1928.

Appleton, Nathaniel. *The Origin of War Examined and Applied.* Boston 1733 (Evans 3623).

Barnard, John. 'Autobiography.' *Massachusetts Historical Society Collections,* 5th ser. 5,6 (1879).

Biggar, H.P. ed. *The Works of Samuel de Champlain.* 6 vols. Toronto: The Champlain Society, 1906.

Boston Courant.

Boston Evening Post.

Boston News-Letter.

Boston Post-Boy.

Church, Thomas. *Entertaining Passages Relating to Philip's War.* Boston, 1716 (Evans 1800).

Collection de documents inédits sur le Canada et l'Amérique publiés par le Canada-Français, tome premier. Quebec: L.J. Demers et Frère, 1888.

Collections of the Massachusetts Historical Society, 1st ser., vol. 3 (Boston, 1794); 2nd ser., vol. 8 (Boston, 1819).

Collections of the Nova Scotia Historical Society, I (Halifax, 1879); IV (Halifax, 1885).

Doughty, Arthur G. *Rapport sur les travaux de la Division des Archives pour l'année 1912.* Ottawa: Imprimeur du roi. 1914.

Douglass, William. *A Summary, Historical and Political, of the First Planting, Progressive Improvements, and Present State of the British Settlements in North America, Volume One.* Boston, 1749 (Evans 6307).

Dudley, Joseph. *A Modest Inquiry into the Grounds and Occasions of a Late Pamphlet.* Reprinted in *Masssachusetts Historical Society Collections,* 5th ser., 6 (1879), 65–95.

Ebacher, Laurie. 'Charles Melanson Letters.' *Mémoires de la Société généalogique canadienne-française,* 6: 6–7 (1955), 313–18.

Fergusson, Charles Bruce, ed. *Minutes of His Majesty's Council at Annapolis Royal 1736–1749.* Halifax, 1967.

Graham, Gerald S., ed. *The Walker Expedition to Quebec, 1711.* Toronto, 1953.

Great Britain, Historical Manuscripts Commission. *Report on the Manuscripts of His Grace the Duke of Portland Preserved at Welbeck Abbey, Vol. 5.* Norwich, 1899.

Great Britain, Public Record Office. *Calendar of State Papers, Colonial Series, America and West Indies.* W. Noel Sainsbury, et al., eds. London, 1860– .

Gyles, John. *Memoirs and Odd Adventures.* Boston, 1736 (Evans 4021).

Hesketh, Thomas. *Divine Providence Asserted and Some Objections Answered.* Boston, 1710 (Evans 1455).

Hubbard, William. *A Narrative of the Troubles with the Indians.* Boston, 1677 (Evans 231).

Independent Advertiser.

Instructions for Samuel Vetch (New York, 1709) (Evans 1353). Reprinted in *Nova Scotia Historical Society Collections*, 4 (1884), 64–8.

Journals of the House of Commons, 1715–1751.

Journals of the House of Representatives of Massachusetts. Boston, 1919– .

Labaree, Leonard Woods, ed. *Royal Instructions to British Colonial Governors, 1670–1776.* 2 vols. New York, 1967; first published 1935.

Leclercq, Chrestien. *New Relation of Gaspesia.* W.F. Ganong, ed. Toronto, 1910.

Lescarbot, Marc. *The History of New France.* W.L. Grant, ed. 3 vols. Toronto, 1907–14; first published 1618.

Little, Otis. *The State of Trade in the Northern Colonies Considered.* London, 1748.

MacMechan, Archibald M., ed. *A Calendar of Two Letter-Books and One Commission-Book in the Possession of the Government of Nova Scotia (Nova Scotia Archives II).* Halifax, 1900.

– ed. *Original Minutes of His Majesty's Council at Annapolis Royal, 1720–1739 (Nova Scotia Archives III).* Halifax, 1888.

Mather, Cotton. *The Deplorable State of New England.* London, 1708, and Boston 1721. Reprinted in *Massachusetts Historical Society Collections*, 5th ser., 6 (1879), 96–131.

[Mather, Cotton]. Philopolites, *A Memorial of the Present Deplorable State of New England.* Boston, 1707 (Evans 1331). Reprinted in *Massachusetts Historical Society Collections*, 5th ser., 6 (1879), 31–64.

Moody, Robert E., ed. *The Letters of Thomas Gorges: Deputy Governor of the Province of Maine, 1640–1643.* Portland, ME, 1978.

Morse, William, ed. *Acadiensa Nova 1598–1779.* London: B. Qauritch, 1935.

Nicholson, Francis. 'Journal of Colonel Nicholson at the Capture of Annapolis, 1710.' *Nova Scotia Historical Society Collections*, 1 (1878).

Parry, Clive, ed. *The Consolidated Treaty Series.* 231 vols. Dobbs Ferry, NY, 1969–81.

Penhallow, Samuel. *The History of the Wars of New England with the Eastern Indians.* Boston, 1726 (Evans 2796).

Report on Canadian Archives, 1894. Ottawa: Queen's Printer, 1895.

Sewall, Samuel. *The Diary of Samuel Sewall.* Thomas M. Halsey, ed. 2 vols. New York, 1973.

Shortt, Adam, ed. *Documents Relating to Currency, Exchange and Finance in Nova Scotia with Prefatory Documents, 1675–1758.* Ottawa, 1933.

To the Honourable The Society for Propagating the Gospel in Foreign Parts. Boston 1713. (Shipton and Mooney 39558).

Webster, John Clarence, ed. *Acadia at the End of the 17th Century: Letters, Journals and Memoirs of Joseph Robineau de Villebon, Commandant in Acadia, 1690–1700, and Other Contemporary Documents.* Saint John, NB, 1934.

Williams, John. *The Redeemed Captive Returning to Zion.* Boston, 1707 (Evans 1340).

Williams, William. *Martial Wisdom Recommended.* Boston, 1737 (Evans 4210).

Winthrop, John. *Winthrop's Journal.* James Kendall Hosmer, ed. 2 vols. New York, 1908.

Winthrop Papers. Massachusetts Historical Society Collections, 4th ser., VI. Boston, 1863.

Secondary Sources

Books

Andrews, Charles McLean. *British Committees, Commissions, and Councils of Trade and Plantations, 1622–1675.* Baltimore: The Johns Hopkins University Press, 1908.

Andrews, Kenneth R. *Trade, Plunder and Settlement: Maritime Enterprise and the Genesis of the British Empire, 1480–1630.* Cambridge: Cambridge University Press, 1984.

Andrews, Kenneth R., N.P. Canny, and P.E.H. Hair, eds. *The Westward Enterprise: English Activities in Ireland, the Atlantic, and America, 1480–1650.* Liverpool: Liverpool University Press, 1978.

Armitage, David, and Michael Braddick, eds. *The British Atlantic World.* Basingstoke, UK: Palgrave Macmillan, 2002.

Arsenault, George. *Les Acadiens de l'Île, 1720–1980.* Moncton: Éditions d'Acadie, 1987.

Baker, Emerson W., and John G. Reid. *The New England Knight: Sir William Phips, 1651–1695.* Toronto: University of Toronto Press, 1998.

Balcom, B.A. *The Cod Fishery of Isle Royale, 1713–58.* Ottawa: Parks Canada, 1984.

Basque, Maurice. *Des hommes de pouvoir: Histoire d'Otho Robichaud et de sa famille, notables acadiens de Port-Royal et de Néguac.* Néguac: Société historique de Néguac, 1996.

Batinski, Michael C. *Jonathan Belcher, Colonial Governor.* Lexington: University of Kentucky Press, 1996.

Bayly, C.A. *Imperial Meridian: The British Empire and the World, 1780–1830.* London: Longman, 1989.

Beck, J. Murray. *Politics of Nova Scotia,* vol. I: *1710–1896.* Tantallon, NS: Four East Publications, 1985.

– *The Government of Nova Scotia.* Toronto: University of Toronto Press, 1957.

Béguin, Katia. *Les princes de Condé: Rebelles, courtisans, et mécènes dans la France du Grand Siècle.* Seyssel: Champ Vallon, 1999.

Benes, Peter, ed. *New England/New France 1600–1850. The Dublin Seminar for New England Folklife, Annual Proceedings, July 1989.* Boston: Boston University, 1992.

Bernard, Antoine. *Le drame acadien depuis 1604.* Montreal: Les clercs de Saint-Viateur, 1936.

– *Histoire de l'Acadie.* Moncton: L'Évangéline, 1938.

Biggar, H.P. *The Early Trading Companies of New France: A Contribution to the History of Commerce and Discovery in North America.* Toronto: University of Toronto Library, 1901.

Black, Jeremy. *British Foreign Policy in the Age of Walpole.* Edinburgh: John Donald, 1985.

Black, Jeremy, and Philip Woodfine, eds. *The British Navy and the Use of Naval Power in the Eighteenth Century.* Leicester: Leicester University Press, 1988.

Blussé, L., and F. Gaastra, eds. *Companies and Trade: Explorations on Overseas Trading Companies during the Ancien Régime.* Leiden: Leiden University Press, 1981.

Bond, Richmond P. *Queen Anne's American Kings.* Oxford: Clarendon Press, 1952.

Bosher, J.F. *Business and Religion in the Age of New France, 1600–1760.* Toronto: Canadian Scholars' Press, 1994.

– *The Canada Merchants, 1713–63.* Oxford: Clarendon Press, 1987.

Boucher, Philip P. *Les nouvelles Frances: France in America, 1500–1815, An Imperial Perspective.* Providence, RI: John Carter Brown Library, 1989.

Boucher, Philip P., and Serge Courville eds. *Proceedings of the Twelfth Meeting of the French Colonial Historical Society, St. Genevieve, May 1986.* Lanham: University Press of America, 1988.

Bowen, H.V. *Elites, Enterprise and the Making of the British Overseas Empire, 1688–1775.* London: Macmillan, 1996.

Braddick, Michael J. *State Formation in Early Modern England, c. 1500–1700.* Cambridge: Cambridge University Press, 2000.

Braudel, Fernand. *Écrits sur l'histoire.* Paris: Flammarion, 1969.

Brebner, John Bartlet. *New England's Outpost: Acadia before the Conquest of Canada.* New York: Columbia University Press, 1927.

Brenner, Robert. *Merchants and Revolution: Commercial Change, Political Conflict, and London's Overseas Traders, 1550–1653.* Princeton: Princeton University Press, 1993.

Brewer, John. *The Sinews of Power: War, Money, and the English State, 1688–1783.* New York: Alfred A. Knopf, 1989.

Brown, George W., et al., eds. *Dictionary of Canadian Biography.* 14 vols. to date. Toronto: University of Toronto Press, 1966– .

Buckner, Phillip A., and John G. Reid, eds. *The Atlantic Region to Confederation:*

A History. Toronto and Fredericton: University of Toronto Press and Acadiensis Press, 1994.

Bushman, Richard L. *The Refinement of America: Persons, Houses, Cities*. New York: Alfred A. Knopf, 1992.

Calnek, W.A. *History of the County of Annapolis*. Belleville: Mika Studio, 1972; first published 1897.

Canny, Nicholas P., ed. *Europeans on the Move: Studies on European Migration, 1500–1800*. Oxford: Clarendon Press, 1994.

– ed. *The Oxford History of the British Empire*, vol. I: *The Origins of Empire*. Oxford: Oxford University Press, 1998.

Campbell, Duncan. *Nova Scotia in Its Historical, Mercantile and Industrial Relations*. Montreal: John Lovell, 1873.

Campbell, J.R. *A History of the County of Yarmouth*. Belleville: Mika Studio, 1972; first published 1876.

Carruthers, Bruce G. *City of Capital: Politics and Markets in the English Financial Revolution*. Princeton: Princeton University Press, 1996.

Casgrain, H.R. *Un pèlerinage au pays d'Évangéline*. Quebec: Demers, 1888.

Cell, Gillian. *English Enterprise in Newfoundland, 1577–1660*. Toronto: University of Toronto Press, 1969.

Charges and Regulations, of the Ancient and Honourable Society of Free and Accepted Masons, Extracted from Ahiman Rezon &c. Together with a Concise Account of the Rise and Progress of Free Masonry in Nova Scotia, from the First Settlement of It to This Time. Halifax: John Howe, 1786.

Choquette, Leslie. *Frenchmen into Peasants: Modernity and Tradition in the Peopling of French Canada*. Cambridge: Harvard University Press, 1997.

Clark, Andrew Hill. *Acadia: The Geography of Early Nova Scotia to 1760*. Madison: University of Wisconsin Press, 1968.

Coleman, Margaret. *The Acadians at Grand Pré*. Ottawa: National and Historic Parks Branch, Department of Indian Affairs and Northern Development, 1968.

– *The Acadians at Port Royal*. Ottawa: National and Historic Parks Branch, Department of Indian Affairs and Northern Development, 1969.

Colley, Linda. *Britons: Forging the Nation, 1707–1837*. New Haven: Yale University Press, 1992.

Conrad, Margaret, ed. *Making Adjustments: Change and Continuity in Planter Nova Scotia, 1759–1800*. Fredericton: Acadiensis Press, 1991.

Cronon, William. *Changes in the Land: Indians, Colonists, and the Ecology of New England*. New York: Hill and Wang, 1983.

Crosby, Alfred W. *Ecological Imperialism: The Biological Expansion of Europe, 900–1900*. Cambridge: Cambridge University Press, 1986.

Couillard-Després, Azarie. *Charles de Saint-Étienne de la Tour, Gouverneur, Lieutenant-Général en Acadie, et son Temps, 1593–1666.* Arthabaska, PQ: L'imprimerie d'Arthabaska, 1930.

Dagneau, Jacques, and Sylvie Pelletier, eds. *Mémoires et histoires dans les sociétés francophones.* Quebec: CÉLAT, 1992.

Daigle, Jean, ed. *Acadia of the Maritimes: Thematic Studies from the Beginning to the Present.* Moncton: Chaire d'études acadiennes, Université de Moncton, 1995.

– ed. *The Acadians of the Maritimes: Thematic Studies.* Moncton: Centre d'études acadiennes, Université de Moncton, 1982.

Daniels, Christine, and Michael Kennedy, eds. *Negotiated Empires: Centers and Peripheries in the New World, 1500–1820.* New York: Routledge, 2002.

Davies, K.G. *The North Atlantic World in the Seventeenth Century.* Minneapolis: University of Minnesota Press, 1974.

Demos, John. *The Unredeemed Captive: A Family Story from Early America.* New York: Alfred A. Knopf, 1994.

D'Entremont, Clarence-Joseph. *Histoire du Cap-Sable de l'an mil au Traité de Paris, 1763,* vol. 3. Eunice, LA: Hébert Publications, 1981.

Dickason, Olive Patricia. *Canada's First Nations: A History of Founding Peoples from Earliest Times.* Toronto: McClelland and Stewart, 1992.

Dunn, Richard S. *Sugar and Slaves: The Rise of the Planter Class in the English West Indies, 1624–1713.* Chapel Hill: University of North Carolina Press, 1972.

Durand, Yves. *Les solidarités dans les sociétés humaines.* Paris: Presses universitaires de France, 1987.

Eales, J. Geoffrey. *The Eel Fisheries of Eastern Canada.* Ottawa: Fisheries Research Board of Canada, 1968.

Eccles, W.J. *France in America,* rev. ed. Markham, ON: Fitzhenry and Whiteside, 1990.

– *The French in North America, 1500–1783.* Markham, ON: Fitzhenry and Whiteside, 1998.

Ertman, Thomas. *Birth of the Leviathan: Building States and Regimes in Medieval and Early Modern Europe.* Cambridge: Cambridge University Press, 1997.

Faulkner, Alaric, and Gretchen Faulkner. *The French at Pentagoet, 1635–1674: An Archaeological Portrait of the Acadian Frontier.* Saint John: New Brunswick Museum; Augusta: Maine Historic Preservation Commission, 1987.

Ferguson, Robert, et al. *Report on the 1979 Field Season at Grassy Island Nova Scotia.* Ottawa: Parks Canada, 1981.

Flemming, David B. *The Canso Islands: An 18th Century Fishing Station.* Ottawa: Parks Canada, 1977.

Garratt, John G. *The Four Indian Kings.* Ottawa: Public Archives of Canada, 1985.

Gipson, L.H. *The British Empire before the American Revolution.* 15 vols.; vols. 1–3, Caldwell, ID: Caxton Printers, 1936; vols. 4–15, New York: Knopf, 1939–70.

Girard, Philip, and Jim Phillips, eds. *Essays in the History of Canadian Law,* vol. III: *Nova Scotia.* Toronto: University of Toronto Press, 1990.

Godfrey, William G. *Pursuit of Profit and Preferment in Colonial North America: John Bradstreet's Quest.* Waterloo: Wilfrid Laurier University Press, 1982.

Greene, Jack P. *Negotiated Authorities: Essays in Colonial Political and Constitutional History.* Charlottesville: University Press of Virginia, 1994.

– *Peripheries and Center: Constitutional Development in the Extended Polities of the British Empire and the United States, 1607–1788.* Athens and London: University of Georgia Press, 1986.

– *The Quest for Power: The Lower Houses of Assembly in the Southern Royal Colonies, 1689–1776.* Chapel Hill: University of North Carolina Press, 1963.

Greengrass, Mark. *France in the Age of Henri IV: The Struggle for Stability,* 2nd ed. London and New York: Longman, 1995.

– ed. *Conquest and Coalescence: The Shaping of the State in Early Modern Europe.* London: Edward Arnold, 1991.

Greer, Allan. *The People of New France.* Toronto: University of Toronto Press, 1997.

Greenwood, F. Murray, and Barry Wright, eds. *Canadian State Trials,* vol. I: *Law Politics and Security Measures, 1608–1837.* Toronto: University of Toronto Press, 1996.

Griffiths, N.E.S. *The Acadians: Creation of a People.* Toronto: McGraw-Hill Ryerson, 1973.

– *The Contexts of Acadian History, 1686–1784.* Montreal and Kingston: McGill-Queen's University Press, 1992.

Haliburton, Thomas C. *An Historical and Statistical Account of Nova-Scotia.* 2 vols. Halifax: Joseph Howe, 1829.

Hansen, Denise. *Eighteenth Century Fine Earthenwares from Grassy Island.* Ottawa: Environment Canada, Parks, 1986.

Harlow, Vincent T. *The Founding of the Second British Empire, 1763–1793.* 2 vols. London and New York: Longmans Green, 1952–64.

Harris, R. Cole, and Geoffrey J. Matthews, eds. *Historical Atlas of Canada,* vol. 1. Toronto: University of Toronto Press, 1987.

Hautecoeur, Jean-Paul. *L'Acadie du discours: Pour une sociologie de la culture acadienne.* Quebec: Presses de l'Université Laval, 1975.

Havard, Gilles. *La Grande Paix de Montréal de 1701: Les voies de la diplomatie franco-amérindienne.* Montreal: Recherches amérindiennes au Québec, 1992.

Head, C. Grant. *Eighteenth Century Newfoundland: A Geographer's Perspective.* Toronto: McClelland and Stewart, 1976.

Hébert, Monique, Nathalie Kermoal, and Phyllis LeBlanc, eds. *Entre le quotidien et le politique: Facettes de l'histoire des femmes francophones en milieu minoritaire.* Gloucester, ON: Réseau national d'action éducation femmes, 1997.

Hickey, Daniel. *The Coming of French Absolutism: The Struggle for Tax Reform in the Province of Dauphiné, 1540–1640.* Toronto: University of Toronto Press, 1986.

History of the Ancient and Honourable Fraternity of Free and Accepted Masons, and Concordant Orders. London: The Fraternity Publishing Co., 1910.

Hutchinson, Thomas. *The History of the Colony and Province of Massachusetts Bay.* 3 vols. Lawrence Shaw Mayo, ed. Cambridge: Harvard University Press, 1936; first published 1765.

Johnson, James Turner. *Ideology, Reason, and the Limitations of War: Religious and Secular Concepts, 1200–1740.* Princeton: Princeton University Press, 1975.

Johnson, Richard R. *John Nelson, Merchant Adventurer: A Life between Empires.* New York: Oxford University Press, 1991.

Johnston, A.J.B. *Control and Order in French Colonial Louisbourg, 1713–1758.* East Lansing: Michigan State University Press, 2001.

– ed. *Essays in French Colonial History: Proceedings of the 21st Annual Meeting of the French Colonial Historical Society.* East Lansing: Michigan State University Press, 1997.

Kettering, Sharon. *Patrons, Brokers, and Clients in Seventeenth-Century France.* New York: Oxford University Press, 1986.

Kettner, James H. *The Development of American Citizenship, 1608–1870.* Chapel Hill: University of North Carolina Press, 1978.

Kimball, Everett. *The Public Life of Joseph Dudley.* New York: Longmans, Green, 1911.

Labaree, Leonard Woods. *Royal Government in America: A Study of the British Colonial System Before 1783.* New Haven: Yale University Press, 1930.

Landau, Norma. *The Justices of the Peace, 1679–1760.* Berkeley: University of California Press, 1984.

Landsman, Ned C., ed. *Nation and Province in the First British Empire: Scotland and the Americas, 1600–1800.* Lewisburg, PA: Bucknell University Press, 2001.

Lauvrière, Émile. *Deux traîtres d'Acadie et leur victime: Les Latour, père et fils et Charles d'Aulnay.* Paris: Plon, 1932.

– *La tragédie d'un peuple: histoire du peuple acadien de ses origines à nos jours,* 2nd ed. 2 vols. Paris: Plon, 1924.

Lawson, Philip. *The East India Company: A History.* London and New York: Longman, 1993.

Lounsbury, Ralph G. *The British Fishery at Newfoundland, 1634–1763.* New Haven: Yale University Press, 1934; reprint, Hampden, CT: Archon, 1969.

MacDonald, M.A. *Fortune and La Tour: The Civil War in Acadia.* Toronto: Methuen, 1983.

Malone, Joseph J. *Pine Trees and Politics: The Naval Stores and Forest Policy in New England, 1691–1775.* Seattle: University of Washington Press, 1964.

Malone, Patrick M. *The Skulking Way of War: Technology and Tactics among the New England Indians.* Baltimore: Johns Hopkins University Press, 1993.

Marshall, Dorothy. *Eighteenth-Century England,* 2nd ed. London: Longman, 1974.

Marshall, P.J., ed. *The Oxford History of the British Empire,* vol. II: *The Eighteenth Century.* Oxford: Oxford University Press, 1998.

Martijn, Charles, ed. *Les Micmacs et la mer.* Montreal: Recherches amérindiennes au Québec, 1986.

Martin, John Frederick. *Profits in the Wilderness: Entrepreneurship and the Founding of New England Towns in the Seventeenth Century.* Chapel Hill: University of North Carolina Press, 1991.

Matthews, Keith. *Lectures on the History of Newfoundland, 1500–1830.* St John's: Breakwater, 1988.

McCusker, John J., and Russell Menard. *The Economy of British America, 1607–1789.* Chapel Hill: University of North Carolina Press, 1991.

McLennan, J.S. *Louisbourg from Its Foundation to Its Fall: 1713–1758.* London: Macmillan, 1918; reprint, Sydney: Fortress Press, 1957.

McNeill, John Robert. *Atlantic Empires of France and Spain: Louisbourg and Havana, 1700–1763.* Chapel Hill: University of North Carolina Press, 1985.

Miquelon, Dale. *Dugard of Rouen: French Trade to Canada and the West Indies, 1729–1770.* Montreal: McGill–Queen's University Press, 1978.

– *New France, 1701–1744: A Supplement to Europe.* Toronto: McClelland and Stewart, 1987.

Morgan, Edmund S. *American Slavery, American Freedom: The Ordeal of Colonial Virginia.* New York: Norton, 1975.

Morrison, Kenneth M. *The Embattled Northeast: The Elusive Ideal of Alliance in Abenaki-Euramerican Relations.* Berkeley: University of California Press, 1984.

Morrison, R. Bruce, and C. Roderick Wilson. *Native Peoples: The Canadian Experience.* Toronto: McClelland and Stewart, 1986.

Moulaison, Glenn, Muriel Comeau, and Édouard Langille, eds. *Les abeilles pillotent: mélanges offerts à René LeBlanc.* Pointe de l'Église: Revue de l'Université Ste-Anne, 1998.

Murdoch, Beamish. *A History of Nova Scotia or Acadie.* 3 vols. Halifax: Barnes, 1865–7.

Olson, Alison G. *Making the Empire Work: London and American Interest Groups, 1690–1790.* Cambridge: Harvard University Press, 1992.

Ommer, Rosemary E. *From Outpost to Outport: A Structural Analysis of the Jersey–*

Gaspé Cod Fishery, 1767–1886. Montreal and Kingston: McGill–Queen's University Press, 1991.

Osgood, Herbert L. *The American Colonies in the Eighteenth Century*. 4 vols. New York: Columbia University Press, 1924.

Paul, Daniel N. *We Were Not the Savages: A Micmac Perspective on the Collision of European and Aboriginal Civilization*. Halifax: Nimbus, 1993.

Pitre, Marie-Claire, and Denise Pelletier. *Les Pays-Bas, Histoire de la région Jemseg-Woodstock sur la rivière Saint-Jean pendant la période française (1604–1759)*. Fredericton: Société d'histoire de la rivière Saint-Jean, 1985.

Plank, Geoffrey. *An Unsettled Conquest: The British Campaign against the Peoples of Acadia*. Philadelphia: University of Pennsylvania Press, 2001.

Pope, Peter E. *The Many Landfalls of John Cabot*. Toronto: University of Toronto Press, 1997.

Pothier, Bernard. *Course à l'Accadie. Journal de campagne de François Du Pont Duvivier en 1744*. Moncton: Éditions d'Acadie, 1982.

Price, Richard, ed. *Maroon Societies: Rebel Slave Communities in the Americas*, 2nd ed. Baltimore: Johns Hopkins University Press, 1979.

Rabb, Theodore K. *Enterprise and Empire: Merchant and Gentry Investment in the Expansion of England, 1575–1630*. Cambridge: Harvard University Press, 1967.

Rameau de Saint-Père, François-Edme. *Une colonie féodale en Amérique: L'Acadie (1604–1881)*, 2nd ed. Paris: Plon, 1889.

Rawlyk, George A. *Nova Scotia's Massachusetts: A Study of Massachusetts–Nova Scotia Relations, 1630 to 1784*. Montreal: McGill–Queen's University Press, 1973.

– *Yankees at Louisbourg*. Orono: University of Maine Press, 1967.

Reid, John G. *Acadia, Maine, and New Scotland: Marginal Colonies in the Seventeenth Century*. Toronto: University of Toronto Press, 1981.

– *Six Crucial Decades: Times of Change in the History of the Maritimes*. Halifax: Nimbus Publishing, 1987.

Richter, Daniel K. *The Ordeal of the Longhouse: The Peoples of the Iroquois League in the Era of European Colonization*. Chapel Hill: University of North Carolina Press, 1992.

Ricker, Jackson. *Historical Sketches of Glenwood and the Argyles, Yarmouth County Nova Scotia*. Truro: Truro Printing and Publishing Co., 1941.

Robichaud, Donat. *Les Robichaud, histoire et généalogie*. Published by author, 1967.

Rolde, Neil. *Sir William Pepperrell of Colonial New England*. Brunswick, ME: Harpswell Press, 1982.

Roy, Michel. *L'Acadie des origines à nos jours: Essai de synthèse historique*. Montreal: Québec/Amérique, 1981.

Rumilly, Robert. *L'Acadie anglaise, 1713–1755*. Montreal: Fides, 1983.

– *L'Acadie française, 1497–1713*. Montreal: Fides, 1981.

Sahlins, Peter. *Boundaries: The Making of France and Spain in the Pyrenees*. Berkeley: University of California Press, 1989.

Sauvageau, Robert. *Acadie: La guerre de cent ans des Français d'Amérique aux Maritimes et en Louisiane, 1670–1769*. Paris: Berger-Levrault, 1987.

Savelle, Max. *The Diplomatic History of the Canadian Boundary, 1749–1763*. New Haven: Yale University Press, 1940.

Schusky, Ernest L., ed. *Political Organization of Native North Americans*. Washington, DC: University Press of America, 1980.

Scott, William Robert. *The Constitution and Finance of English, Scottish and Irish Joint-Stock Companies to 1720*, vol. 2: *Companies for Foreign Trade, Colonization, Fishing and Mining*. Cambridge: Cambridge University Press, 1912; reprinted New York: P. Smith, 1951.

Sévigny, P. André. *Les Abénaquis: Habitat et migrations, 17e–18e siècle*. Montreal: Éditions Bellarmin, 1976.

Silverman, Kenneth. *The Life and Times of Cotton Mather*. New York: Harper & Row, 1984.

Speck, W.A. *Stability and Strife: England, 1714–1760*. Cambridge, MA: Harvard University Press, 1977.

Steele, Ian K. *Politics of Colonial Policy: The Board of Trade in Colonial Administration, 1696–1720*. Oxford: Clarendon Press, 1968.

– *Warpaths: Invasions of North America*. New York: Oxford University Press, 1994.

Stone, Lawrence, ed. *An Imperial State at War: Britain from 1689 to 1815*. London and New York: Routledge, 1994.

Surette, Paul. *Atlas de l'établissement des Acadiens aux trois rivières du Chignectou 1660–1755*. Moncton: Éditions d'Acadie, 1996.

– *Petcoudiac, Colonisation et destruction, 1731–1755*. Moncton: Éditions d'Acadie, 1988.

Taylor, Alan. *Liberty Men and Great Proprietors: The Revolutionary Settlement on the Maine Frontier, 1760–1820*. Chapel Hill: University of North Carolina Press, 1990.

Taylor, M. Brook. *Promoters, Patriots, and Partisans: Historiography in Nineteenth-Century English Canada*. Toronto: University of Toronto Press, 1989.

Teal, John, and Mildred Teal. *Life and Death of the Salt Marsh*. Boston: Little, Brown, 1969.

Theibault, John C. *German villages in crisis: Rural life in Hesse-Kassel and the Thirty Years' War, 1580–1720*. Atlantic Highlands, NJ: Humanities Press, 1995.

Tilly, Charles. *Coercion, Capital, and European States, AD 900–1990*. Cambridge MA: B. Blackwell, 1990.

– ed. *The Formation of National States in Western Europe*. Princeton: Princeton University Press, 1975.

Trevelyan, George Macaulay. *England under Queen Anne*, vol. 3: *The Peace and the Protestant Succession*. London: Longman, 1934.

Trigger, Bruce, ed. *Handbook of North American Indians*, vol. 15: *Northeast*. Washington: Smithsonian Institution, 1978.

– *Natives and Newcomers: Canada's 'Heroic Age' Reconsidered*. Montreal and Kingston: McGill–Queen's University Press, 1985.

Trudel, Marcel. *The Beginnings of New France, 1524–1663*. Toronto: McClelland and Stewart, 1973.

Université de Moncton, Centre d'études acadiennes. *Inventaire général des sources documentaires sur les Acadiens, premier tome*. Moncton: Centre d'études acadiennes/Éditions d'Acadie, 1975.

Upton, L.F.S. *Micmacs and Colonists: Indian–White Relations in the Maritimes, 1713–1867*. Vancouver: University of British Columbia Press, 1979.

Vanderlinden, Jacques. *Se marier en Acadie française: XVIIe et XVIIIe siècles*. Moncton: Éditions d'Acadie et Chaire d'études acadiennes, Université de Moncton, 1998.

Waller, George M. *Samuel Vetch: Colonial Enterpriser*. Chapel Hill: University of North Carolina Press, 1960.

Walzer, Michael. *The Revolution of the Saints: A Study in the Origins of Radical Politics*. Cambridge: Harvard University Press, 1965.

Webb, Stephen Saunders. *Lord Churchill's Coup: The Anglo-American Empire and the Glorious Revolution Reconsidered*. New York: Alfred A. Knopf, 1995.

White, Richard. *The Middle Ground: Indians, Empires, and Republics in the Great Lakes Region, 1650–1815*. Cambridge and New York: Cambridge University Press, 1991.

White, Stephen A. *Dictionnaire généalogique des familles acadiennes: Première partie 1636–1714*, vols. I and II. Moncton: Centre d'études acadiennes, Université de Moncton, 1999.

Wicken, William. *Mi'kmaq Treaties on Trial: History, Land, and Donald Marshall Junior*. Toronto: University of Toronto Press, 2002.

Willcox, William B., and Walter L. Arnstein. *The Age of Aristocracy, 1688–1830*, 6th ed. Toronto: D.C. Heath, 1992.

Williams, Basil. *The Whig Supremacy 1714–1760*, 2nd ed. Oxford: Clarendon Press, 1962.

Williamson, William Durkee. *The History of the State of Maine: From Its First Discovery, A.D. 1602, to the Separation, A.D. 1820*. 2 vols. Hallowell, ME: Glazier and Masters, 1832.

Young, Brian, and John A. Dickinson. *A Short History of Quebec: A Socio-Economic Perspective*. Toronto: Copp Clark Pittman, 1988.

Articles

Adelman, Jeremy, and Stephen Aron. 'From Borderlands to Borders: Empires, Nation-States, and the Peoples in Between in North American History.' *American Historical Review* 104 (1999), 814–41.

Alsop, J.D. 'The Age of the Projectors: British Imperial Strategy in the North Atlantic in the War of Spanish Succession.' *Acadiensis* 21:1 (1991), 30–53.

– 'The Distribution of British Officers in the Colonial Militia for the Canada Expedition of 1709.' *Journal of the Society for Army Historical Research* 65 (1987), 120–1.

– 'Samuel Vetch's "Canada Survey'd": The Formation of a Colonial Strategy, 1706–1710.' *Acadiensis* 12:1 (1982), 39–58.

Armitage, David. 'Greater Britain: A Useful Category of Historical Analysis?' *American Historical Review* 104:2 (1999), 427–45.

Babitch, Rose Mary. 'The English of Acadians in the Seventeenth Century.' In *Atlantic Provinces Linguistic Association.* Université Saint-Anne, 1979, 96–105.

Baker, Emerson W. 'New Evidence on the French Involvement in King Philip's War.' *Maine Historical Society Quarterly* 28:1 (1988) 85–91.

Barnes, Thomas Garden. ' "The Dayly Cry for Justice": The Juridical Failure of the Annapolis Royal Regime, 1713–1749.' In Philip Girard and Jim Phillips, eds., *Essays in the History of Canadian Law,* vol. III: *Nova Scotia.* Toronto: University of Toronto Press, 1990, 10–41.

– ' "Twelve Apostles" or a Dozen Traitors? Acadian Collaborators during King George's War, 1744–48.' In F. Murray Greenwood and Barry Wright, eds., *Canadian State Trials,* vol. I: *Law Politics and Security Measures, 1608–1837.* Toronto: University of Toronto Press, 1996, 98–113.

Bartels, Dennis, and Olaf Uwe Janzen. 'Micmac Migration to Western Newfoundland.' *Canadian Journal of Native Studies,* 10 (1990), 71–96.

Basque, Maurice. 'Genre et gestion du pouvoir communitaire à Annapolis Royal au 18e siècle.' *Dalhousie Law Journal,* 17:2 (1994), 498–508.

Basque, Maurice, and Josette Brun. 'La neutralité à l'épreuve: Des Acadiennes à la défense de leurs intérêts en Nouvelle-Écosse du 18e siècle.' In Monique Hébert, Nathalie Kermoal, and Phyllis LeBlanc, eds., *Entre le quotidien et le politique: Facettes de l'histoire de femmes francophones en milieu minoritaire.* Gloucester, ON: Le Réseau national d'action éducation femmes, 1997, 107–22.

Baugh, Daniel M. 'Maritime Strength and Atlantic Commerce: The Uses of a "Grand Maritime Empire." ' In Lawrence Stone, ed., *An Imperial State at War: Britain from 1689 to 1815.* London and New York: Routledge, 1994, 185–223.

Black, Jeremy. 'Introduction.' In Jeremy Black and Philip Woodfine, eds., *The British Navy and the Use of Naval Power in the Eighteenth Century.* Leicester: Leicester University Press, 1988, 1–31.

Bock, Philip K. 'Micmac.' In Bruce Trigger, ed., *Handbook of North American Indians*, vol. 15: *Northeast.* Washington: Smithsonian Institution, 1978, 109–22.

Bosher, J.F. 'Huguenot Merchants and the Protestant International in the Seventeenth Century.' *William and Mary Quarterly*, 3rd ser. 52:1 (1995), 77–102.

– 'The Imperial Environment of French Trade with Canada, 1660–1685.' *English Historical Review* 108 (1993), 50–81.

– 'The Lyon and Bordeaux Connections of Émmanuel Le Borgne (c. 1605–1681).' *Acadiensis* 23:1 (Autumn 1993), 115–33.

– 'The Political and Religious Origins of La Rochelle's Primacy in Trade with New France, 1627–1685.' *French History* 7:3 (1993), 286–312.

Bottingheimer, Karl S. 'Kingdom and Colony: Ireland in the Westward Enterprise, 1536–1660.' In K.R. Andrews, N.P. Canny, and P.E.H. Hair, eds., *The Westward Enterprise: English Activities in Ireland, the Atlantic, and America, 1480–1650.* Liverpool: Liverpool University Press, 1978, 45–65.

Boulle, Pierre H. 'French Mercantilism, Commercial Companies, and Colonial Profitability.' In L. Blussé and F. Gaastra, eds., *Companies and Trade: Explorations on Overseas Trading Companies during the Ancien Régime.* Leiden: Leiden University Press, 1981, 97–117.

Bowen, H.V. 'British Conceptions of Global Empire, 1756–83.' *Journal of Imperial and Commonwealth History* 26:3 (1998), 1–27.

Braddick, Michael. 'The Early Modern English State and the Question of Differentiation, from 1500 to 1700.' *Comparative Studies in Society and History* 38:1 (1996), 92–111.

– 'The English Government, War, Trade, and Settlement, 1625–1688.' In Nicholas P. Canny, ed., *The Oxford History of the British Empire*, vol. I: *The Origins of Empire.* Oxford: Oxford University Press, 1998, 286–308.

Brewer, John. 'The Eighteenth-Century British State: Contexts and Issues.' In Lawrence Stone, ed., *An Imperial State at War: Britain from 1689 to 1815.* London and New York: Routledge, 1994, 52–71.

Brun, Josette. 'Marie de Saint-Étienne de La Tour.' *Les cahiers de la Société historique acadienne* 25:4 (1994), 244–62.

Buffinton, Arthur H. 'The Puritan View of War.' *Colonial Society of Massachusetts Publications* 28 (1930–3), 67–86.

Calloway, Colin G. 'The Abenakis and the Anglo–French Borderlands.' In Peter Benes, ed., *New England/New France 1600–1850. The Dublin Seminar for New England Folklife, Annual Proceedings, July 1989.* Boston: Boston University, 1992, 18–27.

Campbell, Anita. 'The How Household: A Colonial Merchant's Life-Style in 18th
Century Canso.' *Canadian Collector* 20:2 (1985), 54–7.

Campbell, Joan Bourque. 'The Acadian Seigneury of St-Mathieu at Cobeguid.'
Nova Scotia Historical Review 9:2 (1989), 74–88.

Canny, Nicholas. 'English Migration into and across the Atlantic during the
Seventeenth and Eighteenth Centuries.' In Nicholas Canny, ed., *Europeans on
the Move: Studies on European Migration, 1500–1800*. Oxford: Clarendon Press,
1994, 39–75.

– 'The Origins of Empire: An Introduction.' In Nicholas Canny, ed., *The Oxford
History of the British Empire*, vol. I: *The Origins of Empire*. Oxford: Oxford University Press, 1998, 1–33.

– 'Writing Atlantic History; or Reconfiguring the History of Colonial British
America.' *Journal of American History* 86 (1999–2000), 1093–1114.

Chard, Donald F. 'Canso, 1710–1721: Focal Point of New England–Cape Breton
Rivalry.' *Nova Scotia Historical Society Collections* 39 (1977), 49–77.

– 'The Impact of French Privateering on New England, 1689–1713.' *American
Neptune* 35 (1975), 153–65.

Clarke, P.D. 'Rameau de Saint–Père, Moïse de l'Acadie.' In Jacques Dagneau
and Sylvie Pelletier, eds., *Mémoires et histoires dans les sociétés francophones*.
Quebec: CÉLAT, 1992, 73–106.

Countryman, Edward. 'Indians, the Colonial Order, and the Social Significance
of the American Revolution.' *William and Mary Quarterly*, 3rd ser., 53:2 (1996),
342–62.

Daigle, Jean. 'Acadia from 1604 to 1763: An Historical Synthesis.' In Jean Daigle,
ed., *Acadia of the Maritimes: Thematic Studies from the Beginning to the Present*.
Moncton: Chaire d'études acadiennes, 1995, 1–43.

– 'Acadian Marshland Settlement.' In R. Cole Harris and Geoffrey J. Matthews,
eds., *Historical Atlas of Canada*, vol. I. Toronto: University of Toronto Press,
1987, Plate 29.

– 'Un Acadien devant la cour suprême du Massachusetts, 1697.' *Les cahiers de la
Société historique acadienne* 6:2 (1975), 106–8.

– '1650–1686: "Un pays qui n'est pas fait." ' In Phillip A. Buckner and John G.
Reid, eds., *The Atlantic Region to Confederation: A History*. Toronto and Fredericton: University of Toronto Press and Acadiensis Press, 1994, 61–77.

Delaney, Paul. 'The Husbands and Children of Agathe de La Tour.' *Les cahiers de
la Société historique acadienne* 25:4 (1994), 263–84.

Desserud, Donald. 'Nova Scotia and the American Revolution: A Study of Neu-
trality and Moderation in the Eighteenth Century.' In Margaret Conrad, ed.,
Making Adjustments: Change and Continuity in Planter Nova Scotia, 1759–1800.
Fredericton: Acadiensis Press, 1991, 89–112.

Dickason, Olive P. 'Amerindians between French and English in Nova Scotia, 1716–1763.' *American Indian Culture and Research Journal*, 10:4 (1986), 31–56.

– 'La guerre navale des Micmacs contre les Britanniques.' In Charles Martjin, ed., *Les Micmacs et la mer*. Montreal: Recherches amérindiennes au Québec, 1986, 233–48.

– 'Louisbourg and the Indians: A Study in Imperial Race Relations, 1713–1760.' *History and Archeology/Histoire et Archéologie* 6 (Ottawa: Parks Canada, 1976), 1–132.

Eccles, W.J. 'Sovereignty-Association, 1500–1783.' *Canadian Historical Review* 65:4 (1984), 475–510.

Erickson, Vincent O. 'Maliseet-Passamaquoddy.' In Bruce Trigger, ed., *Handbook of North American Indians*, vol. 15: *Northeast*. Washington: Smithsonian Institution, 1978, 123–36.

Frégault, Guy. 'La Déportation des Acadiens.' *Revue d'histoire de l'Amérique française* 8:3 (1954), 309–58.

– 'L'Empire britannique et la conquête du Canada (1700–1713).' *Revue d'histoire de l'Amérique française* 10:2 (1956), 153–82.

George, Timothy. 'War and Peace in the Puritan Tradition.' *Church History* 53:4 (1984), 492–503.

Greene, Jack P. 'Empire and Identity from the Glorious Revolution to the American Revolution.' In P.J. Marshall, ed., *The Oxford History of the British Empire*, vol. II: *The Eighteenth Century*. Oxford: Oxford University Press, 1998, 208–30.

– 'Negotiated Authorities: The Problem of Governance in the Extended Polities of the Early Modern Atlantic World.' In Jack P. Greene, *Negotiated Authorities: Essays in Colonial Political and Constitutional History*. Charlottesville: University Press of Virginia, 1994, 1–24.

– 'Political Mimesis: A Consideration of the Historical and Cultural Roots of Legislative Behavior in the British Colonies during the Eighteenth Century.' *American Historical Review* 75 (1969), 337–60.

– '"A Posture of Hostility": A Reconsideration of Some Aspects of the Origins of the American Revolution.' *Proceedings of the American Antiquarian Society* 87:1 (1977), 27–68.

Greengrass, Mark. 'Introduction: Conquest and Coalescence.' In Mark Greengrass, ed., *Conquest and Coalescence: The Shaping of the State in Early Modern Europe*. London: Edward Arnold, 1991, 1–24.

Griffiths, N.E.S. 'The Formation of a Community and the Interpretation of Identity: The Acadians, 1604–1997.' *British Journal of Canadian Studies* 13 (1998), 32–46.

- 'The Golden Age: Acadian Life, 1713–1748.' *Histoire sociale/Social History* 17 (1984), 21–34.
- 'Longfellow's *Evangeline*: The Birth and Acceptance of a Legend.' *Acadiensis* 11:2 (1981–2), 28–41.
- 'Subjects and Citizens in the Eighteenth Century: The Question of the Acadian Oaths of Allegiance.' In Glenn Moulaison, Muriel Comeau, and Édouard Langille, eds, *Les abeilles pillotent: mélanges offerts à René LeBlanc*. Pointe-de-l'Église: Revue de l'Université Ste-Anne, 1998, 23–34.
- '1600–1650: Fish, Fur, and Folk.' In Phillip A. Buckner and John G. Reid, eds., *The Atlantic Region to Confederation: A History*. Toronto and Fredericton: University of Toronto Press and Acadiensis Press, 1994, 40–60.
Griffiths, N.E.S., and John G. Reid. 'New Evidence on New Scotland, 1629.' *William and Mary Quarterly*, 3rd ser., 49:3 (1992), 492–508.
Hiller, J.K. 'Utrecht Revisited: The Origins of French Fishing Rights in Newfoundland Waters.' *Newfoundland Studies* 7:1 (1991), 23–39.
Hinderaker, Eric. 'The "Four Indian Kings" and the Imaginative Construction of the First British Empire.' *William and Mary Quarterly*, 3rd ser., 53:3 (1996), 487–526.
Hirsche, Adam J. 'The Collision of Military Cultures in Seventeenth-Century New England.' *Journal of American History* 74:4 (1987–8), 1187–1212.
Hynes, Gisa I. 'Some Aspects of the Demography of Port Royal, 1650–1755.' *Acadiensis* 3:1 (1973–4), 3–17.
Johnson, Richard R. 'The Search for a Usable Indian: An Aspect of the Defense of Colonial New England.' *Journal of American History* 64 (1977), 623–51.
Kelly, Gerald M. 'Louis Allain in Acadia and New England.' *Les cahiers de la Société historique acadienne* 4 (1973), 362–80.
Lanctôt, Gustave. 'L'Acadie et la Nouvelle-Angleterre, 1603–1763.' *Revue de l'Université d'Ottawa* 11 (1941), 182–205, 349–70.
LaPlante, Corinne. 'Pourquoi les Acadiens sont-ils demeurés en Acadie?' *Les cahiers de la Société historique acadienne* 3:1 (1968), 4–17.
- 'Le traité d'Utrecht et la question des limites territoriales de l'Acadie.' *Les cahiers de la Société historique acadienne* 6:1 (1975), 25–42.
Lax, John, and William Pencak. 'The Knowles Riot and the Crisis of the 1740's in Massachusetts.' *Perspectives in American History* 10 (1976), 163–214.
Lynch, Katherine A. 'The Family and the History of Public Life.' *Journal of Interdisciplinary History* 24:4 (1994), 665–84.
Mancke, Elizabeth. 'Another British America: A Canadian Model for the Early Modern British Empire.' *Journal of Imperial and Commonwealth History* 25:1 (1997), 1–36.

– 'Empire and State.' In David Armitage and Michael Braddick, eds., *The British Atlantic World*. Basingstoke, UK: Palgrave Macmillan, 2002, 175–95.

– 'Negotiating an Empire: Britain and Its Overseas Peripheries, c. 1500–1780.' In Christine Daniels and Michael Kennedy, eds., *Negotiated Empires: Centers and Peripheries in the New World, 1500–1820*. New York: Routledge, 2002, 235–65.

Marshall, Ingeborg. 'Beothuk and Micmac: Re-Examining Relationships.' *Acadiensis* 17 (1988), 52–82.

Marshall, P.J. 'Empire and Authority in the Later Eighteenth Century.' *Journal of Imperial and Commonwealth History* 15:2 (1986–7), 105–22.

Massignon, Geneviève. 'La seigneurie de Charles de Menou d'Aulnay, gouverneur de l'Acadie, 1635–1650.' *Revue d'histoire de l'Amérique française* 16:4 (1963), 469–501.

McCully, Bruce T. 'Governor Francis Nicholson, Patron *Par Excellence* of Religion and Learning in Colonial America.' *William and Mary Quarterly*, 3rd ser., 39:2 (1982), 310–33.

Miller, Perry. 'Errand into the Wilderness.' *William and Mary Quarterly*, 3rd ser., 10 (1953), 3–19.

Miller, Virginia. 'The Micmac: A Maritime Woodland Group.' In R. Bruce Morrison and C. Roderick Wilson, eds., *Native Peoples: The Canadian Experience*. Toronto: McClelland and Stewart, 1986, 324–52.

Moody, Barry. 'Growing Up in Granville Township, 1760–1800.' In Margaret Conrad, ed., *Making Adjustments: Change and Continuity in Planter Nova Scotia, 1759–1800*. Fredericton: Acadiensis Press, 1991, 165–79.

Moogk, Peter. 'Ile Royale: The Other New France.' In A.J.B. Johnston, ed., *Essays in French Colonial History: Proceedings of the 21st Annual Meeting of the French Colonial Historical Society*. East Lansing: Michigan State University Press, 1997, 43–52.

Morrison, Kenneth M. 'The Bias of Colonial Law: English Paranoia and the Abenaki Arena of King Philip's War, 1675–1678.' *New England Quarterly* 53 (1980), 363–87.

Pagden, Anthony. 'The Struggle for Legitimacy and the Image of Empire in the Atlantic to c. 1700.' In Nicholas Canny, ed., *The Oxford History of the British Empire*, vol. I: *The Origins of Empire: British Overseas Enterprise to the Close of the Seventeenth Century*. Oxford: Oxford University Press, 1998, 34–54.

Pastore, Ralph. 'The Sixteenth Century: Aboriginal Peoples and European Contact.' In Phillip A. Buckner and John G Reid, eds., *The Atlantic Region to Confederation: A History*. Toronto and Fredericton: University of Toronto Press and Acadiensis Press, 1994, 22–39.

Patterson, Orlando. 'Slavery and Slave Revolts: A Sociohistorical Analysis of the First Maroon War, 1665–1740.' In Richard Price, ed., *Maroon Societies: Rebel*

Slave Communities in the Americas, 3rd ed. Baltimore: Johns Hopkins University
Press, 1996, 246–97.

Patterson, Stephen E. 'Indian–White Relations in Nova Scotia, 1749–61: A Study
in Political Interaction.' *Acadiensis* 23:1 (Autumn 1993), 23–59.

Plank, Geoffrey G. 'The Two Majors Cope: The Boundaries of Nationality in
Mid-18th-Century Nova Scotia.' *Acadiensis* 25:2 (1995–6), 18–40.

Pothier, Bernard. 'Acadian Emigration to Île Royale after the Conquest of
Acadia.' *Histoire sociale/Social History* 3:6 (1970), 116–31.

Prest, Walter H. 'Edible Wild Plants of Nova Scotia.' *Proceedings and Transactions
of the Nova Scotian Institute of Science* 11 (1902–6), 387–416.

Ramirez, Bruno. 'Clio in Words and Motion: Practices of Narrating the Past.'
Journal of American History 86 (1999–2000), 987–1014.

Rawlyk, George A. '1720–1744: Cod, Louisbourg, and the Acadians.' In Phillip A.
Buckner and John G. Reid, eds., *The Atlantic Region to Confederation: A History.*
Toronto and Fredericton: University of Toronto Press and Acadiensis Press,
1994, 107–24.

Reid, John G. 'The Conquest of "Nova Scotia": Cartographic Imperialism and
the Echoes of a Scottish Past.' In Ned C. Landsman, ed., *Nation and Province in
the First British Empire: Scotland and the Americas, 1600–1800.* Lewisburg, PA:
Bucknell University Press, 2001.

– 'Mission to the Micmac.' *The Beaver* 70 (1990), 15–22.

– 'The Scots Crown and the Restitution of Port Royal, 1629–1632.' *Acadiensis* 6:2
(1977), 39–63.

– '1686–1720: Imperial Intrusions.' In Phillip A. Buckner and John G. Reid,
eds., *The Atlantic Region to Confederation: A History.* Toronto and Fredericton:
University of Toronto Press and Acadiensis Press, 1994, 73–103.

Rouet, Damien. 'L'Acadie, du comptoir à la colonie: Migration et colonisation
du bassin des Mines.' *Les cahiers de la Société historique acadienne* 29:1 and 2
(1998), 34–57.

Roy, Muriel K. 'Settlement and Population Growth in Acadia.' In Jean Daigle,
ed., *The Acadians of the Maritimes: Thematic Studies.* Moncton: Centre d'études
acadiennes, Université de Moncton, 1982, 125–96.

Ryan, Shannon. 'Fishery to Colony: A Newfoundland Watershed, 1793–1815.'
Acadiensis 12:2 (1983), 34–52.

Salmond, John W. 'Citizenship and Allegiance.' *Law Quarterly Review* 17 (1901),
270–82.

Shammas, Carole. 'English Commerical Development and American Colonization, 1560–1620.' In K.R. Andrews, N.P. Canny, and P.E.H. Hair, eds., *The
Westward Enterprise: English Activities in Ireland, the Atlantic, and America, 1480–
1650.* Liverpool: University of Liverpool Press, 1978, 151–74.

Snow, Dean R. 'Eastern Abenaki.' In Bruce Trigger, ed., *Handbook of North American Indians*, vol. 15: *Northeast*. Washington: Smithsonian Institution, 1978, 137–48.

Speck, Frank. 'The Eastern Algonkian Wabanaki Confederacy.' *American Anthropologist* 17 (1915), 492–508.

Taylor, Alan. 'Centers and Peripheries: Locating Maine's History.' *Maine History* 39 (2000–1), 3–15.

Tilly, Charles. 'Reflections on the History of European State-Making.' In Charles Tilly, ed., *The Formation of National States in Western Europe*. Princeton: Princeton University Press, 1975, 3–83.

Turgeon, Laurier. 'Basque–Amerindian Trade in the Saint Lawrence during the Sixteenth Century: New Documents, New Perspectives.' *Man in the Northeast* 40 (Fall 1990), 81–7.

– 'Pour redécouvrir notre 16e siècle: Les pêches à Terre-Neuve d'après les archives notariales de Bordeaux.' *Revue d'histoire de l'Amérique française* 39 (1985–6), 523–49.

Vachon, André. 'The Administration of New France.' In George W. Brown et al., eds, *Dictionary of Canadian Biography*. 14 vols to date. Toronto: University of Toronto Press, 1966–, II, xv–xxv.

Vanderlinden, Jacques. 'À la rencontre de l'histoire du droit en Acadie avant le dérangement: Premières impressions d'un nouveau-venu.' *Revue de l'Université de Moncton* 28:1 (1995), 47–80.

Walker, Willard, Robert Conkling, and Gregory Buesing. 'A Chronological Account of the Wabanaki Confederacy.' In Ernest L. Schusky, ed., *Political Organization of Native North Americans*. Washington, DC: University Press of America, 1980, 41–84.

Walters, Mark D. '*Mohegan Indians v. Connecticut* (1705–1773) and the Legal Status of Aboriginal Customary Laws and Government in British North America.' *Osgoode Hall Law Journal* 33:4 (1995), 785–829.

Webb, Stephen Saunders. 'The Strange Career of Francis Nicholson.' *William and Mary Quarterly*, 3rd ser., 23:4 (1966), 513–48.

Wicken, William. 'The Mi'kmaq and Wuastukwiuk Treaties.' *University of New Brunswick Law Journal* 43 (1994), 241–53.

– '26 August 1726: A Case Study in Mi'kmaq–New England Relations in the Early 18th Century.' *Acadiensis* 23:1 (1993), 5–22.

Unpublished Works

Barrieau, Nicole. 'L'évolution du paysage colonial d'un établissement colonial: Le cas de Port-Royal, 1686–1710.' Unpublished research, Université de Moncton, Centre d'études acadiennes, 1994.

Braddick, Michael J. 'Elite Co-Option and State Formation in the British Atlantic World, c. 1530–1700.' Working Paper no. 97–14, International Seminar on the History of the Atlantic World, 1500–1800, Harvard University, 1997.

Chard, Donald F. 'The Impact of Ile Royale on New England, 1713–1763.' PhD thesis, University of Ottawa, 1976.

– ' "Pagans," Privateers, and Propagandists: New England–Acadia Relations, 1690–1710.' MA thesis, Dalhousie University, 1967.

Clarke, P.D. 'The Makers of Acadian History in the Nineteenth Century.' PhD thesis, Université Laval, 1987.

Crowley, Terence Allan. 'Government and Interests: French Colonial Administration at Louisbourg, 1713–1758.' PhD thesis, Duke University, 1975.

Daigle, Jean. 'Michel Le Neuf de La Vallière, seigneur de Beaubassin et gouverneur d'Acadie, 1678–1684.' MA thesis, Université de Montréal, 1970.

– 'Nos amis les ennemis: Relations commerciales de l'Acadie avec le Massachusetts, 1670–1711.' PhD thesis, University of Maine, 1975.

Desbarats, Catherine M. 'Colonial Government Finances in New France, 1700–1750.' PhD thesis, McGill University, 1993.

LeBlanc, Stéphane. 'Neutralité des Acadiens: Étude du discours dans l'historiographie et dans les pétitions.' Unpublished research, Université de Moncton, Centre d'études acadiennes, 1996.

Mancke, Elizabeth. 'Colonial Corporations and the Emergence of the British Imperial State.' Working Paper 97–06, International Seminar on the History of the Atlantic World, Harvard University, 1997.

– 'Spaces of Power in the Early Modern Northeast.' Paper delivered at Conference on 'New England and the Maritime Provinces: Connections and Comparisons,' Orono, ME, April 2000.

Marsaud, Myriam. 'L'étranger qui dérange: Le procès de sorcellerie de Jean Campagna, miroir d'une communauté acadienne, Beaubassin, 1685.' MA thesis, Université de Moncton, 1993.

Moody, Barry. ' "A Just and Disinterested Man": The Nova Scotia Career of Paul Mascarene, 1710–1752.' PhD thesis, Queen's University, 1976.

Morrison, Kenneth M. 'The People of the Dawn: The Abenaki and Their Relations with New England and New France, 1600–1717.' PhD thesis, University of Maine, 1975.

Nagel, Kurt William. 'Empire and Interest: British Colonial Defense Policy, 1689–1748.' PhD thesis, Johns Hopkins University, 1992.

Nietfeld, Patricia. 'Determinants of Aboriginal Micmac Political Organization.' PhD thesis, University of New Mexico, 1981.

Plank, Geoffrey G. 'The Culture of Conquest: The British Colonists and Nova Scotia, 1690–1759.' PhD thesis, Princeton University, 1994.

– 'Samuel Vetch's Imaginary Canada.' Paper delivered to American Society for Eighteenth-Century Studies. Nashville, April 1997.

Plaze, Roland. 'La colonie royale de Plaisance, 1689–1713: Impact du statut de colonie royale sur les structures administratives.' MA thesis, Université de Moncton, 1991.

Pothier, Bernard. 'Acadian Settlement on Île Royale, 1713–1734.' MA thesis, University of Ottawa, 1967.

Prins, Harald E.L. 'Tribulations of a Border Tribe: A Discourse on the Political Ecology of the Aroostook Band of Micmacs (16th–20th Centuries).' PhD thesis, New School for Social Research, 1988.

Ringuet, Isabelle. 'Les stratégies de mobilité sociale des interprètes en Nouvelle-Écosse et à l'Île Royale, 1713–1758.' MA thesis, Université de Moncton, 1999.

Robison, Mark Power. 'Maritime Frontiers: The British, French, and Mi'kmaq in Nova Scotia and Ile Royale.' PhD thesis, University of Colorado, 2000.

Rompillon, Samantha. 'La migration à Beaubassin, village acadien, fruit de la mobilité et de la croissance.' MA thesis, Université de Poitiers, 1998.

Tapie, Edith. 'Les structures socio-économiques de Grand Pré, communauté acadienne.' MA thesis, Université de Poitiers, 2000.

Wicken, William C. 'Encounters with Tall Sails and Tall Tales: Mi'kmaq Society, 1500–1760.' PhD thesis, McGill University, 1994.

Index